A THEORY OF THE
GOOD AND THE RIGHT

A THEORY OF
THE GOOD
AND THE RIGHT

Richard B. Brandt

CLARENDON PRESS · OXFORD
1979

Oxford University Press, Walton Street, Oxford OX2 6DP

OXFORD LONDON GLASGOW
NEW YORK TORONTO MELBOURNE WELLINGTON
NAIROBI DAR ES SALAAM CAPE TOWN
KUALA LUMPUR SINGAPORE JAKARTA HONG KONG TOKYO
DELHI BOMBAY CALCUTTA MADRAS KARACHI

Published in the United States by
Oxford University Press, New York

© *Oxford University Press 1979*

British Library Cataloguing in Publication Data

Brandt, Richard Booker
A theory of the good and the right.
1. Ethics
I. Title
170   BJ1012   78–40647

ISBN 0–19–824550–5

Printed in Great Britain by
Richard Clay (The Chaucer Press) Ltd,
Bungay, Suffolk

PREFACE

THIS BOOK is an expansion of John Locke lectures, delivered at Oxford University in the spring of 1974. A basic thesis of these lectures was, however, put forward much earlier, in a Lindley lecture at the University of Kansas in March, 1963, published by that University under the title, 'Moral Philosophy and the Analysis of Language'. This thesis had both critical and constructive facets. The critical one was that it is misguided to ransack the facts of ordinary use of ethical language in order to identify analytic truths which can be a foundation for normative reasoning (a commitment common to both traditional 'reportive' naturalists and to prescriptivists like R. M. Hare), and that it is at best dubious to suppose there is any 'standard practice' which people use in the appraisal of ethical judgements (what I had assumed in my earlier *Ethical Theory*). The constructive idea was the identification of two questions, different from the ones with which moral philosophers have traditionally been concerned, but which capture at least most of what is clear and important in the traditional questions. The first of these is: 'What would a person (perhaps all persons), if rational in the sense of having made optimal use of all available information, want and choose to do?' The second is: 'What kind of moral system, if any, would such a person support for a society in which he expected to live?'

Reflection on these two questions led me to a rather prolonged inquiry into the facts and theories of empirical psychology, in search of what a 'rational' person might want and choose to do. The results of this were rewarding beyond my initial expectations, and a report of them, and of their implications for the basic questions, formed perhaps the most interesting part of the Locke lectures, and is a central feature of the present book. For these data shed light on how to criticize our basic motivations—a problem which is of urgent practical importance for decision-making, and about which traditional philosophy has had woefully little to say, beyond urging us to inspect what we really want, or to appeal to our 'intuitions'. This material also, as we shall see, throws light on the question of what kind of moral system a rational person would support for his society—and hence on the derivation of basic moral principles.

A great many other topics are discussed in the present book; an earlier version of my proposals on many of these was in the Locke lectures. It may be helpful to alert some readers to one fact about these discussions: that in many important respects they are very different from the views expressed in *Ethical Theory*. Readers of *Ethical Theory* who have commented on parts of the present book have tended to construe it as a consistent expansion or reformulation of the views expressed in *Ethical Theory*. This construction is mistaken and leads to misunderstandings. While almost all the purely critical parts of *Ethical Theory* still seem to me sound, the positive views in the present book are substantially different from those of the earlier book at almost every point. The crucial Chapter 10 of the earlier book ('The Justification of Ethical Beliefs') had to be replaced almost wholly. The psychological account of the earlier book was rather primitive. The present conceptions of 'pleasure' and of hedonism are very different, as is the discussion of what can be counted as basic 'intrinsic goods'. So is the criticism of egoism and act utilitarianism. Again, I no longer affirm that an equal distribution of welfare is itself a basic value, and the account of the utilitarian theory of distributive justice is much elaborated. I still support a form of 'rule-utilitarianism', but the theory now takes a form which seems to me superior not only to the brief sketch in *Ethical Theory* but also to earlier papers on that topic, published in 1963 and 1967. So I urge readers of *Ethical Theory* to forget that book while reading the present one, and to understand this book on the basis simply of what it says.

Comments on the genesis of the present book would be incomplete without mention of the influence of two philosophers: John Rawls and William Frankena. Rawls's work has been a constant stimulus, where I have not been convinced by him, to develop an alternative view. He kindly allowed me to use an earlier version of his book, in mimeograph form, as a text for a course on normative ethics taught, I think, in the spring of 1969. I was much stimulated by the challenge of his view that a derivation of normative principles is impossible except by a restriction on information of the kind contemplated by his concept of a 'veil of ignorance'. At one stage I essentially adopted a form of his proposal about a meaning to be assigned to moral predicates like 'morally right' —that an action is right if and only if it would be permitted by a moral code which all rational persons could accept behind a 'veil of ignorance'—although later, for reasons that will appear below, I came to think that the basic problem for moral philosophy is different from the one implied by this conception, and is one much closer to the suggestion made in my 1963 Lindley lecture. In general, I have been much influenced by Rawls's published work in one way or another. I have also profited from conversations with him, both at luncheons at the University of Michigan during his year here in 1975–6, and over mid-afternoon Coca-Colas at the Center for Advanced Study in the Behavioral Sciences during 1969–70. For all this I am grateful to him.

The benefit I have enjoyed from the work and friendship of William Frankena has been very different, partly because our views are more similar although Frankena cannot swallow my account of distributive justice, or my view of the definition of 'morality', or my convictions about various other topics. Frankena read and criticized earlier versions of many parts of the present book, and we have discussed ethics over a weekly lunch for several years. Where there are mistakes in this book, they occur either in parts which he did not read, or in passages where I perversely declined to accept his good advice. I am very grateful to him for his setting me straight on many points and for his friendship.

There are numerous other persons to whom this book is indebted. There are many whom I cannot possibly mention by name: particularly students at the University of Michigan, and members of two summer seminars supported by the National Endowment for the Humanities, who pressured me to make things clearer or to come up with better reasons. My colleagues have listened to earlier versions of various chapters at colloquia and have criticized them mercilessly. The result is somewhat clearer and more defensible than it otherwise would have been.

Several individuals stand out, as ones to whom my gratitude is due, in addition to Rawls and Frankena. My colleagues John Bennett, Arthur Burks, Holly Goldman, and George Mavrodes have helped either by giving me information about things of which I was ignorant, or by prodding me by their detection of vagueness, inconsistency, or lack of sound argument in pieces which they read. Richard Hare, Derek Parfit, and James Griffin were both encouraging and helpful in many conversations during Trinity term of 1974, when I was in Oxford. Diana Ackerman, in weekly discussions over most of one year, raised numerous difficulties with my discussion of pleasure and desire, which I have done my best to resolve. Philosophers in Scandinavia not only provided a very enjoyable month during the spring of 1977, but their criticisms—especially those of Dag Präwitz, Lars Bergstrom, and Lars Ericsson—enabled me to improve my discussion of the concept of welfare and to clarify the latter half of the chapter on economic justice, although I probably have not met their criticisms fully.

Various philosophers have been helpful to me by their criticisms, in print, of 'rule-utilitarianism': particularly David Lyons (1965), Alan Donagan (1968), B. J. Diggs (1970), D. H. Hodgson (1967), and Joel Feinberg (1967). Fred Feldman and Michael Bayles kindly sent me copies of symposium papers on this topic, and Feldman has helped further in correspondence. I should also mention useful discussions with David Benfield.

Psychologists have been extraordinarily supportive of my venture into psychology. I cannot mention them all, but I must thank a few by name, in view of their criticial commentaries on my manuscript, suggestions made in conversations, and encouragement in the enterprise: John Atkinson, Albert Bandura, Dorwin Cartwright, Martin Hoffman, Howard Kendler, James Papsdorf, Joan Sieber, and Edwin Walker. I herewith excuse them all from any responsibility for mistaken statements I make about psychology in this book. I have done my own picking and choosing, and there may be things I say to which none of them would subscribe.

I am also indebted to Carolyn McKee, who worked for several weeks on a near-final version of my manuscript. She improved its style, showed how to reduce its length without loss of content, and identified obscurities.

Joan Warmbrunn, of the staff at the Center for Advanced Study in the Behavioral Sciences, turned my first draft into a fine-looking typescript, and Alice Gantt has typed repeated versions with incredible speed and accuracy. I thank both of them.

The President and Fellows of Corpus Christi College granted me a temporary fellowship during my residence there, in Trinity term, 1974, and showed most cordial hospitality. A fellowship at the Center for Advanced Study in the Behavioral Sciences, in Stanford, provided unimprovable facilities for working, and an ideally cordial and stimulating atmosphere, during 1969–70. My stay there was partly supported by a fellowship from the Department of Health, Education, and Welfare. The National Endowment for the Humanities granted me a senior fellowship during 1971–2. The University of Michigan has supported my work not only by a sabbatical leave, but by tolerance of my absence on leave during several years. To all of these individuals and institutions I herewith give warm thanks.

RICHARD B. BRANDT

Ann Arbor, Michigan
December, 1977

CONTENTS

Part I

CHAPTER I

THE STRATEGY OF PRACTICAL CRITICISM

MORAL PHILOSOPHY has traditionally been a systematic attempt to answer some questions of apparently universal interest about: what is worth wanting or working for; what is the best thing for an agent to do from his own point of view; what is morally right; and what is morally just. This book aims to clarify these questions and to advance towards an intellectually satisfying answer to them, using non-traditional types of evidence and non-traditional argument.

The book also poses a second set of questions which have played a smaller but recently nonetheless important role in the philosophical tradition. These questions are: 'What is it rational to want, for itself?', and 'What is it rational for an agent to do, from his own point of view?'. Also: 'Which kinds of action is it rational to approve morally?' or better, because clearer, 'What kind of moral system for his society would it be rational for an agent to support?'. The relation of these questions to the previous ones may not be obvious, but answering them will in fact open the way for an answer to the questions of the first set.

The argument in pursuit of these major objectives will have two parts. One is meta-ethical or methodological. It will assign a clear and useful meaning to the term 'rational', explain why the term in that sense will naturally be commendatory, and argue that the above-listed main traditional questions of moral philosophy can be satisfactorily rephrased as questions about what it is rational to want for itself, rational for a person to do from his own point of view, and about which forms of action would be permitted by a moral system for a society which it would be rational for a member of that society to support. The other part of the argument is substantive. It will put forward and defend some generalizations about which kinds of choice or desire or support of a moral system are rational; or, in other words, about the best thing for an agent to do from his own point of view, about the intrinsically good, and about the morally right.

In establishing the substantive principles, I shall make a good deal of use of contemporary psychology. Some philosophers will raise their eyebrows at this. They think the evidential support of psychological theories is poor. Some psychologists will also object, largely because they lack confidence in systems of theory such as flourished in the 1940s. To these doubts my reply is twofold. First, I shall state explicitly the psychological generalizations on which I rely, and where possible shall indicate the evidence for them. I am claiming that these particular generalizations are sound, however dubious some parts of contemporary psychology may be. Second, even if these generalizations turn out to require modification, at least a demonstration of how psychological theory can be used to establish normative principles will be worthwhile in showing how someone can turn, to the same use, the theories of the future. Of course, it is not news that philosophers should think they can squeeze normative conclusions out of psychology: they have been trying to do this since Epicurus, and Hume is a prime example of the psychologizing of moral philosophy.

I. HOW TO PROCEED: APPEAL TO LINGUISTIC INTUITIONS?

Historically philosophers have tried to answer the traditional questions about the good and the right in basically two ways. (Sometimes the two have been combined.) The first way is to rephrase these questions in terminology sufficiently clear and precise for one to answer them by some mode of scientific or observational procedure, or at least by some clearly stateable and familiar mode of reasoning. One then uses this procedure (kind of reasoning) to find answers, sometimes surprising, to the stated questions. J. O. Urmson characterized the basic assumption of this view, when he wrote that if you want to know 'how a certain type of assertion, the moral, the mathematical, or the aesthetic, for example, can be reasonably arrived at or defended, it is clearly necessary to determine the general character of such assertions, to make it explicit what sort of claims in what sort of fields they make.... If we want to know what sort of support a claim needs, we surely need to be clear what sort of claim is being made.' (1968, pp. 10–11.)

The second tradition, which I shall call 'intuitionism', can take quite different forms. Roughly the idea is that we already have presumably well-justified opinions about the answers to the several traditional questions, although these opinions need to be systematized and hence, in some cases, revised to some degree. However, the idea is not first to frame our questions clearly and then go out to find answers, letting the chips fall where they may; but rather that we roughly already know most of the answers, and if we want to know more precisely what our questions are, the best way to find out is by looking at the principles we already know, and seeing what construction of the questions is consistent with the truth or acceptability of these principles.

I shall offer what seem to me conclusive objections to intuitionism in the final section of the present chapter (I gave reasons for dismissing the older form of the theory in 1959, Chapter 8), as well as, to some extent, in Chapter 13 where I shall discuss further the views of Professor Rawls. We must avoid intuitionism even if this were to mean (as it does not) that we must end up as complete sceptics in the area of practice. Therefore we must go along with the first procedure.

This procedure may take two forms. The first I shall call the 'method of appeal to linguistic intuitions'. The second I shall call the 'method of reforming definitions'. I shall opt for the second. In the present section I explain the first, and give reasons why we should not rely on it—although I do not deny that it should be welcomed if, by good luck, reliance upon it were to lead to the same results as use of the second method.

Roughly, according to the method of appeal to linguistic intuitions, we identify the questions of normative ethics by finding which questions people actually raise when they pose the traditional moral questions. It is thought that if we note sufficiently carefully what people (including ourselves) are doing when they raise these questions, we shall be able to paraphrase them in a perspicuous way. Then, to use some terminology of R. M. Hare, having got the 'logic' of normative concepts straight, we can see what kind of argument is a reasonable argument in normative discourse.

This procedure is attractive because it makes clear how normative inquiries can have a firm scientific basis. For how certain words are used, and what raising certain questions does can be known by observation. There is no more reason to deny that these questions can be answered by the methods of science than there is to deny that descriptive grammar, or descriptive semantics, is an empirical science.

Let me state the procedure in more detail. It is supposed that there is some expression synonymous with any normative statement in its ordinary use, which differs from the original enough to make clear what has to be done to confirm or justify the original statement, either by the methods of science or otherwise. For instance, J. S. Mill wrote (not consistently with his main line of thought): 'To think of an object as desirable ... and to think of it as pleasant, are one and the same thing.' G. E. Moore said (1903, pp. 25, 147): 'To assert that a certain line of conduct is, at a given time, absolutely right or obligatory, is obviously to assert that more good or less evil will exist in the world, if it be adopted than if anything else be done instead.' More recently Max Black wrote (1964, p. 173) of the premiss 'Everyone should do anything which is the one and only way to achieve anything that he wants to achieve' that this 'proposed additional premise must be said to be analytic, in the sense of being guaranteed correct by virtue of the meanings or functions of the terms it contains'. And R. M. Hare has offered a paraphrase of a different kind: for 'It is wrong to lie' he suggests the imperative 'Don't anyone, at any time, ever lie!'[1]

How, according to the theory, are these synonymous paraphrases to be identified? By our *linguistic* intuitions. To find whether a

---

[1] Hare does not, however, claim that ordinary language settles how normative questions are to be construed. He thinks reasons can and must be given why language should contain normative expressions paraphrasable in this way. See his 1963, pp. 2, 96 ff., 200 ff.; also my review of this book, 1964, especially pp. 140–2. I am uncomfortable about using the term 'prescriptive' as if its meaning were obvious; but discussion would lead too far afield.

sentence 'S' (containing the term to be analysed) is accurately paraphrased by the more perspicuous 'S''', we ask ourselves if there is any logically possible situation in which we should be content to utter 'S' sincerely but not 'S''', or willing to say 'S''' but not 'S'. If there is such a situation, the proposed paraphrase fails the test. If we cannot find one, then perhaps the paraphrase is accurate, barring a failure of our imagination. Sometimes our linguistic intuitions do not give unambiguous testimony.

The general project, then, is to identify the important questions of ordinary normative language, paraphrase them in a perspicuous way, and with the new statements get on with the business of finding the answers—or else give up the business of finding answers, since the paraphrase might make it clear that there is no answer to be found.[2]

The above procedure makes the work of the philosophical analyst of moral terms sound like empirical inquiry, in which a linguist might well engage if he were interested. Relatively few philosophers, however, actually engage in this sort of activity. Most philosophers who offer definitions of normative terms offer rather 'reforming' definitions, although normally they leave unexplained the course of reasoning they might use to support the definitions they adopt. For instance, R. B. Perry said that the question for philosophers is not how normative words are used, for they are used confusedly, but how they are best to be used. W. K. Frankena has said that the problems of meta-ethics demand for their solution 'clarity and decision about the nature and functions of morality, of moral discourse, and of moral theory, and this requires not only small-scale analytic inquiries but also studies in the history of ethics and morality, in the relation of morality to society and of society to the individual, as well as in epistemology and in the psychology of human motivations'. (1968, p. 80.) Other philosophers who depart from the outlined procedure in one way or another include Elizabeth Anscombe, Philippa Foot, David Falk, C. L. Stevenson, Philip Rice, and P. H. Nowell-Smith.

Why should one not rely on the guidance of ordinary language,

---

[2] The above account is a bit too crude for some theories. For instance, according to the 'emotive' theory of Stevenson, exact paraphrases cannot be found; one can only find approximate paraphrases and then offer an account of what they lack.

following 'linguistic intuitions', for framing the questions to be answered by normative inquiry? There are several reasons, doubtless recognized by many or most philosophers.

(1) The first is simply the common-sense observation that normative words are so vague that reliance on 'linguistic intuitions' can reach no definite results. This fact is reflected in dictionaries, which define normative terms by reference to other normative terms and offer nothing more enlightening. The status of these expressions is in sharp contrast to terms like 'x is the sister of y' which any dictionary or six-year-old will explain. It is no surprise that proposals that have been offered by philosophers have gained no general acceptance from other philosophers. It is true that some normative terms may be more satisfactory than this, for instance 'good' in such expressions as 'good knife', 'good eyesight', 'good swimmer', or 'good time', although I believe (with Rawls) that in fact most of these terms require a more complex paraphrase than might appear at first sight, involving the concept of 'good thing to choose', which itself must be unpacked in a complicated way for which ordinary usage provides no guidance.

One might complain that the suggested vagueness of ordinary normative language just cannot be so—that it is necessary for terms used as frequently as these to bear, in specific contexts, a meaning that is sufficiently precise. But we must remember that the meaning of these terms is never conveyed to children by explicit definitions: the parents would not know what to say. It is true that gross misapplications of normative words by children are corrected, but not the finer details of usage. The usage is not honed in a way that would be necessary for linguistic intuitions to support the perspicuous paraphrases necessary for ordinary language to be a guide for normative moral philosophy.

Even if the usage of some or many individuals is less vague than I suggest (and this may have been true, say, of Bentham), there is no reason to think there is any language-wide single meaning for these terms. In general, our meanings are entwined with our total conceptual system, and as our total beliefs change, our concepts change. Why should this not also be true of practical concepts? Take the moral concepts of religious people. Suppose a religious man says that what he means by 'wrong' is 'prohibited by God'. Now, philosophers have used a dialectical device, as early as Plato in the *Euthyphro*, to show that this theological concept cannot be what is meant by 'wrong'. But the dialectical device at most shows that religious people are confused, not that their moral concepts are identical with those of Bertrand Russell. Nor is there reason to think that the moral concepts of unruly boys from the east side of London or New York are identical with those of Moore or Sidgwick.

(2) Even if linguistic intuitions pointed to more precise paraphrases of normative terminology than they actually do, one would not want to rely on them for guidance in normative reflection. For language might well embody confusing distinctions, or fail to make distinctions it is important to make. In fact, the English language does. Let us see how.

Consider the latter point, in connection with the term 'right'. We use this word in two contexts, in one of which it must be construed as saying one thing, in the other of which, another. Sometimes it must be taken to mean that an action is morally justified; in other contexts it must be taken to mean that an action, although morally unjustified, is nevertheless morally excused, and its agent not reprehensible. The distinction is parallel to one at law, between an act's violating the statutes or common law, and the agent not being subject to a penalty because of absence of *mens rea*. Now there is nothing in English usage which positively excludes recognizing different meanings for the two different contexts. But there is also nothing which encourages it, and one hears the following reasoning used by persons who have an unquestioned competence in English: 'One is not acting wrongly if one does what one sincerely thinks is one's duty. Therefore, if a person does what he thinks is his duty, he is always doing the right thing.' Now it cannot fairly be said that persons who use this reasoning are abusing English.[3] If one sees something

---

[3] A popular columnist who dispenses syndicated advice daily recently answered the following question: 'I'm a nineteen-year-old girl who is getting more and more confused about the word "morality". Who decides what is morally right? My parents? Society? The law? Or should I make the decision myself?' To which the relevant part of the answer was as follows: 'If you feel sufficiently mature and competent to set your own standards for your own reasons, do it. Who decides what is "morally right"? With the help of your learning, examples, experience and conscience—and with an eye for consequences—you decide.' This exchange illustrates more than one point I have been making. I suggest that both the writer and the columnist were competent in English.

mistaken in this argument, it is because one has studied moral philosophy and seen that there are possible different kinds of claim which must be distinguished. Would descriptive semantics force us to recognize a mistake? It may be, of course, that there is no easy line to draw between making distinctions through the guidance of linguistic intuitions, and making them because one is forced into them in order to have a plausible moral philosophy; but if there is not, one would like to see the topic discussed more than it has been.

English also tends to confuse matters in the opposite way, by labouring distinctions without a significant difference. A prime example of this is the existence of terms like 'duty', 'obligation', and 'wrong', all capable of being employed in moral contexts. These words are not exact synonyms; at least one may say it is wrong to commit adultery or be cruel to an animal, but it sounds odd to say it is our moral duty not to. While the associations, suggestions, and flavours of these words are different, there is no difference of substance between what we say with one and with another. The differences of the words, however, provide a standing temptation to suppose there are corresponding differences of substance. Books and articles have been written on this assumption. Some have argued that something is an obligation only if one has made a contract or promise; and others have suggested that a person has a duty or an obligation only where some other person has a right. These claims are dubious, but even if they were not, we can still ask if the difference of terminology does not tend to obscure the moral similarity of the cases. Is there some important sense in which we are morally free to be cruel to animals, if cruelty to animals is merely wrong but there is no obligation to refrain from it?

(3) But suppose the above claims are both mistaken: suppose people use normative terms non-vaguely, and all in the same way. And suppose language does not confuse various jobs, at least in the way suggested. Would an appeal to linguistic intuitions, disclosing perspicuous paraphrases of normative questions, properly set the stage for normative inquiries? Not at all. Let us see why in terms of two examples.

Suppose, to take a currently popular view, that 'You ought to do A' is properly used to make a universal prescription, or perhaps, used to express a pro-attitude towards your doing *A*, with at least the implication that the speaker is prepared to feel the same for relevantly similar cases. How far would this fact take one in a normative debate? Not far. Suppose I demand of myself, on grounds of conscience, that I perform a certain act, but am not prepared to make a similar demand on others for similar cases. One might say this is impossible. But in fact it is well known that some people hold themselves to higher standards than they set for others; and in complex situations their own conclusions about what they morally must do, everything considered, are not prescribed for others. (See Raphael, 1974–5.) We should recall that the judicious Sidgwick thought it a synthetic proposition that an act which is wrong for me is wrong for anyone else in similar circumstances. (1922, p. 99.) Suppose, then, I make my demand, but refuse to universalize it. If I do, the analyst of ordinary language can, assuming the suggested definition of 'ought' is correct, show me that it is a linguistic mistake to express myself by the phrase 'I ought . . .', but I might make the demand on myself, and feel it justified, and worry not at all about the impropriety of using 'I ought . . .'. Where is the sting of being denied the use of a certain English expression?

Consider another example. Suppose 'ideal observer' theorists are right that 'is intrinsically good' means 'would be desired by anybody who was fully informed and otherwise in a normal frame of mind'. And suppose I find myself desiring to achieve something in my life, as an end in itself, and am convinced that many intelligent persons feel the same, but at the same time think that many other persons have virtually no achievement motivation, although they are fully informed and otherwise normal. Is my aspiration shown to be mistaken by allusion to the use of 'is intrinsically good'? Obviously not.

What do these examples prove? One might say: Nothing, beyond the fact that the proposed analyses are mistaken, or at least fail to recognize the flexibility of normative language. What the examples suggest, however, is that the locutions of ordinary language are not always well adapted to say what on reflection we want to say, or to raise questions which on reflection we want to raise. At least they are not infallible guides to framing the questions we want to ask. Reflection on the human situation and what we want to know must be the source of the conceptual framework we want to use; and reliance on paraphrases of ordinary language certified by our linguistic intuitions is a clumsy and often misleading method for identifying the concepts we need for the guidance of practical reflection.

2. A REFORMING DEFINITION: RATIONAL ACTION
   AND THE BEST THING TO DO

If we do not rely, for a perspicuous formulation of the questions the moral philosopher is to answer, on paraphrases of ordinary language normative questions, guided by our linguistic intuitions, where shall we turn for it? Philosophers like R. B. Perry, who agree that reliance on ordinary language is no help, are frustratingly vague about how to proceed, and why.

In the end it seems there is no alternative to reflection on what we *want to know*, for purposes of decision-making. This reflection, of course, might not promise definite results, since what a person wants to know depends on his conceptual framework or system of beliefs—and these will vary from one society, or age, or level of scientific information, to another. But fortunately there are some facts which are fixed points. Every person acts, or makes decisions. Every person has desires, aversions, aspirations. Every society has some kind of moral system. So there are some topics about which everyone will want a question answered; and one question everyone will want answered is how far actions, desires, and moral systems can be criticized by appeal to facts and observation. Some philosophers think that facts and observation cannot take us far, but it would be agreed that if they can take us anywhere, we should find out where. That question everyone will want to answer, although the precise form of the question, and the answer which can be given, will depend on the state of knowledge at the time when it is asked. It is this question on which the remainder of this book will concentrate.

With this question in mind, I shall pre-empt the term 'rational' to refer to actions, desires, or moral systems which survive maximal criticism and correction by facts and logic. We could of course use some other term, like 'fully informed', but the choice of 'rational' seems as good as any, and I do need a term which I can use regularly to refer to actions (etc.) which have this status. But I should make clear at once that 'criticism' of actions, desires, or moral systems is unlike criticism in science; or at least unlike the confirmation or refutation of a scientific belief by confronting it with evidence and principles of logic which support it logically or are incompatible with it. In the case of desires (etc.) there can be 'criticism' only in the sense that the desire or action (etc.) is shown to be what it would (or would not) be if it were maximally influenced by evidence and logic.

It is convenient to distinguish three senses of 'rational', for use in different contexts. First, I shall call a person's action 'rational' in the sense of being rational to a first approximation, if and only if it is what he would have done if all the mechanisms determining action except for his desires and aversions (which are taken as they are)—that is, the *cognitive inputs* influencing decision/action—had been optimal as far as possible. (We shall see later that this condition is met if and only if every item of *relevant available* information is present to awareness, vividly, at the focus of attention, or with an equal share of attention.) Second, I shall call a desire or aversion 'rational' if and only if it is what it would have been had the person undergone *cognitive psychotherapy* (a term which cannot be fully explained before Chapters 5 and 6). Finally, I shall say that an action is 'rational' in the sense of fully rational if and only if the desires and aversions which are involved in the action are rational, and if the condition is met for rationality to a first approximation.

Two examples may serve to make clearer what is meant. First, actions rational to a first approximation. Suppose an anthropologist is deciding whether to spend a leave of absence, planned for a Californian climate, in Berkeley or Palo Alto. He decides to go to Palo Alto, but when deciding overlooks the (possible) fact that a duplicate non-circulating set of periodicals important for his project exists in Berkeley but not at Stanford. If he had remembered this fact at the time of his decision, he would have chosen Berkeley without a doubt. Obviously his action was irrational in the sense explained. Second, an example of an irrational aversion. Let us suppose small Albert refuses to play with the interesting small daughter of a neighbour because she is devoted to a pet rabbit, and he has an intense aversion to rabbits. Let us suppose further that he has an aversion to rabbits because someone once produced a loud noise in his vicinity while he was reaching out to touch a rabbit. (See Watson and Raynor, 1920.) Now suppose that Albert would be disabused of his aversion if he repeated to himself, on a number of occasions and with utter conviction, some justified statement as 'There is no connection between rabbits and loud noises; rabbits are just friendly little beasts.' In this case his aversion would have been removed by cognitive psychotherapy and I shall say his aversion is irrational.

My proposed use for 'rational' may deviate somewhat from ordinary usage, but ordinary usage is vague. Dictionaries suggest vague synonyms like 'agreeable to reason; reasonable; sensible'. The proposed use may also deviate somewhat from that of economists who often talk of 'rational' shoppers; but the usage of economists is also not very clear, since when they say a rational person has a transitive preference ordering and acts so as to maximize expectable personal utility, it is not clear whether they are proposing to define 'rational' in this way, or merely to suggest that persons rational in some undefined sense actually behave in the manner suggested, or perhaps are recommending a kind of behaviour by use of the term 'rational'. In any case, I am proposing to use the terms 'rational' and 'irrational' as explained. Whether or not this proposed usage deviates from that of common speech or economics, it is useful to name an important and interesting concept, and henceforth I shall use it in that sense, with no further meaning or connotation.

Let me now define two of the terms used in the above explanation of rational. First, 'relevant'. A piece of information is relevant if its presence to awareness would make a difference to the person's tendency to perform a certain act, or to the attractiveness of some prospective outcome to him. Hence it is essentially a causal notion. Second, 'all available information'. This concept is intended to capture the idea of the best justified system of beliefs available at the time. It is contrasted with the beliefs the agent actually has, which may be scanty or unjustified, as compared with the science or common-sense knowledge of his day. It is also contrasted with the beliefs an omniscient being might have, beliefs in all true propositions, since we do not know the identity of such beliefs and can hardly use them as a tool of criticism.

(Almost everything a person does would be different if he had the knowledge of an omniscient being made available to him—for instance, if he were informed of the cure for cancer.) We might, however, identify all available information with the factual beliefs an agent would have had at the time of action, if his beliefs had been fixed by his total observational evidence and the principles of logic, both inductive and deductive. It seems more useful, however, to define the concept to include beliefs the agent would have if he obtained evidence which he could obtain at the time. So I prefer to define 'all available information' as the propositions accepted by the science of the agent's day, plus factual propositions justified by publicly accessible evidence (including testimony of others about themselves) and the principles of logic. This conception may need to be extended or sharpened in some directions, but the intent seems reasonably clear. Notice that 'information' in this sense need not be true. It could also be information it would be intolerably expensive to get, so that trying to get it might itself be irrational. But this conception will enable us to criticize the actions or desires of persons today, as being irrational, although they may not themselves be aware of the known facts which make them so.

The proposed definition of 'rational', it is important to see, does not import any substantive value judgements into the concept of 'rational'.

In chapters to come I shall be summarizing what contemporary empirical psychology has to say about how cognitive inputs affect both action and desire. If all goes well we shall then be in a position to defend some general statements about which kinds of action and desire are rational in the relevant sense, by showing what the behaviour and desires would be if the cognitive input were all the relevant available information. We shall then know something about which kinds of behaviour and desire would survive maximal criticism by facts and logic.

I have urged that everyone will want to know how far facts and logic will take us, and where they will take us, in the criticism of actions, desires, and moral systems. But perhaps, as the argument progresses and it becomes clear exactly what kind of criticism I am saying is possible (i.e. finding which actions and desires are rational), the reader may begin to wonder what is proved by the kind of criticism in question. I shall confront this possible doubt in Chapter 8, where I shall explain why, or to what extent, knowing that an action or desire is rational must be a recommendation of it.

Suppose it is agreed that this kind of criticism, the showing that something is rational, is important. It remains to be shown, however, whether to ask whether an action is rational or a desire is rational is to capture everything important in the traditional normative questions: 'What is desirable in itself?' or 'What is the best thing to do?'. In other words, it remains to be shown whether talk of something being rational can serve as a useful replacement for, or explication of, talk of the best thing to do, or the desirable. It is important to know this. For, although I have urged that it is pointless to follow the guidance of our intuitions about ordinary language in deciding what precise questions normative philosophy should try to answer, we want to be sure that a proposal that looks promising does not overlook something important that is asked about in traditional ordinary-language normative questions.

Let us begin with the expression 'the best thing to do', postponing consideration of 'desirable' and 'morally right'.

We should first note that to ask what is the best thing to do is the same as to ask which action is more worthy of being chosen than any other action open to the agent. Let us then consider this second question. Then we can ask: 'In what way may one action be identified as more worthy of being chosen?' Obviously not merely by observing whether the agent in fact chooses it. We come at least closer if we suggest that it is the one that would be chosen, if the causal factors responsible for the choice have been criticized in all possible ways, have been purged of all mistakes. But then, which are the possible modes of criticism? Which kinds of 'mistake' are possible in this area? In chapters to come we shall see what these are. We shall see that awareness of the options open, awareness of the possible outcomes of one action as compared with another, vivid and detailed representation of these outcomes, and so on, all play a role in determining action. When these and other cognitive factors have been corrected as much as possible, the cognitive 'mistakes' relevant to action will have been removed as far as possible, and the resulting actions will have endured maximal criticism. (Is any other mode of criticism possible, if we lay down the restriction that criticism is not to make use of unsupported normative principles?) But evidently action criticized in this sense is exactly what I have been calling 'rational' action. It turns out, then, that when we try to unpack our rough concept of one action being 'more worthy of choice' than another—the best action—in the light of what we know about the causal determinants of action, our only option is to identify it with the action the causal sources of which have been 'corrected' in the light of optimal use of relevant information—precisely the action I have called a rational action. So it looks as if, at least thus far, 'What is the rational thing to do?' does not miss important issues raised by the traditional question 'What is the best thing to do?'

It might be argued that the former question is not an adequate substitute for the latter, because the latter has functions which the former has not. Which functions? It is true that one function of 'the best thing to do' is to recommend. But obviously the same is true of 'the rational thing to do': if a person with a reputation for thoughtfulness says that a certain action is the one I would take if my decision process were fully moulded by available information, he has clearly recommended it to me—as we shall see more fully in Chapter 8. There is no incompatibility between a statement being true or false and with a descriptive meaning, as is true for 'it is rational to do' statements, and its having performative (e.g. recommending) force just on account of that meaning. It is possible that the traditional expression has some other function which the 'it is rational to' does not, but as yet no one has pointed out what it is.

In view of the above, ought we to teach children in school that 'the best thing to do' comes to the same thing as 'the rational thing to do'? Yes, and no. No, in the sense that it is just plain false that the two expressions mean the same, for the former has no definite meaning at all, in ordinary use. Yes, in the sense that the latter expression captures all that is clear in the former, as we see when we try to unpack it; and in the sense that association of the two expressions will help the child, when he asks himself (as he doubtless will continue to do for a long time) what is the best thing to do, to think of the detailed steps he should take in order to determine what is the fully criticized action.[4]

3. HOW TO PROCEED: APPEAL TO ETHICAL INTUITIONS?

We now turn to a wholly different type of theory about how to answer normative questions: intuitionism. Supporters of this view do not think that the proper order of reflection is the one approved by the theories we have been considering: first, a clear formulation of what question is to be answered (viz. if one wishes, a 'definition' of ethical terms); then, use of observation and scientific method or some indicated appropriate mode of argument; leading finally to a normative conclusion, possibly surprising. On the contrary, they think proper ethical reflection roughly goes the other way: antecedently accepted normative beliefs about concrete situations, then information from science or observation, and finally inference to normative generalizations or definitions. Indeed, a very popular method of appraising proposed general normative principles (or definitions) is to find their implications for particular—often very peculiar or even bizarre situations—and to approve the principles if and only if they agree with 'our intuitions' for these cases. Thus J. O. Urmson recently (1974–5) defended a plurality of basic normative principles without any general priority rules, on the grounds that we cannot 'accept' the implications of the alternatives. And John Rawls wrote that 'There is a definite if limited class of facts against which conjectured principles can be checked, namely our considered judgements in reflective equilibrium.' (1971, p. 51.)

---

[4] I have sometimes (1972) suggested that it is a good replacement for 'What is the best thing for me to do, from the point of view of my own welfare?' Professor Mark Overvold, in his dissertation, 'Self-Interest, Self-Sacrifice and the Satisfaction of Desires', 1976, deposited in the Graduate Library of the University of Michigan, has shown that this was a mistake. For possibly, according to my definition, the rational act for me would be to do something which I fully anticipate will cost me my life, for the sake of one of my children. But, whereas it seems sensible to say this is 'the best thing for me to do', it does not seem sensible to say that it is the best thing for me to do, from the point of view of my own welfare. I am not enhancing my own welfare by losing my life for the sake of someone else. According to my earlier definition, it would be logically impossible for a rational act to be a case of self-sacrifice: the present definition allows this, and also provides a useful tool, as we shall see, for explaining the sense in which it can be rational to act morally—where moral action conflicts with self-interest.

What kind of thing do these philosophers have in mind when they speak of 'intuitions' against which normative generalizations can be checked? This is not easy to say. An older view was that there are simple ethical properties (goodness, rightness), the attachment of which to events or states of affairs is logically necessary and mind-independent; and that it is possible to know that something is good or right either because the fact that something of a certain sort is necessarily good or right is self-evident to thoughtful adults or because adults can be directly acquainted with such facts by a special 'sense'. Such knowings were called 'intuitions'. The contemporary philosophers we are now discussing write as if they do not subscribe to this view. What then are these intuitions which can serve as a check for normative generalizations? Some writers may have in mind phenomena which undoubtedly do occur: a person being ready to prescribe something universally; being for or against something; feeling moral disapproval of some action or person; feeling guilty about some deed of his own, and so on. But such phenomena can hardly be a reasonable check of normative generalizations except in the context of some theory about what ethical statements mean, either a prescriptivist theory like Hare's, or some type of 'ideal observer' theory which claims that moral statements can be explicated as statements about how well-informed impartial persons would react (e.g. 'A is morally reprehensible' might be construed to mean 'Any fully informed impartial and otherwise normal person would feel disapproval of A').[5]

Let me now formulate an 'intuitionist' theory which appears to be espoused in influential quarters at the present time. On this view, to say that we have 'intuitions' is roughly to say simply that we do make normative statements sincerely, and believe them in some ordinary sense. So there are beliefs in, and dispositions on occasion to utter, certain normative statements; and to say this is to say there are 'intuitions'. Not quite: these philosophers use 'intuition' to refer to a class of normative beliefs somewhat narrower than the totality of such beliefs. They have wanted to exclude normative beliefs held because of recognized logical relations to other already present normative beliefs, such as

[5] But see Brandt, 1959, Chap. 10; Scheffler, 1954; Morton White, 1956, Chaps. 14, 16.

a belief that this lie is wrong because it is an instance of the already accepted general principle that all lies are wrong. There are further limitations: to judgements which are considered, which are made or could be made in moments of emotional calm, and are not obviously distorted by personal interest. Such beliefs may be of any level of generality; they may be about particular actions or some whole class of actions, for example, all breaches of promise. One very general such belief might be: 'If an action is wrong for one person, it is wrong for everyone in similar circumstances.' The degree of commitment to such normative statements may differ from one case to another; let us call a person's degree of belief in one of these 'intuitions', which it enjoys independently of recognition of its logical relations to other such intuitions, its initial credence level for the person. We could represent this by fractions ranging from o (absence of any inclination to believe) to 1 (the strongest possible belief). Notice that credence level seems to change with time: the moral judgements we utterly accepted in our teens may seem little, or not at all, convincing now.

How, then, are we to test proposed general principles by appeal to intuitions? Historically some philosophers have thought that convictions about specific situations must be allowed to stand no matter what; any principle incompatible with one of these must be rejected. At present a more complicated view appears to be more widely held—to the effect that intuitions about specific cases may require rejection or modification through reflection on their logical relation to other intuitions. More specifically, what some philosophers have in mind is a rough parallel to the procedure Nelson Goodman recommended (1965, p. 64) for logic: that we amend a general principle which yields particular implications we are unwilling to accept, and that we reject a particular judgement if it violates a general principle we are unwilling to amend. One procedure of this sort is this: in case of conflict between a suggested general principle and any intuitions (whether general or particular), we are to reject, amend, or add in such a way that the total resulting system of normative beliefs 'saves' the total amount of initial credence (represented by the sum of the suggested fractions) better than any other system of normative beliefs. Problems arise if we try to push the numerical model too far; and some philosophers probably wish to say nothing more precise than simply that, in case of choice between two sets of normative beliefs, we give preference to the one which we find it easier to believe as a whole. We might call this account a 'coherence theory of justification in ethics'.

The proposal is especially interesting when used to test a simple very general theory. One might think of Henry Sidgwick as having defended utilitarianism in this way.[6] He thought that the lower-level principles of common-sense are beyond repair: vague, incapable of amendment so as to be compatible with intuitions of particular situations, and conflicting with each other. He proposed utilitarianism as a set of basic principles to replace all the rest—principles to which he thought common sense normally appeals when lower-level principles run into trouble of some sort. Of these he said (1922, p. 425): 'Utilitarianism may be presented as the scientifically complete and systematically reflective form of that regulation of conduct, which through the whole course of human history has always tended substantially in the same direction.' Professor Rawls makes a somewhat similar claim for his principle that an action is right if and only if it accords with the principles every rational person would prefer as supreme directives for action in a society in which he expected to live, if he were choosing in ignorance of any facts which could be used to advantage himself as compared with others.

Rawls, however, introduces a further distinction. He speaks of principles satisfying a somewhat Goodman-like condition as in 'reflective equilibrium' (for that person at that time—he does not claim that the equilibria of all persons will agree). He then distinguishes between reflective equilibrium 'in the narrow sense' and 'in the broad sense'. The former contemplates a Goodman-like combination of restructured moral principles of persons (say, at the secondary school level) who have been uninfluenced by philosophical arguments; the latter contemplates a Goodman-like system of intuitions as these are after influence by philosophical arguments, or as they ideally would be after influence by 'all relevant philosophical arguments', presumably such as arguments against act utilitarianism like those presented by Rawls (1971) or

[6] But we must not interpret Sidgwick too simply. (See Peter Singer, 1974.)

Hodgson (1967) or some deontic logicians, or for utilitarianism like those offered by Hare (1963, 1976) or W. S. Vickrey (1973) or J. C. Harsanyi (1973).

How might these philosophers justify their view that a normative principle should be tested against our intuitions in the sense of our considered beliefs, or a given intuition be tested by its compatibility with a system of normative beliefs (say by testing whether it can be included in a system with maximal initial credence level)? One reason is clear enough: if we assume that normative principles have implications for action, it would be self-defeating to espouse inconsistent ones. But this requirement will not take us far: it requires us merely to hold a consistent set— or a causally coherent (non-self-defeating) set—of judgements about types of action. It does not dictate any particular way of adjudicating conflicts between, say, higher-level and lower-level normative 'intuitions'. So proponents of the theory must find some other justification for the procedures of maximizing the sum of initial credence levels[7] or of giving preference to the set of normative beliefs we find it easier to accept as a whole. If it is supposed that normative principles are true or false, it could be that adopting principles so as to maximize initial credence levels (or adopting the set one finds morally most congenial as a whole) leads away from the truth rather than towards it. There is a problem here quite similar to that which faces the traditional coherence theory of justification of belief: that the theory claims that a more coherent system of beliefs is better justified than a less coherent one, but there is no reason to think this claim is true unless some of the beliefs are initially credible—and not merely initially believed—for some reason other than their coherence, say, because they state facts of observation. In the case of normative beliefs, no reason has been offered why we should think that initial credence levels, for a person, correspond to credibilities. The fact that a person has a firm normative conviction gives that belief a status no better than fiction. Is one coherent set of fictions supposed to be better than another?

One problem with appraising the thesis of these 'coherence-

---

[7] Professor I. Scheffler wrote: 'I may be asked how I justify the maximization of commitment. My answer can only be that I am trying to describe what I take to be the meaning of rational justification.' (1954, p. 178.) Compare J. W. N. Watkins, 1963, p. 109.

intuitionist' philosophers is that they do not make clear whether they think that normative statements express any facts. They attempt to be neutral among meta-ethical theories. And if, preserving this neutrality, they maintain that an ethical conviction is only a 'disposition to utter certain normative sentences sincerely', it is unclear why anything should be 'tested' at all—or even why it should be claimed that ethical convictions have logical connections with one another.

Advocacy of testing normative generalizations against ethical intuitions might be combined with the meta-ethical thesis that normative statements express attitudes (that normative 'beliefs' are attitudes, pro or con), or that normative statements are universal prescriptions. Then getting a coherent set of convictions would not be an advance towards knowledge or of justified belief; but it could be a desideratum all the same. Why? There is the reason already mentioned, that an incoherent set of moral commitments may be self-defeating in action. But, in addition, it might just be satisfying to identify a coherent policy. People may just dislike an incoherent set of moral attitudes, just as they dislike harbouring incoherent beliefs—they may dislike this form of *cognitive dissonance* (Festinger, 1957). One might ask why anyone should want this, or why specifically one should aim at reflective equilibrium in the wide sense rather than in the narrow sense. Is it thought that somehow we thereby approach sophistication? It is not clear what answers might be given to these questions.

In summary, it is puzzling why an intuition—a normative conviction—should be supposed to be a test of anything.

Various facts about the genesis of our moral beliefs militate against mere appeal to intuitions in ethics. Our normative beliefs are strongly affected by the particular cultural tradition which nurtured us, and would be different if we had been in a learning situation with different parents, teachers, or peers. Moreover, the moral convictions of some people derive, to use words (1974) of Peter Singer, 'from discarded religious systems, from warped views of sex and bodily functions, or from customs necessary for the survival of the group in social and economic circumstances that now lie in the distant past'. What we should aim to do is step outside our own tradition somehow, see it from the outside, and evaluate it, separating what is only the vestige of a possibly once useful moral tradition from what is justifiable at present. The method of intuitions in principle prohibits our doing this. It is only an internal test of coherence, what may be no more than a re-shuffling of moral prejudices.

Moreover, moral intuitions differ from one individual or culture to another. Where one person thinks promise-keeping or sexual taboos are highly important—these beliefs have high initial credence level—and another does not, the search for reflective equilibrium will only produce different moral systems, and offers no way to relieve the conflict. Nor is this matter trivial. Moral disagreement does not exist only between our own reflective equilibria and those of some primitive tribes, or on relatively super-ficial matters. It exists among sophisticated civilized persons and in core areas; for instance, some persons find Locke's principles about property intuitively appealing, and erect a moral and political theory thereon in which what we might call the 'claims of humanity', espoused by others, are ignored—and the result be practically very influential on policies of taxation.[8] The defender of appeal to intuitions might say that anyone who does this simply has not completed the task of making a coherent system of his intuitions. But has this been shown?

A defender of appeal to intuitions might challenge dissenters to name a better method for establishing normative claims than by appeal to intuitions. But this challenge can be met. There is a viable alternative: to make up our minds what it is we want to know when we are faced with practical problems. I suggested how we might do this when I outlined reasons for thinking we might substitute for the question 'What is the best thing to do?' the clearer question 'Which action would be the fully criticized action?' or 'Which action would be a rational action?'. We shall see later how certain other clear questions emerge, as the ones we want to answer for purposes of action. Once we know what these are, we can use the ordinary methods of science and observation to deter-mine the answers. We need not rely on our antecedent moral commitments.

Intuitionism can be, in addition to being a theory about how

[8] Compare, for instance, the position taken by Robert Nozick, 1974, with that of Allan Gibbard, 1976, or Peter Singer in his review of Nozick in the *New York Review of Books*, 6 March 1975, or that of David Lyons, 1976.

to answer normative questions, also a theory about what normative questions mean. At least it can be if our normative beliefs can be formed into a system, with one supreme principle at the top, and with all other beliefs derivable by straight deduction either from it alone, or from it taken along with factual premisses. For one can then make the supreme principle (which will contain a moral predicate) analytic by construing the meaning of the moral predicate so that the analyticity follows. For instance, if we had the supreme principle 'An act is right if and only if it will produce as much happiness as would any other act open to the agent', we could make the principle analytically true by proposing to define 'is right' as identical with the property on the right-hand side. Such a move is essentially the one made by Rawls (1971, p. 111)—although he explicitly disavows resting any of his conclusions on the definition—when he says that 'the concept of something's being right is the same as, or better, may be replaced by, the concept of its being in accordance with the principles that in the original position would be acknowledged to apply to things of its kind. . . . Explication is elimination: we start with a concept the expression for which is somehow troublesome; but it serves certain ends that cannot be given up. An explication achieves these ends in other ways that are relatively free of difficulty. Thus if the theory of . . . rightness as fairness fits our considered judgements in reflective equilibrium, and if it enables us to say all that on due examination we want to say, then it provides a way of eliminating customary phrases in favour of other expressions.' A philosopher who makes this move, however, has adopted a naturalistic definition of the 'reforming' type, and the question in what sense his total theory is an 'intuitionism' becomes more complex.

CHAPTER II

WANTING AND PLEASURE

THE CONCLUSION of the preceding chapter was that it is of first importance, for practical decisions, to know what it is *rational*, in a certain sense, to do, and want: that is, to know what one would do or want if relevant available information were vividly represented at every point in the decision process where thoughts influence what is done. In the following chapters I shall lay out the parts of psychological theory essential for understanding where and how thoughts or beliefs influence actions and also the formation of desires and aversions. Later I shall put this information to work and state some general principles about when actions (and desires/aversions) are rational. These principles will identify actions and desires which have been *cognitively criticized* as much as possible.

The branches of psychology on which we can draw are the theory of motivation, the theory of learning, and the theory of psychotherapy. These branches overlap, and the divisions were not invented with an eye to our problems. I shall therefore slice the psychological material into two parts, and lay out the theory correspondingly. One part I shall call 'the theory of action': it comprises the lawlike principles which relate an action of the organism to its properties (such as occurrent wants), roughly at the time of action, and on which the action is causally dependent. (This is discussed in Chapter 3.) The other part is 'genetic': it comprises principles relating action-relevant properties of the organism (the ones on which the theory of action relies to explain actions) to preceding experiences and earlier (perhaps native) properties of the organism. (I shall set forth this genetic theory in Chapter 5.)

The main business of the present chapter is to explain two notions, both of great importance for psychology and philosophy. The first is 'wants' and its opposite 'finds aversive'—a term for which I shall often substitute one favoured by some psychologists, 'is valenced for', since 'valence' can take positive and negative values and hence serve both for 'wants' and its opposite. The second is 'pleasant' (and 'unpleasant'). The former terms will be central in the theory of action sketched in the following chapter; the latter will be important in the genetic account in Chapter 5.

These concepts will be important throughout the remainder of this book, and they have been of central philosophical importance since the earliest practical philosophy of the Greeks. Controversies over pleasure theories and desire theories of the meaning of 'good', over whether people desire only pleasure, whether only pleasure is intrinsically good, over interpersonal comparisons of both desire and pleasure, and about the measurement of both—these are very much alive today. They can be clearly formulated and resolved, only if we can give an account of how 'want' and 'pleasant' can be intelligently used. What we need, of course, is not an account of common-sense usage of these terms but an account of concepts suited for a scientific psychological explanatory conceptual framework—just as the philosopher writing about the concept of temperature need not worry about the common-sense use of 'temperature' but about the concept important for physical theory.

1. WANTS AND AVERSIONS (VALENCE)

People *want* events or situations of a certain sort to obtain at some time or times; or they are *aversive* to events or situations in the sense that they want them not to obtain at some time or times. We can speak, meaning the same, of an event or situation obtaining at a certain time as being positively (negatively) *valenced* for a given individual at a certain time.

What is valence? For something to be valenced for a person at a time is for that person to be in a certain 'central motive state' (Bindra, 1974, 1969, 1968; Gallistel, 1964)—perhaps ideally describable in complex physiological-chemical terminology as 'a readiness of certain neuron-sets to fire'. At present, however, we are in no position to describe this state accurately in physiological-chemical terms; and even if we were, we ought not to define 'valence' in this way, but rather by relation to behaviour or experience, since we would not accept a physiological definition that did not identify the same things as being valenced as would a psychological-type definition.

The term 'valence' (and similarly, 'want', 'aversion') is not an observation term, but a theoretical construct in psychological theory, and its meaning is conferred on it by the laws in which it appears. The most important of these is the law relating it to action-tendencies, and we may use this law as giving us a first approximation to an account of its meaning. We shall therefore say that a person 'wants' something O, or that something O 'is valenced for' him at the time, if his central motive state is such that if it were then to occur to him that a certain act of his then would tend to bring O about, his tendency to perform that act would be increased.

What is a *tendency* to perform a certain act? One might incline to say that a tendency to perform a certain act is just the probability that the agent will do it; but this proposal will not work, at least if we have a frequency conception of 'probability' in mind, since we might want to say that a person had a strong tendency to perform a certain act at a time even if, when he has such a tendency, he seldom performs the act on account of the presence of stronger contrary tendencies. It looks as if we can understand the term fully only by seeing its role in the various law statements into which it enters. Nevertheless, we can get an initial idea of it from just one of these laws: that an agent will actually perform an action A if and only if the tendency to perform A is stronger than the tendency to perform any other action B.

So far, then, I am saying that a person *wants* a certain thing if his central state is such that, were a certain thought or judgement to take place, there would be an increase in his tendency to perform a certain act.

But in addition there are other tendencies which are lawfully related to valence, indicative of it, and partially define its meaning. First, consider 'disappointment'. Suppose a child's father has promised to bring him a toy. The child talks about this all day, and towards evening watches at the window for the approach of his father. When the father arrives, it turns out that he has forgotten, and the child bursts into tears. Obviously the disappointed bursting into tears is evidence of positive valence. It is well known that such valence-indicating behaviour is not restricted to the case of human beings; a chimpanzee, for instance, is manifestly frustrated when he finds only lettuce where he had expected a banana. Second, consider elation or elation behaviour. Suppose a man receives an unexpected letter telling him he has won a $10,000 prize and enclosing a cheque. He leaps for joy, stops work, and hurries home to show it to his wife. Third, when some kind of event is valenced there is a disposition to think of such an event, or to notice ways of bringing it about. Thus if I am hungry I notice signs of restaurants along a street, where I may not have noticed them before. Of, if I am asked to make up stories about what is happening in scenes shown in pictures, I am apt to construe the picture in terms of a kind of event that is valenced—an assumption of the Thematic Apperception Test. Fourth, if I am deciding what to do and some outcome is valenced much more strongly than others, I shall decide more quickly than if the margin is smaller. A rat, for instance, when deciding to run down a runway where he will find both food and shock, will reflect on the situation more briefly, the hungrier he is (and the longer, the less food and the more shock he expects). Again, one works more vigorously for something more strongly valenced; hence we expect a rat to run more rapidly when he is very hungry than when he is not (with some qualifications). In some cases the mere thought of a valenced event produces physiological effects: a person wanting breakfast who thinks of bacon and eggs will have motion in the duodenum. Of course, if all these things are lawfully related to valence, it follows that they are to some extent correlated with one another.

These lawful relationships explain the meaning of 'valence' in present psychological theory, at least in large part. Obviously it is a disposition of the central nervous system which can have different degrees of magnitude. Also, again obviously, the degree of wanting can change rapidly; if I sight a luscious-looking eclair on a pastry tray just as I am finishing dinner in a restaurant, my desire for dessert may increase notably in a moment's time.[1]

We need at this point to make certain distinctions: we need to distinguish *occurrent* from normal and effective valence. The account so far has been an account of occurrent valence, and

[1] For psychologists' discussions of the concept, see Lewin, 1938; Ryan, 1970, Chap. 11; Irwin, 1971, Chap. 3; Heider, 1959, Chap. 5; MacCorquodale and Meehl, 1953, 1954; Tolman, 1954, 1955; Vroom, 1964, Chap. 2; Hilgard and Bower, 1975; Atkinson and Birch, 1970; Atkinson and Feather, 1966, Chaps. 1, 11. For elation and frustration behaviour in rats, see Amsel, 1958, 1952; Crespi, 1942; E. C. Jones, 1970; and Tolman, 1932, p. 75.

that is what I mean when I use the term 'valence', unless special notice is given. The idea has been that a person at a time t occurrently wants a certain situation if all that is required at t, in order for a relevant change in an action-tendency to occur, is that he have a thought at t, to the effect that this action would tend to produce the situation. But we also want to recognize such a thing as a *normal* valence. Take a person's interest in eating apple pie. We know that the occurrent valence of eating apple pie will be low at a particular time if the person is food-satiated, or if on recent days he has eaten many pieces of apple pie. So we may wish to say that although a person's occurrent desire for apple pie is low, normally eating apple pie is highly valenced. There is also *effective* valence. When something is occurrently valenced, it is true that if a certain thought were to occur, then a certain action-tendency would be increased. But suppose no such thought occurs. It seems useful to distinguish the status of occur-rently valenced events which are not in any way before the mind at the time, from those which in some way are. When the object is before the mind, an occurrently valenced event will be called effectively valenced. (Something effectively valenced need not be affecting action-tendencies, because it may be before the mind in the absence of a belief relating it to action, e.g. daydreaming about apple pie.) Obviously many things can be normally valenced for a person at t which are not occurrently valenced at t; and many things can be occurrently valenced at t which are not effectively valenced at t—since only as many things (three or four?) can be effectively valenced as can be before the mind, in thought, at once.

With these distinctions in hand, we can turn to the contention that the above account of valence needs at least some addition, bringing it closer to being a quality of conscious experience (and hence tending to make 'valence' an observation term). David McClelland (in McClelland, Atkinson, Clark, and Lowell, 1953, pp. 28 ff., 1951, pp. 227 ff.) wrote that when some state of affairs S is positively valenced 'the thought of S produces or reinstates a favourable affective tone'. Karl Duncker (1951, p. 416) pro-posed that if a situation is desired, then it, as presented in anticipation, 'becomes aglow with an empathetical feeling tone of pleasantness'. Alvin Goldman (1970, pp. 92–8; also Gosling, 1969, pp. 97, 105, 121, 124) has gone further, saying that when a state of affairs is valenced, there is a 'favourable regarding, viewing, or taking of the prospect' of it; he actually identifies wanting with this kind of conscious event, said to be phenomenally unlocated, not a sensation, feeling, impulse or flash.

What should one say about such proposals? It does seem that some effective valences may make a difference to direct experience. When a hungry person thinks of eating bacon and eggs, his thought arouses motion in the duodenum, not to mention a 'watering mouth'; and the thought does seem to have a glow of excitement about it. So there is some plausibility in supposing that some effective valences are accompanied by 'glows'. It is clear, however, that normal valences and occurrent valences cannot all be represented in this way—there are just far too many. One could, of course, define 'valence' so as to be identical with just 'effective valence'; in that case 'occurrent' valence' would be explained as a disposition for effective valence to occur in certain conditions, when the thing is thought about.

There is an epistemological attraction in the idea that at least effective valences are represented in conscious experience, since this would explain what we are tempted to believe, that we know whether we want something without observing our behaviour and without waiting to see if we are delighted or disappointed by news we may acquire about the prospects of the state of affairs in question. For if wanting is reliably correlated with some introspectible experience, then we can know whether we want just by introspecting. But the epistemological argument is inconclusive. Even if we suppose that knowledge of what we want is non-inferential—and it may not be so—we need not postulate an introspectible experience as the only available explanation of the facts. For one thing, it is possible that, when we reflect on some outcome we want, we just do believe that we want that outcome, because a tendency to say 'I want that ...' has become conditioned to the fact of wanting. There are analogues to this, such as knowing where one's limbs are without inferring the location from some special sensation.

Furthermore, there are some objections to the claim that *effective* valences always have such a correlate in experience. (1) If intentional behaviour is always directed by thoughts of outcomes with these tell-tale glows, it seems we should understand our own motivation better than at least some analysts think we do. There is a special puzzle if there is evidence that behaviour is influenced by wants which are entirely unconscious. (2) It is doubtful whether introspection reveals these experiences to vary in intensity with the known intensity of the corresponding valences. At least, we are sometimes surprised to find, after making a decision to forego a certain outcome, how deeply disappointed we are at the loss. If these 'glows' are, or accurately represent, the valences, this disparity seemingly should not occur.

It may be that such conscious events sometimes occur when something valenced is thought about. But it does not follow that they always do, or that they always occur when there is purposive behaviour, much less are causally sufficient for it. Indeed, it is doubtful whether they occur very frequently in the course of normal behaviour—for instance, in my own experience while writing the preceding lines. It looks as if the brain is able to control behaviour so as to bring about valenced situations, quite often, without the intervention of any conscious 'glowing' representations of the situation, just as it is able to manage typing a certain sentence without thinking of the letters.

It appears, then, that the concept of 'valence' which is important for psychological laws predictive of behaviour is the one explained earlier: the concept of occurrent valence as a disposition (roughly) of the central nervous system such that, if the thought were to occur that a certain action would tend to produce a certain situation, then the tendency to perform that act would be increased.

A further distinction is needed: between what is wanted or valenced for itself—what is in this book always meant by 'valenced' unless otherwise indicated—and what is in a sense wanted because it is seen to be a means to something wanted for itself. The distinction is an important one. It is required for any clear explanation of the philosophical debates about the distinction between intrinsic and extrinsic value. (See Quinn, 1974.) Failure to make it has seduced some philosophers into a proliferation of conscious 'wanting-experiences'. There is a temptation to do this, since 'I want' in English is ordinarily used not only to refer to the status of things wanted or aversive in themselves, but also to events with only the status of means or routes to valenced outcomes. For instance, asked why I am not watching football on television, I might reply that 'I want to read X's dissertation'; but it might be the opposite of the truth to suppose I am drawn to read that dissertation—I read it only because I am averse to neglecting my duties. The distinction is also important for psychology (Olds, 1956, p. 56). As Kurt Lewin pointed out (1938, pp. 93 f.), if you say that every means to an end is valenced and at the same time assert that action-tendencies are a function of the valenced situations of which one is aware, then the tendency to reach an end-goal (e.g. hearing a symphony) would diminish as one traversed the route, and one would perhaps find oneself in conflict en route, with as many valenced situations behind one as situations in the direction of the end-goal.[2] Failure to make a sharp distinction appears to infect the animal literature of 'secondary reward' and 'secondary re-inforcement'.

There is a problem, however, of stating exactly what is the difference—and the subsequent one of finding operational criteria for distinguishing it. There are clear cases of both statuses. An appendectomy is something a person could hardly want for itself; people have them only to avoid pain or nausea or threat to life. In contrast pain is something aversive in itself to normal people; people normally want to get rid of it for no further reason, although they may have further reasons, for instance if pain prevents working at top efficiency. Again, listening to a symphony or walking in the woods are clear examples of experiences wanted for themselves; a person can well want these for no further reason, although he may also want them for further reasons, for instance, to please a friend. The distinction, then, is familiar. But how may we formulate the difference? I propose the following, with the understanding that the described relation between valence and action-tendency is to be generalized to other tendencies (e.g. to feel joy or disappointment) which are criteria of valence. I suggest,

---

[2] Some psychologists wish to dispense with the whole route-goal distinction, and say that behaviour is explained by the fact that classical conditioning makes the next stage of the route, beyond where one is, attractive—so that the rat keeps running because the position immediately ahead of him is positively valenced. This theory, however, cannot explain why, when a rat has, prior to being placed on the runway, been put in a familiar goal-box and found it empty, he shows little or no interest in running the maze. It is evident that what he thinks is in the goal-box is highly relevant to what he does.

then, that an outcome O is occurrently *intrinsically* valenced for a person at a time t if and only if his central nervous system at t is such that if he judged (thought with belief) that a certain act by him at t would tend to bring about O, then, even in the absence of any further judgements about O (such as its probable further effects) not contained in the concept of O, there would be an increase in his tendency to perform that act. We must also require that the O said to be intrinsically valenced be stripped down so as not to include elements irrelevant to the increase of the person's tendency to perform the act.

This conception of 'valence' makes it difficult to identify what is valenced, since it requires knowing a certain judgement, without the help of other judgements, would elicit an increment in action-tendency. But the difficulty should have been expected, for it is not clear whether the company of other human beings, being liked and respected by others, having power over others, or having money are really wanted for themselves, or only because of an expectation that they will bring other benefits.

To say that something is wanted for itself is not, of course, to say that its being so is 'functionally autonomous' in the sense that its status will persist without occasional 'reinforcements' in the sense of support, say, by occasional gratifications from experience with the valenced entity or situations like it.

Families of Valenced Objects: Motive and Incentive Value[3]

When something is occurrently valenced for me, the fact is usually not isolated. If eating a bowl of bean soup is occurrently positively valenced for me, the chances are that eating any one of many other foods is also valenced. Two facts about these valences must be noted. First, the longer the time since my last meal, the larger the number of foods the eating of which is positively valenced. Second, there is an order among these valences: eating a large bowl of soup may be preferred to eating a small bowl, or steak preferred to bean soup. (There are complications: there are foods valenced for the beginning of a meal, and others valenced only for the end of a meal.) This preference ordering correlates roughly with the order in which eating them becomes positively

---

[3] For helpful discussions see Atkinson and Birch, 1970, Chap. 2; Ryan, 1970, pp. 473 ff.; and Atkinson and Feather, 1966, Chaps. 1, 11.

valenced the hungrier I get. Some things (e.g. Swiss chocolates) I want to eat pretty much irrespective of my level of satiation; other things (the least preferred) I want to eat only when I am starved. The total situation might be represented by a stick protruding through a surface, with names of foods listed on it in order of preference from top to bottom, and the distance between any point above the surface and the surface representing the degree of occurrent valence of the item listed at that point. As time passes since my last meal, the stick rises, with more and more foods emerging above the surface. When I eat, the stick sinks, until when I have eaten my fill its top end is at or near or even below the surface. Obviously the occurrent valence of a particular food depends on two things: how much of the stick as a whole protrudes, and the distance of a given item from the bottom of the stick. No food has positive valence when the top of the stick has sunk to the level of the surface.

When the valences of states of affairs are related in this way we may say they form a 'family'. (Some psychologists would prefer to say they manifest a 'drive'.) Several relationships define membership in a family. (1) The valences rise and fall together (not exactly: when I have consumed a steak, the meat section has declined sharply, but the valence of eating cherry pie only slightly). (2) The valence of each member falls roughly when any member of the family occurs (e.g. when a steak is eaten). In this sense, we can say that any member of a family is substitutable for any other. (Any food somewhat satisfies hunger.) (3) The valences of all members of a family begin to rise, after a definite time interval since the occurrence of any member of the set. The time interval since this occurrence (since satiation, if at that time the most preferred member of the family fell to zero valence) may be called 'deprivation time'. In the case of the physical desires, this fact of the rise of all valences with deprivation time derives from physiological facts such as cellular depletion and a consequent difference between the chemistry of venous and arterial blood, and the reaction to this of sensors in the brain. The rise of valences with deprivation time, however, seems not to be characteristic only of physical desires; it seems to be characteristic also of the valence of having human company or of receiving admiration or approval. (Eisenberger, 1970; Kimble, 1961, pp. 254, 433; Gewirtz and

Baer, 1958.) (4) In many cases when a certain deprivation time has elapsed some disliked stimuli appear, e.g. hunger pangs or faintness. Lewin speculated that disliked stimuli occur with every family, when the deprivation interval is great enough (1938, p. 135).[4] (5) When the set of valences has risen because of a period of deprivation, the level of physical activity—restlessness or exploratory activity—increases.

Some 'families' are tighter-knit than others. If valenced situations do not have the first two of the above relations, it is pointless to call them 'members of a family' at all. But members of some families will have more of the above properties than others.

Are there positively valenced states of affairs which do not belong to some family or other? Some psychologists appear to think there are none. But surely some seem to have this status: say, having a grandfather clock, which is occurrently positively valenced for the present writer.

It is obvious from the stick metaphor that the valence of any member of a family depends on two factors: the relative strength of the motivation of the whole family, and the relative standing of the item among members of the family. The first factor I shall call 'motive' (some would prefer 'drive'); the second I shall call 'incentive value'. The factors are experimentally separable: for instance, we know that a rat will run faster down an alley the hungrier he is (motive), or the more he likes the goody he happens to know is in the goal-box (incentive value). In Chapter 5 we shall be concerned with the genesis of incentive values.

It is controversial whether total occurrent valence is the sum, or a multiplicative function of motive and incentive value; the latter theory implies that the valence is zero in case either factor is zero (e.g. if the rat is satiated, or detests the substance known to be in the goal-box).

Thus far the discussion of families has made little mention of negative valences. Is there any relation among tasting castor oil, loud sound, blinding light, or electric shocks which makes it help-

---

[4] What do we say if it turns out that something very different from the standard goals of a certain family behaves as if it belongs—substitutes for other members of the family? For instance, suppose hearing music, or scientific activity, can substitute for sexual activity? The supposition that this happens is embodied in the concept of 'sublimation'.

ful to talk of 'families'? Some, but relatively little. Repetition of a negatively valenced event reduces dislike (Grossman, 1973; Zajonc, 1968) of future events of identical kind, and also of similar ones—a bit like satiation. Further, there is spontaneous recovery of dislike after a time lapse, an effect which might be likened to that of recovery of satiated desire after some deprivation time. There is no parallel to the relation between physiological need states and the cycle of changes in valence corresponding to deprivation and satiation, since most aversive states involve external stimuli or tissue damage (loud noise or injury to a cartilage). Psychologists find little use for the distinction between motive and incentive value for the case of aversive outcomes.

2. THE PLEASANT AND THE UNPLEASANT

A second concept it is essential to discuss is that of the pleasant (and unpleasant). We could as well discuss what it is for something to be *liked* by someone, or for someone to be *enjoying* something. Any one of these terms must be understood, for present purposes, in the occurrent sense, not in the dispositional sense in which we might say of a man who is sound asleep that he likes or enjoys hearing Beethoven's music. We are using the terms in an occurrent sense when we are stroking a cat and he purrs and we say, 'He likes that' or 'He is enjoying that'. We can ignore possible differences among these terms in ordinary English usage, and we are not even interested in what 'pleasant' means in ordinary speech, but rather in how we should conceive of it in a defensible psychological conceptual scheme.

A basic fact from which we can start is that we know many things are pleasant (or unpleasant), and we must aim at a theory of the pleasant which is consistent with this knowledge. Among the pleasant things are: sniffing a perfume, eating a steak, dozing in a deck-chair, playing tennis, a general euphoria or sense of well-being or content, announcing to someone else that he is receiving an award, listening to a symphony, watching a football game, making preparations for a trip, day-dreaming about some hoped-for event, and so on. I shall think, however, in terms of two simple examples: liking a sweet taste, and disliking the taste of quinine in the mouth—reactions common to many animals. The hope is that an account of these will, with minor modifications, be found adequate also to the other cases. Disliking the taste of quinine is an unlearned liking, whereas liking a compliment (or disliking being treated in a contemptuous manner) presupposes a great deal of learning. We should aim at an account of pleasure which will cover both.

What is present when a person likes the taste of a chocolate? (1) Often there is expressive behaviour, like purring or smiling; but we can smile without liking and can like without smiling. (2) There are autonomic changes, but there is no distinctive pattern characteristic of liking or disliking. (3) There are electro-chemical processes in the brain. About these our knowledge is growing rapidly. For instance, there is firing of certain neurons in a certain area of the hypothalamus when a hungry animal has a morsel of food in his mouth (and can be presumed to be liking that), apparently the same neurons that are activated by intracranial electrical stimulation to obtain which a hungry animal will keep pressing a bar until exhausted. (Rolls, 1975.) There is some evidence that the presence of dopamine and adrenalin is involved in the occurrence of such events. (Stein, 1969; Laverty, 1975.) But we must set aside a physiological account of pleasantness for the same reasons as those mentioned above for the case of 'valence': the data are such that at present such an account would be premature, and in any case some other account must remain basic, since we identify a neuron's firing as indicative of liking only when there is other reason to think the animal is enjoying something.

Only two further possibilities suggest themselves: (4) that being pleasant is identical with some introspectible fact of experience, or (5) that it is what is designated by some theoretical construct defined by its relation to behaviour.[5] I shall consider these in turn.

Quality-of-experience theories. This view has assumed various forms. One form identifies being pleasant with the occurrence of a bodily sensation, either localized (e.g. bright feelings in the

---

[5] Good reviews of historically influential theories are to be found in Alston, 1967, and Beebe-Center, 1932. Useful discussions are to be found in Duncker, 1941; Gosling, 1969; Penelhum, 1957; Taylor, 1963; Berlyne and Madsen, 1973; Glickman and Schiff, 1967; Rolls, 1975.

upper chest), or more diffuse, like feeling fatigued or buoyant. One trouble with the localized sensation form is that it is implausible to identify the sensation with any particular location; one cannot identify any localized sensation present whenever anything is pleasant. It is also implausible to affirm that the unpleasantness of pain is a sensation occurring somewhere else. The trouble with the 'diffused feeling' theory is that when we try to fix attention on the alleged feeling, we cannot do it in the way we can on drowsiness or feeling energetic. Moreover, as Gosling (1969, p. 36) has pointed out, we cannot explain the meaning of 'feelings of pleasure' in the way we can other experiences like drowsiness, by pointing to the usual cause or occasion of the feeling or to a specific standard response to it (as the standard response to an itch is a desire to scratch), or by pointing to analogies (e.g. talk of 'sinking' sensations, or 'butterflies' in the stomach).

One possibility is that 'is pleasant' is a multivalent phrase having different meanings in different contexts. When one is half-dozing in a deck-chair, there is a pervasive feeling of peaceful drowsiness. When one is devouring a good steak, there is some excitement around the mouth which may be the way it feels to be salivating heavily. When one hears good news there is an emotion of joy, and an enthusiasm for living. These feelings undoubtedly do occur. On this view one could claim that it is a mistake to look for some special feeling or quality of feeling, identical among all these, the intensity of which correlates with our judgement about how pleasant something is. We could say that, although 'is pleasant' is multivalent, we know quite well when the term is properly used in certain contexts, since we have been taught to use it in that context only when feelings/sensations like the described ones are present.

This proposal has the virtue of not postulating the existence of dubious sensations. But in principle it must leave unanswered the questions why we happen to apply 'is pleasant' to this particular set of experiences. Moreover, on this view presumably the unpleasantness of pain would not be distinguishable from the sensation of pain itself; but there is surgery which apparently leaves the sensation intact but reduces the unpleasantness of it to a rather mild level, so that it appears we must distinguish between the intensity of pain and the unpleasantness of it, just as we must distinguish (as Plato pointed out) the pleasantness of the sensations of sexual intercourse from their intensity.

These reflections lead us to the proposal that pleasantness is a quality or attribute of a sensation, emotion, feeling, or complex of these—the view defended by Karl Duncker. It is said to be a quality which enables us to order the experience it qualifies in an order of more and less. It is, Duncker says, a 'tone pervading experience', incomplete by itself, essentially of something else, adjectival. The conception becomes more elusive, however, when we are told that 'Being merely the tone of something, it has no properties of its own aside from its algedonic character and its intensity ranging from extreme pleasantness through indifference to extreme unpleasantness' (1941, p. 408).

Most of the objections which have been raised against most quality-of-experience theories do not apply to this one. Still, the alleged quality seems elusive, although some may disagree. C. D. Broad wrote that hedonic tone is a quality 'which we cannot define but are perfectly acquainted with' (1934, p. 229). Furthermore, the proposal does not serve to integrate psychological or physiological theory. However, it would be consistent to affirm such a quality as the way it feels when the causal process is going on which I shall now identify as what it is to be pleasant.

A motivational theoretical-construct theory. The theory to which we come is, roughly, that for an experience to be pleasant is for it to make the person want its continuation.

Many years ago E. L. Thorndike proposed a definition of a 'satisfactory' state of affairs, suitable for application to animal experimentation. His idea was that a satisfactory state of affairs is one the animal does nothing to avoid, but often does things to attain and preserve; whereas an uncomfortable state is one the animal commonly avoids or abandons. This explanation, however, is sensible only for 'being pleasant' in the dispositional sense. A suggestion (typically not pellucid) along the same line, usable for the occurrent sense, was offered by Kurt Lewin (1938, p. 175) who said that tendencies not to leave the psychological region 'are exactly the description of the situation of a person enjoying himself in [the region] G. The positive valence of the present region G does not include a tendency to a directed locomotion. However, it includes the resistance against a force in the direction of leaving G in case such a force should come up.'

Lewin's statement requires interpretation. Presumably he means by 'region' some kind of experience (taken in a broad sense) the person is having at the time. When he says that a region is positively (occurrently) valenced, what he means is that a continuation of that kind of experience is positively valenced. What kind of action-tendencies might such positive valence involve? A tendency not to do anything which would extinguish the experience which is pleasant; and, if the person thinks that the experience will continue only if he does something, there will be a tendency to do that. So a child, enjoying eating an ice-cream cone, will continue eating and not throw down the cone, and will resist if someone else tries to take it away. (My definition of 'valence' may be too intellectual for a neonate, who does not represent the effects of his acts on future outcomes; hence, for his case 'pleasantness' may better be explained just as a disposition for native maintaining sequences to occur. What it is for the child to be enjoying his milk is that he continues to suck, and hangs on to the bottle if someone tries to tug it away. Presumably such sequences have been established by survival value.)

In contrast, if some kind of experience is unpleasant, the continuation of it will be negatively valenced, and hence there will be action-tendencies to do whatever is believed likely to remove, expunge, or produce its non-existence. (On the level of the neonate, displeasure must be defined in terms of native action-tendencies to reject, spit out, get away from the object involved in the experience, such as the quinine in the mouth which is producing the bitter taste.)[6]

It may be that our conception of the action-tendencies involved in pleasant experiences should be enlarged. An article by Albert Silverstein (1973) *suggests* (he is making the point for something different from pleasure) that a pleasant experience not only involves a positive valence of its continuation, but also a

---

[6] The above remarks sound as if valence were related only to action-tendencies. We must therefore remind ourselves that valence, as explained (p. 26 f.), is related lawfully to other phenomena or tendencies, although some of these are hardly relevant when what is valenced is just the continuation of an experience already present. If 'pleasant' is explained in terms of valence, it follows that a pleasant experience is related to these other tendencies in the ways in which anything occurrently valenced is.

desire to improve receptor orientation towards the object. Thus, if one is enjoying looking at a picture, one might try to improve one's view, in general improve the articulation of the experience. So, if you are liking some food, you may begin to savour it more carefully. Or, if your favourite football team is reported to have won a game, you may buy a newspaper with a fuller account, so that you may enjoy the story in more detail. Perhaps we ought to say that when some state of affairs is pleasant, a fuller experience of the same sort is positively valenced.

There is a final feature that should be included in an account of pleasantness. When an experience is pleasant, the (increased) occurrent valence of the continuation of that experience is *causally dependent* on the experience already going on, say, the taste of ice-cream. We might say that the taste of ice-cream energizes an increased valence of continuing to taste ice-cream, or, at the neonatal level, energizes the actual retention and swallowing tendencies. To be less metaphorical, we could say that the occurring experience is the *differential cause*,[7] of the increased positive valence of the continuation of that experience. It follows that the pleasantness of an experience has a definite time-span—the length of time during which the experience is going on and energizing the valence of its continuation. It also follows that the pleasantness of something is always the pleasantness *of* something—the experience which is its differential cause.

If we put all the foregoing together we have the following definition of 'the experience E of the person P is pleasant for P at t': 'an experience of the kind E is going on in the person P at t; and the experience E is the differential cause at t of an increment in the positive valence of the continuation of E beyond t, or at the neonate level, of the occurrence of tendencies to act in a way likely to result in the continuation of E'. In short, an experience is pleasant if and only if it makes its continuation more

---

[7] To say that an experience E at t is the differential cause of an increased valence $+V$ at t is *not* to say that E by itself is a sufficient, or a necessary, condition of $+V$. What is meant is that E, plus the presence of some conditions present at or before t, is a sufficient condition of $+V$, so that the occurrence of E completed the set of factors sufficient for $+V$. Some other set of conditions (and without E) might have been sufficient to produce $+V$ (so that E is not necessary), but in fact these conditions were not present at t. When all these conditions are met, we can say that E is the differential cause of $+V$. (See Mackie, 1965, and Kim, 1971.)

wanted. The transposition for being unpleasant will be obvious. When an experience is pleasant for a person in the above sense, there presumably is a corresponding story to be told about electro-chemical processes in the brain.[8]

Why not this motivational theory of pleasure? The main objection is epistemological. It is thought that the suggested explanation implies that (a) a person needs evidence and inference to know whether an experience is pleasant (he must know whether something is the differential cause of something else), and (b) that a person can be mistaken about whether an experience is pleasant. But in fact, it is supposed, evidence and inference are not needed for knowing whether an experience is pleasant; and we cannot make mistakes about whether some experience is pleasant. However, the assumptions of these objections are mistaken. First, inductive reasoning may not be necessary, on the conception, to produce the belief that some experience is pleasant; it may be that—as was suggested with 'valence'—the phrase 'is pleasant' is keyed in, by conditioning, with the very processes which the above theory views as the pleasantness of something. In that case we would find ourselves inclining to say 'That is pleasant' without any inferential process. Suppose I sample some red wine from a partially used bottle, and find the taste sour and bitter, and

---

[8] There is a metaphysical problem here which may disturb some readers. I have been talking as if an experience can be a differential cause of valence or action-tendencies, where the latter notions are at least partly concepts of behaviour-tendencies. Some readers may think that experiences are unqualified to be causes of anything, and in particular unqualified to be causes of physical behaviour. There is of course a deep issue here, which I shall not try to resolve; I shall merely take steps to avoid it, and to placate critical readers, by providing alternative readings. Let us then interpret 'an experience making' in any one of the following ways, whichever suits the reader best. (1) For dualistic readers, let us just bear in mind the notion of a conscious state—like the taste of ice-cream—and say that it can be a cause, as readily as any physical state of affairs. (2). Alternatively, we may suppose there is a brain-state correlated with but not identical with the conscious state, and read, where I talk of 'experience making', rather 'the brain-state correlated with the experience making'. In case the correlated brain-state cannot occur unless the conscious state does, the conscious state will be a necessary condition of the effect of the correlated brain-state. This interpretation will suit epiphenomenalists. (3) Finally, identity theorists may think of the conscious state as being identical with a brain-state, and in that case there will be no problem in supposing that the mind-brain-state causes a behavioural tendency. For the reader unconcerned with such metaphysical problems, it will be most convenient to forget these distinctions, since they will play little or no part in what is to follow.

know I do not wish to be drinking that with my meal. I would say, 'It doesn't taste good, let's open another bottle'. The motivational account of this does not seem strange or forced. It is true that evidence and inference are needed to justify the belief which psychologically may be immediate; but normally the logic is quite simple, since the inference depends mostly just on the observation of a novel feature added to the situation, e.g. introducing quinine into the mouth. It is also true that, according to motivational theory, we can make mistakes about what is pleasant. But so we do. Suppose a child is offered a piece of cod as his first experience in eating fish, and he spits out the first mouthful and refuses to continue. What is it that is unpleasant? The texture of the meat, the slight oiliness, the specific taste of cod? We do not know, and neither does he; the way to discover is for him to try a bite of trout. Here our first guess might well be mistaken, and to find the fact we do need to use inductive inference. (It is certain, of course, that it was something in his mouth that was unpleasant.) Consider another case. Suppose you are talking to someone at a cocktail party and want to continue the conversation. You ask yourself, 'What is pleasant?' It might be the novel ideas the person is expressing, or the vivacious personality, or the fact that he is flattering you, or just sex appeal. Your opinion on this matter is a hypothesis which can be tested, say, by noting under which circumstances you move on to talk with someone else—or by noting which reflections about the person motivate you to seek his company further.

3. SOME IMPLICATIONS

The foregoing account of 'valence' makes dubious the proposal that people desire only pleasure. The thoughts which increase action-tendencies normally seem to be thoughts of very concrete things, like eating a piece of pie, or hearing a symphony, or visiting one's daughter, or one's daughter being delighted by something. It seems unlikely that action-tendencies will be increased only by the thought that an unspecified experience will be the differential cause of maintenance activities, although, as Bishop Butler rightly pointed out, a child can be motivated by the promise of something pleasant, with no specification what the pleasant thing is to be. J. S. Mill was not even remotely correct when he said that 'desiring a thing and finding it pleasant' are 'two modes of naming the same psychological fact'. He would have been closer had he said that desiring a thing and its conception being motivating are the same thing. He would have been wrong had he even said that 'desiring a thing and finding the idea of its occurrence pleasant' are the same. Surely the idea need not be pleasant in the sense that I am inclined to dwell on it, daydream about it. I may want a good wine for dinner, but dwelling on the prospective taste of the wine is not a rewarding enterprise. So much for the relation of desire and enjoyment implied by the above account. We shall return later to the possible truth of a more sophisticated hedonist proposal.

It follows from the theory that if one wants to compare two experiences for pleasantness, one must compare the strength of the augmented-action-tendencies to continue. The test is not, of course, which action-tendency to continue is stronger, for the whole action-tendency to continue need not be attributed to the influence of the ongoing experience: I might be enjoying writing an examination, but be very well motivated to complete the examination apart from the pleasure of it. There is a subtler point to note. Suppose I ask myself how much I am enjoying a symphony. It would be too simple just to ask myself how much resistance I would put up to the suggestion of leaving. For my resistance to leaving is not just a function of the experience going on now, but my anticipation of what is coming in that movement or the next. The simplest problem of comparison of pleasures is the case of two experiences going on simultaneously, e.g. listening to a record and looking at a gorgeous sunset through the window. Would I prefer someone to turn off the music, or pull the curtains? If one wants to compare a present with a past experience, for pleasantness, of course memory is involved. One has to justify believing that one would have been more resistant to interruption of something, owing to the experience going on, alone, in the one case than in the other. Sometimes this will be easy, sometimes difficult. Of course, what is shown by such comparisons is simply that an experience at some moment was more intensely pleasant than another at some moment; not yet that an hour of one experience was the equivalent in pleasure of fifteen minutes of another. This problem will be considered later, along with the question of interpersonal comparisons.

I conclude with some remarks about the senses in which, according to the above, pleasures of the same intensity might have different 'qualities', as J. S. Mill thought they do, and whether these qualities might make them differ in desirability.

What might be meant by saying that experiences identical in degree of pleasantness—the strength of added valence to continue they arouse—may be different in 'quality'? (1) One thing that might be meant is just that there are different experiences which may be equally pleasant, like dozing in a deck-chair, making a fine stroke in tennis, or savouring a fine Burgundy. Undoubtedly these experiences are all different, but they may be pleasant to the same degree. (2) It could be that experiences which are pleasant always contain a 'subjective' element in the sense of bodily-sensations or emotions or feelings (tickles or itches, fatigue-feelings or feelings of well-being or energy), and that this subjective element can differ from one case to another even when the pleasantness is the same. It is not merely that dozing in a deck-chair is different from eating steak, although these experiences are equally pleasant. It could be that the relaxed drowsiness essential to pleasant dozing is different from the sensory complex essential to the pleasant savouring of a steak. There seems no reason to deny that two experiences might be equally pleasant but differ with respect to their subjective components, and have different 'qualities' in that sense. There are other senses in which two experiences equal in pleasantness might differ in 'quality'.

Clearly, one of two experiences, identical in degree of pleasantness, might be preferable, or even just preferred, on account of its particular quality. To take a quite obvious case, although eating a piece of pie and listening to a record were equally pleasant, now, having just completed eating an entire pie, I can surely want more strongly to hear a record than to consume yet another piece of pie. And it would seem a bit absurd to say it is not preferable. So much is obvious. But it is not consistent to affirm both (a) that the pleasantness of a state of affairs is the only thing relevant to the desirability of a state of affairs, and also to affirm (b) that the quality of a pleasure is relevant to the goodness of a state of affairs. For the one affirmation is that it is the property of pleasantness to a certain degree that is the one thing relevant to desirability; whereas the other affirmation is that the feelings or emotions of sensation-complexes (etc.) to which the relevant causal property attaches are also relevant. The dual claim is inconsistent.

CHAPTER III

THE COGNITIVE THEORY OF ACTION

ONE THEME of Chapter I was that the question 'What is the best thing to do?' can helpfully be reformulated as 'What would I do now if my decision processes had been subject to criticism by facts and reason to a maximal extent?' or, given that terms are suitably defined, as 'What is the rational thing for me to do?'. I pointed out that decisions are a function of both cognitive factors and desires/aversions, and that therefore an answer to the question what is the fully rational thing to do must come in two stages. In the first stage, we concentrate on determining what is the rational thing to do, as a first approximation, concentrating on the cognitive factors, and taking for granted that the desires/aversions are given, not needing criticism. In the second stage, the desires and aversions themselves are criticized, and thereafter it may be determined what fully rational action would be.

All this sounds quite programmatic, and the reader may wonder whether we can make any general statements at all about what is the rational thing to do, even as a first approximation. In Chapter 4 I shall produce some such general statements, suitably supported. In the present chapter, I set out the psychological basis for the reasoning of Chapter 4.

It may not be clear what kind of 'psychological basis', if any, is needed. But consider the following possibility: suppose we had a psychological theory telling us of which properties of an agent his decisions/actions are a function. Then if some of these properties were cognitive (beliefs, percepts, etc.), we might be able to say what his behaviour would be like if these cognitive factors were optimal—incorporating available evidence and optimally vivid. For this kind of reasoning, it is evident that psychological theory is necessary. Conceivably psychology might tell us that cognitions have no influence on behaviour, and in that case a study of the psychological theory of action would leave us empty-handed. But we shall find that this is not the case. I shall call any psychological theory which holds that cognitions play a significant role in determining action, a *cognitive theory*. Hence the title of the present chapter.

Readers may wish to know which psychologists I am classifying as cognitive theorists, and which are associated with the summary of the theory which I shall provide. I classify the following as cognitive theorists: E. C. Tolman, Kurt Lewin, John Atkinson, F. W. Irwin, T. A. Ryan, writers on rational decision theory; and probably A. Bindra and J. A. Deutsch, writers largely interested in physiology. [1]

We shall see that, despite the incompleteness and defective precision of cognitive theories of action at the present time, we do know enough to identify certain types of action as *irrational*, to identify certain types of information as necessary in order for rational action to occur, and to support some important generalizations about types of action that are rational or irrational. That is something: and it is something which we can justify affirming without relying on normative 'intuitions'.

I shall summarize the cognitive theory by stating five laws.

i. The Law of Action

Among the actions which occur to a person as ones he might perform, he performs that one which at the time there is the *strongest net tendency* to perform (or towards the performance of which there is the strongest 'performance vector', to use a term popular in Tolman's later writings).

What is to count as an 'action'? It is convenient (but not necessary) to limit 'action' to intentional bodily movements and mental occurrences: like waving one's arm, putting on one's hat and so on. Exactly how complex a piece of behaviour is to count as a single bodily movement is a question we can ignore. For an experienced typist the typing of one word or even one sentence might qualify as a single act; whereas for a beginner the striking of

[1] For a general survey of theories of this type and a review of some applications, see Vroom, 1964, and Mitchell, 1974. For an excellent general discussion embedded in a general account of theories of learning, see Hilgard and Bower, 1975. Another good general account is Atkinson, 1964; see also Weiner, 1973; Atkinson, 1958; and Bolles, 1967. Especially worthy of careful study are Tolman, 1955 and 1959. The literature on decision theory can be tracked down by looking in Edwards and Tversky, 1967; Luce and Raiffa, 1957; Luce and Suppes, 1965; and reviews by Becker and McClintock, 1967, and Rapaport and Wallstein, 1972.

one key would be the appropriate simple action. For the most part, however, deliberation is concerned with the selection and execution of a sequence of acts comprising a complex plan. First there is the selection of a sequence (its later stages left a bit imprecise); then the initiation of its first stages; and finally the monitoring, maintenance, or modification of its later stages. Obviously the selection and execution of such a plan involves many different bodily movements, connected by the belief that the sequence of actions will accomplish certain results.

ii.   The Law of the Effect of Valence and Expectancy on Action-Tendency.

Let us for the present suppose that a person anticipates that an action he might perform will alter the probability of only one event or outcome which is of interest to him. The 'law' then asserts the following: If an individual expects, to a degree E, that a consequence of an action A by him now will bring about an outcome O, then, if O has a positive valence V for him, his tendency (T) to perform $A(T_A)$ will have the magnitude of the product $E \times V$. If O has a negative valence V, the tendency $(\bar{T})$ *not* to do $A(\bar{T}_A)$ will have the magnitude $E \times$ (the absolute value of) V.

The foregoing law does not tell us what the total effect will be if several different outcomes are involved. There is the question 'How simply do they sum?' One answer to this question will appear later as another law. Evidently, however, the two laws stated do have implications for simple situations. Suppose you are enjoying being in bed; remaining in bed (by the definition of 'enjoy', defended in Chapter 2) then is itself a valenced outcome. Suppose the only reason for getting up, at least right now, is that you are hungry. Evidently it follows from the above laws that if someone offers to serve you breakfast in bed you will remain in bed. It is also evident that you believe that if you get up you will no longer be enjoying the comforts of bed (probability $= 1$), and that if you do get up you will be able to assuage your hunger (probability approximately $= 1$). Therefore you will get up when the valence of eating certain things is stronger than the valence of staying in bed.[2]

---

[2] It may be that you will not change your situation (get up) unless the tendency to get up exceeds the tendency to continue doing what you are doing (stay in bed) by some definite amount. (You may have to think that *The Times* is on your doorstep before you can climb out.) See Cartwright and Festinger, 1943.

A statement like the above law appeared in my earlier explanation of the meaning of 'valence'; one might therefore ask if the above law is a synthetic empirical thesis at all. The answer is twofold: first, it was pointed out earlier that valence is related to various other tendencies, so that the truth of the law has implications for correlation of action with those other tendencies; and second, the law introduces the notion of subjective probability, which can be identified and measured independently. So the law is synthetic and empirically disconfirmable; and there is in fact reason to doubt whether as stated it is exactly true.

How seriously are we to take talk of the 'product $E \times V$'? Some psychologists, e.g. Tolman (1959, p. 135), appear to construe it in a way compatible only with ordinal measurement; that is, the effect of the law is simply to affirm only that (a) where either E or V is altogether absent there is no increase of action-tendency at all, and (b) that an increase in E when V is held constant, or an increase in V when E is held constant, will produce a greater action tendency. Some writers, however, would wish to take a more strongly quantitative interpretation.

What kind of evidence is there that this 'law' is at least approximately true—if we take it as asserting at least as much as does the interpretation just suggested? It looks as if the common-sense evidence is so strong that we hardly need experimental data to know that such a principle is somewhere near the truth: it is quite obvious, for instance, that a person will pay more for a lottery ticket the fewer competing tickets he knows there are, and the larger the prize. Clearly if a person will pay $X for one chance in a hundred to acquire $1,000, he will pay more—$X + Y—for a ticket that gives him one chance in ten for the same prize. If he will pay $X for a ticket giving him one chance in a hundred for $1,000, he will pay $X + Y for one chance in a hundred for $2,000; and he will pay more than either of these for one chance in ten at $2,000. For sceptics who want hard figures to support common sense, they are available. For instance, studies show that a person's choice of occupation is strongly influenced by features of an occupation which he values, but also influenced by his judgement of the likelihood of finding a position in that field: a person might prefer teaching philosophy to working as a lawyer, everything considered, but go into the law because of the dim prospects of a position teaching philosophy.[3] Experimental work with human beings has been done with achievement motivation more than with any other motive (Atkinson and Raynor, 1974). The general upshot of this research is that an individual's achievement behaviour is a function of his general motivation to achieve or avoid failure (= Motive, see above p. 34), his estimate of the likelihood of success or failure, and of the significance (= Incentive Value, see above p. 34) of a particular success or failure to him (a success is insignificant if it is easy, and a failure insignificant if the task is so demanding that hardly anyone would succeed). There is also animal evidence supporting the general law. A rat will run for the food-box faster and take less time getting started (decrease in 'latency'), when he is hungry or knows there are goodies in the goal-box than when he has eaten recently or knows there is little, or less-liked, food in the goal-box. His action-tendency, then, declines with a decline in valence. Again, if he is rewarded only infrequently (say, one time in five) in the goal-box, in other words if his expectancy is lowered, again he will run less rapidly and take more time in starting. This seems expectable enough. More interesting is the fact that animals which have been randomly and infrequently rewarded ('partial reinforcement on a variable schedule') will continue performing the hitherto reward-producing behaviour longer, after rewards have been stopped altogether, than will animals which have been regularly rewarded in the past. Why? Suppose the animal had only a one in five expectation of reward. When reward ceases altogether, his expectation is not necessarily changed, since a one in five expectancy is compatible with quite long runs of no reward. So, if his behaviour is a function of $E \times V$ and E remains subjectively constant despite a long period of no reward, the animal will continue his behaviour. On the other hand, the regularly rewarded animal might have an expectancy, say, of 100 per cent. Then, when rewards are discontinued, his expectancy is quickly modified; he guesses right away that the situation is different from what it was. The law that action-tendency is a function of $V \times E$ explains why his hitherto reward-producing behaviour extinguishes rapidly in this situation. (Logan and Wagner, 1965, pp. 31–50; Kimble, 1961, pp. 287, 319; Hilgard

[3] A large amount of evidence is summarized by Vroom, 1964, and Mitchell, 1974. See also Rotter, 1954, Chaps. 5, 6; Atkinson, 1964, Chaps. 8, 9; Bresnahan, Hilliard, and Shapiro, 1973.

and Bower, 1975, pp. 140–4, 567 f., 192 ff.)

It may be thought that the proposed law is in principle not susceptible of evaluation for human beings because there is no way of determining precisely the values of E or V. There is extensive literature on this subject, following the pioneering work of J. von Neumann and O. Morgenstern (1944; see Davidson, Suppes, and Siegel, 1957). The thought has been that if a person's subjective probability expectations could be identified, a procedure is available for assigning numbers to his desire-strength, unique up to a linear transformation. The reasoning is as follows. Suppose we have a list of outcomes, rated by the person in the preference order A followed by B followed by C. Suppose further we arbitrarily assign a valence value to C (say 1) and an arbitrary larger value to A, say 10. We assume, since B rates between A and C, that there is some gamble involving a probability mix of A and C (the prospect of getting A with probability p, otherwise C with probability $1-p$) such that the person will be indifferent (operationally: he will choose one with frequency about equal to the other) between getting B for certain, and gambling for A or C with the odds as mentioned. (The probabilities are his expectations, not necessarily the objectively correct probability values.) If the person is indifferent between the options, we can assume his action-tendencies are the same.

Let us for the moment assume that our law implies the following equation, as representing the situation when two action-tendencies are equal:

$$V(B) = p(V(A) + (1 - p)V(C)$$

Since, for the purposes of our example, we assigned valence to A and C of 10 and 1, we get the equation:

$$V(B) = p(10) + (1-p)1$$

Let us suppose, for simplicity, that $p = \frac{1}{2}$. Then $V(B) = \frac{1}{2}(10) + \frac{1}{2}(1) = 5\frac{1}{2}$. Evidently a different initial assignment of numbers would have resulted in a different value for B, but the ratio of the intervals would be the same: here 10, $5\frac{1}{2}$, 1. (If we had initially given the values, 4 and 1, the value of B would have worked out at $2\frac{1}{2}$, with the several values now 4, $2\frac{1}{2}$, 1. The intervals in the former case are $4\frac{1}{2}$, $4\frac{1}{2}$, and in the second case $1\frac{1}{2}$, $1\frac{1}{2}$, or equal.)

I have said that the equation might be taken as implied by our law; but it is only if it is assumed that the strength of the action-tendency T to take a gamble involving two events is the algebraic sum of $V \times E$ for each prospective event individually. I shall return to this question shortly.

A repetition of the procedure ideally would enable us to assign a valence number to every state of affairs for a given individual. That done, we could use our $E \times V$ formula to make predictions about choices between options, and thereby test the theory. In fact, however, the test would come at a much earlier stage. For there is nothing in the described procedure to guarantee that its application will yield consistent results. Let us see how this is.

Suppose, we suggested, the valence ($= V$) numbers got so far are $A = 10$, $B = 5\frac{1}{2}$, $C = 1$. Let us then go on to another event D, which let us suppose is, like B, located in the preference ordering between A and C. And let us suppose that the person is indifferent between D and the gamble involving A and C only when $p = \frac{3}{4}$. Thus the valence number for D will be $\frac{3}{4}(10) + \frac{1}{4}(1) = 7\frac{3}{4}$. Its valence, then, is greater than that of B. Suppose, however, we use our procedure relating D to A and B, as we can, assuming D falls between A and B in the preference ordering. Then $V(D)$ will $= p(10) + (1-p)(5\frac{1}{2})$. What must the value of this p be, in order that the consistent result be $7\frac{3}{4}$? Evidently, $7\frac{3}{4} = p(10) + (1-p)5\frac{1}{2}$, or $10p + 5\frac{1}{2} - 5\frac{1}{2}(p)$. Thus $p = \frac{1}{2}$. But there is no guarantee that the individual will be indifferent between D and a gamble involving A and B when p is set at $\frac{1}{2}$. If he is not, something has gone wrong, and possibly the 'law' $E \times V = T$, or the assumption about summing, is the culprit.

Suppose, however, the individual is indifferent at that point; and suppose we can identify a valence for each event he might wish or be aversive to, and that his attitudes to gambles involving these events are all consistent in the sense explained, and that with the numbers at hand, and information about his subjective probabilities, we can predict which gambles he takes in every instance. Then we could clearly say that his choice behaviour is as if $V \times E = T$.

Is this ideal state of affairs what we find in fact? The experimental data are few, and although in a narrow range of cases (bets on small sums of money) some results generally support the theory, much more needs to be done. There are experimentally-based doubts: evidence that persons like to place bets at certain odds and not others, some preferring to take 'long shots' and others to avoid these, some persons preferring to place bets involving a specific probability level (say, $\frac{1}{2}$), and to avoid ones involving some other specific probability level (say, $\frac{3}{4}$). (The reply, however, may be made that these experiments dealt with *objective* probabilities, and not *subjective* probabilities E, as they should have done.) Furthermore, many (including economists) would prefer a certain gift of $500,000 to a 10 per cent chance of $2,500,000 plus an 89 per cent chance of $500,000 plus a 1 per cent chance of nothing, although they prefer a 10 per cent chance of $2,500,000 plus a 90 per cent chance of nothing to an 11 per cent chance of $500,000 plus an 89 per cent chance of nothing, thus setting store by a 1 per cent risk of nothing in one case which they do not set store by in the other. The experimental data on gambling give one the impression of very considerable complexity.[4] It seems advisable to insist only on a weak interpretation of our law, keeping our minds open about future developments which might make possible acceptance of a stronger (and perhaps more complex) form.

It may be useful to describe a simple model depicting how this 'law' might work. Let us think of a rat in a maze, and suppose that he knows that if he makes a left turn at a certain point he will eventually come to a cup which contains food 25 per cent of the time ($E = \frac{1}{4}$), whereas if he makes a right turn at the same point he will eventually come to a cup which contains water 50 per cent of the time ($E = \frac{1}{2}$). We think of two sensing systems in the hypothalamus which detect water deficiency and food deficiency; and as a result of the operation of these systems at the time water has a valence V_w for him, and the expected mash a valence V_f. Now we can think of these valences as being like levels of charge in a battery, one battery for each valenced outcome. We can think further that there are wires connecting these batteries to a solenoid, which can switch on a motor system operating so as to produce a left turn or a right turn, i.e. take one route to one outcome or the other route to a different outcome. We can think of the resistance of these wires as representing the reciprocal of the probability of the outcome, given respectively the left or the right turn—this depending on past experience of finding a valenced object in the food cup. Now let us

[4] See Ellsberg, 1954; papers by Edwards in Edwards and Tversky, 1967; Allais, 1953; Irwin, 1971, pp. 149 ff.; Rothenberg, 1961, Chaps. 9, 10; Slovik, 1964; Payne and Braunstein, 1971.

suppose that when the rat is faced with the option of turning right or left (or doing nothing), a switch is turned which permits current to flow along these wires from the battery. How much current comes through will be a function of the charge-level of the battery at the moment, and of the resistance of the wire. We can think of the current from these wires entering the solenoid and activating a switch in such a way that the more current will result in the solenoid's directing the motor activity to making one or the other turn. Evidently the stronger current in the solenoid, which will direct behaviour to one option or the other, will be fixed by whether $E \times V$ is greater. The model can be complicated to allow for further relevant variables.[5]

A needed complication is different batteries feeding into the same terminal of the solenoid (different valenced outcomes supporting the same action-tendency); and also, in order to allow for negative valences (e.g. a rat knowing that the only route to the food cup leads across a grid by which he will be strongly shocked), the conception of negatively charged batteries (ones that will draw off current at a given terminal and hence facilitate the relevant action *not* being performed).

The suggested model comports reasonably well with what we know of the brain-physiology of motivation. Some physiological psychologists prefer a different model. They first point out that, if objects are visible which in the past have satisfied a certain physiological need, a native approach-and-consummate mechanism will be set in motion towards the object most highly valenced at the moment. The rat in the maze, however, cannot actually see the food or water; so this mechanism does not work as simply in his case. However, it is said, suppose the visual cues on the left-hand side have been associated with food $\frac{1}{4}$ of the time, and those on the right-hand side with water $\frac{1}{2}$ the time, then these cues will function, by conditioning, as surrogates for visible goal objects. They set the approach-and-consummate mechanism in motion, and those cues will be approached for which the expectable valence is higher. The animal would eat the maze wall if he could, but, since he cannot, the same process is repeated for cues further down the

[5] If this 'model' is sensible, then it is mistaken to think that the Hullian conception of a 'fractional anticipatory goal response' is the only intelligible model for the operation of incentive motivation. See Bolles, 1967, p. 336.

alley, so that he is led, a step at a time as it were, to the goal-box. An objection to this model is that if a rat is placed at a choice point just after having been put at the end of the maze and having observed both cups to be empty, he will not show enthusiasm for running the maze either way, despite the fact that the associations with the alley-cues are unaffected by his information.[6]

It might be objected to the whole foregoing account that it does not recognize the (alleged) fact that bodily movement is always preceded by and caused by, a conscious experience, a willing (volition) in some sense of that movement, which occurs after a survey of the options for action and their likely consequences. The theory sketched above, however, does not deny that there are such conscious events antedating and causing bodily movements, whether volitions, felt impulses to act, conscious 'desires', or whatever. Neither does it affirm them. The view that there are such intervening occurrences, however, cannot seriously be claimed to have obvious support from introspection, and in any case the theory that there are such occurrences, far from solving any problem about the causation of bodily movement, simply duplicates that problem. The theory duplicates the problem, because while perhaps useful in a causal explanation of bodily movement, it raises the problem: what is the causal explanation of these volitions (etc.)? Any scientific theory of action must view some sequences as just instances of a lawful relationship. The theory outlined above treats actions like raising one's arm as basic and unanalysable and affirms their causal dependence, roughly, on valences and anticipated probable outcomes at the time. If we complicate the story by introducing conscious volitions, these will be the causes (in part) of the movements (and a constituent of the 'action'), but they will presumably be explained by appeal to those same valences and anticipations of outcomes by which our theory explains the movement. Thus, from the point of view of a causal theory, the conception of a volition seems to serve no purpose, although, if volitions are asserted on grounds of introspection, they can be absorbed into the foregoing conceptual framework.

It may add to the plausibility of the proposed theory to reflect on how William James's ideo-motor theory of action can be in-

---

[6] See Bindra, 1974, 1969, 1968; also R. W. Black, 1969; and Logan and Wagner, 1965, pp. 98 ff.

corporated within it. James's theory,[7] we may recall, is that 'every representation of a movement awakens in some degree the actual movement which is its object; and awakens it in a maximum degree whenever it is not kept from so doing by an antagonistic representation present simultaneously to the mind'. We can construe 'a representation of a movement' as an image of the sensory feedback when a certain movement is made. Now I have suggested that, for deliberate action to take place, there must be awareness that that act would (probably) lead to a desired outcome; but I have so far left open what must be in mind when we make a judgement about 'that act'. It could be that, in order for action to take place, there must be a thought of an action taking place now, which includes an image of sensory feedback—from muscles, tendons, joints, skin, etc. James does not require this: in the case of familiar acts he thinks it is enough to think of the remoter sensory effects of motion, e.g. the visual appearance, the sound, in fact just any sensory image which is directly associated with one particular movement. The interest to us of the ideo-motor theory, however, is its claim that this representation is a sufficient condition for the corresponding action to take place, whereas I have been suggesting that the thought of a causal relation of this action to a (valenced) goal is a necessary condition for deliberate action to take place. Now it would be consistent for an advocate of the $E \times V = T_A$ theory to allow that the thought of the act must contain sensory components, at least of the remoter sensory effects of an act, but also even of the direct kinesthetic data. This concession might fill out the conception of a thought leading to action in a way convincing to some people. It would follow that if I cannot produce an image of sensory feedback for some action (because no such experience has occurred before), that action cannot be performed at will, however much I wish to. It is interesting to note that James's famous description (1913, Vol. II, p. 524) of how we manage to get out of a comfortable bed in the morning includes reference to no conscious events beyond those insisted upon in the preceding account:

Now how do we *ever* get up under such circumstances? If I may generalize from my own experience, we more often than not get up without any struggle or decision at all. We suddenly find that we *have* got up. A

---

[7] James, 1913, II, 522 f. I have benefited from A. Goldman's 1976.

fortunate lapse of consciousness occurs; we forget both the warmth and the cold; we fall into some revery connected with the day's life, in the course of which the idea flashes across us, 'Hello! I must lie here no longer'—an idea which at that lucky instant awakens no contradictory or paralyzing suggestions, and consequently produces immediately its appropriate motor effects. It was our acute consciousness of both the warmth and the cold during the period of struggle, which paralyzed our activity then and kept our idea of rising in the condition of *wish* and not of *will*. The moment these inhibitory ideas ceased, the original idea exerted its effects.

This case seems to me to contain in miniature form the data for an entire psychology of volition. It was in fact through meditating on the phenomenon in my own person that I first became convinced of the truth of the doctrine which these pages present. . . .

My conclusion is that the $E \times V = T$, when construed short of its quantitative form, is a well-supported theory. It comports with the evidence from brain physiology, and we can construct a plausible model of brain processes which can explain its truth. It does not imply the absence of any conscious processes which we know to be essential for action, and it can accommodate what is plausible in the ideo-motor theory of action.[8]

iii. The Dependence of Valence on Motive.

If a state of affairs belongs to a 'family', the positive valence normally increases with the time elapsed since the last occurrence of a member of that family, and is diminished by the occurrence of any other member of the family.[9] For instance, the valence of eating steak increases with the lapse of time since food was last ingested, and is diminished by eating something. (The term 'normally' in the

---

[8] The $E \times V = T$ theory does not explain why, or predict that, it occurs to an agent that a particular action might be taken, and if it were that it would lead to a certain action. For our purposes, a theory on this point is not essential. It is well known, however, that if an animal is hungry it tends to explore—and when a human being is hungry reflections on food sources tend to come to mind.

The interested reader may find profit in looking at some further discussions of this topic: Deutsch and Deutsch, 1966, pp. 116 ff.; McClelland, Atkinson, Clark, and Lowell, 1953, pp. 90 ff.; Sheffield, 1966; Atkinson and Birch, 1970, pp. 145–6; Bitterman, 1967; Prokasy, 1965, pp. 302–22.

[9] The above 'law' is not straightforwardly a synthetic statement, since the notion of a 'family' of valences includes reference to increases of valence with deprivation time and decreases by substitute satisfactions. The 'law' does bring out some important relationships of which we should be aware.

'law' is intended to provide for the fact that intravenous feeding—
or relevantly similar events for other families—is not really a case of
eating food, but affects valences of the eating-family.) In some cases
the valence of some event is a function of the condition of the cells of
the body or the amount of some substance in the blood. These
physiological states are themselves influenced by the recency of,
say, occasions of ingesting fluid, and hence reference to them would
be involved in explaining why the 'law' is true. In other cases,
however, there is no known physiological correlate of valence,
underlying the relationship of members of a 'family'; thus the
interest in congenial human company increases with the time-
interval since the last human interactions, but there is no evidence
that there is a physiological deprivation state in the absence of
human interactions. And the same for the 'need' for compliments
or admiration, and for sensory stimulation. Presumably the
valence of human interaction, and of admiration by others, is
learned; but there is no explaining why these events should have
valences corresponding somewhat with deprivation time.[10]

For the cases of negative valences, I have mentioned earlier the
facts of habituation and recovery time.

The above law does not explain the preference ordering among
members of a family, or the valence of states of affairs not belonging
to a family, or the degree of valence of family-members relative to
other families in specific circumstances.

It follows from the foregoing that a person's valence, say, for
eating steak, varies from one time to another. When our second law
speaks of $T_A = E \times V$, obviously the 'V' must refer to the valence at
the time; a person's 'utility-function' is not a fixed permanent fact
about him.

iv. The Dependence of Action-Tendency on Representation.

The preceding description of the '$E \times V = T_A$' principle assumed
that E is the subjective expectancy that a certain event (O) will occur
in case a certain action (A) is performed, e.g. that if I toss this coin it
will come up heads with a probability of $\frac{1}{2}$. Now, as formulated, this
principle does not require that an occurrent expectancy of this sort

---

[10] For some different views about physiology, deprivation time, and valence, see Tolman,
1959, especially pp. 100 ff., 131–2; Wagner and Carey, 1973; Rolls, 1975, especially pp. 147 ff.;
Deutsch, 1960, Chap. 3; Bindra, 1969.

actually be a conscious thought; 'expectancy' like 'valence' can be defined behaviourally. There is reason, however, to think we must give more attention, in some way, to the role of *conscious* representations in the theory of action.

There is a long tradition of philosophers who have, to put their views in my terminology, believed that the mode of representation of *E*—of an action's probable consequences—is important for the impact of that representation on action. They have thought, for instance, that if the object of potential consummatory gratification is immediately before one's eyes, the tendency to seize that gratification is augmented. Aristotle, in his discussion of weakness of the will, says that a person can believe that a given action will affect important remote outcomes unfavourably, but choose immediate gratification because, under the influence of anger or sexual appetite, he holds his belief (about remote outcomes) only in the way a man believes something when he is 'asleep, mad, or drunk'. Such a person may report his belief in words, but his speech 'means no more than its utterance by actors on the stage'. (1954, pp. 1147a 15–24.) David Hume, in his chapter 'On the influence of the imagination on the passions' (1854, Bk. 2, Pt. 3), dilates upon the relative inefficacy of abstract conceptions in arousing motivation as compared with vivid depictions, a phenomenon he cites as parallel to the greater motivational efficacy of the recent memory of an enjoyment as compared with the pallid memory of a more remote occasion. Hume regards this fact as the reason why we are less excited about events distant either in space or time: 'Contiguous objects must have an influence much superior to the distant and remote. . . . Talk to a man of his condition thirty years hence and he will not regard you. Speak of what is to happen tomorrow, and he will lend you his attention.' Again, Henry Sidgwick, observing that a person often desires what he knows is on the whole bad for him, explains that 'these bad effects, though fore-*seen* are not fore-*felt*: the representation of them does not adequately modify the predominant direction of desire as a present fact'. He was therefore led to say that a person's good on the whole is identical with what 'he would now desire and seek on the whole if all the consequences of all the different lines of conduct open to him were accurately foreseen and adequately realised in imagination at the present point of time'. (1922, pp. 110–12.)

It is not only philosophers who have thought the mode of representation has something to do with the impact on action of a thought-about outcome. Kurt Lewin (1938, pp. 148, 163, 203–6) thought we can explain how we are able to get children to do things they do not want to do (e.g. eat a disliked food) by distracting attention, by removing the disliked outcomes to the periphery of attention. He also suggested we must make the same sort of appeal to explain how indecision sometimes gets resolved by a momentary drift of attention away from one set of outcomes, a proposal we have just seen was made by William James in his explanation of how we are able to climb out of bed on a chilly morning. Contemporary experimental work on what psychologists now call the problem of 'delayed gratification' (essentially the hoary philosophical problem of 'weakness of the will') has led Professor Walter Mischel (1974) to write that 'it is remarkable how little is known about the effects of the mental representation of rewards upon the subject's pursuit of them'.

Should we modify the simple '$E \times V = T_A$' principle in some way? The foregoing views hint that we might introduce another variable 'R' to refer to the *adequacy of representation* of the belief that an action A probably will eventuate in an outcome O; thus we might restate our principle as $T = E \times V \times R$. The idea, of course, is that E and R can vary independently (I may represent to myself very vividly that an act will have only a slight tendency to produce a certain outcome). The new principle would be no more (or less) quantitative than the old one, although it does introduce complications.

What might be meant by talk of 'more adequate representation'? One thing would be centrality, being at the focus, of attention. During reflection only a few things can be attended to. Lewin speculated that we must think of the fraction of attention given to all objects at a time as summing to 1. But there are other aspects of representation. A. A. Lazarus (1964, p. 66) writing on de-sensitization procedures, stresses the importance for success whether situations are imagined 'sufficiently clearly, vividly, and realistically'. Presumably 'clarity' refers here to amount of detail. For instance, if a person is imagining a house, he may be able to tell exactly how many windows there are on a side, what shape they are, and so on. Vividness seems to be further unanalysable, but some persons are known to have more vivid images right across the various sense modalities. It may seem to some philosophers that the term 'image' is one that ought not to find a place in any scientific discourse, but there is burgeoning experimental literature on the subject, and imagery can be a part of an explanatory theory, e.g. of paired-associate learning. Indeed, imagery is now recognized as 'one of the primary modes of representation of information in memory'. There have been impressive proposals relating the brain-circuitry involved in imagery to that involved in perception.[11]

It is beyond doubt that the expected time-interval before an anticipated event strongly influences the reaction to the anticipation of that event. For instance, data support what every sensible person would expect, that students are more concerned about, and motivated by the prospect of, an important examination to take place in three weeks, than they were a year prior. (Hechhausen, 1968.) Again, the data clearly support what virtually everyone would expect, that novices at parachute-jumping are more anxious (as shown by changes in galvanic skin response to words associated with the dangers of the forthcoming episode) on the morning of the scheduled jump than they were several days before. (Epstein and Fenz, 1962; Epstein, 1962.) It is also clear that children are more ready to exchange a five cent Hershey bar available now, for a twenty-five cent one available in an hour, as compared with the twenty-five cent one available only in several days or weeks. (Mischel and Metzner, 1962.) That these things happen no one will doubt. But it is far from clear why they happen. Is it because the representation of present or near events is more vivid, more adequate? Various pieces of evidence are relevant to a conclusion on this point.

A substantial amount of research on children has been conducted by Walter Mischel and his students precisely with the intention of answering this question. It has been established that older children and children with a higher I.Q., and probably children with a clearer perception of time-intervals (and possibly a wider time-perspective) tend to be more successful in waiting for a larger

---

[11] See Hilgard and Bower, 1975, pp. 588–9; Hebb, 1968; J. L. Singer, 1970; Neisser, 1970; Ernest and Paivio, 1969; Eysenck and Beech, 1971. For how vividness of information influences its role in inferences, see Nisbett, Borgida, Crandall, and Reed, 1975. For a contemporary experimental study of attention, see Davies and Trine, 1969.

reward as compared with seizing an immediate gratification. This fact is some support for the view that it is better awareness of the remote event that is crucial. Other facts which Mischel and his associates have brought to light show that the mode of representation of the future reward is important. Most of their experiments involved choices between a less preferred food now, and a more preferred food for which the child might have to wait twenty minutes. The child had the option, during the wait of twenty minutes, of either eating the less preferred food or waiting for the return of the experimenter when he could have the more preferred food. They had no doubt that the more preferred food would be forthcoming: in some of the experiments it was on the table to be seen. (Thus, evidently, the degree of expectation is not the only thing besides valence that affects action-tendencies.) Some of the results were: (1) Surprisingly, when both foods were on the table the child less frequently found it possible to delay. A plausible explanation of this (not the one Mischel and his associates support, which is a frustration theory) is that, both objects being food, the presence of both increased the action-tendency to eat something so much that delay for the more preferred food did not take place. (2) Being shown slides of the preferred food increased ability to delay, presumably because it made the representation of the future preferred event more vivid. One might ask why the slides did not have the same effect as perception of actual food on the table, and the answer seems to be that, being perceived as pictures, they served to remind without causing a high level of arousal. (3) When the two kinds of food were actually before the child, in a later experiment, the instruction to the child was either (a) to think of the consummatory qualities of the objects (e.g. the chewy, sweet, soft taste of a marshmallow), or (b) to think of them in other ways (e.g. the marshmallows as cotton balls). With the former instruction the children did not delay gratification; with the latter almost all of them did. (4) In a very similar experiment, some children were facing the real rewards but were told to think of them as pictures, whereas other children were shown slides but instructed to think of the objects depicted as really being there. The children instructed to think of the real objects as only pictures succeeded in delay of gratification much longer than those told to think of the pictures as being real. The authors conclude that 'the crucial determinant of delay behaviour was the subject's cognitive representation, regardless of what was actually in front of the child'.[12]

We must conclude that probably the adequacy of representation is a factor, along with expectation and valence, in the production of action-tendencies, although many details and puzzles remain to be worked out. One question might be: 'Which ones of the various dimensions of images—detail, vividness, and realism—are involved? Or must other features of representation be emphasized?'

Animal data give some support to the same conclusion. One experiment you can perform for yourself: you command a dog, which likes to play with a ball, to 'sit', and gradually move a ball close to him. As the ball comes closer, his muscles bulge, and he is obviously restraining himself with difficulty, if he does succeed in not grabbing the ball or running and barking. There are well-known laboratory data to the same effect: the 'goal gradient' behaviour of rats—in particular the fact that they run faster towards the food-box the closer they are (except for a terminal slowdown); and the vigour with which they pull, in a harness, towards an attractive goal or away from a charged grid, is a function of proximity. Here the facts are beyond dispute; and a plausible proposal is that adequacy of representation is part of the best explanation. (Alternative explanations, in the case of rats, were offered by Clark Hull and Neal Miller, to the effect that the pulling and running responses are more strongly conditioned to environmental stimuli close to the goal-box, partly because of greater similarity to the goal-box stimuli, but mostly because the reward occurred almost immediately after the contiguity of stimulus and response.[13] If, however, one rejects the entire Hullian conceptual structure, the data have to be explained along different lines.) Assuming that the vigour of the pulling (and probably also the running) activities correlates with the action-tendency strength at the time, and assuming that action-tendency is at least largely a function of the valence of the anticipated goal and the expectancy that it will result from the action, both of which variables are

[12] Mischel, 1974, especially pp. 42–8. This paper contains a bibliography of related experimental work. An explanation of (1), somewhat similar to mine, is offered by J. W. Atkinson and David Birch in the same volume, p. 97.

[13] For a review see Kimble, 1961, pp. 140–50. See the discussion by Lewin, 1938, pp. 165 f.; also that by Neal Miller, 1944, pp. 431–65; Kelleher and Gollub, 1962, especially p. 571; and Cofer and Appley, 1967, pp. 821, 830, 832.

probably mostly fixed over the distances involved, there seems no obvious candidate for an explanation other than adequacy of representation of the situation. The phenomenon is not surprising if we suppose that the familiar stimuli in the alley near the goal remind the rat more vividly of the goal than do those further away—much as the actual sight of home, when a commuter turns a corner and sees his house before him, apparently reminds him of the comforts within and quickens his steps. Of course, degree of representation could have effects where goal-distance is constant: as Heckhausen (1968) has remarked of human reaction to time-distance of a goal, 'Even if the time distance to the goal event is negligibly short, arousal may be diminished if the critical event is anticipated only vaguely or faintly. On the other hand, even if the time distance is still very long, a vivid anticipation of the goal event would raise the arousal level since man, as we know, is eminently capable of pulling "future time elements" into the present.'

My conclusion is that the philosophers, beginning with Aristotle, were nearly right in the first place. But, considering the complications and the short time in which there has been experimental interest in the matter and the possibility of other proposals, it seems we should assert the 'law' of dependence of action-tendencies on the adequacy of representation only with a considerable degree of caution.

v. Action-Tendency and Plurality of Expected Outcomes.

Our unamended second law asserted that there will be a tendency to perform an action, in view of an anticipated outcome, of a magnitude $T_A = V \times E$. But suppose the person anticipates several different outcomes, perhaps with different valences and different degrees of expectation. What will be the magnitude of the action-tendency in this case? If we construed our second law in its strong quantitative form, a simple answer suggests itself: just the algebraic sum of the $E \times V$ products, summed over the several outcomes. This appears to be the conclusion of many psychologists. J. W. Atkinson and W. Reitman, for instance, suggested (1958, p. 279) that 'the resultant motivation is the algebraic summation of approach and avoidance'; and Atkinson wrote (1958, p. 324) that 'the total motivation for performance of that act will be the sum of the contributions made by the particular motives which have been engaged'. The same view is adopted by Joel Raynor (1974; also Littig and Petty, 1971).

In view of the reasons provided earlier for a more ordinal construction of the principle, and in the apparent absence of any accurate summing device for the $V \times E$ products in actual situations,[14] it is the part of wisdom to opt for a principle short of the suggested algebraic summation of those hoped-for 'quantities'. In the absence of acquaintance with any simple more conservative formulation in the literature, I shall say it is a 'law' that if several distinct outcomes are expected to flow from an act, with the products $(E \times V)$ all positive, then each anticipated outcome adds something to the strength of the action-tendency, taking the largest 'product' as a base; and the same, *mutatis mutandis*, for the tendency not to do something, if the products are all negative (the valence negative). If the valences of the anticipated outcomes are mixed, the most I would suggest as a possibility is that if each negative product can be matched with a larger positive product there will be a residual action-tendency to perform the act; and if each positive product can be matched with a larger negative product there will be a residual action-tendency not to perform the act. But what might the meaning of talk of comparison of these 'products' be? Perhaps we can know that if a certain anticipated outcome had been the only motivating factor, there would have been an action-tendency stronger (or weaker) than would have been an action-tendency if some other anticipated outcome had been the only motivating factor. That counterfactual statement might provide the wanted meaning. Of course, if one opts for the possibility of utility numbers along the lines of the thinking of von Neumann and Morgenstern, one could with good conscience make things more simply quantitative.

In any case, a serious complication is introduced by the Law of Dependence of Action-Tendency on Representation. For if the action-tendency deriving from a given anticipated outcome is a function of the degree of representation of the outcome, or its likely production, at the time of choice, then the influence of each outcome on the total action-tendency may correspond less to the algebraic sum of the 'products' than to the degree of representation the relevant outcome happens to have at the time of choice. This

[14] R. N. Shepard; reprinted in Edwards and Tversky, 1967.

result appears to correspond with common-sense observation of decision-making, to the effect that if a consideration bulks large in one's mind at the time of decision, it will carry a weight far out of proportion to what it would have been if all the outcomes had been equally well represented. At the time of decision only a few items can be before the mind, and it is these that determine the decision. If you are deciding whether to move to New York, and what is before your mind when you are deciding is primarily theatres and restaurants, you will probably decide to move, even though you would not have, if other considerations had had a fair share of attention at the time the decision was made.

The above set of 'laws' is incomplete. For instance, one might include a 'law' to the effect that the valence of a goal is enhanced if the agent was interrupted before reaching it and thinks he could have reached it successfully.[15] And possibly there are some laws about aspiration level. The ones stated, however, are the only ones known to me which are relevant to our purpose.

Whether one should say these laws are part of a 'deterministic' theory of human behaviour could be debated. The 'laws' are mostly not quantitative laws and hence, even if it were possible to fix precise values for the independent variables, no prediction of behaviour—at least, no precise prediction of behaviour—is possible, although in simple situations there is a prediction whether the agent will or will not do a certain general type of thing, viz. take the first steps along the route which he thinks leads to a goal, when the action-tendency associated with that route is strongest.

Even so weak a set of principles has interesting normative implications. These will be developed in the following chapter. One of these implications, worth noticing here, derives from the fact that action-tendencies are a multiplicative function of valences (occurrent desires and aversions), and hence that an action-tendency is always zero in magnitude if there is no valence attached to the contemplated action itself or its expected outcome. This thesis has an implication about the scope of effective criticism of action. For, if our 'laws' are true, no intentional action will occur without desire or aversion directed at it or its outcome, and hence no *rational, ideally criticized* action will take place without desire or aversion. (If some philosophers have thought, as some seem to have done, that a

[15] See, for instance, Cartwright, 1942.

person can do his duty even if so doing is not positively valenced for him (or failure negatively valenced), perhaps 'out of respect' for duty in some sense, they were wrong; and their psychology of morality needs basic revision.) Thus the best, the rational, the fully criticized choice is necessarily one which aims at realizing some valenced goals somehow. A person's wants and aversions (possibly altered from what they now are, in a way to be discussed at a later stage) are necessarily relevant to what is the best or rational thing to do. *In that sense*, J. S. Mill was right that what is desired is a clue to what is desirable.

This conclusion might appear unpalatable because it suggests an earthy naturalism: that the basic physical wants, such as for food or drink or sex, define what is the best thing to do, according to the above conclusion. This would be a mistake. People want all sorts of things. They may want to do the will of God, acquire self-control, or realize some Platonic transcendent good. We know they may because they *have* so wanted. I have not suggested, so far, that such desires are mistaken in any way. If anyone wants to criticize desires like these, he must do more than the psychological theory of action has done or can do.

You may object that rats are not human beings, and that laws that account for the behaviour of a rat may not apply to the deliberative actions of men. Let us see how the principles stated above apply to human decision and action, by considering a story about a human being in the process of making a decision.

Let us suppose a graduate student receives offers of two posts— an unlikely event, but a logical possibility. If one is much more attractive than the other, so that there is no feature of the one as valenced as the comparable feature of the other, and if there is no serious prospect of an offer from a still more interesting institution, no deliberation will go on except how to accept the offer in a dignified manner, without unseemly haste. The reason is that each $V \times E$ product for each feature of one job will be greater than a matched product of the other. Suppose, however, the institutions are more nearly equal in their attractive features: salary, climate, quality of students, teaching load, library facilities, stimulating colleagues, and so on. How people behave in such a situation will vary, depending on intelligence and conceptual schemes, including thoughts about how to make rational decisions. There are some persons who, at a time of decision, find only one consideration importantly valenced—how happy they will be with the situation after the decision is made; and they think that the way to determine this is to sleep one night on the matter and then do whatever they feel inclined to do in the morning—inclinations, not reflection, being the guide. Of course many other things are in fact valenced for these people, but their preconceptions have the effect that these outcomes simply do not get represented—to use Lewinian terminology, their 'psychological fields' shrink—and so play no role in forming the action-tendency. All of this is perfectly consistent with the above 'laws', although the laws do not say anything about why certain outcomes are not represented. But we must recall that going over the relevant outcomes is itself a prolonged action which must be motivated, and in the situation of the hypothetical persons there is no motivation to perform that act. Some people find delay and deliberation quite aversive, and as a result the option of postponement for more deliberation is negatively valenced, and their decision is controlled by the valences of the outcomes which occur to them at the time.

People for whom delay for deliberation is not aversive will find at least four options open in the above case: to take one post, accept the other, think longer about the issue, or put the whole matter out of mind for later action. When a person is deliberating, he reflects on the various features of one position and the other, and each of these tempts him to accept in accordance with the degree of valence and the probability that the outcome will really be present. These reflections do not lead to action immediately, because of at least vague awareness of the possibility of catastrophic features not yet thought of. The careful decision-maker turns the matter over in his mind frequently, hoping that decisive considerations will occur to him. He will then take pencil and paper, knowing the limitations of his capacity to sum the various 'products', and try to match up equally tempting opposite considerations and drop them from mind, concentrating on the remaining features. If he is unfortunate, strongly valenced considerations will tempt him in one direction, and other strongly valenced ones tempt him in the other direction. He may try to remove undesirable features of one or the other position, thus making the decision easier.

Eventually his prospective employers will set a deadline and the delay must end; two options are removed, and only the choice between the two positions is left. The decision then is made, on the basis of the winnowed set of important unmatched considerations which crowd into awareness at the time sufficiently to engage valences and lead to action-tendencies. Why certain factors happen to be in awareness at the time with the degree of representation they have is a complex question: some may have become emphasized in the process of deliberation—just cognitively salient; some may be influenced by the fact that one's spouse is sitting nearby expressing views; some may be influenced by a temporary frame of mind—a restricted set if one is tired. (Remember that the degree of representation plays a role in determining how large an influence any consideration will have.) The strength of a particular motive at the time will play a role in the valence which attaches to a consideration: if one is at a moment of high achievement motivation, challenges may be strongly valenced; if one is at a moment of high need for affiliation, the fact that one has good friends at one institution will appear attractive. At any rate, the valences of these considerations, influenced by motive, and the degree to which the considerations vividly enter awareness, will fix the action-tendencies. And in this simplified situation, where the thought of further at the moment unconsidered features is prevented from playing its normal inhibiting role, the '$E \times V$ products'—however inaccurately summed, in comparison with the force each would have if taken singly—turn out to be stronger in one direction, and one acts accordingly.

All the principles listed above clearly play a role in a process of deliberation of this sort. The story of what goes on seems a realistic one.

CHAPTER IV

THE CRITICISM OF ACTIONS

WE HAVE now identified to what extent, and how, the beliefs, judgements, or thoughts of an agent influence what he does. Hence we can now inquire what a person's actions would be like if his thoughts were what they would have been if they were ideal in the sense of including available relevant information, and in the sense of representing this information adequately—being vivid, enjoying an equal share of attention, and so on.

Action which is ideal in this sense I have called 'rational action'—only to a first approximation, of course. I have raised a hope that more psychological knowledge, of a different sort, might enable us to criticize our wants and aversions, which for the present we are taking as given and not themselves the object of criticism. We must remember also that action which is rational in this sense is action we can properly call 'the best thing to do'—also as a first approximation, of course, pending criticism of our desires and aversions. So, in using our psychological theory to find ideal or informed or rational action, we are at the same time finding what is the *best* action—the action which has been criticized as fully as possible by appeal to facts and logic.

In the present chapter I shall exploit the results of the preceding one and identify various types of mistake in action, that is, types of action that would not have taken place had the action been 'rational', the choice mechanisms fully suffused by available knowledge.

The reader should not expect that these mistakes will be very specifically identified. Specific identification could hardly be expected in a general account; nor does one find it in the literature of moral philosophy generally. For the most part, the mistakes will be identified only by directing the reader to notice what he would not have done if he had been careful to do such-and-such. In some cases, however, for instance in the discussion of 'discounting the future', it will be possible to be more definite.

Some persons have thought that it is impossible in principle to show that certain actions are mistaken. A long tradition has held that whereas we can show reasons for thinking that something is justifiably believed, we cannot show reasons for thinking something is justifiably done. This tradition is mistaken if the present project is successful.

If we know what is the best thing to do, for purposes of action we do not need to inquire further what things are good. For instance, if I know that it is rational for me to buy a certain car, it is not to the point to debate whether it is a good car or a car better than other cars. If the best thing for me to do, if I am going to buy a car, is to take this one, then the question which is the best one for me is already answered. It is true that some other questions are so far unanswered: what it is best for other people, or people with standard needs, to do if they are about to buy a car. The question what is the best, or a good, thing of a certain kind is a derivative question, and the answer to it is always derivable from answers to the questions what it is best for me to do, or for persons with standard interests and situations to do. Our question is the fundamental one.

i. The mistake of overlooked options. The principles of the theory of action tell us that the tendency to perform a certain act is fixed by the subjective probability of various outcomes to which it may contribute, the valence of these outcomes for the agent, and perhaps other things. It follows that there will be no tendency to perform a certain act, if its performance is not brought to mind at all. Hence overlooking a certain option may have the consequence that one does something very different from what one would have done if one had considered that option. If a person who considered an option would have taken it, he has made a mistake if he does something else because he failed to consider it.

Virtually every action could turn out to be a mistake if we broadened the conception of 'available information' to the point of omniscience; doubtless there is something that could be done that would cure cancer if we only knew what to do. But there are other action-programmes which are realistically called mistaken because the relevant options could be, or have been, thought of. The most obvious of these is a plan for a *sequence* of acts so ordered that the wanted outcomes are realized at minimal cost; for instance, going home via the post office to mail a letter versus going home first (the most attractive goal at the moment since one is hungry), and then making a lengthy trip to the post office. What a rational person will always do is adopt an efficient schedule providing for a sequential achievement of things he wants, not necessarily in order of importance.[1] Such plans are, of course, always among the options.

How complex and far-reaching plans are among the options? Obviously we need to plan ahead more than a day—witness airline reservations. One trouble with not planning far ahead is that actions not taken now may rule out possibilities much later; for instance, a choice of business courses in secondary school may rule out entering the medical profession years later. Sometimes people talk of whole 'life-plans', but clearly any life-plan must be kept schematic enough to allow for changes of preference, and for the fact that there is simply not available evidence to evaluate a detailed life-plan.

In assessing how far-reaching our plans should be, we must recall an earlier point (p. 12 f.) that 'rational' might be defined in more than one way, depending on what is meant by 'all available information'. I decided to say that an action is rational (we might call this 'objectively rational') only if it is what it would have been if the agent had utilized all relevant information available at the time, including what he might not easily find out. In this sense, we might say that a person made an 'objective' mistake because he would have made a different plan—say, opted for a medical preparatory course in secondary school—if he had canvassed the options as thoroughly as a knowledgeable person would have done. But we might also have decided to say that an action is rational (we might call this 'subjectively rational') if it was based on the full use of beliefs rationally supported by the evidence the agent actually had at the time. It might, therefore, not be subjectively irrational for a person to fail to take a medical preparatory course in secondary school, even if objectively it is irrational to do so. But we must remember that a person usually has one option obviously open to him: to postpone action in order to reflect more or gather more information. Taking this option is of course itself an action, which may be either

---

[1] This point has been a favourite with writers influenced by the idealist tradition. For a relatively recent discussion see Mabbott, 1953.

objectively or subjectively rational or irrational. A person might decide, rationally both objectively and subjectively, that the cost of further reflection and information would be greater than the difference between the best and worst options for the basic decision. (It would be irrational, both subjectively and objectively, for a person to spend a week trying to plan savings on his income tax, if he knew at the outset that his maximal saving would be $10.) With this distinction in mind, what can we say about how far-reaching plans we ought to make? The answer is that we are not in a position to generalize: many schematic long-term plans are easy to make and leave options open and are manifestly superior to comparable alternatives; of others this may not be true and it would be irrational both subjectively and objectively to spend much time appraising them.

Some writers appear to think that we should not call an action irrational in any sense just because it falls short of the ideal of objective rationality, or even if it would have been subjectively rational to postpone decision for more information. What thoughtful people aim to do, it is said, is merely to scrutinize plans until one is found which meets rather loose criteria of being good enough. (Simon, 1955 and 1957; see Arrow, 1951.) Their claim about what thoughtful people aim to do need not, however, be accepted. For it is open to us to suppose that when people accept a plan which meets rather loose criteria of being good enough, it is accepted because there is rough background information that other plans are likely to be only slightly better and that it is not worth the time to canvass possibilities further when the most that can be hoped for is a minor improvement. Their ultimate plan of action, then, can be defended as subjectively but possibly not objectively, rational; and their decision to act without more information is subjectively rational and possibly also objectively so. It is worth noting that a person may employ a secretary, with the thought it is not worth the time to look further in view of past experience with the market, but later, in hindsight, say that the decision was a 'mistake', i.e. was objectively irrational.

ii. The mistake of overlooked outcomes. The laws of the theory of action assert that the magnitude of the tendency to perform a certain act is a function of the outcomes subjectively expected from that action in the circumstances. A person who had all the relevant available information would presumably be able to identify the expectable outcomes with considerable accuracy. A person without such information may overlook the possibility of a certain outcome altogether; if he does, he may well perform an act he would not have performed if he had had that outcome in mind and appraised its likelihood. If he does, we can call that action a mistake.

The sources of such a mistake may take various forms. Sometimes an agent knows about a certain outcome perfectly well but simply forgets at the moment of decision. In order to prevent such accidents intelligent people keep paper and pencil lists of pros and cons relevant to an important decision. Sometimes a person does not think of an outcome at all throughout the entire period of reflection, simply from an insufficiently careful or imaginative analysis of the situation on the basis of available information. For instance, a faculty member of a university in a small town, who values social life with his academic colleagues highly, might decide to move to another university located in New York or London, without thinking of the obstacles to social life with his colleagues where they live scattered around a large city. Suppose that, if our faculty member had thought of this, he would not have moved; we would then properly call his action a mistake, not being the action he would have taken on the basis of relevant available information.

One particular form of this general kind of mistake is so pervasive as to merit special notice. It arises from considering an outcome only in a somewhat vague and abstract way, either throughout the period of deliberation or at the time of decision. (Of course, sometimes the filling in of more detail is itself an effort which, as we saw above, it may be irrational to put forward in view of our estimate of the importance of what is at stake.) Consider an example. You are strongly tempted to move to another university in view of the scholarly merits of your prospective colleagues; but you do not inquire whether they spend their time in their offices, are willing to discuss the theoretical problems agitating other people or are wholly engrossed in their own work. If these more detailed questions were considered and answered, the move might be much less tempting, and we would have to call it a mistake if it were made.

iii. The mistake of erroneous degrees of expectation. The theory of action, as explained above, implies that, when valence is held constant, increase in the degree of expectation of an envisaged outcome will raise (if the valence is positive, lower if the valence is negative) the magnitude of the tendency to perform the relevant act.

We must assume that, for most and probably all actions, there is a best justified degree of expectation given the available evidence. The evidence may not permit a quantitative formulation, if no relevant frequencies of past events are in the evidence. Even so, rough odds can be put in quantitative terms. We must assume, then, that there is a correct degree of expectation of an outcome if a given action takes place, on the evidence, even though the 'correct degree' can be no better than a rough range, say, between 25 per cent and 50 per cent likelihood.

Decisions should be made with the correct degree of expectation—with the usual reservation about the cost of information—and ones made on the basis of an incorrect estimate are mistaken. We think this in practical life: we would think a baseball manager out of his mind if he sent a .050 hitter rather than a .500 hitter to bat at a crucial point in a ball game.

Sometimes a person faces special obstacles to acting with correct degrees of expectation. A person contemplating suicide, in a mood of deep depression, may repress evidence favourable to optimistic forecasts of his future; he may fail to project the past data accurately (he may forecast complete failure despite a record of regular past success); he may overlook the fact that future happiness is likely despite the fact that in his depressed mood now nothing seems attractive.

iv. Mistakes in adding increments to action-tendencies. We know that the strength of the tendency to perform an action with an anticipated valenced outcome corresponds with the product $V \times E$ in an appropriate sense. But suppose an action—one among several options—is expected to have several outcomes. Then what do we do? In the preceding chapter I extemporized a 'law' (p. 65) about what we *do* do, but there is surely a question whether we might not find a way to do it better—'fairer' to all the considerations involved. A familiar proposal, which assumes we can assign numbers to the valences and probabilities, is that we simply sum the $V \times E$

products over all the anticipated outcomes, and that this sum represents the relative desirability of the action. But, theoretical problems aside, we simply do not have these numbers. Are we then simply to throw up our hands in complex situations? The matter is worth scrutiny.

The first thing to notice is that there is a problem about choices, even when the outcomes are all certain or probable to the same degree. Let me quote the conclusion of one study of consumer choices, by R. N. Shepard:

Many practical decision problems require that a choice be made among alternatives, each of which consists of a number of subjectively disparate attributes. But, after a choice of this kind has been made, the decision maker sometimes comes to the realization that his particular choice was not the best even by his own subjective standards. One source of the subjective nonoptimality of such decisions seems to be man's demonstrable inability to take proper account, simultaneously, of the various component attributes of the alternatives; that is, although he will probably experience little difficulty in evaluating the alternatives with respect to any one of these subjective attributes, a considerable number of experiments reviewed here indicate that his ability to arrive at an over-all evaluation by weighing and combining or 'trading off' all of these separate attributes at the same time is likely to be less impressive.[2]

Evidently there is a problem about simultaneous adequate representation of the various features or elements of the alternatives, an inability to get everything adequately, or even equally, before the mind at the same time. We need this for 'rational' choice between options, since we know that inadequate representation renders an option less likely to be chosen, and because rational choice is choice as it would be if the choice were made with vivid and equal representation of the relevant outcomes. Further, we do have a conception what this might be like for complex choices, e.g. for products with complicated distinct features—in the example of a person who has used such complex products for a long time and has gradually formed a decided preference. His experience has given him a kind of 'holistic' view of the options. Presumably a person

---

[2]Shepard, 1964. R. E. Quandt (1956) has suggested that buyers often fail to pay attention to features of an article they most of the time think significant for choice, and sometimes base their decision on a feature they normally think is irrelevant.

approximates to this if he has mulled over various outcomes of options before him for a long time and has formed a firm preference.

Is there any procedure by which we can approximate, when the probabilities are equal and can be ignored, to the ideal of a simultaneous adequate representation of the complex outcomes of options between which we are choosing? We can properly reduce the complexity of the problem by a matching procedure. If some features can be paired off as equal, and a 'holistic' view of the remainder leads to a predominant action-tendency for one action, presumably a holistic view of the whole, were it possible, would have led in the same direction. Alternatively, if some outcomes of option A overmatch paired outcomes of option B, and a holistic view of the remaining outcomes of A with those of B favours A, again an ideal holistic view of the whole set would presumably favour A. Such matching may not be easy if the issue is not one of immediate consumption, say, of a banana-split versus that of some other complex goodie, but is a matter of choice of a long-term mode of life (for instance, teaching in the sunny climate of Palo Alto versus teaching in the more rigorous atmosphere of Ann Arbor), especially since the outcomes must be broken down into detail, such as playing tennis outdoors versus indoors, taking walks, and so on. And there is the question of how much of one's time would be spent in one location, doing something necessarily different from what one would be doing in the other location. Such reflection is time-consuming and not easy; but it seems to be used by thoughtful people for important decisions, and so it should be.

The items mentioned above were all near-certainties. Can any such matching be done when different outcomes are expected, but with different degrees of probability? Some choices involve probabilities at virtually every point: say a decision to marry a certain person, or to employ a certain person as a secretary. Even here it seems there can be appropriate matching. Miss Jones's bad typing may be more objectionable than Mr. Smith's spelling, but the former may get better as she promises it will. In this case one inclines to go for Miss Jones with her probably improved typing, rather than for Mr. Smith with his unimprovable spelling. So, if Miss Jones comes out ahead in a 'holistic' view of other matters, we can forget the spelling and the typing. It even seems reasonable in some cases to equate a $V \times E$ product for Miss Jones with a different

$V \times E$ product for Mr. Smith, if, when we consider both by themselves, we are indifferent which to choose.

Suppose we have exhausted the possibilities for matching, what are we then to do, and how reliable will it be as a 'holistic' response? The obvious answer is that we try to get the outcomes, and their probabilities, as vividly (and equally) before the mind as possible. If we have done that then we have to rely on internal processes (like an analogue computer, or like the batteries and wires in the model suggested on p. 53 f.), to give us a 'holistic' response, fair to the valences of the several anticipated outcomes, and to the probabilities of each. As the outcomes involved become more numerous, the problems of getting them all vividly before the mind increase, since obviously only a very few things can be got vividly before the mind, and responded to, at once. We necessarily depart from ideal 'rationality' because of this finite capacity of our minds. Something can be done to mitigate the probable errors: we can get the more important factors before the mind at the moment of decision. If we do this the hope is that our conclusion will be closer to what an ideal 'holistic' view would favour, than if the issue were settled by having the less important factors before the mind. But we cannot be sure. Evidently there is here a limitation to the scope of rationality in decision-making.

v. The mistake of discounting the future.   A person 'discounts' future events if he behaves in the following way: given that he would perform action A with an expectancy E of producing outcome O as compared with action A' with an expectancy E' of producing outcome O' if O and O' were to occur at roughly *the same time*, he would perform A' rather than A if the outcome O' were expected to occur significantly *earlier* than O, everything else being the same. In the preceding chapter we observed an example of this: children often do what will enable them to eat a sweet now, rather than what will enable them to eat a much more desirable sweet (as ascertained by their preferences between the two, for immediate consumption) an hour or more from now. The economist Jevons thought that adults behave in the same way, and suggested that generally, the more remote from the present a pleasure is, the less important it seems to a person. This time-preference became the basis of some economists' theory of interest. (Georgescu-Roegen,

1968, p. 250.) Psychologists generally suppose that the curve of concern about aversive events falls off more steeply with time-separation than does interest in desired events.[3] (This may explain why the threat of punishment is often ineffective.)

It is not obvious that everyone discounts the future; indeed, some people save so much of their income in order to provide for their old age that earlier parts of life are neglected, and from excess prudential zeal they fall short of the economist's ideal of maximizing utility over a lifetime. We need not question, however, that some persons do discount future events at least some of the time.

In recent years philosophers have debated whether choice of a lesser good because of closer time-position is rational, or consistent with firmly rooted beliefs such as that we are continuing persons. Some philosophers have attempted to show that something is radically mistaken about pure time-discounting, and other philosophers have doubted whether any such thing has been proved. One writer, after quoting the biblical 'Take no thought for the morrow; for the morrow shall take thought for the things of itself', goes on to argue that it has not been shown that there is anything wrong with an extreme policy of 'aprudentialism', which recommends that one always do, at any moment, what will maximize gratification at that moment (we can extend the time-slice a bit—talk in terms of an hour), absolutely irrespective of the consequences for later times.[4]

Why do people sometimes discount future events? The preceding chapter reviewed evidence indicating that mode of representation of a fact affects the magnitude of the action-tendency aroused by it. Mode of representation, we saw, might be inadequate because of lack of attention, absence of detail, lack of vivid imagery, and so on. If we assume that future events tend to be less adequately represented than facts of the immediate present, especially aversive

---

[3] See Neal Miller, 1944. There may be individual differences in the magnitude of these effects. See Foley and Banford, 1968; also Berkowitz, 1964, pp. 83–94.

[4] Trebilcot, 1974. See Rawls, 1971, pp. 293–5, 420, 423; Nagel, 1970, especially Chap. 8. Henry Sidgwick affirmed a maxim of Rational Prudence, that 'the mere difference of priority and posteriority in time is not a reasonable ground for having more regard to the consciousness of one moment than to that of another. The form in which it practically presents itself to most men is "that a smaller present good is not to be preferred to a greater future good" (allowing for difference of certainty).' (1922, p. 381.)

features of future events (thus ill health twenty years from now as compared with the delights of a cigarette now), our principle would provide at least a partial explanation why people 'discount' future events, especially aversive ones. Something of the sort has been proposed by various philosophers, as we noted in the preceding chapter. Incidentally, F. P. Ramsey remarked that discounting later enjoyments 'is ethically indefensible and arises merely from the weakness of the imagination'.[5]

If discounting future events arises wholly from inadequacy of representation, then obviously it is irrational in my sense, since it would not occur in a person with ideally adequate representation of available facts. We must admit that, since the preceding chapter was not ideally clear on just how 'adequate representation' should be explained, and further did not present empirical evidence that the various factors mentioned do reduce the relevant action-tendencies according to some specific function, the proposal is not precise. Furthermore, even if we know that inadequacy of representation is probably at least a partial explanation of time-discounting, we do not have conclusive evidence that nothing else is involved. In fact, some other partial explanations have been proposed: for instance, that conflict in the individual is one thing that reduces 'delay of gratification'. Again, it is logically possible that it is a basic fact about human beings that action-tendencies (or, perhaps the valences of events) depend on a time-distance variable; perhaps our basic formulation should be

$$T_A = f\left(E, V, R, \frac{1}{\text{time-distance}}\right).$$

But there is no evidence for such a fact, and psychologists regard time-discounting as something that requires explanation. If we are cautious, however, what we shall say is that *to the extent* to which preference for a nearer event derives from inadequate representation of the temporally more remote event, *then it is irrational*.

Is absence of time-discounting a part of 'prudence'? The term 'prudent' seems to have a slightly bad name at the moment,

[5] Ramsey, 1928, pp. 543–59. Much the same point is made by G. H. von Wright, 1963b, p. 113. Sidgwick has a superb discussion of the difficulties of forecasting and comparing future enjoyments, 1922, Bk. II, Chap. 3.

suggesting too much calculation, and weighting future goals too heavily in comparison with present enjoyments. It might be useful to rehabilitate the term, and if we do we should put down not discounting future events, as such, as one of the elements of prudence. We might, of course, just identify prudence with rationality in my sense.

One might wonder whether it is possible to benefit from this theoretical lesson and overcome the processes that lead to time-discounting. Actually, it is: psychologists' self-help manuals suggest many remedies. For instance, if a person is trying to lose weight, he can place forbidden goodies at the back of the refrigerator where he does not see them and hence his desire is not aroused by vivid visual perception. Or, one can develop habits of verbal response to situations of 'temptation', since it is not difficult to postpone action long enough for some verbalizing. And once the verbalizing has its nose in the motivational tent, the remoter goals can be made more vivid—by just repeating statements about them to oneself, by summoning up images (e.g. of confrontation with a weight-watcher's group tomorrow), and so on. The same thing can be done, doubtless with more difficulty, about aversive features of future events, which in the ordinary course of events influence choice much less than by their fair share. A human being can, then, intervene in his own motivational system and come some distance towards equal recognition of future states of affairs, whether attractive or aversive.

It is not merely future states of affairs which tend to be unfairly treated because they are under-represented. Outcomes tend to be under-represented also because of the state of one's motives. If a person is sated with human company, it is hard for him to represent adequately his enjoying a convivial gathering; and the same if he is sated with sex. The reverse, of course, if the person is in a state of deprivation with respect to some family of valenced outcomes.

vi. The mistake of ignoring future desires. It is probably irrational, then, to prefer one outcome to another just because it will come sooner, when preference would go the other way if the outcomes would be simultaneous. There is another issue, however, which is often confused with this one. Suppose one now (time t) desires an outcome to occur at the later time t'; suppose further there is another outcome which is incompatible with this one at t' (and there is no way to combine them sequentially), which one does not desire now although one knows that one will desire it later, beginning at some time between t and t', rather more than one desires the other outcome now. Would it be rational to arrange for the occurrence of the now not desired outcome? In general, how far is it rational to pay attention, in action, to desires we do not now have, but know we shall have later?

Writers sometimes behave as if they thought this situation cannot arise—as if an agent's desires and aversions for various outcomes are fixed over a lifetime. It is quite obvious, however, that desires and aversions do vary. Some desires, for instance, are cyclical. I drink my fill of water and do not want another drop, but I know I shall want water three hours from now, when I finish a game of tennis. Or, I have just chatted with colleagues over coffee and am sated with that and wish to return to work, but I know that in a few hours I shall again want the company of congenial human beings. Desires are temporarily affected by mood or emotion; if I am grief-stricken nothing will seem important or exciting except the object lost. Desires also change with maturation or novel circumstances. We can predict that when a man has produced a family, he will have affection for his children and want their welfare. Every time a person acquires a friend or falls in love he develops desires he did not have before, for the company or affection of a certain other person. Moreover, as a child grows older, he loses some of his childhood aspirations; he may have wanted to become a policeman, but ceases to do so by the time he is old enough to qualify. So it is far from true that desires and aversions are fixed, although some change only rather slowly.

There are two interesting, but mistaken, answers one might give to our general question how far it is rational to provide in action for the satisfaction of desires we know we shall have but do not have now. One is that knowledge of any desire, present or future, would be motivating to a rational person, roughly to a degree corresponding to the expected strength of the desire. The second is that a rational person would pay attention to, and only to, his knowledge of desires approximately simultaneous with the outcomes they are desires for; thus a child's desire now to become a policeman at the age of twenty-five does not count now, but the knowledge that he will desire the same at twenty-five will (or might) count.[6] According to this view, it seems to follow that one thing a rational person would pay attention to is his own happiness or enjoyment at any time, if we assume, as I have argued one should, that to enjoy oneself is to be wanting the continuation of one's experience or activity then going on.

These views that a rational person would aim to maximize satisfaction of known desires, or aim to satisfy a selected segment of known desires, are less simple than might appear. A person has many desires and aversions at the same time. The various desires endure for different periods of time, and have varying intensities during these times. For instance, I may know that I shall want to learn French six months from now, but that after a year of study of French I shall have lost interest. Again, consider the putative fact that during the last week of life people sometimes wish very strongly to have lived an ascetic, wholly achievement-oriented kind of life. May I ignore a desire I shall have only a week or a year? In deciding how much weight a desire deserves, shall I count its average intensity over a lifetime, its peak intensity, or what? Should I draw a curve for each desire, its height above the x-axis showing its intensity at any time, and then weigh the desire in accordance with the area under the curve over a lifetime? When one tries to think through what it would be like to plan now, as far as possible, for maximizing desire-satisfaction over a lifetime, one finds oneself unable to get a firm grip on the supposed conception. We shall be returning to these problems later (in Chapter 13).

Fortunately, these puzzling conceptions may be ignored because, if our 'laws' of the theory of action are correct, what an agent does is always a function of his desires at the time; there is no such thing as motivation by beliefs alone. Present desires for outcomes (and beliefs about how acts will produce them), and never thoughts of future desires alone, motivate persons.

The recognition of this fact does not preclude discussion of our original question about how far it is rational to pay attention to knowledge that we shall have certain desires at a later time. We do need to rephrase it and divide it into two parts. (1) How can a person

---

[6] This view seems to be held by Thomas Nagel, 1970. Nagel does not explain what he means by 'desire', 'reason', and 'justified'—central terms in his conception—and hence it is difficult to be sure.

take future desires into account in his present actions? (2) To what extent would a fully informed or rational person actually do this? The answer to the first question is that a person must have a present desire to satisfy future desires, or an aversion to frustrating them, or else a present desire for the effects of satisfying future desires or a present aversion to the effects of frustrating future desires.

Let us consider how this works out. Suppose I am going on a hike and am not thirsty now, but decide to take a flask of water. Why? The answer is that I *now* have an aversion to being uncomfortably thirsty four hours from now. However we acquire such aversions, the fact is that we have them. Again, although I am not thirsty now, perhaps the idea of a cool draught when thirsty later is attractive to me now. (My aversion, and this attraction, may later become more intense when I am actually thirsty.) This example can be generalized. When a want which passes a threshold of intensity is frustrated, a person experiences some discomfort like thirst, or at least what Karl Duncker (1941, pp. 417–18) called 'the sorrow of want'. If so, then for every type of want previously experienced, there will be (at least in good visualizers) a present aversion to its being frustrated when aroused, and possibly a present desire for its satisfaction. It looks, then, as if there is at least a fixed present aversion to frustration of almost any desire, and often a fixed desire for its satisfaction. This fact explains in part how known future desires can be taken into account in present action.

Some philosophers have developed a somewhat different conception. Bishop Butler (1729, Sermon 1) affirmed that every human being with a reasonably adequate conceptual apparatus necessarily develops a second-order desire for his own long-range happiness, a desire which Butler called 'self-love'. Such a desire, he says, 'seems inseparable from all sensible creatures, who can reflect upon themselves and their own interest or happiness, so as to have that interest an object to their minds....' Butler seems to mean by 'happiness' or 'interest' the being in some internal state one likes, everything considered, whereas unhappiness is being in some state which one dislikes. Sometimes, however, he suggests a more restricted notion, when he implies that happiness is a state in which some *antecedent desire* for something has been gratified. 'Happiness', he says, 'consists of the gratification of particular

passions, which supposes the having of them.' (Ibid.) The restriction, however, is a mistake, because there are states of affairs we
like, such as coming on an unexpected view of a sunset, which are
not the satisfaction of any identifiable antecedent desire. In what
sense is a person's own happiness the object of a desire, according to
him? He is not merely saying what I have just pointed out, that we
have aversions and desires for specific liked or disliked states of
affairs, such as being thirsty or enjoying a cool draught when hot.
He seems to be saying that all thoughtful persons have a desire for
their own happiness *in the abstract*, independently of any representation of some specific form of discomfort or enjoyment. Butler
points out rightly that a person 'may go through some laborious
work upon promise of a great reward, without any distinct
knowledge what the reward will be'.[7] So he seems to be saying that
there is a desire for enjoyment and aversion to discomfort, *just as
such, and as abstractly* represented; and this he calls 'self-love'.

It seems, then, that we have a dual means of answering our
question how we can act so as to satisfy anticipated future desires
now. On the one hand, people, at least good visualizers, have
standing aversions to specific frustrations and standing interests in
enjoyments of satisfaction, and these can be action-guiding for
people who make use of vivid information about how they may feel
later; and on the other hand intelligent people have a standing
interest in future happiness as such. So a thoughtful person will
make some provision, at some cost, for the satisfaction of future
desire either because he is averse to specific frustrations, or because
he knows it will add to his happiness. Nothing has been said about
how strong these present desires will be.

Do these considerations show that a rational person will be
motivated to satisfy his known future desires equally as much as his
present desires? It seems doubtful that they do. Suppose I have a
desire now for an outcome O at time t, and know I shall later have a
desire of equal intensity for O' to occur also at t. In the situation we

---

[7] 1729, Sermon 1, footnote. We should note that the English usage of 'happiness' is
complex and not accurately represented by an analysis in terms of enjoyment/discomfort. In
an article, 1967, I suggested that what it is to be a 'happy person' is (a) not to be dissatisfied
with the major outlines of one's life, which one thinks important, including future prospects,
and (b) to have enjoyments from time to time. But the word 'happy' is used in many contexts
('the happiest hour of my life'), and the various nuances of meanings in different contexts
have not, to my knowledge, been analysed.

may presume I shall also have some aversion now to the specific discomfort of being frustrated at t if O does not occur, and the same for O'; and I shall have some interest in the specific enjoyment of getting the desired O at t, and the same for O'; and in the abstract I shall want both O and O' to occur at t because I know each will add to my happiness. So far my desire now for O, and my future desire for O', appear to come out equally; at least, let us suppose this. But it is also true that the idea of O now motivates me in a way in which the idea of O' does not. That it does is implied by the fact that I do desire it now. In view of this fact, does it not seem plausible to say that the total motivation or action-tendency to do what is expected to bring about O will be greater than the total motivation or action-tendency to do what is expected to bring about O', at the time? The answer must be affirmative. However much we insist that a fully informed person will visualize future states of affairs as vividly as present ones, I do not see how one will show that a fully informed person will be as much motivated now to produce O' which he knows he will desire in the future, as he is now motivated to produce O. If so, then there is built into human nature something that many persons would regard as a basic irrationality. Butler may have been aware of the problem. For he acknowledged that particular passions are often more strongly motivating than considerations of 'self-love'. He went on to say that the principle of self-love has rightful authority over the 'passions', saying that 'it is manifest that self-love is in human nature a superior principle to passion'. (1722, Sermon 3.) But he did not attempt to show that motivation by self-love would be stronger than motivation by competing particular desires, in a case like the one we have been considering, *in a rational person*—which may be necessary for a solution of the problem satisfactory to some persons.

   An informed or rational person, then, will be motivated to some extent by the knowledge that he will desire something at a future time; but it cannot be shown that this motivation will be equal to the motivation arising from an equally strong present desire.

   An important special case of this problem of the proper weight of a known future desire is that of a below-normal (or above-normal) strength of some variable desire. Suppose a person is now, at the time of decision, fully satiated (or deprived) in respect of his sex desire, or affiliation desire, etc., then the normal or average level of these desires is not operative in the decision. A rational person would to some extent compensate for this by representing to himself vividly the frustrations or joys associated with these desires, in which we assume he takes a somewhat steady interest. But he might not fully compensate, if the above reasoning is correct. Philosophers have sometimes thought that an optimal decision would be guided by a 'normal' state of desires. It is not clear, however, how this predilection can be justified. The problem has disturbing scope, since human decisions are almost always made in a state of satiation or deprivation of some desire, often one bearing on the decision. As a result, it seems required to conclude that a decision made today, in one state of deprivation or satiation, might be a *rational* one—corrected in all the ways full and vivid knowledge would correct it—but be different from a decision made tomorrow which also would be rational. It is not clear how this kind of 'relativism' can be avoided.

CHAPTER V

THE PSYCHOLOGY OF PLEASURE AND DESIRES

THE IDEA that *actions* can be mistaken in some way I have now supported as best I can. But can *pleasures*, or *desires*, be mistaken in some way? A good many people have thought they can be. The idea that a pleasure can be 'false' is as old as Plato, and it is at least natural to say that a thrill of enjoyment has something wrong with it if it is a response to false information or a misreading of information. And the idea that some desires are defective also goes back to the Greeks: for instance, intense desire for reputation, or power, or wealth.

In the present and the following chapter I shall explore and defend the view that there are some desires and some pleasures which a fully rational person would not experience. We shall see that the conception of a 'fully rational' person must be slightly modified for the present context, but it will be roughly the same: the idea of a person in whom the mechanisms underlying desire, pleasure, and action have been fully suffused by relevant available information. Precisely what the concept is will be explained in the following chapter.

What is the importance of identifying desires, aversions, or pleasures which a person would not experience if he were fully rational? The answer to this question is not self-evident. Should one, or even can one, act as if one did have a desire one in fact does not have? If one does experience irrational pleasures or desires, is it rational to try to get rid of them? And at what expense? I shall discuss these matters in Chapter 8. But two preliminary observations are in order now. First, most of us would, if it were really shown that a desire, say, for reputation, is based on a cognitive mistake in an important sense, be less inclined to expend effort in seeking to satisfy it. Second, at least some of us are troubled by the fact that some things we desire in life are probably never going to happen, and we would feel less troubled if we knew that these desires were irrational in the first place. Our question, then, does seem to have some practical importance.

How might it ever be shown that a given person, if he were 'fully rational', would not desire certain situations just for themselves, or enjoy certain things or situations? Obviously this can be shown only if beliefs or thoughts play an essential role in the genesis of desires and enjoyments. If they do, and if we knew that an essential belief or thought was itself unreasonable or incompatible with available information, we could conclude that the desire or pleasure was irrational—it would not have occurred in a fully rational person. The first thing we must do, then, is to explore the psychological theory of the genesis of desire and dispositions to like or take pleasure in certain things or situations, and find out to what extent beliefs or thoughts are involved in this genesis. That is the task of the present chapter. The following chapter will put these results to work.

1. INNATE AND CONDITIONED DISPOSITIONS TO LIKE AND DISLIKE

It is convenient to begin with learning dispositions to enjoy (like) certain experiences, since enjoyments are basic to acquiring normal desires or valences, or incentive values (p. 34), and not the other way around. (Throughout, except when the context indicates otherwise, when I speak of pleasure or liking, I intend also to be talking of displeasure or disliking.)

We should remind ourselves of the agreed definition of 'pleasant' or 'likes'. Roughly, we said that what it is for an experience to be pleasant for a person is for it to make him want its continuation (or to make him tend to act in a way which normally would contribute to its continuation). Notice that pleasantness is conceptually related to wanting or valence: the experience makes one want something. We must distinguish pleasant experiences from what is often called 'consummatory activity' like eating, drinking, or copulating. These activities—all typical interactions with goal objects of a suitable kind—are normally pleasant (in so far as the person wants to continue them), but some experiences are pleasant which are not consummatory activities, for example, viewing a sunset.

Is the pleasantness or unpleasantness of any experience an

unlearned, or native, response to it?[1] It is generally supposed that some experiences are natively either pleasant or unpleasant. It is generally thought that it is natively pleasant, other things being equal, to eat when hungry, explore the environment, solve a puzzle, taste sweetened water, see a smiling face. And it is generally thought that some experiences are natively unpleasant, such as pain, loud noise, the taste of castor oil, loss of support for an infant, thirst, inability to breathe, having an overfull bladder, constraint on action, and the absence of sensory stimulation. Some psychologists would have a longer list (e.g. adding cuddling); others would make it shorter. Psychologists who think that pleasure responses are unlearned often believe that their occurrence has survival value for the person's gene-stream and hence has an evolutionary explanation.

In some cases the best explanation of the hedonic quality of an experience is that it is learned. For example, drinking scotch and water or receiving a compliment are learned pleasures (the writer has not yet learned the former). Such an explanation is especially convincing when people differ markedly in the pleasure they take in a certain experience, and when we find a possible explanation in their individual life histories. This is the case with achievement motivation (Rosen and d'Andrade, 1959), and the same for the discomfort of being alone or the liking for being with others (Schachter, 1959, Chap. 5), in view of the data that first-born children like being with others more intensely, at least in certain sorts of situation.

[1] It may seem odd to regard the pleasantness of something as a *response*, the sort of thing we are accustomed to think of as being conditionable. But a rather broad use of this term seems to be accepted. Some years ago Miller and Dollard wrote: 'It is obvious that "response", as here used, is not restricted to the conventional usage, in which a response is defined as a muscular contraction or a glandular secretion. It is also obvious that "stimulation" is not restricted to the conventional usage, in which a stimulus is defined as an energy change activating receptors. According to the present usage, a response is any activity by or within the individual which can become functionally connected with an antecedent event through learning; a stimulus is any event to which a response can be so connected.' (See Miller and Dollard, 1941, p. 59. Also Eysenck and Beech, 1971, pp. 597–8.)

It seems that an experience being pleasant qualifies as a response. For an experience to be pleasant is for it to make the person want to continue it at the time. The 'making the person want to continue' can be viewed as a response to the experience, which is the 'antecedent event.' If a person's enjoyment of an experience E is learned, he at one time experienced E without wanting to continue it; then, after some 'learning' events, his experiencing E makes this wanting take place.

Since evidently a theory of acquiring likes and dislikes by learning is necessary, it is economical to rely on this process as far as possible, and to minimize postulation of native tendencies. Most psychologists think this learning process is one of conditioning. We must go into this.

Suppose that the pleasantness, say, of a tune is learned by conditioning. We shall then think of it as having essentially the status of the salivation of Pavlov's dogs. In their case, meat powder was first blown into their mouths (unconditioned stimulus) and this elicited salivation (unconditioned response). Then the meat powder was preceded by the sound of a buzzer (conditioned stimulus). After a few occasions of this pairing of the buzzer with the subsequent appearance of the meat powder, salivation commenced at the sound of the buzzer. When an initially neutral stimulus comes in this way to elicit a response at first elicited only by the unconditioned stimulus, it is said that the process is one of *classical conditioning*. It seems just a basic law of organisms that classical conditioning takes place. In the case of the pleasantness of a tune being a result of conditioning, the unconditioned stimulus would be some already liked experience (like the meat powder blown into the mouths of Pavlov's dogs); the conditioned stimulus would be the tune (in Pavlov's case, the sound of a buzzer); the unconditioned response would be the pleasantness-resonse to the unconditioned stimulus (corresponding to native salivation in response to the presence of the meat powder in their mouths); the conditioned response would be the pleasantness-response to the unconditioned salivation of the dogs at the sound of the buzzer). If we want the formulation of a law relating the acquisition of pleasantness to other factors, we have this: if a neutral experience of the kind E is closely associated either with reduction of unpleasant sensations characteristic of some deprivation state, or with the production of already liked exciting sensations, then E experiences come to be pleasant; and if Es are closely associated either with the onset of already unpleasant experiences like pain, or with the offset of already liked experiences like play, Es come to be unpleasant. On the basis of animal data we can fill this out to say: (1) as an increasing function (a) of the number of pairings and (b) of the intensity of the affective quality of the primary reward; and (2) as a decreasing function of the delay of the primary reward. Such pleasantness appears to extinguish readily, and its maintenance requires occasional futher pairings with the primary reward. Incidentally, an experience can become pleasant when it has been paired with intracranial stimulation of the 'pleasure centres'.[2]

However, is there solid evidence that pleasantness can be conditioned to an initially neutral experience? There is a large animal literature under the title of 'secondary reinforcement' or 'secondary incentives', but although the animal evidence is consistent with an interpretation in terms of the conditioning of pleasantness, it does not require it, and one would prefer not to lean heavily on that evidence.

Other kinds of evidence indicate that learned pleasantness is a result of conditioning. Common-sense information supports the view. For instance, people like the food they have eaten since childhood—presumably because it has been associated with reduction of hunger-pangs or the various pleasures of eating.[3] Again, almost everyone in the Western tradition enjoys hearing Christmas carols. We like them presumably not because they are great as music but because we associate them with happy times and receipt of gifts in childhood. Furthermore, many practitioners of behaviour therapy assume that pleasantness can be conditioned. For example, they try to remove a child's fear of dogs by rendering the percept of a dog pleasant by conditioning—allowing the child, in the arms of its mother, and eating ice-cream, to see the dog at a distance, and then gradually bringing the dog closer. This procedure is thought to cure a conditioned anxiety originally attached to the dog percept, by attaching an incompatible favourable affect to the same stimulus. It has also been shown that favourable affect can be conditioned to nonsense syllables, or to picture post cards

---

[2] See Kimble, 1961, Chap. 7; Kelleher and Gollub, 1962; Young, 1961, p. 170; Staats, 1970, especially pp. 119 ff.; Atkinson and Birch, 1970, pp. 157 ff. and 251 ff.; Wike, 1966, Chap. 3, also pp. 25–7.
Most psychologists find no difficulty in the idea of conditioning of parts of the consummatory response, e.g. salivation, to associated stimuli. Indeed, R. C. Bolles has said (1967, p. 336) that this conception is 'the only serious proposal that has been made for a mechanism to account for incentive motivation'. Wanting to continue the experience (cf. eating, copulating), or maintenance activities, would seem to be part of the consummatory 'behaviour' which could be conditioned.

[3] The *Palo Alto Times* on 22 July 1970 depicted a woman with a broad smile on her face, eating a newspaper. She said she had developed a craving while pregnant nineteen years ago, and had been enjoying consuming newspaper ever since.

previously rated as indifferent.[4] Furthermore, it has been found that babies develop a preference for the presence of a red light when it has been shown during feeding.[5] It is generally supposed that a child's liking for the presence of his mother derives from her prior presence during tension-reducing events such as feeding, changing napkins, removing safety-pins, etc., as well as the positive pleasures of being fed, cuddled, and carried about. (Mussen and Conger, 1956, p. 137.)

Parallel evidence supports the conditioning of unpleasantness. First, every reader can provide his own common-sense evidence for the view. The writer can only ascribe the unpleasantness of touching any living creature with feathers, of the thought of the San Francisco airport, of the interior of any public school building, of the sight of someone else having a knee injury, and of many other things, to conditioning by past events. There are more 'scientific' data. Behaviour therapists widely use 'aversive conditioning' in the treatment of alcoholism, obesity, and sexual deviance, for example, by giving the patient a nauseous drug and letting him rehearse the deviant behaviour when he begins to feel discomfort. The claim is that the behaviour loses its attractiveness or becomes plain aversive.[6] Sometimes an electric shock is used instead of a nauseous drug. Some psychologists question, however, whether the behavioural evidence must be construed as indicating conditioned aversiveness.[7]

Some animal experimentation supports the view. Rats can be made to reject their otherwise preferred liquid—water sweetened with saccharin—by injections of apomorhine (a nauseous drug) after drinking the sweetened water.[8]

Some psychologists incline to the view that no autonomic conditioning is just a matter of contiguity (as the above-stated law implies it is), but rather involves awareness of the relation between

[4] There is a critical review of some studies along these general lines in Bandura, 1969, pp. 602 ff. and 513 f.; see also A. Silverstein, 1973.

[5] Lee, 1967. Reshevsky (1967, pp. 109–10) found that rats came to prefer grape juice to milk when they were fed the former only when hungry, the latter when sated.

[6] There is a review of material prior to 1969 in Bandura, 1969, Chap. 8. A discussion of the data from a very different point of view is to be found in Brown and Farber, 1968; see also Neal Miller, 1951; Levy and Martin, 1975; and Eysenck and Beech, 1971.

[7] See, for instance, Hallam and Rachman, 1972; P. M. Miller, et al., 1973; Marmor, 1971.

[8] Revensky and Gorry, 1973; Hargrave and Bolles, 1971; Rachman and Teasdale, 1969.

the conditioned and the unconditioned stimulus, so that the former has become a signal for the latter. If this view is correct, then conditioned salivation could be salivation at the anticipation of food, and a child's 'conditioned' pleasure could be pleasure at the anticipation of being cuddled and fed. The experimental data indicate, however, that awareness of such a relation facilitates the conditioned response but is not necessary for it, and that re-cognition that the connection no longer obtains facilitates but does not accomplish extinction of the response. (Kimble, 1962; Grings, 1973; Brandeis and Lubow, 1975.)

The reasonable conclusion seems to be that experiences become pleasant (or unpleasant) as a result of contiguity with other experiences already pleasant.

Psychologists seem relatively satisfied that at least the less important of our non-native likes and dislikes, for example food preferences, can be explained by conditioning. Psychologists worry, however, about whether important likes and dislikes can be explained in this way. Does conditioning explain our enjoyment of the plaudits of the multitudes, the discomfort of knowing that a person has a very negative reaction towards one, and so on? Why do some psychologists have doubts? For one thing, classical aversive conditioning (as distinct from avoidance behaviour) extinguishes easily; so do 'secondary incentives'. Again, the effects of condition-ing of incentives, at least in animals, seem fairly weak; while we know that we can condition a positive response to previously neutral picture postcards, it remains to be shown that a person would pay fifty cents, rather than ten, to obtain one of these. Furthermore, in the case of the conditioning of pleasure, the strength of the effect seems to depend on whether the desire, the satisfaction of which did the conditioning, is in force. In view of this, how can we think that classical conditioning explains, say, our dislike of being the target of negative attitudes of another person—a dislike which seems strong, not easily extinguished, and inde-pendent of the state of other 'drives'?

Various psychologists have interested themselves in this prob-lem.[9] It is clear that real-life conditioning of pleasantness differs

[9] See Hill, 1968; McClelland, 1958, 1965; Brown and Farber, 1968; Neal Miller, 1951; Bandura, 1969, pp. 224–8, 602–6; Amsel, 1972; McClelland and McGown, 1953; Wike, 1966, pp. 477 ff.; Nevin, 1966.

from controlled conditioning in the laboratory, which may explain why the former is strong and durable, the latter weak and short-lived. For one thing, the associations which support the pleasantness of achievement and the unpleasantness of rejection by others continue sporadically through life—for instance, material rewards, and the praise and admiration that go with achievement. These associations are not cut off at the end of a laboratory session. Moreover, the associations are in varied directions: in the case of achievement, praise and affection from parents, money, privileges, and the promise of future rewards. Furthermore, the supporting associations do not come regularly but infrequently and at unpredictable intervals—a situation which in the laboratory we know to be favourable to resistance of extinction of behaviour, although the impact on the extinction of incentives is not clear. Of great importance is the fact that these basic associations occur in childhood, when the affective force of experiences like praise and rejection is apt to be high, partly because the child's time-perception does not give him a clear view of when a given situation will terminate. Further, partly because the child lacks facility with symbolism, he does not discriminate the various contingencies—that achievement brings specifically praise mostly from parents, or that it has been given specifically for certain kinds of achievement. When at a later stage these particular relations no longer obtain, or are no longer emotionally important to the person, the altered situation may have little extinctive effect.

Everything considered, classical conditioning seems a reasonable explanation of the pleasantness of experiences, in so far as this is learned and not native, whether the cases be rather trivial like food preferences, or important like the pain of rejection.

2. DESIRE AND PLEASANT EXPERIENCES

What has all this to do with desires and aversions? Let us first recall what it is for something to be desired. Chapter 2 argued (roughly) that what it is for a person to desire some situation O occurrently, for its own sake, is for the person to be in such a central state that, were he at that time to think that performing a certain action would make the occurrence of O more likely, he would be more inclined to perform that act. In other words, if a person desires

O, then, if he sees an available route to approach O, he will be more inclined to move along that route.

It is manifest that pleasures, whether native or learned, have much to do with the development of desires. For instance, there was a time when the suggestion that I should buy hearts-of-palm would have left me unmoved. Then one evening I ate hearts-of-palm salad in a Paris restaurant and found it delicious. On returning to the U.S.A., I went to a delicatessen and inquired for hearts-of-palm, and have frequently since produced hearts-of-palm salads myself. It looks as if, as a result of the taste of hearts-of-palm (natively) eliciting maintenance tendencies (= being pleasant), now the thought, image, or representation of eating hearts-of-palm produces in the agent a *tendency to approach*, which is the nearest thing there can be to a maintenance-tendency when the object is not there. I say it looks as if this is what happens. But how might we conceptualize this relationship in terms of psychological theory? Some psychologists (Logan and Wagner, 1965, p. 102) have suggested that a fundamental weakness of Tolman's and similar theories is that they are unable to explain how valences change.

What we want is some plausible way to conceptualize the relationship between an antecedent pleasant experience, and a subsequent desire for experience of that kind. There are two possibilities, the first of which seems more plausible, but both of which could be involved.

The first possibility is that the new desire results from conditioning. The person eats the salad, and there is a (native) pleasure-response to the taste. While he is eating, the person also has thoughts, images, or some kind of representation of the eating experience (along with percepts of the tablecloth, etc.). The pleasure-response disposes him (this is true by definition) to do what will prolong the taste or eating experience. The principle of classical conditioning then implies that the disposition to prolong the activity or experience will attach to contiguous percepts, ideas, or representations. This means that the thought or image of a hearts-of-palm salad acquires the capacity to dispose the person to approach hearts-of-palm (the nearest thing to maintaining the taste-experience when one does not yet have it) by whatever route presents itself. This is the same thing as desiring hearts-of-palm. (In this case a repetition of pairings was not required; one somewhat prolonged experience was enough.) Doubtless verbalization is important in the process in some way.

In a previous chapter (p. 34) we noticed that valences are a function of two variables, which we called 'drive' or 'motive' on the one hand, and 'incentive value' on the other. In other words, when we are hungry the valence of hearts-of-palm is greater than when we are food-satiated (the effect of the state of 'drive' or 'motive'); but given that we are hungry, eating hearts-of-palm is more strongly valenced than either plain lettuce or carrots (incentive value). The process of conditioning we are here considering fixes the *incentive value* of something. If the incentive value belongs to something in a family (see above, Chapter 2), then we have to think of its valence as a condition of the central nervous system which is determined by both factors: the state of deprivation-satiation of the family, and the conditioned incentive value of the particular kind of experience. The neurophysiology of this relationship is at the moment speculative, but it is worthwhile observing that when we are not hungry we have less desire for a hearts-of-palm salad, and if we do eat it, the experience is less pleasant than it would be if we were hungry—a fact which is emphasized in the theory of the brain physiology of motivation and pleasure held by Rolls (1975).

Do cognitive motivation theorists accept this conception of the influence of pleasant experiences on desire by conditioning? Some do. P. T. Young writes that 'stimulus situations acquire incentive value by virtue of their association with affective arousals'—which comes to the same thing if we can construe 'stimulus situation' to mean not 'percept' of the object but 'representation' of it. Young further says: 'The strength of motives depends upon the intensity of the affective processes that organized them. . . . The strength of a motive depends not only upon affective intensity but also upon the duration of an affective arousal, upon the frequency of occurrence of the affective process, and probably also upon its recency.'[10] A rather similar view was held by D. C. McClelland, who suggested that the thought of a situation, previously liked, partially reinstates (because of association) the affective tone which accompanied the past situation. The reinstatement comprises motivation, on his

---

[10] Young, 1961, 172–3. Clark Hull and K. W. Spence came as close to this as a stimulus-response theory can, in their view of fractional anticipatory goal response. See Hull, 1952, 124–50; Spence, 1956, 130 ff.; and critical discussion by Weiner, 1973, 81–6.

theory. (McClelland, Atkinson, Clark, and Lowell, 1953, p. 28.) A recent book by Atkinson and Birch, following suggestions by Sheffield, takes a somewhat similar line.[11]

So much for a conditioning theory of how enjoying a certain kind of experience can lead to a normal desire for hearts-of-palm.

There is a principle about conditioning which must be taken to apply to all the processes of conditioning discussed in the present chapter: the principle of stimulus generalization. The principle is essentially this: If a person has acquired a tendency to make a certain response (e.g. an autonomic response like galvanic skin response) to a certain stimulus S, then he will tend to make the same response to another stimulus S' not exactly like S, corresponding to the degree of similarity of S' to S. Roughly, the more S' resembles S, the more he will tend to make the same response and (if the response can have different degrees of magnitude) the more the size of the response will approximate to the size of the response to S.

3. DIRECT CONDITIONING OF DESIRES

I have been explaining how a person's enjoying a certain experience in the past results in experiences of that type being desired or positively valenced. The explanation was via conditioning of approach-tendencies to the representation of an experience. Thus the *target* of present desires is something like what was enjoyed before.

Let us now look at a different and simpler process by which desires/aversions may be instituted. I call it 'direct conditioning'.

Many psychotherapists hold that behaviour can be made aversive, or desired, by conditioning withdrawal or approach tendencies directly to the *thought* of that behaviour—a conception

[11] They suggest that a left turn on the route to an anticipated goal (eating a hearts-of-palm salad) occurs because beginning that movement (towards that anticipated end) has had conditioned to it (because it arouses expectation of the reward) the excitement of the consummatory activity (enjoyment) of eating the salad. This conditioned excitement gives moving along that route a 'boost' as compared with other actions the person might take. Thus the conditioned excitement of enjoyable consummatory activity is what gives moving force to the reflection that doing *this* will lead to *that* (eating the salad). (Atkinson and Birch, 1970, Chaps. 5, 6, 8, especially pp. 145–52, 157–8, 251, 177 f., 182 f.; Sheffield, 1965, especially pp. 314–21; Bindra, 1972.) Sheffield proposes that what a conditioned stimulus essentially does is produce some kind of central representation of the unconditioned stimulus (p. 163).

which has been applied frequently in recent years to the treatment of alcoholism, homosexuality, and obesity.

The treatment procedure is simple. Consider an alcoholic. Any of several things may be done. Either (1) the patient takes a sip (say) of martini and keeps it in his mouth while (a) he is (physiological treatment) given an electric shock (or becomes nauseous from an injection of apomorphine), or else (b) he brings vividly to mind (psychological treatment) how he felt when (say) he vomited the last time he drank too many martinis. Or else (2) he imagines vividly having a sip of martini in his mouth and then, as before, either (a) he is given a shock or made nauseous, or (b) he brings to mind how he felt when he vomited the last time he drank. In any of these ways, it is affirmed, the idea of a martini gets associated with an aversive state, either nausea or shock. After such treatments, patients report that they are either unable to get an image of a martini at all, or that any image they get is repulsive. The success rate of such 'aversive conditioning therapy' is alleged to be reasonably high.

The reverse treatment associates a pleasant experience or the thought of one, or relaxation feelings, to percepts or thoughts or images hitherto neutral or phobic. It is said that the association makes such percepts attractive or at least no longer aversive.[15]

What is going on in such cases? One thing is already familiar: a certain taste becomes pleasant or unpleasant by association with something already pleasant or unpleasant. Furthermore, the thought of having martini in the mouth is, by conditioning, directly made an unpleasant thought. It is this latter, novel feature which I have in mind in labelling the process '*direct* conditioning'. In other words, the thought of some situation or behaviour is made unpleasant, not by association with a situation or behaviour of that sort which is itself unpleasant, but by the occurrence, temporally contiguous with the thought, of something unpleasant (the thought of martini and a powerful shock). The difference is not so very great, since in the form of conditioning discussed above, there was a thought at the time of the pleasant (unpleasant) experience, and the prolongation tendency of the experience rubbed off on to the thought, as approach (avoidance) tendency; whereas in direct

[15] For a summary of the experimental data, see Bandura, 1969, Chap. 8; also, Evans, 1968; Thorpe, Schmidt, Brown, and Castell, 1964; Rachman and Teasdale, 1969; Davison, 1968b, pp. 91–9.

conditioning the withdrawal tendency which rubs off on to the thought comes from a shock, or from thoughts about consequences such as vomiting, not from the experience thought about. In either case, a later thought of an experience or activity will be attractive or repellent (valenced), because of the conditioned approach (withdrawal) tendencies.[16]

4. OTHER BASIC MECHANISMS?

Are the above described processes the only fundamental ones involved in the learning of desires, aversions, and dispositions to like or dislike? It appears that they are. Some other, apparently different, processes or laws are frequently mentioned as important, however; they deserve brief description, in the course of which I shall explain why they are not basic processes.

i. Identification and Imitation of a Model.

One proposal is that children acquire desires/aversions as a result of 'identification' with someone, or because of observation of a model. Obviously, some desires (etc.) are acquired in this way; but the question is whether this process is somehow a new basic type of genesis, or only a variation of the basic processes already described.

I shall describe three somewhat different accounts—the most plausible I have seen—about what goes on. Writers on this topic often do not sharply distinguish copying behaviour from copying desires and aversions. We are interested only in the latter.

(1) Sometimes it is said that the child values the affection of the model (parent or psychoanalyst) but feels insecure about its permanence, for instance when the model withholds affection when the child misbehaves. He comes to think he must do something, e.g. achieve in school, to retain his model's love. As a result of acting or being motivated to act in this way (and presumably being pleased or relieved if he succeeds in getting the result), he eventually comes

---

[16] A conceptual difficulty may be raised. It may be said that if what is done is simply to make the thought of martinis unpleasant, why does not the patient simply think of something else—why should he avoid martinis? For something to be unpleasant is for there to be a tendency to escape from *it* not from something else. Professor Diana Ackerman raised this point in conversation some years ago. We must remember, however, that thoughts, images, and percepts are very alike, and if a certain autonomic response is conditioned to an image, it will be aroused by the corresponding percept by stimulus generalization.

to want the outcome (e.g. achievement) itself. The crucial problem in this account is the last stage: how do we get from doing, or being motivated to do, or being pleased with having done, something as a means, to wanting it as an end? The question is how some situation or object, frequently a means to certain pleasurable outcomes and frequently thought of in connection with them, comes to be valenced in itself.[17] Very probably it is a matter of conditioning: there is no basic process here beyond those already discussed. (A somewhat different proposal is one put forward by MacCorquodale and Meehl (1953) in their formalization of Tolman, p. 58—that of a special 'law' asserting that increased 'cathexis' goes to a means, utilization of which in action leads to an already valenced end.)

(2) The child notices that certain events make the model happy (or the reverse), as shown by the model's expressive behaviour. Now it is said that persons who are happy tend to make those around them happy, since they behave in a friendly and helpful manner. So the happy model tends to act so as to make a happy child. The happiness-expressive behaviour of the model thus gets paired with a happy state in the child, and by conditioning the child's perception of the happiness-expressive behaviour of the model is able to arouse happiness in the child. By a further step in conditioning, perception of the event which is known to make the model happy also becomes capable of arousing a happy state in the child. So the child comes to want this state for itself. Evidently this theory makes use of the conditioning principles described earlier.

(3) The behaviour of a nurturant model tends to be copied in his/her absence since such behaviour is a partial substitute for the presence of the model, the presence of whom has become rewarding—because of connection with nurturant behaviour—and the absence of whom has become anxiety-arousing. Seeking the things the model seeks is one aspect of this copying; so these things are sought because of the satisfaction seeking them brings, as a substitute for the absent model. Later these happiness-producing

---

[17] See J. S. Mill in *Utilitarianism*, Chap. 4: the stongest natural attraction, he says, comes to fame and power from 'the strong association thus generated between them and all our objects of desire. . . .' And he speaks of the 'provision of nature, by which things originally indifferent, but conducive to, or otherwise associated with, the satisfaction of our primitive desires, become in themselves sources of pleasure more valuable than the primitive pleasures, both in permanency, in the space of human existence that they are capable of covering, and even in intensity'.

things are wanted for themselves. In this process the last stage, again, is the crucial one; a transition is required which appears to be identical with the one required by the first model described above. It looks as if this transition can be explained in terms of conditioning, by the principles stated above; and again it looks as if the description of the total process does not involve interesting novel principles.[18]

Identification and imitation of models apparently do not exemplify fundamentally new processes of learning valences. Still, it is important to be aware of the types of syndrome described above. For a description of them draws attention to something we might not have noticed. They bring out how a conjunction of processes results in the desires and aversions of one person tending to be duplicated in another person. So people often do not just acquire their likes/dislikes and valences from their own experience; they often rather take over such features of models, usually their parents or leaders in their peer group. Thus, even if we do not need to say that there is some fundamentally different type of learning process here, there is a process well worth attention in its own right—just as Kepler's laws are worthy of attention even if they are implications of Newton's laws for the special case of the planetary system.

ii. The Role of Affect-conditioned Words, in the Development of Desires/Aversions.

It is worthwhile noting briefly the role of language and communication in the development of desires/aversions. Obviously, communication affects behaviour and the learning of desires in several ways. First, it is informational. It may comprise testimony and hence evidence about the probable outcome of some kind of behaviour, and of how well this will be received by some persons. Second, language can express the attitude of a speaker (or his group); and in so far as a person is interested in the favourable attitudes of others, this expressive behaviour conveys useful information.

A more interesting question is whether certain words can elicit certain affective states in an auditor, just by themselves and apart

[18] For discussions of identification and modelling phenomena, see Bandura, 1969, Chap. 3; Bandura and Huston, 1961; Kagan, 1958; Martin, 1954; Baldwin, 1968, especially pp. 428–80; Stoke, 1950; Berkowitz, 1964; Aronfreed, 1968.

from any information they convey. If I reflect that a certain action is classified as 'immoral' or 'bad', will this reflection produce unpleasant anxiety, irrespective of inferences about the probable attitudes of others? There is no good theoretical reason for denying that this may be so. For if, as we know is the case, fur coats can become aversive to a child by stimulus generalization, because an aversive loud sound has been associated with petting a rabbit, why may not 'wrong' be aversive through association with punishment, disapproving glances, and so on? If so, and if these words are applied to certain kinds of behaviour or situations, is it plausible to suppose that these behaviours and situations become aversive, as another step in conditioning? It is widely believed by psychologists that this does happen.[19] All this, of course, does not require any fundamental principles different from those described above.

5. DE-CONDITIONING

The processes described in the preceding pages can be summed up in four words: contiguity conditioning, and stimulus generalization. Previously neutral types of experience become pleasant or unpleasant by contiguity conditioning; anticipated outcomes previously neutral become valenced either by conditioning of the pleasantness of samples of such outcomes to the idea of them, or by stimulus generalization, or else because the idea of them has been associated with some pleasant or aversive experience simultaneous with the thought ('direct' conditioning).

We have yet to assess the impact of beliefs or judgements on what is already pleasant or valenced. While the preceding pages give us some idea what thought can do to bring about conditioning or generalization of conditioned responses, we have not surveyed what thought can do to extinguish or diminish them. In order to understand this, we need a general account of de-conditioning. I shall discuss three causal mechanisms.

Psychologists agree that when a response has been conditioned to some stimulus, the probability of the response, when the stimulus occurs, does not diminish just with the passage of time. In human beings conditioned eyelid reactions and salivation have occurred

[19] See, for example, Brown, 1961, pp. 168 ff.; Bandura, 1969, pp. 227–8; Neal Miller, 1951, pp. 463–5; Grings, 1965.

after an interval of four months with no intervening conditioning trials. So, decrement in the probability of the response must be explained in some other way. What are the processes?

i. Counterconditioning. This is the functional extinction of a response R to a situation by conditioning the person to have a different response R' to the same situation, which is stronger than the conditioning to have R and where the response R' is incompatible with the occurrence of R. To take a historical example, when Pavlov's dogs first heard a buzzer, they pricked up their ears and turned their heads towards the buzzer; after the salivation response had been established by the sound being followed by meat, the dogs responded to the buzzer by licking their chops and turning towards the meat pan. The same thing can occur with autonomic responses. Suppose a child has a strong anxiety response to the perception of a dog. The anxiety can be 'cured' by producing the percept of a distant dog, while the child is securely in the arms of its mother being fed goodies. The pleasurable response to the total situation prevents the recurrence of anxiety responses and tends to get attached to the percept of the dog. The dog is gradually moved closer. In the end the percept of the dog has developed a strong tendency to elicit relaxation and approach responses incompatible with the anxiety response. The anxiety response has been functionally extinguished, although strictly it may be merely overlaid and might recur if something happened to extinguish the new favourable responses. The principle of this procedure is widely used in therapy, and is central in the 'desensitization' techniques developed by Dr. J. Wolpe.[20]

The application of counterconditioning to the cases of the pleasant/unpleasant, and to desire/aversion, is obvious. If the earlier proposal about how to attach pleasantness (or the opposite) to a neutral experience is correct, then we presumably can reverse the pleasantness (unpleasantness) already attaching to the experience by introducing surrounding experiences which condition in the opposite way. The same for valence. We recall that, very roughly, for some outcome to be valenced is for the person to be disposed to approach that state of affairs. We can functionally

[20] See M. C. Jones, 1924; Weitzman, 1967; Staats, 1970; Eysenck and Beech, 1971; Wolpe, 1958; Bandura, 1969, pp. 357–9, Chap. 5, and pp. 431, 439; Grings and Uno, 1968; Gale, Sturmfels, and Gale, 1966; Cooke, 1968; Davison, 1968b, pp. 91–9 and 1968a pp. 84–90.

extinguish this valence by building up a disposition for the thought of that outcome to produce avoidant responses. And the reverse if we wish to extinguish negative valence. We build up this counter-disposition by means of the two processes already described. Our earlier account, then, already contains a partial story about how desires and aversions may be extinguished.

Verbal self-stimulation, we have seen, is one way in which conditioning can be brought about. The student may condition himself to like receiving a high grade in a course by saying, 'This shows I'll be able to get into medical school'; and in general comments about the positive or negative future effects of a given outcome will affect the valence of that outcome by conditioning, in one way or another.

ii. Inhibition. A second process may be best explained by returning to the case of Pavlov's dogs. When meat powder was blown into their mouths there was an unconditioned salivation response. Then, after a number of sessions during which a buzzer was sounded a few seconds before the appearance of the meat, the animals began to salivate shortly after the sound of the buzzer. The salivation was a conditioned response to the sound. Next, the practice of following the sounding of the buzzer by blowing in meat powder was discontinued. For a time, the animals continued to salivate whenever the buzzer was activated. But the buzzer produced less and less salivation on subsequent trials, until finally it produced none at all. This process is de-conditioning by inhibition, and it seems characteristic of responses produced by classical conditioning.

It may be that cognitive processes are involved in this effect: the dogs may have salivated originally because the buzzer caused them to expect food, and when this expectation was extinguished by the repeated non-appearance of food following the sound of the buzzer, there was no longer an expectancy producing salivation. This cognitive account, however, is at most only part of the story.

How shall we define 'de-conditioning by inhibition'? Suppose a regular response has been conditioned to a certain stimulus, because the latter has been followed by another (unconditioned) stimulus already able to elicit the response. Then if the conditioned stimulus is presented, usually or often followed by the conditioned response, but in the absence of the unconditioned stimulus, the probability or magnitude of the response to the conditioned stimulus will diminish, the more the greater the number of 'extinction trials'. When the probability or magnitude of the conditioned response does diminish as part of this process, we call it 'de-conditioning by inhibition'.

Let us see how this 'law' would work for the phenomena of interest to us: pleasure and desire. Take a conditioned displeasure first. Suppose aversiveness has become conditioned to the appearance of the interior of a public school building, by early experiences of boredom, anxiety, or humiliation when a child. Then the 'law' states that repeated exposure to views of the interior of a school building in the absence of boredom, anxiety, etc., would gradually cause the displeasure response to disappear. In this case what counts as an extinction trial is clear: the exposure to the conditioned stimulus. (Presumably one could get somewhat the same effect imaginatively. One could conjure up a vivid image of the school interior, and then assure oneself that nothing threatening or boring any longer goes on there. This would be a 'covert' extinction trial.)

Now consider desire or aversion. Suppose a person has an achievement desire—say always to be the first person to finish arithmetic problems in school—because of pleasant parental praise and reward of school achievement. Then there can be overt or covert extinction trials. An overt trial is one in which he sees what he can do to achieve that end, is motivated to do it, and succeeds in doing it—but no reward occurs—say, no one congratulates him or even notices that he finished first. (There may be further covert events: he says to himself, 'No one pays any attention', or 'That didn't get me anywhere'.) A covert trial is one in which—but here I am speculating in order to accommodate what seems to happen— he thinks about achievement of this sort, or daydreams about it, and is motivated to achieve or perhaps even feels a thrill of pride in his daydream, although he sees no opportunity for action (maybe he is not even in school that day) and hence does nothing to that end, but then reminds himself that achievement of that sort gets him no further goods such as praise or admiration, from teachers or peers. Either way, there is an extinction trial. The 'law' of extinction by inhibition tells us that as these extinction trials mount up, the response in question will diminish, in magnitude or frequency, and eventually disappear altogether.[21]

Can we say anything further about why conditioned pleasure or valence should extinguish after 'trials' of these sort? Some writers regard overt behavioural extinction trials as a special case of counterconditioning, on the ground that effort is involved, and since effort is disliked there is gradually built up an aversion to behaving in this way. (Clark Hull introduced the concepts of 'reactive inhibition' and 'conditioned inhibition' in this connection.) Since autonomic responses, and in particular the kinds of responses in which we are interested, require no expenditure of effort, that suggestion is hardly helpful for their case. It appears that we must regard extinction by inhibition as just a natural and basic process, like conditioning itself.

iii. Discrimination. Our final question is whether de-conditioning occurs as a result of awareness of differences.

We recall that in classical conditioning a stimulus initially elicits a response; then when this stimulus has been regularly preceded by another stimulus for a time, the latter stimulus also elicits something very like the response to the unconditioned stimulus. Now, according to the principle of 'stimulus generalization' the (conditioned) response can also be elicited by a range of stimuli rather like the ones present in the conditioning trials. For instance, it may be elicited by some part of the original conditioned stimulus. The 'generalization' is not of indefinitely wide scope. For instance, if conditioning makes a baby like red things, because red things were presented to him during feedings, he generalizes the favourable response mostly to shades of red rather like the original one. There is then a question: 'If a person becomes aware of—perhaps comes to verbalize—the difference between the stimuli in the original trials, and parts of them or stimuli rather like them, will the response tend to narrow so as to occur only in response to the

---

[21] Psychologists mostly concern themselves with extinction of patterns of overt behaviour, e.g. avoidance behaviour. What is most pertinent to our purposes, however, is experimentation with conditioned autonomic responses. I have extrapolated to conclusions about extinction of desires and aversions primarily from data on extinction of involuntary or autonomic behaviour, anxiety, and other emotions. See Bandura, 1969, Chap. 6; Kimble, 1961, Chap. 10 and pp. 180–2; Atkinson and Birch, 1970, pp. 157, 251; Lang, 1969; Buchwald and Young, 1969; F. Nelson, 1966; Eysenck, 1973; Brady, 1967, especially 307 f.; and Amsel, 1972.

stimuli in the original conditioning "trials"?'

It is clear that introduction of a clear discrimination between two situations tends to reduce the generalization of responses from the one to the other. For instance, some subjects were read a list of words, and were shocked after each colour word. The result was that subsequently an altered galvanic skin response occurred each time a word of any kind was read out. This was a result of conditioning. Then it was pointed out that shocks came only after the colour words. There was then a gradual reduction, after six trials, of the galvanic skin response to non-colour words. There was reduction of generalization, then, but it was neither immediate nor complete.[22]

There has been considerable experimentation with animals, but it obviously operates under difficulties: we are not privy to their inner 'insights'; nor can we point out distinctions to them, but must leave it to the poor things to make their own discriminations on the basis of what happens to them. The type of experiment that has been performed is as follows. After the trials in which the conditioned response was established to a type of stimulus, trials followed in which some varieties of the conditioned stimuli occurred, followed by the unconditioned stimuli, and some varieties not. The result was that the varieties of conditioned stimulus not paired with the unconditioned stimulus were less able to elicit the response—there was inhibition (along the lines of the 'law' stated in preceding pages), and this tendency not to respond itself generalized (or spread to similar stimuli) in the normal way. The responses of the animals, after the total series, represent a normal generalization of the original series plus the later pairings with the unconditioned stimulus, and a normal generalization of the inhibition sequence.

Transposition of these laboratory data to human experiences of the sort of interest to us is somewhat precarious. It seems we might expect an effect which we can call 'partial inhibition'. That is, if a person becomes aware of the fact that the unconditioned stimulus usually follows a certain range of conditioned stimuli but seldom a certain rather similar range of stimuli, the conditioned response will

---

[22] Cole and Sippreth, 1967. Bandura discusses how the theory can be used to prevent undesirable generalizations of conditioning, 1969, pp. 510–11.

tend to narrow to the former set. So if there is some reason to use 'direct aversive conditioning' to make distasteful to a person not all alcoholic beverages as such, but only gin and whisky, then shocks could be applied when he has in his mouth, or is thinking of, a sip of whisky or gin, but not when he has a sip of tequila (all this could also be explained to him)—and then this last he would able to enjoy.

The laboratory data also suggest that we should be open-minded towards reports of therapists that discriminations often make a difference to emotional reactions. For instance, one therapist testifies that a child with a domineering father had generalized the response he had developed to his father, to his employer; and he reports further that therapy was able to eliminate the generalization by dwelling on the differences, by pointing out how the patient is not dependent on his employer as he was on his father (and so on). Another has remarked that a patient can sometimes be brought to see that his 'anxiety is meaningless, that is, unrealistic, because of the accidental nature of its association with some harmful stimulus, and insight is nothing other than the recognition of which associations are meaningful and which are not'.[23] These emotional phenomena are different from those of direct concern to us, but an extension of the theory to the phenomena which do concern us is quite plausible.

[23] See Brady, 1967; London, 1964, pp. 97–8; Amsel, 1972.

CHAPTER VI

THE CRITICISM OF PLEASURES AND INTRINSIC DESIRES

IN THIS and the following chapter, we shall see whether all our tilling of the soil of psychology yields us any harvest.

The general project of the first part of this book has been to see how far logic and evidence can take us in criticizing actions, pleasures, and desires. We have already discussed how far they can take us in criticizing actions to a first approximation, that is, while ignoring the question whether the desires or aversions involved in action can themselves be criticized on the basis of information. We now consider how we can appraise actions to a second approximation by providing a critique of desires and aversions.

This critique, based on the theory of the genesis of pleasures and desires, will tell us which things a fully rational—roughly, a fully informed—person would want or enjoy. I shall show that certain and only certain kinds of things would be rationally desired by certain kinds of persons or in certain kinds of situation, and in some cases that a certain kind of thing would be enjoyed or desired by *every* rational person.

Most philosophers have supposed that such a critique of desires and pleasures is impossible; it is thought that facts and logic cannot show, say, that an intrinsic desire is mistaken. Hume, it is supposed, had the last word (1854, Bk. II, Pt. III, Sec. 3):

... it is only in two senses that any affection can be called unreasonable. First, when a passion such as hope or fear, grief or joy, despair or security, is founded on the supposition of the existence of objects, which really do not exist. Secondly, when in exerting any passion in action, we choose means insufficient for the designed end, and deceive ourselves in our judgment of causes and effects. Where a passion is neither founded on false suppositions, nor chooses means insufficient for the end, the understanding can neither justify nor condemn it. It is not contrary to reason to prefer the destruction of the whole world to the scratching of my finger. It is not contrary to reason for me to choose my total ruin, to prevent the least uneasiness of an Indian, or person wholly unknown to me. It is as little contrary to reason to prefer even my own acknowledged lesser good to my greater, and have a more ardent affection for the former than the latter. A trivial good may, from certain circumstances, produce a desire superior to what arises from the greatest and most valuable enjoyment. . . .

Of course, we are here concerned only with at least partly intrinsic desires and aversions—desires for some outcome at least partly *for itself*, not just because it is in some way a means to something else that is desired.

Earlier conclusions have already shown that some desires or aversions are in a sense mistaken. For they show that a rational person, with his desires just as they are, had sometimes better undertake psychological treatment to *remove* a certain desire. A member of Congress might find that the whole set of outcomes he most wants can be realized only if he gives up drinking excessive amounts of alcohol. So the drinking has to go. And, if that has to go, the desire had also better be changed; removal of the desire will make him more comfortable. So, if he is rational, he will see to the removal of the desire. Such reflections do not show, however, that there is anything wrong with a desire for alcohol itself. All that is shown is the relation between this desire and the satisfaction of a large set of other desires. In what follows, however, I shall show something very different from this: that there is something mistaken about certain desires or aversions, just in themselves, or at least in their occurring with an intensity beyond a certain point.

The critique to come will show that some desires, aversions, or pleasures would be present (or absent) in some persons if their total motivational machinery were fully suffused by available information; and will show how to identify such desires, aversions, or pleasures for a given person. Less metaphorically, the aim is to show that some intrinsic desires and aversions would be present in some persons if relevant available information registered fully, that is, if the persons repeatedly represented to themselves, in an ideally vivid way, and at an appropriate time, the available information which is relevant in the sense that it would make a difference to desires and aversions if they thought of it. By 'ideally vivid way' I mean that the person gets the information at the focus of attention, with maximal vividness and detail, and with no hesitation or doubt about its truth. I mean by 'available information' the beliefs associated with this term in Chapter 1: relevant beliefs which are a part of the 'scientific knowledge' of the day, or which are justified on the basis of publicly available evidence in accordance with the canons of inductive or deductive logic, or justified on the basis of evidence which could now be obtained by procedures known to science.

We need to restrict further the kind of information that qualifies as 'relevant', in order to guarantee that the effectiveness of the information is a function of its content. If every time I thought of having a martini, I made myself go through multiplication tables for five minutes, the valence of a martini might well decline. But obviously the desire for a martini is not misdirected simply if it fails to survive confrontation with the multiplication table in this way. Any desire would be discouraged by this procedure. We want to say that a thought is functioning properly in the criticism of desires only if its effect is not one its occurrence would have on any desire, and only if its effect is a function of its content. It must be a thought in some fairly restricted way about the thing desired; for instance, a thought about the expectable effects of the thing, or about the kind of thing it is, or about how well one would like it if it happened, and so on.

The claim is that relevant available information, if confronted on repeated occasions, affects our desires. But how often is 'repeated'? We cannot be, and need not be, precise on this. If several representations have no effect, we can reasonably infer that more of them would do no better. But if several representations have some effect, the question arises what would happen if there were more? Presumably what we are after is the asymptote: what desires, aversions, and pleasures a person would have if the number of representations increased without limit, if the reflection had maximal impact by representation as often as you like.

Finally, I have said that the self-stimulation by representation of relevant information should come at 'an appropriate time'. When is that? Obviously, when the effect will maximize counterconditioning, inhibition, or relevant discrimination. For instance, the appropriate times for a smoker to reflect on the bad consequences of his habit are (1) just after inhaling, when the reflection may destroy any pleasure he ordinarily takes in the cigarette; (2) when he wants or is thinking about lighting a cigarette, when the reflection will tend (a) to set up an association between the idea of the state of affairs and contrary motivation, or (b) to make it clear that the total outcome will in fact not be pleasant with the inhibiting effect of that reflection; and (3) when he is having thoughts or images which tend to make the idea of smoking exciting, so that the reflection will associate these mental occurrences with a less glamorous image. But it is not clear that such reflections will be fruitless on any occasion when one is thinking about an outcome.

This whole process of confronting desires with relevant information, by repeatedly representing it, in an ideally vivid way, and at an appropriate time, I call *cognitive psychotherapy*. I call it so because the process relies simply upon reflection on available information, without influence by prestige of someone, use of evaluative language, extrinsic reward or punishment, or use of artificially induced feeling-states like relaxation. It is *value-free reflection*.

I shall call a person's desire, aversion, or pleasure 'rational' if it would survive or be produced by careful 'cognitive psychotherapy' for that person. I shall call a desire 'irrational' if it cannot survive compatibly with clear and repeated judgements about established facts. What this means is that rational desire (etc.) can confront, or will even be produced by, awareness of the truth; irrational desire cannot. It is obvious, of course, that desires do not logically follow from the awareness which supports them; the relation is causal and sometimes involves other desires, aversions, or pleasures.[1]

One implication of our definitions may be surprising. It arises from the fact that some valences, or dispositions to enjoy something, may resist extinction by inhibition and anything else, since they have been so firmly learned at an early age. By my definition these qualify as rational. For I use 'rational' as the contradictory of 'irrational' and have defined an 'irrational' desire (etc.) as one that would extinguish after cognitive psychotherapy. If a desire will not extinguish, then it is not irrational. This result is consistent with the general view that a desire (etc.) is rational if it has been influenced by facts and logic as much as possible. Unextinguishable desires meet this condition.

---

[1] If a desire required to support another desire, the rationality of which is being assessed, is itself irrational, we must say that the desire being appraised is irrational.

What reason do we have for thinking that optimal exposure to certain information, such as contemplated in cognitive psychotherapy, will affect desires/aversions in specified ways? First there is theoretical reason. In the examples to follow I shall in each case present first a theory of the genesis of the relevant desires/aversions. In some cases this will be obvious, hardly open to controversy; in other cases I shall cite evidence to show that certain desires in fact have developed in a certain way. Then I shall show that desires/aversions produced in these ways are bound to extinguish by repeated self-stimulation by information, given the facts about how desires (etc.) extinguish as described in the preceding chapter. The procedure will therefore be deductive; it will be like showing how a physical particle of a given description must move under specified conditions, given what we know of gravitational attraction, electromagnetism, and the theory of motion under forces.

There is also empirical support from the clinical reports of psychotherapists for the view that exposure to relevant information will affect desires/aversions in the ways to be suggested. There is less of this kind of support than we would like and one reason for this is probably that psychotherapists aim primarily to help the patient, at least mostly in the direction in which the patient himself asks for help, and not to help the patient find his ideal value-system. Usually the therapist is more engaged in reducing anxieties than he is in changing desires, or finding rational desires; and he uses whatever devices, from cognitive self-stimulations to electric shocks, will reach the intended goal. Nevertheless many therapists have had a good deal of success in changing desires through patient self-stimulation by true statements—for example, making excessive alcohol consumption aversive, reducing the craving for the approval of other people, mitigating the aversiveness of being alone, reducing the aversiveness of being self-assertive in relation to one's spouse or employer, reducing the intensity of the desire to achieve in all situations, and reducing the desire to smoke.[2] So we have fairly direct observational evidence that self-stimulation can change desires (etc.) in the anticipated way. In fact, we hardly

[2] See, for instance, L. and A. W. Birk, 1974; Brady, 1967; Ellis, 1962; Ellis and Harper, 1961; Goldfried and Merbaum (eds.), 1973; Heller and Marlatt, 1960; Murray and Jacobson, 1971.

need to turn to therapists to know that reflections can change intrinsic desires and pleasures. What woman does not know that repeating to herself the facts that a beloved male is inflexible, selfish, unloving, not very bright, and wholly concerned with success in business, will over time reduce her emotional commitment to him, and make her enjoy his company less?

I. SOME TYPES OF 'MISTAKEN' DESIRES, AVERSIONS, OR PLEASURES

Let us now look at some types of likes/dislikes, or desires/ aversions and see how it is that we must view them as irrational. The various types are neither exhaustive nor mutually exclusive. They are to be viewed as collections of examples, and should be used as a guide in thinking about cases of particular concern.

i. First Mistake: Dependence on False Beliefs.

It is obvious that persons often desire outcomes now as a result of having (falsely) thought them means to ends already wanted or enjoyed: associating the means with the end or with the thought of the end, or associating the thought of the means with the liked end or the thought of the liked end. For instance, a student may have begun to work for a Ph.D. and an academic profession because he thought his parents (themselves professors) would be disappointed in him if he did not; and now he wants an academic life for itself (but not because he has found it satisfying). Or, a person may have developed an aversion to the taste of a certain food because he thought it made him ill. A person may now feel uncomfortable about enjoying himself because he thought God (or his parents) wanted him to work hard and eschew indulgences; and he wanted to please God (or his parents).

Let us suppose (as often happens) that the relevant beliefs are false. Parents wish a child only to be happy, not to enter an academic life; certain foods do not make one ill; there may be no God, or if there is one, he may not disapprove of personal indulgence. Assuming that there are no other facts, not involved in the genesis, reflection upon which supports the desire, a desire with such a genesis will extinguish in cognitive psychotherapy. Why?

Extinction will occur primarily through inhibition. If the person repeats to himself the fact that he will not achieve the goals involved in instituting the desire by doing a certain thing, the intrinsic desire for doing that thing will diminish. Consider the parallel with the salivation of Pavlov's dogs. The thought of the instrumental outcome (the Ph.D.) is like the sound of the buzzer; the desire for it to occur is like the salivation; the pleasant thought that its occurrence would please parents is like being offered the food. Then, as the dogs stopped salivating at the sound of the buzzer when the food was regularly omitted, so the student will stop being motivated to go for the Ph.D. when he regularly reminds himself that doing so will not please his parents. (Of course, the desire to get the Ph.D. will not extinguish if by this time the student has other reasons—for instance, finds academic work inherently satisfying.) Counterconditioning can presumably also play some role: if the student reminds himself that a Ph.D. is for him very hard work, that he was not cut out to be an academic, and so on.

ii. Second Mistake: Artificial Desire-Arousal in Culture-Transmission.

An important factor in the genesis of desires, aversions, likes, dislikes, is a child's observation of the attitudes and values of other persons—parents, teachers, or peers, not to mention films and television—producing ambition perhaps to own a powerful sports car, aspiration (to belong to a prestige occupation) or aversion (to belonging to a low-prestige one).

How does the observation of the attitudes of others produce these likes and dislikes, desires and aversions? In part the process is one of direct conditioning: the child feels anxiety when another child is the target of the critical attitudes of others (why he feels anxiety at this will be explained in Chapter 7); and this anxiety becomes attached by conditioning to the idea of the situation for which the other child is criticized. Alternatively, the process may be one of those roughly classified as 'desire acquisition by identification' (see above, pp. 100 ff.). Still again, there may be beliefs essentially involved. For instance, the statements of parents may make the child believe there are unspecified unpleasant consequences of being in a certain situation, from which the child will infer that the situation itself must be unpleasant in some way. Given any of these cases, an *intrinsic* aversion (desire, etc.) is produced after conditioning has done its work.

The production of these intrinsic desires/aversions is artificial if they could not have been brought about by experience with actual situations which the desires are for and the aversions against. Take, for instance, a non-prestige occupation like garbage collection, or marriage to a person of another race, religion or nationality. Actual experience with these situations could be highly satisfying (and there is no reason to suppose it would be aversive), and would not produce an intrinsic aversion. So, naturally produced desires/ aversions would not coincide with those produced in these artificial ways. I shall call a desire/aversion artificial if it could not have been produced naturally. (A desire/aversion which could be produced naturally may be called 'authentic'.)

These attitudes do derive from the realities of the situation in one sense, for the firm attitudes of others are real facts with which people have to deal. But intense concern with the attitudes of other people is itself founded on error—the false belief that the attitudes of others are crucially important for an adult, especially if the attitudes in question are those of one's own parents only. An independent adult need not fear the sanctions his parents might try to impose; for, realistically, a person will not lose the affection of his parents through doing some of the things of which they disapprove. Of course, if a person wishes not to upset his parents, then their reaction is a fact to be taken into account like any other; just as, if all one's friends strongly dislike someone one is considering for marriage, that fact is one to be taken into account too. The situation arising from favourable or unfavourable attitudes of others is complex, but on the whole the attitudes of others hardly serve by themselves to render a desire realistic.

All artificial desires are prime candidates for extinction or diminution, by cognitive psychotherapy, through inhibition or counterconditioning, or both. Why? Partly because the usually essential supporting beliefs are false; and in so far as they are, the attitude will tend to extinguish for reasons already explained. Partly also because any anxiety conditioned through the attitudes of others will tend to extinguish by inhibition after a review of the relative unimportance of such attitudes for the mature adult. And partly by counterconditioning: through reflection on the fact that one's aversion is preventing one from having some potentially very satisfying experiences or relationships, or that one's desire is leading one into experiences or relationships one simply does not like. For instance, a person might want, as a result of these artificial processes, to be in the academic profession; but he might have good reason also to believe—if he thought about it—that he would be bored by the scholarly work involved, that he would not be effective as a teacher and therefore would dislike teaching, and that he would not like the limited financial prospects of the academic life. If he did reflect on these things, he would tend to establish an aversion which would be incompatible with his ambition to hold an academic post.

Since such 'artificial' desires/aversions would extinguish by this kind of reflection, in 'cognitive psychotherapy', they are irrational.

Let us pause and apply our results so far to a desire which has received more attention in the psychological literature than any other, except perhaps sex: the desire for achievement. Unfortunately, when we say that a person has a strong desire to achieve, it is not clear precisely what we mean. Psychologists seem to agree on a rather broad but vague definition. Desire to achieve is said to be desire for 'success in competition with some standards of excellence'.[3] But a comparative notion gives us a more interesting conception. On this conception, the desire to achieve is not just a desire to do difficult things well, or make some important contribution in life, or reach some long-term professional goal. It is a desire to be, and to appear, superior in many areas in which one is emotionally involved—such as tennis, argument, doing well professionally, and so on.

Where might this general desire come from? It could come from native satisfaction from doing difficult things. Children take pleasure in learning to stand or turn over; they enjoy exploring the

---

[3] J. W. Atkinson, 1958, p. 181; also pp. 76, 324, 497, 516–17. R. R. Sears once said, 'There are many names for this learned drive: pride, craving for superiority, ego-impulse, self-esteem, self-approval, self-assertion; but these terms represent different emphases or different terminological systems, not fundamentally different concepts. Common to all is the notion that the feeling of success depends on the gratification of this drive, and failure results from its frustration.' (1942, p. 236.) These terms do not appear to me at all to be only names for different aspects of the same 'drive': craving for superiority, self-esteem, self-approval, and self-assertion are quite different, although there may be a loose relationship. When we say that Americans are distinctively motivated to achieve, what do we have in mind, if anything?

environment, constructing things, solving puzzles. In summary, they enjoy learning skills which enable effective interaction with their environment. (R. W. White, 1959.) Insofar as a desire to achieve is a desire just to do difficult things well, it derives from native liking, and is not artificial; but some persons desire achievement in my explained sense because they think it brings respect if not affection—a belief which is partially false, since achievement is apt to produce irritation; or, they think that achievement will lead to satisfaction of various sorts. Empirical studies suggest that the desire comes from early experiences, especially from demands made by, and rewards given by, parents who are anxious about the performance of their children. A middle-class family, concerned for the child's later success, is apt to welcome any sign of precocity with delight and praise, and to be uncomfortably rejecting if the child fails to do well. One study has shown that children high in achievement motivation had mothers who (1) made demands on them for mastery of various forms of behaviour at a relatively early age (going outside to play, knowing their way about the city, doing well in competition), (2) gave more physically expressed affection for success, and (3) set relatively fewer restrictions on behaviour (such as forbidding sloppiness at the table, leaving clothes about, or failing in school).[4]

If the desire for achievement must be explained in this way—primarily by the congratulations, rejections, and training practices of concerned parents—is it authentic and rational? Consider motivation to be superior in tennis. Could it have been produced realistically by contact with the costs and satisfactions to which such motivation leads? The motivation to be superior may lead to a determination to win (which can put off partners or opponents who merely want to enjoy the game), or to a choice of partners and opponents who are at least one's equal in competence (to the irritation of the others). Hence, being so motivated may be a loss. On the other hand, a reputation for competence will bring invitations to play from abler players and one will enjoy more exciting competition. This is a gain. Such losses and gains have

[4] See Winterbottom, 1958, pp. 453–78. Since this study employed the broader conception of achievement motivation as desire for 'success in competition with some standards of excellence', however, the results should be treated with caution, in relation to the definition I have offered. See also, in the same volume, B. C. Rosen, and E. Douvan.

their analogues in professional or business life. Only here there are further costs: of encompassing absorption in getting ahead, which diminishes other benefits of living; of disappointment, because of the difficulty of being superior to everyone. Achievement motivation in this sense is very different from the desire just to work well, or to make a contribution to social life. In reviewing his motivation, a person must ask himself in detail where the total activity is leading. If, when he does this, his fever diminishes, his desire is shown to be at too high a pitch. At that level it is irrational.

Some business firms have thought it worthwhile to encourage achievement motivation (in some sense) among their executives, and they have employed psychologists to bring about that motivation, apparently with some success. (McClelland, 1965.) The reported methods raise some doubts about the rationality of the heightened motivation. The new level of motivation is neither authentic nor rational if it can be reached only by a mixture of threats, misinformation, and good company.

iii. Third Mistake: Generalization from Untypical Examples.

Some further values which would extinguish in cognitive psychotherapy are neither artificial attitudes, nor based on mistaken beliefs. Rather, they are attitudes which have developed from familiarity with samples of liked/disliked situations but from *untypical* samples, or in an untypical context. For instance, I may dislike dogs because in childhood one attacked me; or I may feel uncomfortable inside public school buildings because in my childhood I was punished or wholly bored there; or, on a simpler level, as a small boy I may refuse a serving of any kind of fish because I have eaten a piece of cod (my first and only experience of fish) and disliked it heartily, saying now, 'I can't stand fish.'

How do such attitudes come about? All learning involves some generalization. Much to our advantage we do not learn a response only to stimuli exactly like those in the original learning situation, but to a *range* of stimuli more or less like the originals. Thus, if I acquire a conditioned like or dislike (etc.) because of one or more experiences, the attitude will be directed towards some *type* of object, and this type may be much broader than the kind of example which was the source of that attitude. If I am attacked by a dog, I could develop an attitude towards all dogs or all mammals, or at least all mammals outside my house.

It is obvious that attitudes which are the result of wild generalizations from a narrow set of experiences—say an aversion to all dogs as a result of being bitten by a terrier which I had provoked—will extinguish in cognitive psychotherapy. Why will they? Partly by counterconditioning because, say, interaction with a friendly well-behaved intelligent poodle will elicit warm attitudes towards dogs of this type, incompatible with my aversion towards *all* dogs. But partly it will diminish by inhibition, since the aversion to all dogs will receive little or no support from further experience with dogs. As we broaden the set of samples of interaction with dogs, the conditioned disliking response will rarely be given new support by another unfortunate experience. So much is clear.[5]

But not all attitudes resulting from generalization are irrational. Let us try to state more exactly which such attitudes would extinguish in psychotherapy and which would not. It is plausible to suppose that an attitude towards something which has its genesis in an experience not likely to repeat itself would extinguish. This generalization can be more precisely formulated if we define the notion of a 'typical experience' as one producing an attitude which would not extinguish if the agent reflected on the percentage of experiences which could rationally be expected with things of that sort over the course of his lifetime. Take my aversion towards dogs because of being bitten by a terrier which I had provoked by tramping on its nose. Suppose the aversion would extinguish after repeated reflection on the fact that only .0001 per cent of terriers will attack me if I do not provoke them. Or suppose that only .0001 per cent of St. Bernards will attack me even if I do step on both nose and tail, and reflection on this would extinguish my terrier-based aversion to St. Bernards. Then my actual aversion to all dogs is based on untypical experiences.[6] If we adopt this definition, then we can say of the attitudes based on generalization, only those

---

[5] One might ask why, then, seriously disabling aversions based on early unrepeated traumatic experiences do not extinguish readily. Part of the answer to this is that the early experience produces avoidance behaviour so that there are no further experiences which could reduce the impact of the original. (See Eysenck, 1973, especially pp. 145 f.)

[6] There is a kind of person-relativism here: what would count as an untypical experience for an Oxford don (meeting a rattlesnake) might be typical for a Navajo Indian.

which are untypical will extinguish in cognitive psychotherapy and hence are irrational.[7]

J. S. Mill stated in *Utilitarianism* that power, fame, and money come to be wanted for themselves and indeed come to be part of one's 'happiness' (one really does like them for themselves and would be unhappy in their absence), because of associations with the good things to which they lead. Let us suppose he is right in this. Are the valence and liking irrational? To answer, we must first determine as best we can (on the basis of available information) the frequency and consistency with which money will provide us with the things we already like. Then, we must see if a clear awareness of these facts will extinguish our desire for money. Money does buy a good many things, and absence of it can have unpleasant consequences. But how much can it buy, and how universally does a merely modest income have unpleasant consequences? When we get the answer to these questions firmly in mind we shall be well on the way to knowing whether a desire for money is irrational.

Some critics might say that any desire for money *for itself* is irrational. It is obviously irrational to want money for any other reason than for what it buys. Our theory need not lead to this consequence; at least it does not if it is just a fact of human nature that we learn to like (want) for themselves things which reliably lead to other things we already like (want). But this consequence need not be dismaying; for we can discriminate various situations involving money, and our theory certainly does not imply that it is rational to prefer money to various other goods in life with which it might be in competition—quite the contrary.

iv. Fourth Mistake: Exaggerated Valences Produced by Early Deprivation

Some people, especially children, appear to have a virtually insatiable craving for attention. And there are abnormally high desires for commendation or admiration from others, or for the company of others. Sometimes these desires seem similar to the condition of

---

[7] A related point is that our likes and desires are sometimes fixed not by untypical *experiences* but by *memory-traces* which may be unrepresentative of the experiences. If I have selectively forgotten the aversive aspects of some experience, my present attitude may be more positive than is rational. So my attitudes to sea-voyages may be more positive than the actual past combination of fun and nausea would lead one to expect. Presumably they would change after firm and repeated reminders of how things typically were and are.

persons who literally do not know when they have had enough to eat or drink, although the physiology cannot be parallel.[8]

Similarly there are abnormal aversions, say to spending money except for necessities, like that noted in the following letter to a columnist:

Dear Abby: My husband grew up fatherless during the depression. Now, at age 50, his net worth is around the half-million dollar mark. He is a professor with tenure, and has an excellent retirement and insurance program. Yet he buys second-hand clothes, day-old bread, and refuses to spend any money on a decent car, vacations or travel.

The reason? He wants to be sure he has enough money for his old age. What could be the matter with him?

HIS WIFE.

This case is extreme, but in milder forms the syndrome is not infrequent. It appears among rats. Rats which have been deprived of food, especially shortly after the time of weaning, respond to restriction of food intake for a week or more, by massive hoarding when food becomes abundant, acquiring and storing as many as several hundred pellets an hour as compared with the normal practice of storing half-a-dozen pellets.[9]

There is testimony that the absence of affection and warm cuddling early in a child's life can lead to insatiable demands for attention. (Mussen and Conger, 1956, p. 157.)

These cases suggest a syndrome whereby an early and prolonged deprivation of something wanted—enough for discomfort and anxiety to be involved—results in an abnormally high development of desire for that thing in later years. It looks as if anxiety gets associated with its absence or with the expectation, even quite small, of its absence. The anxiety then drives the person to relieve

---

[8] The desires to eat and drink arise partly from the activation of sensing devices in the brain, by the content of the blood. Eating or drinking does not bring the content of the blood up to standard for some period of time, but a person stops eating or drinking long before elapse of such a period. Hence we know there is a system of signalling which renders the sensing device temporarily impervious to the relevant deficiency in the blood and thereby shuts off the desire for food or water—say a signal from a wet throat, or from a full stomach. If this system of signals does not work properly, the person may continue to feel like eating or drinking, and enjoy eating or drinking, almost indefinitely.

[9] C. T. Morgan, 1947; C. T. Morgan and E. Stellar, 1950; Hunt, 1941, 1960; Hunt, Schlosberg, Solomon, and Stellar, 1947. The influence of other factors on rat behaviour, however, complicates the data.

it, by securing the object the absence of which arouses it. Thus a child who has been deprived of affection and esteem may, even very shortly after a friendly compliment, become anxious about the attitudes of others and can be made unanxious only by a steady stream of attention or praise. Or, a man who has been economically deprived during childhood will experience conditioned anxiety with the thought of absence of economic means, so that expenditure of money is a threatening experience. We may recall McClelland's point (p. 94 f.) that the experience of deprivation is apt to be very emotionally disturbing at an early age, when the child does not have any clear expectation about when the deprivation will end.

It is not suggested that all 'insatiable' desires derive from early deprivation.[10]

It seems that such abnormally strong desires would extinguish in cognitive psychotherapy. Some traditional psychoanalysts would say that if a person brought to consciousness the connection of early deprivation with his intense desire (= insight), the abnormally strong desire would abate. (Alexander, 1956, p. 55.) On the theory of learning and conditioning adopted earlier, the question is whether cognitive procedures can extinguish the connection between anxiety and the thought of the absence, or possible absence, of something. The answer is that if a person repeatedly reminds himself when he feels rejected, that others warmly accept him and will continue to do so in the foreseeable future, his anxiety in the absence of an expression of affection will diminish by inhibition. (One might also say that the thoughts will produce pleasant relaxation, so that the anxiety tends to be extinguished by counterconditioning.) Of course, the extinction process may take time. So, in so far as the suggested theory about these abnormal desires is correct, vivid repeated representation of knowable facts should bring about a reduction in intensity. We must conclude that a desire of this abnormal sort is 'irrational'.

What sorts of desires might be related to anxiety in this way? It would seem that desire for any situation thought to help secure the presence of an object of which one was once deprived might be a result. So, if the deprivation was of affection or acceptance, the

[10] D. C. McClelland suggested that a desire for achievement can become insatiable because the goal is so vague that no matter what is accomplished there will still be cues suggesting a further possible improvement. (1951, pp. 466–75.)

desire might be to conform with conventional proprieties (others dislike unconventionality), to work for financial security (money buys affection), or to achieve in professional work (achievement buys love).[11]

The whole issue whether some desires or pleasures can be identified as irrational may seem purely theoretical. It may be thought that important decisions are so complex that, even if we became convinced that some desire was irrational, the discovery could make no significant difference to the decision process. This view, however, is a profound mistake. Very often difficult decisions are difficult because, although a great many pros point in one direction, and almost all cons can be overmatched by pros, there is one consideration which remains a serious matter. For instance, suppose a Harvard professor is offered a position in Los Angeles, and is tempted to take it: his salary will be better, the research facilities equal, the graduate students and colleagues equal, the climate appealing, and he likes surfing. There is one difficulty: he is appalled by the thought of detaching himself from Harvard. Not that he thinks his stature in his profession would be diminished if he were to move; he knows that this is not the case. But he 'identifies' with Harvard; he feels himself part of a great tradition, the historically most important educational institution in the United States. Furthermore, his father would have wanted him to be at Harvard. Now undoubtedly most persons have very good reasons for hesitating to leave Harvard, but it could well be that *his* reason, his 'identification' with Harvard, is just irrational. However that may be, the point is that if he found that his basic reason for preferring to stay at Harvard is irrational, his practical problem would be resolved. For a decision to move had been blocked by one

---

[11] Could a rational person desire a logically impossible state of affairs (for example, to prove that π is a rational number), or a state of affairs describable only in meaningless language (for example, his being reincarnated 100 years from now), or a causally impossible state of affairs (for example, the past being different)? Desire is an 'intentional attitude' and can occur when its object is unreal or even impossible. Obviously people do desire such things. But would they if they were rational in my sense? And if not, why not? Obviously people do not stop desiring such things the instant they see the states of affairs are impossible —a man in love may know full well that his heart's desire is something that cannot be.

In my view, a rational person would not desire these things, but because the desire would disappear in cognitive psychotherapy—by inhibition, or counterconditioning after repeated reminders that the situation cannot possibly obtain. There is no simpler reason for thinking that such desires are irrational.

particular concern. And, when he identifies this concern as irrational, he will be clear that the rational thing is to make the move. Thus the identification of a single desire as irrational may have profound importance for a large personal decision.

2. RATIONAL DESIRES AND THE CONCEPT OF THE INTRINSICALLY GOOD

We now have before us the concept of an irrational desire or aversion: one that would not survive cognitive psychotherapy, at least with its present strength. And we have the concept of a rational desire or aversion: one that is not irrational. How nearly does the notion of the rationally desired approximate to the concept of the *good*?

One might say that it makes no difference how close it is. For, if we want to desire and act with reason, we want to know what is a rational desire—one that is maximally criticized by facts and logic. When we have identified a rational desire, we have that: a desire in which all the changes confrontation with available information will bring have been wrought. If we are dedicated to rational desiring and acting, we have what we want. If the term 'good' does not refer to what is rationally desired, so much the worse for the concept of the 'good'.

Even so, it is of interest whether the term 'rationally desired', or some longer phrase incorporating it, means the same as 'good', or if not, would be a useful replacement for that term. If so, it might be wise to conduct primary education so as to give a new meaning to 'good'—in terms of 'rationally desired'.

The word 'good', of course, appears in many different constructions, and the meaning or use of the term in these several constructions is not identical. Consider, for instance: 'a good car', 'a good father', 'good at swimming', 'good for making jelly'. Historically, philosophers have been most concerned with its use in such sentences as 'Knowledge is intrinsically good.'

Recently, some philosophers have thought that no expression in which no value word occurs is either exactly or even approximately synonymous with 'good', at least in its important uses. In contrast, many other philosophers, from Aristotle to Sidgwick and Rawls, have thought that there are expressions approximately synonymous with 'good' in its important uses, or at least functionally good replacements for it. In particular, some have thought that for something to be intrinsically good is just for somebody, or everybody, to like it or want it for itself. On this view, if fame were what someone or everyone wants, it would be good. Others have thought that for something to be intrinsically good is for it to be wanted or liked by persons (or perhaps some individual person) ,with certain qualifications, perhaps knowledge or virtue. Obviously the proposal I have been making belongs with this latter group. We should notice, however, that the altruistic or at least non-self-interested desires pose a problem, for while something may be a good thing if it is the object of a rational altruistic desire, we should clearly hesitate to say that the object of someone's rational altruistic desire is necessarily something good for him, something that is a part of the person's welfare or well-being. This problem will arise again later.

We need not deliberate whether 'rationally desired' in my sense is exactly or approximately synonymous with 'intrinsically good' in its ordinary meaning. I have not argued that it is: in fact I think it is not. Whether it is a useful replacement I shall not debate at this juncture. By this time the reader has probably formed his own opinion, and in any case there is no point in anticipating the discussion of this topic in Chapter 8, where I shall consider whether saying that a desire is rational in my sense is a recommendation of it.

I wish now, however, to put forward two claims on behalf of the conception of rational desire and its utility.

The first is that there is no sentence in which the word 'good' appears, at least in that core complex of uses which have been important for philosophy, which makes an identifiable point which cannot be made by a sentence containing 'rationally desired', doubtless in some complex clause but in which no 'value-word' is present. The claim is a large one. I shall not try to support it further, but merely offer two examples to make clear what claim is being made. Take: 'The Oldsmobile Cutlass is a good car for turnpike driving.' The meaning of this could be quite well construed as 'The Cutlass has a relatively large proportion of those qualities a fully rational person planning on turnpike driving would seek in a car.' In fact, this construction may be an over-kill. It would seem we may not need to appeal to a *fully* rational person in the sense which involves cognitive psychotherapy (and hence goes beyond rationality to a first approximation) unless it is to exclude desires to drive at speeds of 150 m.p.h. Or take: 'Knowledge is good in itself.' The meaning of this could be construed as 'Knowledge is something any fully rational person would want for himself, for no further reason.'

The second claim is that there are various things we want to say, on reflection, which can be said by talk of 'rational desire', but which cannot be said by 'good' or 'intrinsically good' in the ordinary use of these terms.

Suppose I ask myself whether, if I were fully rational, I would want fame for myself, or my own enjoyment. This seems a perfectly good and sensible question for anyone to raise. Yet how is one to raise it if one must do so with the terminology of 'good' in some of its constructions? It has been widely held that when we say that something is intrinsically good, we are committed to saying that anything just like it in respect of abstract properties is also good. As W. K. Frankena has said, 'A particular value judgement, however, is always implicitly general: when one says that X is good, one must be prepared to say that anything just like it is good and good in the same degree. Also, we must be prepared to give reasons why it is good, and this can only be done in the light of more general value judgements about what is good or at least prima facie good.' (1963, p. 64.) But, if this is what 'good' implies, then we are in trouble with our original question whether I would want fame or enjoyment for myself, if I were fully rational. For I was not asking about everybody's fame or enjoyment. In fact, if I want fame for myself, what I precisely do not want, usually, is for everyone else to be famous. (What would fame be if everyone were famous?) Suppose I do want fame for myself but not for others, even after cognitive psychotherapy. What then am I to say, if I want to express the situation by 'good'? Not that fame is a good thing, which suggests it is good for everybody. Not that my being famous is a good thing, but not the fame of others. How about that my fame is a good thing for me? This sounds odd: it suggests that my fame would benefit my health, or promote my other interests. It is possible that some apt phrasing can be found, but it is doubtful.

It might be replied that if a question about what would be desired by a rational person cannot well be put in a familiar phrase involving 'good', then so much the worse for the importance of the question. It is true that 'good' is an old word, and that we might expect that phrases involving it would have developed meanings to permit us to make all the appraisive statements we want to make. But this seems not to be the case. 'Good' seems to be not flexible enough, in its standard English uses, for us to be able to raise the important questions we want to raise about desires.

CHAPTER VII

SOME RATIONAL PLEASURES AND DESIRES

WE HAVE now shown how a person may identify which ones of his desires are rational; but we have not come to specific conclusions about the status of any desire for a given person, much less for everybody. The present chapter will attempt to remedy this lack on a modest scale, by appraising a few specific likes/dislikes and desires/aversions: native likes and dislikes and especially the dislike of pain; the desire for pleasure; and the desire for the happiness of others (benevolence).

1. DESIRES FOR WHAT IS NATIVELY LIKED

The theory of the acquisition of desires, aversions, likes, and dislikes presupposes that some things are natively liked or disliked, that is, are liked or disliked not as a result of association with something already liked or disliked. For the theory postulates, as an essential part of the learning of a desire or liking, association with something already liked or aversive; and while this something already liked or aversive could be so on account of association with something else already liked or aversive, we must assume, if we are to avoid vicious regress, that some situations are liked or disliked independently of association with what is already liked or disliked, i.e. are *natively* liked or disliked. Being in pain, being too cold or too hot, being unable to breathe, having to stay awake when sleepy, being bored, stubbing one's toe, receiving an electric shock, are examples of natively unpleasant experiences; dozing when tired, eliminating, eating good food, having novel stimuli, tasting something sweet, are examples of natively pleasant ones.

Could such likes or dislikes be irrational? Or could anything happen, aside from surgical intervention, that could make our response to such experiences different from what it natively is? If the answer to the latter question is negative, then of course the answer to the former is also negative.

Evidently nothing natively pleasant or unpleasant can be rendered indifferent by inhibition or discrimination. Since it was not learned by association with pleasant (unpleasant) things in the first place, its status will not be lost by withholding further associations with pleasant situations. But counterconditioning is another story. If homosexual experiences, martinis, smoking, and over-eating can be made aversive by pairing with shock or nausea, it is not obvious that conditioning cannot alter the pleasantness of events natively pleasant or unpleasant. In fact dogs which have learned that after a buzzer they will be first shocked and then fed, come to wag their tails and drool while being shocked; hopefully they no longer dislike the shock. In principle it is possible that self-stimulation in cognitive psychotherapy could have such an effect.

It is of course not clear what thoughts could, by counterconditioning, extinguish unlearned likes and dislikes for most of the events listed above. So these likes and dislikes are likely to be accepted as rational. Let us see how these general reflections work out for a prime example of the natively disliked: pain.

First of all, what is meant by 'pain'? Not every aversive experience is painful: having castor oil in the mouth is aversive but not painful. Nor can we say that pain is a sensation caused by stimulation of special receptors; matters are much more complex than that.[1] In any case we can not investigate which physiological processes are connected with pain unless we can already identify experiences as painful. Normally the use of 'pain' is learned by being assured one is in pain when at the time one is having a noticeable sensation arising from tissue damage or pressure. (Some people are congenitally insensitive to pain in the sense that the sensation from tissue damage is not noticeably different from tickles or tingling, so they do not learn the use of 'painful'.) Such sensations are not exactly alike: they may be sharp or dull, big or small, throbbing or steady. Other sensations not caused by tissue damage or pressure are sufficiently similar to those which are for pain terminology to be extended to these: headaches, toothaches, and so on.

Pain sensations are normally unpleasant, apart from slight pains. However, prefrontal leucotomy apparently leaves the pain sen-

[1] See Sternbach, 1968; Melzack and Wall, 1965; Melzack, 1961, pp. 41–9; Hilgard, 1969; Trigg, 1970.

sations intact, but greatly reduces the aversiveness. (Surgery in the hypothalamus can remove the pain sensation altogether.) The pain sensation is thus distinct from its unpleasantness.

The question therefore arises whether, apart from the use of surgery or other physical interventions, pain could be rendered indifferent or even pleasant. Could a person be trained to like headaches, if these elicited praise or chocolates or sex? (Conceivably a masochist is a person who has come to associate pain with reduction in guilt-feelings and hence by conditioning has come to like it for itself.) Since it is not a logical necessity that pain be disliked, it is a matter for observation to determine how far conditioning can affect the liking/disliking of pain. And, if conditioned extinction of disliking, or conditioned liking of pain, is at all possible, there is no reason in principle why the effect might not be produced by thoughts. Hence it is logically possible that cognitive psychotherapy might influence the pleasantness/unpleasantness of at least some kinds of pain, although it is hard to imagine what reasonable thoughts might have such an effect.

A different question is whether (future) pain is bound to be negatively valenced. Normally, as we have seen, an experience unpleasant in the past comes by conditioning to be negatively valenced. But we also know that we can change the 'natural' valence of an experience by associating the idea of it with pleasant (unpleasant) situations or thoughts. Thus it is possible that the idea of being burned at the stake be so frequently associated with the pleasant thought of glory in heaven that the envisaged outcome becomes positively valenced.

Could this ever happen in a rational person? If a person knew that enduring some pain would produce a great contribution to science, and reflected on this repeatedly, it is logically possible that the prospect of at least modestly severe pains might not be unattractive. Such situations must surely be rare, but their possibility shows that pain is not necessarily negatively valenced, even for a fully rational person, in conceivable circumstances.

2. PLEASURE AND ETHICAL HEDONISM

The status of pleasure is very different from that of pain; obviously the question whether every pleasant experience is pleasant can hardly arise. It is a tautology to say that pleasant experiences are pleasant, so the question whether a rational person would enjoy pleasant experiences is one we cannot sensibly raise. There is, however, the other question, about the valence of pleasant experiences for a rational person. This question can sensibly be raised and essentially has been discussed, in somewhat different terminology, from the time of the early Greeks. The hedonistic ethical philosophers have urged that a rational person would want, for itself, one and only one kind of thing: pleasant experiences, and usually pleasant experiences for himself.

Do the conceptual scheme and the psychological theory we have been urging have any implications for this long-standing controversy?

Our conceptual framework at once prompts the following question: Is it seriously being urged that a rational person would not want to defeat his favourite opponent, read a book, or play tennis well? Is it being urged that the only thought of an outcome which would be positively motivating in a rational person is the thought of a pleasant experience? If that is what is being urged, it surely does not have the support of the psychological theory of motivation. That theory explains how it comes about that the thought of savouring a hearts-of-palm salad is motivating. What it absolutely does not say is that this thought is *not* motivating; or that the only thought that is motivating is the thought that something will be pleasant! And the same for a rational person. How would any true thoughts about the experience of eating a hearts-of-palm salad disabuse me of my interest in this kind of activity?

It seems, then, that if ethical hedonism is to deserve serious appraisal, we must find a more subtle formulation, one sympathetic to the traditional ideas but not identical. What might this be? Unfortunately any formulation one chooses to explore risks a possible objection: that there is some other one, closer to the spirit of ethical hedonism, which would do better (or worse). I shall, however, have the temerity to propose a formulation which I think it would be illuminating to assess. It is one which may strike persons sympathetic to hedonism as too artificial to merit attention, but I believe it is more attractive on further reflection. In any case, appraisal of this proposal may suggest fruitful ways of thinking about any better one.

The suggested thesis for ethical hedonists is this: a rational person would want something for itself if and only if it would be rational for him to believe that its occurrence would bring him (directly or indirectly) net pleasure; and he would desire it with an intensity corresponding to the magnitude of this net pleasure (and correspondingly for rational aversion and displeasure).

This thesis has a consequence we should note at once. Suppose I want a certain person to think well of me during all of next month, and I also want to win three sets of tennis from Mr. X tomorrow morning; but my desire for the former is stronger than that for the latter. The interesting consequence is as follows. The thesis of hedonism says that, if my rational preference ordering of the outcomes mentioned is as stated, then it must be rational for me to think the first will be more pleasure-productive than the second. But this relative pleasantness is obviously not the relative pleasantness of just some particular moment of each; it must be the relative enjoyment summed over a period of time, and indeed different periods of time. And this conception seems to require that enjoyments be capable of measurement in some strong sense. We must be ready to compare some moments of one intensity with a different duration of a different intensity. I am not suggesting this is not possible; Chapter 13 will assert that it is. But we should be aware of the fact that the possibility of measurement is required by the thesis of hedonism, as stated.

Is there good reason to believe the ethical hedonist theory, as formulated? On a common-sense level we do accept some of the propositions it implies; for instance, we think it would not be rational to want to eat a piece of pie if there was not good reason to think doing so would be pleasant. But other simple cases are less clear. It is not obvious to me that it is rational for me to want to defeat Mr. X in tennis only with an intensity corresponding with the rational pleasure-promise of that event. If my previous argument has been correct, what we shall want to know is whether the intensity of my desire, after cognitive psychotherapy, would be what the hedonist thesis says it would be. In order to decide such matters, it looks as if we shall have to depart from the level of common sense, and see what psychological theory can tell us. Does it tell us anything? In Chapter 5 we saw that pleasant and unpleasant experiences are involved in the genesis of desires and aversions. But the thesis put forward there was too imprecise to enable us to appraise the hedonist's contention.

A more specific form of genetic psychological theory might permit such appraisive inferences. One theory was put forward by L. T. Troland (1928, reprinted 1967),[2] and he called it 'hedonism of the past'. His proposal was roughly that the valence of a prospective experience for a person is a simple function of the past pleasantness of similar experiences, specifically of the total net pleasure a person has had from similar experiences over his lifetime (1928, especially p. 299). This proposal seems to imply that the degree of a person's desire for something now will correspond with how pleasant the desired experience's occurrence must rationally be expected to be, on the basis of an inductive projection of past occasions. Not exactly: for the present desire is supposed to be a function not only of the average pleasantness of such experiences in the past, but also of the sheer number of them. But a theory like Troland's clearly could be exploited for an appraisal of hedonism.

Troland's theory, as stated, oversimplifies the facts. First, as we saw in Chapter 3, valence is a function of at least three variables: incentive value, deprivation time, and degree of representation. Only one of these (incentive value) can reasonably be explained as the result of past 'reinforcements', that is, past pleasure or distress from situations of the same kind as the one now valenced. Troland's theory, then, can be applied at most to incentive value. Another problem is that his theory overlooks 'direct conditioning': the incentive value of an outcome traceable to past associations of the *idea* of an outcome with pleasant or unpleasant states. Thus it is just not true that the incentive value of an outcome O is a function solely of the magnitude of the pleasantness/unpleasantness of situations like O in the past.

In spite of these difficulties the truth in Troland's theory might support the hedonist's view that in a rational person the valence of an anticipated outcome will vary with its hedonic promise, that is, the net enjoyment a rational person would expect from it. For the hedonist can admit that Troland's theory holds only for incentive value, but still maintain that this does not undermine the hedonist's

---

[2] A somewhat similar point of view is put forward by B. F. Skinner, 1971, Chap. 6. We must remember that to be pleasant is not for some specific feeling to occur.

claim that valence for a rational person will correspond with (rational) hedonic promise.

First consider degree of representation. It is true that valence varies with degree of representation—but not in a rational person, for a rational person by definition will always represent the outcome with maximal vividness. How about deprivation time? The hedonist will presumably agree that valence, even in a rational person, will vary with deprivation time. But the hedonist will reply that the same thing will be true of hedonic promise. For a rational person will know about, and allow for, the influence of deprivation time in his prediction about pleasantness; he will know quite well from past experience that when hungry we enjoy a steak more than when not hungry. This fact has been part of the lore of hedonism since the early Greeks. So, the Hedonist can say that psychology substantially supports his theory, if Troland's hypothesis correctly accounts for incentive value.

The second difficulty is that Troland's theory overlooks direct conditioning, which plays an important role in the transmission of cultural values to the young. Direct conditioning, we have seen, produces valence by pairing the *idea* of an outcome with some pleasant or unpleasant state (e.g. the idea of a martini with unpleasant nausea). This fact seems incompatible with the hedonist's claim that the incentive value of any outcome correlates with the hedonic promise of that outcome. Why? Because the past pairing of the idea of an outcome with some pleasant or unpleasant state was artificial, and hence the incentive value which the conditioning has attached to the idea of the outcome need not correspond with what a rational person would project as the hedonic promise of that kind of outcome, in its natural setting. So, it seems, valence and hedonic promise fall apart, and the hedonist principle must be mistaken.

But, the hedonist may argue, as we saw in Chapter 6, that incentive value left by direct conditioning will normally extinguish in cognitive psychotherapy and therefore will not be present in a rational person. Rational persons will disabuse themselves, at least in good part, of incentive value from direct conditioning which could not have been produced by interaction with typical samples of the type of outcome in question. So, the hedonist may say, we may ignore the discrepancy between incentive value and hedonic promise on account of direct conditioning, because in a rational person the incentive value which does not correspond will have been extinguished.

One difficulty with the hedonist's counter-argument is that the assumption about the effects of cognitive psychotherapy reaches beyond the evidence. What seems true is that there is a tendency for incentive value to extinguish when it has been produced by direct conditioning and diverges from what it would have been had it been produced only by natural interaction with typical examples of the kind of outcome. But it is by no means clear that it will always extinguish to that extent: for instance, if the conditioning occurred in early childhood, when various features are present which make conditioning quite stable (see above, p. 94 f.). In so far as incentive value deriving from direct conditioning resists extinction, its magnitude will diverge from hedonic promise even in a rational person. The hedonist's defence, then, does not quite succeed.

Let us now leave direct conditioning on one side, and ask what is implied by what is known about the principles of *classical conditioning* by pleasant or unpleasant natural experiences, in the way discussed in Chapter 5, Section 2. Do these principles support the theory that incentive value is a simple increasing function of the total net pleasantness of experiences with the kind of outcome, over the person's lifetime? Or of the *average* pleasantness? Or do they somehow imply a correlation between incentive value and hedonic promise, in the case of a rational person?

Taking into account the dearth of empirical data in this area, we can still say that psychologists who have been interested in the problem seem to think that incentive value is at least primarily a result of classical conditioning of approach (etc.) responses to the idea of an outcome. If so, the magnitude of incentive value is subject to all the complexities involved in classical conditioning—the frequency of the association, the temporal gaps between idea and pleasant experience on particular occasions, the recency and in general the dating of these associations (including the fact that some occurred very early in childhood)—all factors involved in the total set of principles about classical conditioning. If, as I suggested in Chapter 5, the principle of stimulus generalization is involved in an important way, we must take into account another set of variables.

When all these complexities are taken into account, it is difficult to affirm that the principles of classical conditioning or stimulus generalization predict that the valence, in a rational person, of a prospective outcome is such a function of past pleasant (or unpleasant) experiences that its intensity would correspond with a rational promise of pleasure from that outcome, based on past experience.

One lesson is clear: if reasoning of this sort is what is required for a serious defence of the principle of ethical hedonism, things are far less simple than those philosophers have thought, who have embraced it just because they thought that any sensible person in a cool hour would find himself attracted by nothing but the prospect of pleasant experiences.

3. BENEVOLENCE[3]

The shorter Oxford Dictionary defines 'benevolent' as 'desirous of the good of others'. Bishop Butler said it is 'an affection to the good of our fellow-creatures'. The term seems to encompass both motivational and affective elements; so I shall say a person is benevolent if it is a relatively permanent trait of his personality that (1) he is intrinsically motivated to produce happiness or welfare in others and to avoid decreasing it, (2) tends to be pleased if informed that someone has moved to a higher level, and (3) tends to be displeased if informed that someone is unhappy or not well off or has moved to a lower level. So defined, it is both a disposition to like or dislike something, and also a related desire or aversion. The definition does not state how much a person must be motivated (etc.) in order to deserve the title 'benevolent'; we can leave this open and will discuss the status of *some* degree of benevolence, perhaps only a little more than none. Besides ranging over various degrees, benevolence also has wider or narrower extension: some people may be benevolent only with respect to their immediate family, whereas God is said to love all sentient creatures as his children. Benevolence connects only loosely with helping behaviour; the latter can have ulterior motives, and having the former even to a high degree does not guarantee helping behaviour in all situations.

Why should we take a special interest in this particular

[3] This section incorporates some points made in a paper (Brandt, 1976).

motive? Benevolence is important in the theory both of the justification of moral standards and the motivation to conform with them. We shall see (Chapter 10) that the most important question for the justification of a moral principle is 'Which moral principles would be supported by fully *rational* persons?' and that means persons with a rational degree of benevolence. In order to answer this question, ideally we should known exactly *how* benevolent a fully rational person would be; realistically, we should be satisfied simply with knowing whether a fully rational person would be devoid of benevolence, or would have a significant degree of it, or would value the welfare of others equally with his own.

Theorists are divided on whether benevolence is native or learned, and those who hold it is learned diverge on the question of how it is learned. According to the theory outlined in Chapter 5, all motivation is learned (except that involved in liking or disliking certain experiences); so, if anything about benevolence is native, it must be the affective (liking-disliking), not the motivational element.

Historically the idea that benevolence is native has had support. Hume, in the *Inquiry*, may have been favourable to the view, writing that 'there is some benevolence, however small, infused into our bosom; some spark of friendship for human kind; some particle of the dove kneaded into our frame, along with the elements of the wolf and the serpent'.[4] Darwin, in Chapter 4 of *The Descent of Man*, supported the nativist view by outlining evidence for altruistic behaviour in subhuman species. The nativist view has not been popular in the present century, however, until recently, when it has been revived by some evolutionary theorists, who have argued that benevolence could have survival value for the gene-stream which fixed it in the individual, particularly in the conditions of primitive life, in small largely related groups with frequent situations of danger and opportunities to help.[5]

If one is a nativist, the question is open what is native. A possible answer is that it is a disposition to have, or easily to learn to have, empathic and sympathetic responses. The terms 'empathic'

[4] David Hume, *An Inquiry Concerning the Principles of Morals*, Sec. 9 (many editions). In the *Treatise* he developed a learning account, rather similar to the one I describe below, except that he seems to hold that a person acts 'benevolently' in order to remove distress, or produce joy, in himself.

[5] See the influential paper by R. L. Trivers, 1971; also Donald Campbell, 1972.

and 'sympathetic' do not appear to have a precise common meaning in the literature. I shall employ them in the following way. First, an empathic response is a response to another's expression of emotion (e.g. a cry of fear) or to perception of a situation of another which has aroused a certain emotion in the perceiver in the past, by having that emotion, say fear. Second, a sympathetic response is disliking the situation of another when and because one believes he is in an aversive conscious state, or liking his situation when and because one believes he likes his conscious state.

If one views benevolence as learned, then one has a choice between two types of theory (or some combination of them): first, a classical conditioning theory in which human models (and identification) do not play a role, and second, one in which human models are central. Let us look first at the former, which explains the evidence better. It begins with an explanation of *empathic* responses, after a Pavlovian model. We recall that Pavlov's dogs first salivated (unconditioned response—UR) when meat powder was blown into their mouths (unconditioned stimulus —US). Then a buzzer was rung shortly before the appearance of the food; and after a time the dogs salivated in much the same way (conditioned response—CR) at the sound of the buzzer (conditioned stimulus—CS). Consider now a child in pain (US). We distinguish from the pain sensation itself (US) a native aversive response to (including dislike of) pain: fear, autonomic changes, crying, withdrawal responses (UR). Now, while the child is in pain and crying, he hears his own cry (CS) and by conditioning (just as with salivation and the sound of a buzzer) the native responses to pain, or some thing like them, occur (CR). So, when a baby hears another baby cry (CS), he will have these same responses (CR), including crying himself. At a more advanced level the child may cut himself and feel pain (US), to which he responds aversively; but while all this goes on he is seeing the blood flow (CS) to which stimulus the aversive reponses of pain become conditioned (CR), so that when he sees another child cut and the blood flow, he gets the same aversive response as if to his own pain (CR) by conditioning. We can work out a conditioning theory of liking responses along the same lines—say the liking of seeing another child delighted by getting an ice-cream cone.

Classical conditioning can also explain *sympathetic* liking and distress. This can occur only after a cognitive advance in the child, however; for by definition of 'sympathetic' he must be able to believe that another person has an internal life of his own with experiences of pain and joy sometimes made manifest in his behaviour. His developing conception includes the idea that others have complex emotional states like his own, including longing, disappointment, and aspiration. But how does he come to like the other being in a state which he enjoys, and dislike another being in a state of distress? There seem to be two possible lines of explanation. The first is a straight extension of the conditioning theory of empathy, with the expressive behaviour and situation of another (already able to arouse conditioned liking and disliking responses) getting linked cognitively with a representation of correlated internal states of the other, so that by an extension of conditioning the representation of these internal states of the other (CS) comes to elicit the same liking/disliking responses (CR). At this more developed state the child is also able to identify what it is he is liking or disliking, in his awareness of the state of the other person; and his earlier rather undirected escape responses become specifically related to the proper target and become attempts to alleviate the distress of the other. [6]

The second line of explanation, less favoured among psychologists, would employ the mechanism of stimulus generalization. This explanation points out that at the higher level of cognitive development the pleasant or distressful states of another are represented in the child. When he represents to himself that another is in an unpleasant state of some sort, he is thinking that someone else is having a certain sort of experience, and that this sort of experience is one he has had himself, and disliked. By the principle of stimulus generalization we may expect this representation to elicit the closest possible thing, in the circum-

[6] I am heavily indebted to Professor Martin Hoffman, of the University of Michigan Department of Psychology, for the substance of this account about empathy and sympathy, although something at least close to it is held by various contemporary psychologists (and it is not far from Hume in the *Treatise*). See his 1975; also Krebs, 1970; the articles in the *Journal of Social Issues* 28, 1972, no. 3, an issue devoted to altruism; and Macauley and Berkowitz, 1970. The last-named contains a paper by J. Aronfreed which describes experimental work which I take to support the above account of empathy and sympathy.

stances, to the responses that experience would elicit if it were occurring in oneself—that is, in case the response to the experience in oneself would be escape tendencies, there may be expected to be tendencies to avoid that experience in another, specifically to alleviate the distress of another. There is no reason why this second explanation of sympathetic liking and distress is incompatible with the classical conditioning explanation; each may be a partial explanation of the phenomenon.

The above explanation is framed in terms of responses to persons we can actually see, or whose internal states are made vivid to us. It does not take us to full-blown benevolence, towards the states of individuals at any point in space and time. But there seems no reason why generalization may not work so that the representation of the states of another, irrespective of whether we can see him or he is near us in space and time, will arouse liking and disliking responses, and corresponding motivation.

Social learning theory conceptions, unlike the empathy-sympathy theory, uses social norms, models, and sanctions to explain how benevolence is learned. The essential difference between the two theories is like the difference between a child learning not to touch a hot stove because it has previously been burned, and learning not to touch a hot stove because it has previously been spanked for coming close to a hot stove.

The social learning theory, using conceptions described above (p. 100 f.), may suppose that children 'identify' with models such as parents, and that identification involves adopting values—including, of course, benevolence. There is empirical support for the view that the behaviour of nurturant models influences children in the direction of helping behaviour—for instance, one study showing that the degree of altruism in children correlates with the degree of altruism in the same-sex parent. Various forms of identification theory explain how all this works. A popular one holds that a child tends to be anxious in the absence of a nurturant parent, and then finds he can make himself feel better by behaving like the parent, thus making himself a kind of parent-substitute, something which reduces his anxiety. He succeeds the better, the more he acts like the parent—and acting like the parent is at its fullest when the child takes over even the value-system of the parent, including his degree of altruism.

These social learning theories doubtless complement the empathy-sympathy theory in describing processes that influence the development of benevolence in the child. But there are reasons for thinking that the empathy-sympathy account is more important (Hoffman, 1975), such as the following: sympathetic behaviour is identifiable in the second year, earlier than the social learning models can explain. Very young children show signs of distress at the distress of other children, when too young to be able to do anything about it, or else to which they respond by improvised attempts, say by offering a doll to an unhappy playmate. Benevolent behaviour is increased by training in role-playing, which the empathy-sympathy theory predicts, but not the social learning theory. Helping behaviour is a negative function of the number of observers and a positive function of the number of distress cues. When a person witnesses another in pain (etc.) he has a measurable physiological affective reaction, which is reduced when he goes to the relief of the distress. The social learning theories offer no explanation of these facts.

Having considered the genesis of benevolence, we are now in a better position to say whether a rational person would be benevolent. Let us consider three questions: (1) Would benevolence extinguish in a fully rational person? (2) Could a perfectly rational person be without benevolence altogether? (3) What form would benevolence take in a fully rational person?

(1) Our question whether benevolence would extinguish in a fully rational person is at least partly a question whether its continuance involves any of the 'mistakes' we have discussed. Of course, if dislike of the distress of others is native, it will not extinguish by inhibition. But let us, to avoid complexities, ignore this theory in favour of the empathy-sympathy learning theory. On this view, sympathy has a status very like being native; it is conditioned early, identifiable in the second year of some children. As such, it is likely to be highly resistant to extinction (see above, p. 94 f.), irrespective of what is done to reduce it. In that case it will automatically qualify as rational (p. 113). And, since the contingencies required for the development of empathy and sympathy are apparently present in any intelligent child who has an adequate conception of other persons, empathy and sympathy would seem immune to differences in the 'socializing' practices of

different families or groups. The genesis of benevolence, if we adopt the conditioning theory, is not artificial, in the sense (explained, p. 116 f.) in which attitudes are artificial when they arise from identification, fear of one's parents, and so on. But benevolence does arise from generalization of an aversive response, from hearing oneself cry or seeing one's own blood flow, to the sound of another's cry or seeing his blood flow—and eventually to a representation of the other's internal distressful states. Is there not here a confusion or 'mistake' of sorts, at least the result of a failure to make a relevant discrimination? One might argue that seeing one's own blood flow is connected with one's own pain (the unconditioned stimulus), but seeing another person's blood is not connected with one's own pain. Perhaps repeated self-stimulation to the effect that another's blood is not connected with one's own pain would lead to at least partial extinction of sympathetic response by inhibition?

Should we then say that benevolence is an irrational liking/desire because its existence rests on failure to make a discrimination? If benevolence is irrational on this ground, then so are virtually all our desires! For seemingly all of them depend on classical conditioning. And in effect classical conditioning results in the occurrence of a response to something different from the unconditioned stimulus—for instance, a negative response to a stimulus that occurred in connection with electric shock. It is not that classical conditioning tends to increase sensitivity to shocks (on the contrary, as shocks go on, sensitivity to them tends to diminish by habituation); it increases negative response to something different. Conditioning is in a sense unfair; for it produces a positive or negative response to something *not guilty except by association*. But how many responses would turn out to be irrational if one affirmed that any response is irrational if *conceivably*, according to the theory of extinction, it could narrow in its scope or partially extinguish if one repeatedly reminded oneself of the difference between the conditioned and the unconditioned stimulus? A liking for Christmas carols; affection for one's mother; desire for things one likes, desire even for one's own happiness. So, ruling out likes/desires as irrational on so broad a basis would imply the irrationality of virtually all learned likes and desires. For this reason I explained 'cognitive psychotherapy' in such a way as to keep some touch with reality; so that a desire or liking ends up as irrational only to the extent that repeated self-stimulations would actually diminish it. Some likes and desires extinguish in this way; but many (partly because of early conditioning) will not: among them, presumably, my liking for the company of my mother, or my horror at seeing someone tortured.

A person's benevolent responses, then, are irrational only if he *can* (causally) get rid of them by saying to himself things like 'His suffering does not hurt me.' Otherwise, they are rational.

(2) Our second question was whether an adult could be fully rational and be without benevolence altogether. The answer to this may seem obvious: that there are such persons and there is no reason to think them irrational—for instance, the operators of Hitler's concentration camps. But we must repeat that a person may be benevolent to some degree, but seldom act so as to help another, because of the presence of stronger motives, such as a desire to please superiors.

Can we identify circumstances in which benevolence might not develop at all? Surely every infant experiences pain and joy, so one requirement for empathy and sympathy is present. But if he is an only child, and others around him interact with him in such a way that the perception of their joy (distress) is seldom paired with his joy (distress), the tendency to sympathy may develop little. Or suppose his earliest fumbling attempts to help others are met with rebuffs, or even (in some societies) with rebukes from his parents; or suppose his play is in the streets, where peers are aggressive and unkindly, and adults are threats. Then discrimination between his own distress and that of others is encouraged, and the conditioned empathic-sympathetic response may be quite small.

Might cognitive psychotherapy produce benevolent motivation in a person who was largely without it? It might remove a block to its development by removing the assumption that other people are unfriendly and threatening. But it may be that a stable motive of benevolence—like other 'social' motives—must be formed in the early years. In that case cognitive psychotherapy will not produce it. On the other hand, it could well be that cognitive psychotherapy would greatly enlarge the range of sympathy. Some people seem capable of sympathy towards a small group, but not towards a larger group because they are discriminated as strange, dangerous, or inferior. More information might achieve a widening of the range of sympathy by removing these misconceptions.

(3) Our final question is what form benevolence will take in a fully rational person.

(3a) A rational person will take into account the whole anticipated future of the persons towards whom his benevolence is directed. For a rational person will represent future states as vividly as present ones and will presumably therefore be as much moved by them. Thus he will not give a child a tasty bar of chocolate if he knows that the child will suffer as a result from painful indigestion later. A rational person presumably will for the same reason have as much concern about future as for present generations, although of course his behaviour will be affected by our greater ignorance of the problems and prospects of future generations.

(3b) It is reasonable to suppose that the degree of a rational person's motivation to improve the welfare level of another will be a function of at least partly the conceived difference, or interval, between the present state and the anticipated improved state (or the present state and an anticipated lowered state which can be prevented).

(3c) It seems to be a common-sense fact that benevolent people are more motivated, other things being equal, to prevent what they think is rational rather than irrational distress, and to produce what they think is rational than what they think is irrational satisfaction. For instance, it would be hard to work up sympathetic concern for a woman's distress at being omitted from the list of the ten best-dressed women in the world, or for a person's distress because a Japanese family has moved next-door.

(3d) So far I have avoided precision about exactly what it is that a rational benevolent person would want for others. One possibility is that he wishes to maximize net enjoyment over a lifetime (possibly excepting irrational enjoyments). Let us call this the *happiness theory*. Alternatively, it may be held that he wishes to maximize desire-satisfaction over a lifetime, where 'satisfaction' means just the occurrence of the states of affairs the person wants or wanted or will want during his lifetime, with no implications about his enjoyment of, or even knowledge about, them. Let us call this the *desire theory*. This theory can take several forms, depending on whether it is actual occurrent desires that are meant, or the desires that would occur after cognitive psychotherapy or in the face of some level of information; but I will postpone these complications for Chapter 13, where I shall argue against the desire theory on the grounds that it cannot be made a conceptually intelligible programme. At that point it will also be made clear why the issue between the two theories is such an important one: that there turns on it the question of whether the kind of moral system a rational person would support (and what is right or wrong we shall see depends on this) is one which promises to maximize enjoyment-happiness or desire-satisfaction.

The practical difference between the two theories is not great, partly because a person always wants the continuation of any experience he is enjoying, partly because it is unpleasant for one's desires to be frustrated. But there are some differences: for instance, a person may want some event to occur after his death, when he will surely get no enjoyment from it; or a person, because of the states of his 'drives' at a certain time, may want an outcome for a later time quite out of line with the enjoyment he will actually obtain from it.

Which theory about the aim of benevolence is right?

Let us begin with a common-sense observation, which anyone can test for himself. I suggest we are interested in other people getting what they want only because we think they will be distressed if they do not, and will be pleased if they do. If we think the satisfaction of a desire will give little pleasure and that non-occurrence of the desired event will frustrate little, we have little motivation to bring about the wanted event. Obviously in the case of children, animals, and mental defectives we want to make them happy and avoid distress, and take known desires into account only as indicators of how this may be done. Matters are different with adults: we think respect for them requires permitting them to make their own mistakes. It is not, however, that we want to help them attain their goals when we think there will be no net increase in happiness.

Psychological theory, in particular the basic theory of sympathetic responses, supports this common-sense view. We remember that some stimuli (sound of a child's own cry), by association with unconditioned stimuli (e.g. his pain), are able to elicit the response natively elicited by the latter; say, disliking, withdrawal responses. By stimulus generalization, the sound of another child's cry will be able to elicit the same disliking, withdrawal responses. Then, at a higher stage, the child believes that others have internal states causally related, say, to his crying. By more conditioning, then, the representation of these is able to elicit the disliking, withdrawal responses. But which internal states of others do we come to believe are behind the expressive behaviour (etc.) of another, so that by conditioning the representation of them is able to evoke a disliking response for them in us? Necessarily (a philosopher would justify it by appeal to some kind of argument from analogy) the very kind we find associated with expressive behaviour (etc.) in ourselves: pain, the taste of quinine, the taste of chocolate, the exhilaration of activity. Basically, it is experiences in others which we like or dislike in ourselves—pleasant or unpleasant states of mind. It is the thought that others are in these states that is able to elicit sympathetic (benevolent) reponses in us.

Is there any reason to think that pure satisfaction of desire—that is, the occurrence of some event at time t of a kind for which there is a desire in the other person at some time t'—hypothesized for another person, can do the same? Remember that for satisfaction of desire in this sense to occur, it is not necessary for the person desiring it even to know about its occurrence, much less to enjoy it. According to the above theory of sympathy, there seems no reason at all to think that the representation of the pure satisfaction of another's desire will be the target of sympathetic/benevolent motivation.

What a rational benevolent person will basically want for others, then, is their welfare or utility in the sense of liked experiences or activities, but not in the sense of the occurrence of events desired, as such, independent of their influence on liked occurrent states.

CHAPTER VIII

THE FORCE OF KNOWING WHAT IS RATIONAL

THE PRECEDING chapters have mostly been attempts to identify which wants or enjoyments or actions are *rational* in a special, explained sense of that word. More specifically, first we inquired which types of action are *rational to a first approximation*: which types of action a person would perform if, taking his desires at the time as given, he were to have all relevant available information vividly before his mind at the moment of decision. Then, second, we inquired which situations a person would enjoy or want (or the opposite) if his motivational mechanisms had been maximally influenced by available information—if, in terms we used, he had undergone cognitive psychotherapy with respect to any want or enjoyment that is in question. We called such fumigated desires or enjoyments 'rational' ones. Finally, we have the ideal of actions which are fully rational, *rational to a second approximation*: those a person would perform if his desires were rational, and if at the moment of decision he were to have all relevant information vividly before his mind.

If a person were already rational in my sense, he would act rationally: this is true by definition of 'rational'. Similarly, if a person had undergone cognitive psychotherapy, he would have rational desires, aversions, and enjoyments. Most of us, however, are not rational in that sense. We simply know, or have very good reason to believe, that certain actions or desires are rational for us, and others irrational.

Suppose one knew a certain action or desire to be rational. What would one's attitude be towards the action or desire? People's attitudes may be different. Some persons, like the writer, will be quite ready to perform the rational act if they know which it is; and they will be favourably disposed towards desires and aversions it would be rational for them to have, and unfavourably disposed towards those it would be irrational to have. They will be disposed to stop regretting the unattainability of goals they know it is irrational for them to aspire towards. Furthermore, they will be willing to spend some time and money to find out which actions or desires are rational for them.

Others, however, may feel differently. The reader may agree that he would perform certain actions if fully rational, and that some of his desires might change if he underwent cognitive psychotherapy, but this concession might leave him unmoved, unaffected in his attitudes and intentions. He might say: 'Why ought I to do, or even try to do, what I would do if I were fully rational? Why should I stop regretting not getting things I want, just because the want is irrational in your sense? Is there any reason why I should stop wanting what it is irrational to want in your sense? Moreover, why I should spend time or energy trying to make my desires and aversions rational?'

At this point it would be helpful to have some dialogue with the sceptic, in order to disclose the exact nature of his puzzlement, in particular, what kind of facts or reasoning might in principle satisfy him. The questions as stated above use terms like 'ought', 'should', and 'reason'. To clear up the puzzle, we need to know what the sceptic means by these terms, in order to locate exactly which questions he is asking. Some philosophers would regard the questions as improper, involving concealed contradictions: if 'ought' means 'would choose if fully rational', then the question why I ought to do what I would do if fully rational makes no sense. Such a response, however, seems unsympathetic; a person may be genuinely puzzled but be unable to articulate his reasons.

Such a sceptic about what it is rational to do in my sense cannot very well deny that the same puzzle arises about knowledge that one 'ought' to do something, or that something is 'the best thing to do', or that something one happens to be desiring is 'undesirable'. If he denies that there are parallel puzzles about the latter expressions, it is probably because he has no clear idea of what these phrases mean, unless, of course, he takes the statements (e.g. 'That is the best thing to do') simply to express already-formed intentions to act, or actual desires. In that case, of course, there could be no gap between intention/desire and these judgements—but then there would be a cost elsewhere, since apparently there would be no such thing as appraisal of intentions and desires, or at least no language in which such appraisals could be expressed.

What might be the source of the sceptic's attitude about rational action and rational desire? One possibility is that he shares the currently widespread scepticism about criticism of values: the belief that each person has his own set of values, his own style of living and acting, and that no one can criticize it objectively. A proper retort to this might be: 'Is showing that a person's values would be different if he had undergone cognitive psychotherapy not a showing that they are in an important sense mistaken? If not, why not? Is there anything that you would conceivably accept as a successful showing that a desire or action is in an important sense mistaken?' A second possible source is a view at the opposite pole: the view that we all know a set of values and principles for action, and that showing what a person would want or choose to do if he were rational is only a feeble affirmation as compared with what we know. The proper response to this is the arguments of Chapter 1, to the effect that: even the learned among us lack self-evident knowledge of truths on these matters; that neither the most careful scrutiny of the ordinary uses of central normative words (ideally disclosing how scientific support for, or at last coercive argument about, normative statements can proceed), nor deliberation in 'reflective equilibrium', will yield knowledge of the kind intended. Maybe the account of what it is rational to want or do fails to give the answer to all our questions; but there is no other authoritative body of knowledge which can do so.

Given that the conceptual framework and source of puzzlement may differ from person to person, is there anything which may help with this possible puzzlement? There is one thing that can be done and which I shall do—that is point to some facts which will recommend rational action and rational desire to everyone or virtually everyone. In other words, I shall cite some facts, awareness of which will make the reader more favourably disposed towards rational action and desire; motivate him to some degree to try to do the rational thing; make him tend to lose interest in goals which are known to be irrational for him, and to want to conform his desires and aversions to what they would be if he were rational.

If these remarks have their intended effect on some readers, then for them 'It is rational to do A' and 'It is rational to desire O' will acquire recommending force. Then 'rational', in my sense, would be both a descriptive term, and a recommending term. In the latter respect it would then be like 'ought' and 'good' and 'best reasons' (in the uses relevant here), although these are unlike 'rational' in my usage in not having any definite descriptive meaning.

1. THE FORCE OF KNOWING WHAT IS RATIONAL TO DO (DESIRES TAKEN AS THEY ARE)

The facts which recommend rational action (as a first approximation—with desires taken as given, as they are) are slightly different from those which recommend rational desire, and they should be examined separately. I begin with the former. What I shall do is cite some considerations which will confer recommending force on 'It is rational to do A' for everyone who understands them.

The first point to be made is that very few people would advocate no use of facts and logic in the guidance of action. The only question is about the precise role of facts and logic, and how far their use should go and be authoritative for action.

We can imagine a world in which information and logic were not used at all in the guidance of action. Suppose 'human beings' had no memories, and hence could not anticipate from past experience the probable consequences of actions, and hence could not guide behaviour by anticipation of its outcomes. Suppose further that the mental processes of these beings were all free associations and that, in line with a pure ideo-motor theory of action, they forthwith performed any action the idea of performing which happened to pop into their heads. In this world action could not be controlled by rational expectation about outcomes, and the distinction between impulsive and reflective action would not be made.

Actually we are beings who know that we exist through time and will have future experiences, know something of the causal order of nature so that we can anticipate the probable outcomes of our behaviour; who have at one time many desires and aversions which draw us towards or repel us from anticipated outcomes of possible actions; and whose momentary impulses to act can be inhibited by reflection on other possible actions and their probable outcomes. We thus both can and do make a clear distinction between an impulse action and a considered one, and at the furthest remove from an impulsive action is the one which has been maximally considered, on which all relevant knowledge has had its impact.

It is a fact that people are uncomfortable if a decision they make turns out to have distressing consequences, when they know it would have been avoided by fuller or more careful reflection. For instance, if one buys a car which turns out to hold the road poorly and to consume large quantities of petrol, and if one knows one could have anticipated these facts by perusing an easily available copy of *Consumers Reports*, one is quite annoyed with oneself. Moreover, we can assume that people generally want to avoid mistakes of this sort. Now a rational action is by definition one which avoids all mistakes deriving from inadequate reflection. So will one not want to do the rational thing?

A person might be moved to avoid only some kinds of mistake, for example about the most efficient means to his identified goals. But it is arbitrary for him to stop deliberation at that point, short of all relevant facts, short of bringing to mind all outcomes which might bring out and engage his desires, short of determining all the options for action and which sets of outcome appeal to him more than which other sets, and so on. So, whether one brings only a few facts to bear on the decision, or all those that are relevant in the sense that it would make a difference if one did, is a matter of doing the job half-way or doing it fully. If one favours deliberation at all, must one not go on to favour fully deliberate action, of the kind I am calling 'rational'?

A second line of reasoning which will add to the recommending force of 'It is rational to . . .', is as follows: Everyone has desires. Acting on the basis of full vivid information (= rational action) is the policy which may be expected to satisfy the system of desires as fully as possible. Why? Awareness of all the options for action secures that there is no other action beyond ones considered, which might have satisfied desires more fully. Awareness of all the outcomes assures that one is repelled by all the aversive outcomes of one option, and attracted by all the positive outcomes of another. This prevents choosing one option when satisfaction of one's desires would have been fuller with another. Attention to the 'addition' of increments to action-tendencies has the effect that various desires receive attention corresponding to their intensity in the choice among action-options; and the same for avoiding the mistake of discounting the future. And it will hardly be questioned that one's choices should be affected by right estimates of the probability of certain outcomes, given certain actions.

In summary, then, by acting rationally (= avoiding cognitive defects at the moment of decision) we assure that our desires, present and future, are satisfied as fully as possible in the circumstances, irrespective of what they are. By showing that a given action is rational, then, by implication we show that it is chosen by a procedure fitted to maximize satisfaction of desires for the agent. Thus the showing that an action is rational must recommend the act—to any agent, since every agent is an agent with desires. The showing does not accidentally recommend to some people; when we consider that all agents are creatures with desires, it recommends of *necessity*.

The argument has not been: there is a premiss, justified by intuition, definition, or reflective equilibrium, to the effect that the best thing to do is to act so as to satisfy desires maximally, and therefore that an action with this effect is best. Use of such an argument with a normative generalization as a premiss is precisely what the reasoning of the present book is intended to avoid. Rather, the argument has been: (1) the policy of acting rationally is apt to result, in the long run, in maximizing the satisfaction of desires—that set of outcomes occurring which an agent prefers to all other sets; (2) hence the policy of rational actions can be recommended successfully to agents, because if the theory described in Chapter 3 is correct they do aim to satisfy their desires maximally, as they are at any given time.

2. THE FORCE OF KNOWING WHAT IT IS RATIONAL TO WANT

A recommendation of doing the rational thing (as a first approximation, with actual desires taken as given) is of course no answer to some other questions a sceptic may raise: 'Why should I *want* only those things it is rational in your sense to want?' and 'Why should I *do* those things it would be rational for me to do if my wants and aversions were rational?' I shall deal in turn with each of these sceptical questions. (I shall take an answer to the first question to constitute an answer to the question whether one should enjoy only what it is rational to enjoy.)

In answer to these questions I shall argue that there are considerations awareness of which will incline every person to want just those things it is rational to want, and to favour doing just those things it would be rational for him to do if his wants and aversions were all rational.

But first it is interesting to note that similar questions might be raised if we supposed it possible to know, in some other way than by determining what it is rational to want in my sense, which possible outcomes are good or worthwhile in themselves. For there is no definitional connection between being good in itself, and either action or desire. Philosophers sometimes take it for granted that a person should seek only what is intrinsically good, but there is no contradiction in conceding that something (e.g. knowledge) is good, but in saying that one is not interested and hence sees no point in seeking it. Ought a person, at least, to desire everything that is good in itself? If 'ought' and 'good' both name un-analysable notions, obviously there can be a question. Even if one defines 'desirable' in an 'ideal observer' fashion much as Sidgwick did, as what a person with full knowledge and vivid imagination would desire, there can be a question why a person ought to desire it. Why ought I to desire what I would desire if I were fully informed and vividly imaginative? One could adopt a view in which these gaps could not be present. For instance, one might take the 'internalist' view that to say something is desirable is in part to express an actual desire and some readiness to act; and if this view is correct, then a person could hardly sensibly say 'This is desirable but ought I to desire it or act as if I did?' At least this question would require a great deal of explanation. But this view, while it closes one gap, opens other problems. For instance, another person can say 'You say (and doubtless correctly from your point of view) that X is desirable, but ought I to desire it?' With this view, again, it is not clear how we would raise a question we all do want to raise: 'Although I know I desire X, is X really desirable?'

Let us now turn to our own problem, how we can recommend to persons the things I have said we can recommend. I begin with how we can recommend *wanting* what it is rational to want.

Let us begin by noting a parallel with beliefs. We know that people do not like having beliefs which they know to be inconsistent with one another, or even just arbitrary. Psychological literature under the title of 'cognitive dissonance theory' (e.g. Festinger, 1957) assembles evidence to support this, showing that a person's awareness of the incoherence of his total set of beliefs and experiences is uncomfortable, and motivates activity to remove the 'dissonance'. The distaste for incoherence does not seem to be simply practical concern that some false belief might produce false predictions of events, reliance on which could be personally costly. Even when the incoherence involves purely theoretical beliefs, such as theories of the origin of the universe or about the relation of mental events to the brain, people are uncomfortable about it and motivated to remove it.

The discomfort and motivating force of 'dissonance' do not, however, arise solely from awareness of incoherence of beliefs. Dissonance theorists, at any rate, claim that they also arise from awareness that actions are discrepant with beliefs about the values of objectives; or from awareness that one is afraid although there are only friends in the vicinity—apparently awareness that this is conditioned fear in a situation where there is no objective threat. (Festinger, 1957, p. 13.)

Irrational desires are very similar to incoherent beliefs and conditioned but unjustified fears. If we survey types of irrational desires, we remember that they are desires which develop from false beliefs; or from the artificial process of culture transmission in the sense I have explained; or from unfortunate experiences during childhood which are uncharacteristic of the way things normally are; or from childhood deprivations. By definition 'irrational' desires are one and all ones that the person would lose if he repeatedly reminded himself of known facts about himself or the world. As such, they contrast sharply with desire and aversions that have developed from sensitive interaction with the world, from discovery of what one likes or dislikes at first hand.

The proposal here is that awareness of the fact that one has irrational desires works in a way similar to awareness that one has incoherent beliefs or unjustified fears. One is made uncomfortable by the awareness, and is motivated to remove its source. I am not offering any reason why this should be the case. I am asserting that, as a fact, people—including the reader—do dislike having to think that their desires are irrational in my sense, not derived from sensitive reaction with the real world, but the accidents of past experience or 'manipulations' of the socializing process. People in fact prefer rational desires, just as they do justified or coherent beliefs. (Birk and Birk, 1974.)

Since they do have this preference, a showing that a desire is rational will be a recommendation: a showing that it is irrational a discommendation.

A second consideration will make people favour having only rational desires, when they think of it—what can be called a 'pragmatic' consideration. The fact is that both irrational desires and irrational versions are apt to be costly, or to stand in the way of benefits, in one way or another. I begin with irrational aversions, which are the more serious culprits.

Irrational *aversions* are of various types. The type on which I wish to concentrate is aversions to situations which in fact one would quite like if one were in them. For instance, one might not want to become a garage mechanic because one has learned from one's parents that it is a low-status occupation which a person with one's education and talents need not enter, and which would be a 'step down'. In fact, however, if one were in that occupation one might like it, whereas one might strongly dislike the recommended alternative, say teaching economics.

All such aversions seem to be sheer loss: they are sources of distress, because of the anxiety aroused at the prospect of the aversive situation. There is the time, effort or expenditure involved in avoidance. There is no gain in the avoidance, since one succeeds only in avoiding situations one would not dislike if one were in them. Indeed, there may be loss of enjoyment in not being in them—for instance, an aversion to dogs cuts one off from all the satisfactions pertaining to interaction with friendly and supportive animals. There is no pleasure of anticipation—there is at best only relief at learning that one is not going to be in the aversive situation. Nor is there pleasant daydreaming about not being in aversive situations. It would seem that the fewer the aversions of this type, the better.

Irrational aversions seem at least mostly to be of this type, since by definition they are ones that would extinguish in cognitive psychotherapy, which will not be the case if experience with the aversive situation is typically unpleasant. Irrational aversions are not built on first-hand experience with, or adequate information about, situations or experiences which are unpleasant.

With irrational *desires* the picture is less bleak. If a person does desire some situation, however irrationally, he is apt to enjoy its occurrence to some extent, to experience some pleasure of anticipation, even some pleasure in daydreaming about its realization. But the very fact of the irrationality of the desire restricts the possible benefit from the goal. For irrational desires could not derive from enjoyments of typical examples of the kind of thing wanted, or else they would not extinguish in cognitive psychotherapy; and hence the expectation must be that the enjoyment level of the situation wanted will, at best, in the normal case be low.

There is a further possible problem with irrational desires, suggested by the Epicureans, although their concept of 'unnatural' and 'unnecessary' pleasure is different from my concept of irrational desire. The Epicureans suggested that satisfaction of irrational desires may tend to be costly. Take reputation or high achievement. If one wants a monument erected in one's honour, one has to do something difficult—make a large gift, achieve a major and difficult scientific break-through, risk or actually lose one's life in battle. It is at least worth considering whether the rational (and simple) desires may not be satisfied at relatively less cost.

It is clear from earlier discussions (p. 84 f.) that probably everyone with an adequate conceptual scheme (with the concept of long-range happiness) will take a positive interest in his net happiness over a lifetime, and hence the above facts about the consequences of irrational desires or aversions will lead to disfavouring irrational desires or aversions in himself. If a person is benevolent, he will also deprecate such desires or aversions in others.

The considerations discussed above should also tend to dispel the gloom a person might feel over failure to attain wanted but irrational goals. It is not a causal necessity that they will: one can want someone to return one's affection when one knows quite well than only unhappiness can come of it. But when a person can both tell himself that a certain desire is irrational (in my sense) and also that the foregoing things are true of irrational desires, we may expect sadness at disappointed aspirations to diminish. Why? Because sadness at non-attainment of a goal is a response to a belief that something valuable was not attained, or that some loss occurred, especially if very easily matters could have been otherwise. But it will be hard to convince oneself that there has been a loss of something of value, when the desire for it is recognized as having been irrational in the first place—and these other things true of it as well.

The reader may have recognized that the foregoing recommendation of rational desires depends on the prevalence of other desires: of a desire to avoid the discomfort of 'dissonance' or of desires being founded on cognitive mistakes of some sort, and of the desire to be happy in the long run. So the argument might be said to be: You do in fact want to avoid the discomfort of dissonance and you do want long-term happiness. Having rational and not irrational desires is a necessary condition of (or at least helps in) avoiding dissonance and unhappiness. Therefore you should be favourable towards rational desires and take an unfavourable attitude towards irrational ones. Of course, if you are uninterested in happiness or avoiding dissonance, the 'argument' does not work.

There is another question: whether a person should take some trouble to rid himself of irrational desires, perhaps seek professional assistance to that purpose. A person might, or course, recognize the irrationality of one of his desires, and rather dislike having it on that account, but not take steps to get rid of it. Should he? There is no reason why the kind of reflection described in Chapter 4 should not be employed to reach a rational decision on the point. Among the costs of extinguishing the desire are the time and expense required; among the benefits are the favourable impact on long-term happiness, and, of course, the absence of a desire which is disliked for itself because it is founded on a mistake.

3. SHOULD ONE ACT AS IF ONE'S DESIRES WERE RATIONAL?

Let us turn now to our final question: whether a person has reason to perform the 'fully rational' act, that is, the act he would (if rational to a first approximation) perform if his desires were fully rational, even if his desires are by no means fully rational. Should I perform acts of compulsive ambition, or should I omit them, in view of the fact that compulsive ambition is irrational?

One might say that the question has no point, since on my own showing (Chapter 3) what a person does is a function of his actual desires, and certainly not of ones he does not have. This inference from the theory of action, however, is misleading. It is true that action is a function of one's desires at the time of action, but we must remember also, from Chapter 3, that the force of a desire is a function also of the degree of representation of the object wanted; and degree of representation can be manipulated. Further, the success of a desire in controlling behaviour will depend on the presence of other also-desired outcomes at the time of action, and a person may be in a position now to control that situation. Suppose I think now that my rational desires may not be strong enough to control action at a later time. If my rational desire now is strong enough to control behaviour now, I can devise a strategy so that it can do so later. I can arrange now, when the irrational desire is weak and the rational one strong, that later, when the irrational desire is strong, either the conduct it would normally instigate cannot occur, or that it will not occur because of uncomfortable barriers in the way. For instance, like Ulysses, I can have myself strapped to a mast so that it is physically impossible to succumb to the blandishments of the Sirens. At a less grand level, if I wish not to smoke, I can see to it that there are no cigarettes in the house so that in the evening when the desire for a cigarette would normally overwhelm my firmest resolution, I can indulge myself only after a cold walk to a store. Or, if I know in what circumstances an irrational desire will begin to gather strength, I can prepare a plan to fill my mind with thoughts of the dangers or disadvantages of the act at an optimal moment in the future, thus, among other things, preventing the delicious image of the outcome from attaining the degree of vividness which would bring the desire for it to its fullest strength. Manuals of self-help or self-control are full of advice to smokers, alcoholics, compulsive eaters; and their advice can be transposed for use with any irrational desire.

Irrational desires, then, at least can often be prevented from erupting into action. But there are circumstances in which it would be irrational to stifle an irrational desire, if the desire is so strong that the individual would be made deeply unhappy, perhaps even neurotic, by its suppression. Let us consider an example. Suppose the friendship and admiration of a certain group of persons (writers, artists, or philosophers, etc.) is extremely important to a person. Suppose further that the individual is justifiably convinced that this value is a vestige of a disadvantaged childhood, in which he suffered from being ignored by the circle of peers whom he most respected; and suppose he is convinced that, everything considered, the desire is an irrational one. Nevertheless, such a person might also conclude that the desire is so deep-seated in him that it would extinguish only after lengthy professionally conducted psychotherapy which he cannot afford. Suppose he then asks himself whether it would be rational for him to contract a marriage which, because of the race or religion of the other individual, would cost him the friendship or admiration of the persons whose regard he craves. The realistic fact is that his desire, rational or not, is going to be with him. Is it rational in the circumstances for him to accommodate himself to it, and avoid making himself unhappy by frustrating it? In this case, it may be rational to avoid the effects of suppressing the desire and thus to do what it would not be rational to do if he did not have this irrational desire.

Are there considerations, however, which for the normal case, will recommend to a person his taking steps, if he can, to avoid acting on the basis of a desire he knows to be irrational, even though he still has the desire? If he thinks his compulsive achievement motivation is irrational, are there any reasons which will dispose him to avoid expressing this motivation in behaviour? Of course there are: any reason there is for wanting to be rid of irrational desires is also a reason for avoiding action motivated by an irrational desire. For if a desire is founded on a 'cognitive mistake', it carries the mistake with it into the action it motivates: we have to say the action was founded on a cognitive mistake if the motivating desire is so. Thus, if the existence of a desire known to be irrational leads to uncomfortable 'dissonance', so will the action based on it. And if the existence of irrational aversions tends to lead to unhappiness, so does action based on them—indeed, it was largely the welfare effects of action on irrational aversions that was the basis of my claim that for an aversion to be recognized as irrational is necessarily for a dis-commendation to have been made.

Part II

CHAPTER IX

THE CONCEPT OF A MORAL CODE

AT THE beginning of this book it was promised that there would be discussion of both the main questions which philosophers concerned with practical matters have considered: questions about the *good*, and questions about the *morally right* or *morality*. The remainder of this book will be devoted essentially to the second question.

How shall we criticize, or justify, moral principles? We recall that the conclusions of Chapter I initially seemed to make difficult the criticism and justification of any normative principle. For they ruled out appeal to ordinary linguistic usage as the source of the normative concepts to be used. If only we could have relied on ordinary linguistic usage to give us a concept of the morally right, then our task would have been the more circumscribed one of establishing some principles about the morally right in that sense. In the second place, the conclusions of Chapter I ruled out appeal to our moral 'intuitions', even those in some sort of 'reflective equilibrium', as a check on either the concept or the substantive principles of the morally right. How then are we to proceed?

The preceding chapters have contained the story of how one can surmount the parallel problem for questions about what is intrinsically desirable and about what is the best thing to do from the agent's point of view. But there the problem was somewhat simpler, there being a natural way to construe these basic terms. For we do make choices, and we do have desires. And it is easy to see that a person might well wonder when a choice, or a desire, is as fully guided by available information as it possibly can be. And it is plausible then to argue that our normative questions are best construed as questions about what a fully 'rational' person would, on the one hand, *choose*, and on the other hand, *want*. In the case of the morally right, there is no obviously relevant human activity the guidance of which by facts and reason is what we are asking for when we raise questions about the morally right and wrong. We shall see in the end, however, that the normative problems about right and wrong can be construed as very like those about the good and the best thing to do.

Before we can inquire how a moral code may be criticized or justified, we must first establish what is 'the morality' or 'moral code' of a person or a society. In order to do this we can simply ask ourselves what instructions we might give an anthropologist embarking on a field trip to investigate the moral code of a primitive people, in detailing what he is to look for. Our instructions should explain the difference between the moral code of a society, on the one hand, and its customs and the 'norms' of its institutions on the other. There are, ideally, some rather fine lines to be drawn, although it will become clear as we proceed that any mistake we might make here can be rectified, for practical purposes, at a later stage.

1. THE NATURE OF A SOCIAL MORAL SYSTEM

It is agreed that virtually all societies, if not all, have systems of constraints on behaviour different from legal ones. I am going to describe one of these fully in the present section (others more briefly in the following one) and call it 'the moral code' of a society.

What is the 'social moral code'? For a group to have a certain moral code is for something to be true of individuals in the group. So let us begin with the moral code of the individual, what we may also call his 'conscience', taken broadly. One might initially be tempted to say that everyone has a moral code, but obviously that is not the case. Babies have not; and a child of three may refrain from raiding the refrigerator only because he knows such activity tends to produce a spanking. If so, we do not want to say that he has a moral code. In fact, some adults never seem to get beyond this level, and it is simpler to say they have no moral code at all, although if we wanted to we could say they do have one, but at a primitive level. What do they lack? I propose six features, and suggest that a person who has all six certainly has a moral code, and that normally adults do have all six; but we must concede that individuals differ considerably, and if someone lacks some of the following we may or may not say that he has a 'moral code', depending on our linguistic taste.

i. Intrinsic motivation. The person has occurrent intrinsic desires or aversions for acting (or failing to act) in certain ways, for instance, an aversion to breaking his promise, to injuring another person, or to failing to give him needed aid. These desires and aversions have different strengths. I am more averse to killing someone than to breaking a promise to attend a large tea party where I shall not be missed. They affect behaviour just as any instrinsic motivations do, according to the laws described in Chapter 3. Moreover, when an agent is asked about the reason for behaviour motivated by one of these, he will normally be able to cite the relevant valenced action: 'I did it because I would have been breaking my promise if I hadn't.'

When a person has an aversion to behaving in a certain way himself, he normally also has an aversion to other people behaving in that way. And, just as when he is averse to performing a certain action himself, he will develop an action-tendency to avoid that action when he sees that one of the things he might do is that very thing, so, if he thinks that another person is about to perform such an action, he will often develop some action-tendency to prevent him. (Although today there is also a 'moral' aversion to interfering with the behaviour of others, except to prevent injury.) The normal extension of aversion to oneself behaving in a certain way does not always extend to others behaving that way. Some kinds of behaviour are thought to be matters of 'personal standards' (e.g. some forms of sexual behaviour), and then the extension does not take place. Again, a person may be motivated to make large personal sacrifices for the sake of others and even averse to himself not doing so; but he is not averse to others failing to make them. Or, when his moral motivations conflict (e.g. aversion to breach of promise and to failing to give aid) and one is stronger and directs his conduct, he will often not expect, or want, the same desire/aversion to be stronger in another person in the same circumstances, or to direct his conduct then. (MacIntyre, 1957; Raphael, 1974–5.)

The most important of these intrinsic motivations—I am not saying that any of them is a necessary constituent of a moral code—is aversion to injuring others and failing to give aid, behind which is the basic motive of benevolence, discussed in Chapter 7. Benevolence we shall see is also important for teaching other moral motivations by the 'inductive' method (explaining to a child how some form of behaviour typically is injurious or helpful to others).

Some people are inclined to give first and even exclusive importance to another motivation: conscientiousness, in the sense of aversion to doing what is thought morally wrong. For they have thought that identifying which acts are morally right or wrong is primarily an intellectual matter, and that the important motivation, from the point of view of morality, is simply aversion to any action already identified as wrong. It is true that for most people coming to believe (by whatever method) that some possible action is morally required motivates them more strongly to perform that act; but in most if not all societies people are also independently motivated to avoid injuring others, keep promises, avoid certain forms of sexual behaviour, and so on. So we do not wish to regard conscientiousness as the only 'moral' motivation.

To be motivated, up to a 'standard' level, to perform or avoid certain actions is to have corresponding *traits of character*—a trait of character essentially being a standing desire/aversion of some sort. (Brandt, 1970.) So the just or truthful or conscientious person is precisely one motivated (up to a certain level) to act justly, tell the truth, and discharge his duty. (Not every trait of character is just motivation concerned with behaviour of a certain sort. Some are just desires/aversions directed at states of affairs, e.g. benevolence with the welfare or happiness of other people. Nor need a trait of character necessarily have to do with moral motivation: consider ambition or greed.)

ii. Guilt-feelings and disapproval. When a person acts contrary to such motivation, he feels uncomfortable: guilty or remorseful. And if another person acts contrary to an observer's motivation (acts in a way the observer is motivated to avoid), the observer will tend to have an anti-attitude towards him: annoyance, disgust, indignation, or resentment (in case he happens to be the victim of the agent's unacceptable action).[1] In sophisticated individuals and societies at least, only actions showing a deficient level of the relevant motivation evoke these responses. The reaction is not aroused if the behaviour occurred inadvertently, or as a result of unavoidable mistake about the facts of the situation, or if the person was at the time unable to do what he thought was right, and so on. In that case, the behaviour is 'excused'. But even if it is, the agent will normally feel uncomfortable about his act and offer some restitution if someone has been injured.

People do not like to have others disapprove of their behaviour; and, if a person knows others disapprove of what he did, he will feel some discomfort which we could also call 'feeling guilty'. (When people disapprove, they may act coldly towards one, or even engage in sanctions such as not giving a good recommendation for a position; so there are reasons beyond just the dislike of anti-attitudes why people wish to escape the disapproval of others.) Knowledge that others will disapprove increases the effectiveness of the moral code as a deterrent to behaviour; moreover, it plays a part in the acquisition of an individual's own moral code, through the process of conditioning. But it is confusing if we count a person's tendency to feel uncomfortable when he knows others disapprove as a part of *his* individual moral code—that is precisely what it is not. *His* moral code is evidenced by his autonomous guilt-feelings—those arising from failure to act in accord with his own moral motivation.

iii. Believed importance. Behaviour to which these motivations lead is thought by the individual to be important, so much so that he thinks it proper that some degree of coercion be brought on a person (perhaps only by the pressure of his own conscience) to induce the relevant form of behaviour in him. In contrast, people do not think others ought to feel threats of something unpleasant if they double-fault in tennis, or that any educative process

---

[1] P. F. Strawson (1974, Chap. 1) makes perceptive remarks on this and some following points. I do not underwrite the principal contentions in that paper.

should be summoned to make them feel guilty about their double-faults.

iv. Admiration or esteem. The reverse of the negative attitudes which others tend to have towards a person who shows a deficient degree of 'moral' motivation is esteem or admiration for a person who manifests in action one of the basic motivations to an unusually high degree. Take a highly considerate person who often acts in a kindly way in which most people would not think to act, or be motivated to act; or a soldier who falls on a live hand-grenade in order to protect his comrades; or a missionary who stays in a plague-ridden area to treat the stricken, when doing so was not one of the requirements of his position. In each of these cases an individual has acted in a socially desirable way beyond the call of duty, manifesting a level of relevant motivation beyond the standard falling short of which elicits disapproval. Such acts are sometimes called 'acts of supererogation'.

v. Special terminology. It is logically possible that an individual may have these intrinsic motivations, guilt-feelings, and so on, but have no linguistic devices specifically adapted to giving expression to them. In fact, however, all or virtually all societies have such devices: in English, terms like 'morally ought', 'morally reprehensible', 'moral obligation', the terminology of moral rights, and so on. It is not merely accidental that there are such devices. The moral code could hardly control interpersonal behaviour if individuals could not communicate the relevant motivations and feelings; and a special terminology is necessary for directing and articulating the basic motivations, as when an agent must think through whether his moral motivation is on balance in support of a bill before the legislature. I therefore add the existence of such a terminology as a fifth feature of what it is to have an individual moral code.

A moral code also requires a rather complex conceptual framework. For instance, a person must have and be able to apply certain concepts such as injury and promise. Moreover, he must have a conception of the consequences of actions (or omissions); and he must have the concept of other persons with states of enjoyment, pain, and desire. Without the latter a child cannot develop the motive of benevolence. Further, we know that people acquire moral motivations mostly by what psychologists call 'inductive methods', that is, by having pointed out the consequences of certain forms of behaviour for the good or ill of other people; hence the child who acquires these moral motivations must have the concept of a causal tendency.[2] A system of excuses, allowing for the discrimination of cases in which disapproval or admiration of an agent is inappropriate, requires yet another set of concepts: an agent's desires and aversions, his intentions, his anticipation of outcomes, inadvertence, mistakes of fact, and traits of character, among others.

vi. Believed justification. A final piece must be added to our conception of an individual moral code. The individual must think that his motivation, guilt-feelings, attitudes of approval, admiration, and disapproval of agents on account of their behaviour, and his estimates of the importance of the relevant forms of behaviour, are justified—not arbitrary but in some sense proper. What kind of 'justification' is wanted? I shall have a good deal to say later about what kind of justification people are looking for, and what they can reasonably get. We ought not to assume that people are clear in their own minds just what would count as a 'justification'. People do think that their morality is not just conventional; they think there are some considerations which would enable them to be intellectually comfortable with it, but normally do not know what these are and cannot even articulate the sort of thing they are looking for. One of the tasks of philosophy is to help get clear what the options are. An example of such justification is religion. If a religious person thinks his moral principles are requirements of God, then, given his structure of theological beliefs and his consequent attitudes towards God (reverence, love, obedience), he may be satisfied with his morality and think it rational for him to do what appears contrary to his long-range personal welfare.

In summary, for an individual to have a personal moral code is for him (1) to have intrinsic motivation for or against his, and to a large extent, others performing certain kinds of action; (2) to experience guilt-feelings when his action shows a deficiency of such motivation, disapproval when another person's does, and

[2] See Hoffman, 1970, for an excellent survey of contemporary knowledge about the acquisition of moral standards. For an interesting speculation see Kohlberg, 1969 and 1971.

admiration or esteem when another person's actions show a super-abundance of such motivation; (3) to think the forms of behaviour he is motivated to perform or feels guilty about not performing (etc.) are important; (4) to think his attitudes of all the foregoing types are justified; and (5) to have the linguistic capability to give all this verbal expression.

In later chapters I shall occasionally depart somewhat from this conception of a 'moral code'. That is, I shall often use 'a person's moral code' to refer only to the *conative-emotional components* of the above, namely (1) and (2). I shall then be free to talk of a person's belief that his moral code (in that sense) is justified, and to talk of a person's normative statements as expressing his moral code. It will be clear in context in which sense I am using the expression, and I trust no one will find the dual usage confusing. The reason for having both usages will be clear. We shall see why it is important to have a usage referring only to the conative-emotional components; but it is also true that we would hardly think a person had a moral code of the normal sort unless he believed his conative-emotional attitudes were justified in an appropriate way. It is perhaps less natural to say that a person has a moral code only if he has the linguistic capacity to express it; if a person does not want to include this concept in any definition of 'a person's moral code', I would not object. I include it because it is a fact and makes a neater package.

The foregoing account may be imperfect, perhaps because among other things it omits reference to personal ideals. But it has the advantage of being a formal conception: it defines 'moral code' without reference to any content. The concept, then, can be accepted by persons with very different personal codes. In fact, there seems no good reason why we should deny that this syndrome appears in all cultures: Greek, Hebrew, and contemporary Western.

The above depiction of a person's moral code is very different from a popular traditional picture, because of its conative-emotional emphasis. I have described a person's moral code as an internal monitor of behaviour: primarily as intrinsic desires or aversions directed at types of conduct, with corresponding feelings of guilt and attitudes of disapproval. In the traditional picture a person's moral code is primarily knowledge or at least belief about which kinds of action are morally right or wrong, with motivation and emotion appearing as responses to this knowledge. Thus, in the traditional picture the intellectual component is causally primary; conative-emotional phenomena are responses to it. Traditional writers have generally found the conative-emotional side of moral experience not very important, and have had relatively little to say about it. What they wanted to know is how to justify the intellectual component, the beliefs about what is right or wrong.

This book is hardly the place to dilate upon the disastrous problems of the intellectualist picture, to which the last century of moral philosophy bears testimony. On the one hand it has not been possible for intellectualists to give a convincing account of what the alleged prior beliefs are supposed to be about, or of the reasoning by which they can be supported or confirmed.[3] A source of these problems, as we saw in Chapter 1, is just that ordinary normative concepts are vague and obscure; and when they are such, obviously there is bound to be a problem about how to support them. For present purposes, however, it is more important to notice how unconvincing the intellectualist picture of human conscience is, from a psychological point of view. The theory supposes that the conative-emotional response is a response to a moral judgement (e.g. that to do A would be wrong), but it is puzzling how there could be such a response when the judgement ('A would be wrong') to which it is supposed to be a response is so vague and obscure. Actually, it seems that what we respond to is primarily the thought that a certain act would be the telling of a lie or injuring someone. That is what is repugnant, not the thought that the action would be wrong. Or, when we reflect on having injured another person it is the thought of how we injured him that elicits remorse or guilt-feeling; it is not the thought that what we did was wrong. Indeed, 'is wrong' is the same predicate in all situations, and it would seem that if the conative-emotional response is just to that, it would be identical in all situations, whereas in fact it appears that the conative-emotional response differs from one case to another, according to the character of the situation (how much injury, how egregious a lie, what kind of promise). It looks, then, as if the intellectualist tradition had things

[3] I have reviewed these problems in 1959, Chaps. 7 and 8.

backwards in viewing moral motivation and guilt-feelings and disapproval as parasitic on beliefs or knowledge that acts are or would
be wrong, and hence a secondary phenomenon. We need not be
alarmed, then, about disparity between the intellectualist tradition
and the above picture of human conscience.

In a given society individuals' moral codes will very largely be
the same. There are differences; there were even in primitive
societies. In our own society, individuals disagree about the
propriety of nude intermingling of the sexes at a beach, or about
the propriety of smoking marijuana; but we do not disagree about a
list of central things (most of the things punished by the criminal
law) such as murder, armed robbery, kidnapping, assault, rape,
infanticide, child-abuse, breach of promise; as well as failure to
render assistance in the dire need of another when this can
be given at negligible cost to oneself, and so on.

The similarity or overlapping of individual moral codes allows us
to define 'the moral code' of a given society, by listing all types
of behaviour enjoined or prohibited by the moral code of at least
one person, and then arranging the items on the list in order
according to the frequency with which they appear in the individual
moral codes in that society. We can then pick out those items which
are virtually universal among adults, and entitle them 'the social
moral code'. Another, equally useful, way of using this expression
would be to take the profile (percentage with an indication of the
range of intensities) for all the items, for the whole group, and
speak of this as 'the social moral code'. Usually I shall have the
former sense in mind when I use this term.

A 'social moral code' defined in this way has some similarities
to the criminal law. Both are systems of control of behaviour. The
law aims to prevent certain things (injury to persons, breach of
contract) just as the moral code does; these aims sometimes conflict and then a decision must be made over which is weightier
(a 'justified' act is not penalized). Both have a system of excuses,
mitigating or exculpating at law—like pleas of insanity or ignorance
of fact. But the two systems differ in some ways. The criminal
law has no part corresponding to the approval of acts of supererogation. More important is the difference in motivation: the motivation of the moral man is primarily just basic desires and aversions
directed at certain forms of behaviour. It is true that normally

people are averse to breaking the law as such (respect for law), just as they are to doing anything believed to be immoral. But the legal system motivates primarily by threat of punishment. Furthermore, while actions can be made illegal by decision, behaviour cannot be made morally wrong by decision.

There is also a difference in the ways in which law and morality are 'in force'. If a law has been passed by the governing body, has not fallen into desuetude or been outlawed by the courts, it is the standard for individual behaviour on pain of punishment. If the law declares something illegal, the individual must regard it as such. If the social moral code declares something wrong, however, the individual need not infer that it is wrong. An individual will normally be disapproved of and criticized by others if he infringes the prohibition; but he need not regard the social code as fixing what his moral obligations really are. He may regard it as inconsistent, irrational, or unjustifiable, and regard what he does as right. If he expresses such a view, other persons may respect his individual code and not criticize him for following it, although of course they may think his code is unjustified or inconsistent. The point is that the social moral code does not define what is morally right for an individual in the way in which the law defines what is legally right for the individual.[4]

Should we define 'social moral code' so that no prohibition or requirement is part of it unless it is well known among adults of the society that the prohibition or requirement obtains? In other words, must a social moral code be publicly known? It is beyond doubt that in fact most widely shared features of a moral code are well known, especially those enforced at law, such as the prohibition of murder and assualt, and so on; but it also seems evident that features of what I have been calling the social moral code may not be publicly known. Suppose it is generally believed that it is part of the moral code in the State of Michigan that homosexual contacts, adultery, incest, and perhaps abortion are prohibited, but that a carefully conducted survey of individual views shows that not more than 50 per cent of the adults disapprove of these forms of behaviour. Presumably we would then want to say that

---

[4] For interesting claims that some of these contrasts are unduly simple, and for references to the literature, see C. D. Johnson, 1975a, 1975b.

these things do not belong in the moral code; for evidently it being generally believed that something is disapproved of is insufficient to make the prohibition part of the code. Suppose, again, that people are asked whether individuals in Michigan disapprove of breaking into a queue for tickets for a popular film, and their answer is doubtful, indicating that it is not publicly known whether this behaviour is disapproved of; but suppose further that a careful survey shows that virtually everyone does disapprove. Would we not then say that this prohibition is part of the code? It seems convenient to define 'social moral code' so that it is not necessary for some prohibition to be a matter of public knowledge, in order for it to belong to the code. I shall use the term accordingly. Of course, some of the benefit of a moral code is lost when it is not public: a deterrent effect of the prospect of disapproval by others requires knowledge that the contemplated conduct is disapproved. Normally, most of the social moral code is public; but it is needless to require publicity as part of the definition.

Little has been said so far about how an individual acquires his moral code. However, we get a better view of the nature of a moral code by seeing how we come by it, and I shall therefore sketch a few outlines, although a full account would be quite complex.[5] I will mention two things: acquisition of the basic motivations, and of tendencies to have guilt-feelings. First the former. Since these are after all desires and aversions, the account of their genesis will incorporate principles involved (Chapter 5) in the development of desires and aversions in general, and in particular the principles of classical conditioning. Not all moral motives are acquired in the same way. In particular, the concern to help and not injure others is virtually identical with benevolence, the genesis of which I have already discussed in Chapter 7; whereas if the aversions to breach of promise and theft are learned by the 'inductive method' (showing the unfavourable effects on welfare), they must be regarded as 'secondary' motives or incentives as a result of association with thought of these ill effects. But there are still other processes. For one thing, it seems likely that for a deeply religious person the example of Jesus, the commandments of God, or the story of God's dealings with the Jewish people may play a large role in the learning of some moral motivation. Again, an aversion to homo-

[5] See Martin Hoffman, 1970, for a review.

sexual behaviour is hardly learned like the aversion to injuring other persons, and cannot well be learned by the 'inductive' process (since it is not usually supposed that anyone is harmed by it). How then is it learned? Here apparently we must appeal to the principle of direct conditioning, or to 'identification', or to the effect via conditioning of the suggestions by teachers (parents, peers, etc.) that homosexual relationships are horrible in some unspecified way. Of course different processes may be combined in producing these outcomes, in different ways for different items of the code—and perhaps differently with different parents who may utilize diverse techniques of 'socialization'.

The learning of tendencies to feel guilt or feel remorse is a different story, since at least some of them are not a natural part of the basic intrinsic aversions and desires—not in the way in which a feeling of disappointment is a natural consequence of frustration of a desire. (Disappointment is, as we saw in Chapter 2, lawfully or even definitionally related to desire.) Since what we call 'guilt-feelings' are not identical in quality, they may require different types of causal explanation. Remorse, for instance, may be classified as a guilt-feeling; but it seems to be a direct and 'natural' response to the perceived situation (just as feeling fear is a natural response to thinking one's life is in danger), in this case a response to regarding oneself as the cause of injury to a sentient creature one does not want injured and with whom one empathizes and who perhaps is responding with resentment to the injury. Different from remorse are guilt-feelings about actions with no identifiable observable victim—say actions with no victim at all, such as is the case with some sexual offences, or when the victim is some corporate entity with whom one cannot empathize, as in the case of theft from a corporation or perjury on an income tax return. How do we get these feelings? The guilt-feelings are apparently not just anxiety about punishment. One possibility is that we have a basic response (like fear of danger) to the expressed disapproval of others or to their expressed unfavourable inferences about character. This 'natural' guilt-feeling response may then become conditioned to the behaviour (or to the thought that it occurred). We could go further back and say that the 'natural' guilt-feeling is itself an anxiety-feeling conditioned to expressions of disapproval because of past associations with punishment or the withdrawal of affection by parents. It is probably important to the child's reactions/attitudes that he does not perceive the punishment or disapproval of others just as an arbitrary annoyance at his behaviour on the part of others. He learns that the others regard their moral standards as having some justification, and that these standards are ones to which the teachers subject their own conduct as well as being ones to which the conduct of children is expected to conform.

The foregoing proposal of what it is for there to be a 'social moral code' is not intended to win any normative battles. The question is completely open whether a particular moral code of that kind is a good one and whether fully rational persons would support it for a society in which they expected to live. If anyone feels that his favourite moral principle is somehow excluded by the definition, he can re-introduce it under another name; in fact, I should be happy to let him take 'morality' and 'moral principle' and I shall use 'system of internal constraints on behaviour' or something of the sort. The terminology certainly does not exclude the possibility that his policy for action is a good one, perhaps the best. I have defined 'moral code' as I have because the present world has a cultural structure of the kind I have described and it seems useful to employ 'moral code' to refer to it.

Philosophers have debated at length in recent years about the proper use of 'morality', 'moral judgement', and 'morally ought'. Evidently some believe that certain normative arguments are strengthened if some principles are made analytic by the use of 'moral', e.g. if egoism does not qualify as a morality at all, or if a social rule is a mere taboo and not a moral principle unless it is somehow important for human welfare. But it should be clear by now that such arguments cannot succeed. Why should the egoist care whether, in good English, his view should be classified as a morality?[6]

2. MORAL CODES AND INSTITUTIONAL EXPECTATIONS

A society has cultural features rather like its moral code, with

[6] See Peter Singer, 1973.

corresponding dispositions in the individual: codes of etiquette, custom, honour, and so on. The phenomena are so similar that in some cases they are not easy to distinguish. (Anyone who thinks my definition of a 'moral code' admits rules of etiquette as 'moral' need not be alarmed, since we shall see later that rational persons would presumably not support sanctioning such rules as if they were moral principles.) There is one structure that is different from a moral code but likely to be confused with it, and in this case it is important to make the distinction: *institutional expectations*, which sociologists sometimes call 'role norms'.

I shall use the term 'institution' to refer to organized groups, of which a family, a university, a church, or General Motors would be paradigm examples. This usage differs from that which takes monogamous marriage, Christianity, and capitalism as paradigm cases; I prefer to refer to these as 'cultural forms' in the society. Obviously the two phenomena are closely related.

Let us first observe that all institutions in my sense (educational, political, religious, economic) comprise individuals who occupy distinguishable nameable positions, with which certain privileges and duties are associated. In other words, in organizations individuals occupy nameable offices, and, as such, are expected to do certain things (their jobs); and in return they expect that certain things will be done for them by others. The individuals occupying these positions co-operate in an organization which as a whole confers benefits on people—its members, other persons, society. People conforming to role-expectations constitute the working of the system; the members of an organization roughly know how the system works and what their contribution is.

Consider a university. The benefits provided by the organization are such things as education, research, and scholarly publication. It includes various different offices: student, president, professor, librarian, and so on. The professor is expected to do certain things such as teach a specified number of courses, assign marks, hold office hours. Who expects these things? Primarily the other members of the organization. However, we must not regard matters as more structured than they are. The By-laws of the Regents may set forth the central expectations which can be legally enforced (although few faculty members have ever read them); the faculty code sets out other widely recognized expectations; but other matters are less clear. Professors and students may have different views about what proper professorial activity involves, e.g. how many office hours, whether professors are to hand out mimeographed lecture outlines, whether lectures should be written out. Professors find out what the norms are, partly from recollection of their own observations as students, partly from reading codes, and partly from conversation with colleagues. It is not easy to find what some groups in the organization expect; one may easily defeat student expectations because there are so many and it is not so easy to find out what they are accustomed to.

What motivates a professor to do what he is expected to do? Neglect of his central duties may cost him his salary. Neglect of other things will cost him the esteem of his colleagues and students. Some professors are devoted to the institution, which may be their alma mater. Others care about students and want to contribute to their education. Some enjoy the work. Others are motivated by moral considerations: accepting a post is tantamount to promising to do the job, thereby incurring the moral obligation of a promise; further, accepting a salary binds one in fairness to doing something which merits the reward.

Obviously these job-expectations differ completely from the morality of the society. If a parent failed to tell his children that at the local university the professors are expected to teach two courses per semester, he could hardly be accused of failing to teach them morality. And the same applies if he did not teach his daughter anything about the role norms of housewives.

There is, however, some similarity between a person's attitude towards the expectations of his role, and his personal moral code. Normally a person is intrinsically motivated to discharge the duties of his job and will feel uncomfortable if he fails, for whatever reason. Most people want to be good professors or good whatever-it-is they are; that is tied to their ego-ideal. Their performance is thought important; it is considered properly to affect decisions about salary. We use much the same language to describe it as about behaviour regarded as a matter of morals: 'duty', 'obligation', 'responsibility'.

But there are differences. A person need not think that the 'norm' for his position is justified: a professor may think formal lectures a bad thing, but they are his job until the Faculty or Regents vote otherwise. Nor do other people generally disapprove of a person's not coming up to expectation. The others in the organization will, but not necessarily the general public.

There are some similarities, then, between a moral code and an institutional expectation or duty or obligation; but there are also marked differences.[7]

Once this difference is clear, we are free to say, if we wish, that rational persons would prefer one moral code over another for a given society, because its currency would have better consequences in view of the institutional expectations in that society. For instance, we might want to say that 'Children should care for their elderly parents' would be part of an optimal moral code for a society, given the whole system of institutional duties and expectations surrounding the family—an imperative supporting what is already expected and in most but not all cases already being done. If the concept of an institutional expectation were not distinct from that of the social moral code, it would make no sense to say that a given moral code should be preferred, if in view of the existing institutions it would do most good. Of course, we also want to be able to say sensibly that a preferred moral code would require change in some existing institutions.

3. COULD A UNIVERSAL MORAL CODE BE EFFECTIVE?

Reflection on the above conception of a social moral code will inevitably raise the question: 'Could all people have the *same* moral code, as an internal, effective yet informal instrument of social control?' This question deserves exploration, since the above conception has some interesting but not widely understood implications for an answer.

The idea that one set of moral principles is universally binding has been attractive and persuasive to many people. W. D. Ross not only accepted the idea, but he believed he could essentially state

[7] The reader may be interested in J. A. Jackson (ed.), 1972, which discusses some controversial matters and refers to the important literature. Ralph Linton, 1936, Chap. 15, has a very sensible discussion of social systems.

the principles: there is a prima facie duty to keep promises, make reparations for wrongful injury, repay debts of gratitude, promote distribution of happiness in accordance with merit, improve one's own mind and character, improve the lot of others with respect not only to mind and character but also to enjoyment, and refrain from injuring others. (Possibly he needed to add some principles, including one about a prima facie duty to fulfil the expectations of one's role in an institution, when one has enjoyed its benefits or expects to do so.)[8]

Why might not one moral code be an effective and useful instrument of social control for all peoples? The question is whether principles abstract enough to be universally valid might be too abstract to function as an actual moral code—recalling that the items of a moral code are to be matters to which intrinsic motivation is to be connected, along with guilt-feelings, and so on. Ross's principles are certainly different from historical moral codes. Take the Ten Commandments. These enjoin people not to steal, commit adultery, or bear false witness, and require honouring one's father and mother; and every one of these acts presupposes a specific, local institutional or cultural structure—of private property, monogamous marriage, courts of law with sworn testimony, and a family structure with husband and wife sharing roughly equal status and one above that of any other family members. The Commandments are not suitable to be of world-wide application, for all social systems. (How might they be reformulated so as to serve that end?) Ross's principles are (at least some of them) much more abstract than actual codes. To try to teach some of his principles would be like putting up a sign in an aeroplane, saying 'Don't do anything offensive to other people who are not in a position to move out of range.' This sign would be ineffective as compared with 'No cigar smoking!' The latter is an implicate of the former for the specific situation of persons in an aeroplane, but the latter is an effective sign and the former is not.

What makes a moral code effective in a society? It must be suited to the level of intelligence and education of the society; so its

---

[8] For an interesting treatment of the relations between moral duties and institutional duties see Michael Stocker, 1970.

application must not demand logical facility beyond the capacities of all but potentially good scientists or philosophers. It must provide in detail for problems of frequent occurrence in the society, without the necessity for long trains of inference. It must not contain items too numerous to be taught by the methods (e.g. classical conditioning) which must be used to interiorize moral principles; so it will probably restrict itself to matters of some importance in the society. (Special 'codes of ethics' for physicians and lawyers seem to do this: they speak directly of complex situations with which the relevant persons are often faced, and give direction for these which do not require deduction from abstract principles.) It looks as if a working moral code must comprise a set of specific directives like 'No cigar smoking!' These directives might not guide people to do exactly what ideally anyone would like them to do, but they are the best that can be done by the instrument of a moral code.

It would be absurd to say that no moral principles which are suitable for universal application could function effectively in a moral code: prohibitions of injury to others and breach of promise (provided with suitable exceptions) are obvious examples. However, actual moral codes could hardly consist exclusively of such principles; an effective moral code will require principles only of local application. There is another concession that may be made to those who think the basic moral principles must be universally applicable. It is conceivable that there should be some stateable universally valid moral principles, which could serve as a moral code for intelligent, well-educated, logically acute persons, although not as a moral code for actual societies. Then we might deduce what would be the requirements of these abstract principles for a specific society, with its particular situation and its special institutions. We might then select some of these principles—the more important ones for that group—and teach them as the moral code for that society, and they might function very well. These principles would not, of course, be universally binding but their status, as being implied by universally valid principles for the specific situation, might be satisfying to philosophers who think moral principles should be binding for all if binding for any.[9]

[9] A useful paper which somewhat develops this conception is R. M. Hare, 1976.

The content of such principles, of course, would change from time to time, along with relevant modifications in the conditions of the society or the structure of its institutions.[10]

[10] One might ask how responsiveness to such changes might be arranged, since my description of a moral code is the description of a product and not of how the product will be modified to meet changing needs. In part, the answer to this question has already been provided. If moral motivation is taught, in good part, by the inductive method, then there must be some responsiveness to change—since it will not be possible to teach aversion to a certain form of behaviour because of its tendency to injure others (etc.), after changes in the situation which have the effect that no one is any longer injured by it. Conversely, as forms of behaviour become harmful, which were not so before, the 'inductive method' is available to introduce new aversions, i.e. new obligations.

Moreover, if morality as described is to function well, as a good system for regulating behaviour, there should be some awareness by the teachers of morality—the parents, educators in the early grades—of what morality is, what its built-in aversions are for, when changes are called for, how these changes may be introduced, and so on. Briefly, in the long-run a system of morality cannot function well in the absence of a philosophy of morality and of moral education (and of a psychology of moral education as well). I shall be coming back to this.

CHAPTER X

JUSTIFICATION AND THE CONCEPT OF THE MORALLY RIGHT

THE PRECEDING chapter postponed the attempt to answer the question whether and how moral principles might be criticized or justified, in favour of an explanation of what it is for an individual, or society, to have a moral code or to subscribe to a moral principle. We now have this explanation before us: I have argued that for an individual to have a moral code or subscribe to a moral principle is primarily for something to be true about his motivation and dispositions to have guilt-feelings. So I am supposing that the reader has a moral code in the sense that he recoils at the idea of harming, much less killing, another human being without the strongest justifying reasons; that he has guilt-feelings about his conduct from time to time; that he feels disturbed when others trample on sentient beings thoughtlessly and is moved to reprimand or rebuke them; and that he occasionally expresses this whole conative-emotional fact about himself, in statements like 'It is wrong to kill another human being except in order to avoid certain very grave evils' (or something of the sort).

We can now return to the question initially of interest, and ask whether and how and in what sense moral codes or principles, as now understood, can be criticized or justified. I suggested above that part of what it is for a person to have a moral code is to believe that his relevant conative-emotional dispositions are justified in some sense or other. We must now pursue the question of what form this justification could take in the present state of knowledge.

1. THE JUSTIFICATION OF MORAL CODES

Sometimes philosophers suggest that we can justify or appraise a moral code by considering whether it is adapted to the function of morality, just as we appraise a carving-knife favourably if it is sharp and therefore able to perform its function well. For instance, G. J. Warnock comments, in a recent volume, that the ' "general object" of morality, appreciation of which may enable us to *understand* the basis of moral evaluation, is to contribute to betterment . . . of the human predicament by seeking to countervail "limited sympathies" and their potentially most damaging effects. . . . Its proper business is to expand our sympathies, or, better, to reduce the liability to damage inherent in their natural tendency to be narrowly restricted.'[1] But how are we to interpret talk of the 'object' or 'function' of morality? We might construe it as we do talk of the function or purpose of carving-knives— the capacity for which they are designed and manufactured, such as the ability to cut a roast cleanly. In general, we know what artifacts are for; they are made for a certain end. If we pursue this parallel, we do no worse than Aristotle when he made assertions about what man is for. The trouble, however, is that the very designation 'carving-knife' tells us what it is for, but the designation 'morality' does not tell us what it is for. Moreover, morality is hardly a manufactured product. We might say that parents 'produce' it in giving their children moral education, but it can be doubted that they have any particular purpose or use in mind. So the parallel between morality and artifacts does not work out, as a device for appraising moral codes.

But we can construe talk of the object or function of morality, doubtless as Warnock intended we should, as talk about the *good* of morality, its utility in relation to the purposes of someone or everyone. We can ask about morality, what use—given our desires and aversions—it can be to us. Or better, since moralities are of different forms, a person can ask: 'What use is this particular moral code to me?' Or, 'What use could it be to me if it were changed, within the limits imposed by the psychological restrictions on moral learning, so that it served my purposes optimally?' And we could deliberate also on which kind of morality would serve best the purposes of sentient beings generally.

In an earlier chapter, however, I concluded that the concepts of

---

[1] Warnock, 1971, p. 26; see also Toulmin, 1950, Chaps. 10, 11; Rawls, 1971, pp. 131 ff.; Whiteley, 1976, especially p. 90. I do not suggest all these writers have the same thing in mind when they talk of 'the function' of morality.

rational choice and rational desire are useful replacements, or ex-
plications, for talk of 'the best thing to do' and 'a good thing'.
So it is good strategy to rephrase our question in these terms. I
suggest, then, that we consider: 'What kind of social moral code,
if any, would you most tend to support for a society in which
you expected to live, if you were *fully rational?*' This question
does not exactly approximate the sense of: 'Which moral code, if
any, would be *best* for you?', but it is preferable. For the latter
suggests the meaning 'Which would serve your welfare best?' and
that suggests 'your self-interest best?' The former question is preferable because less restrictive. It allows that if, as a fully rational
person, you had benevolent desires, you might reject a moral code
which best served your self-interest—you might want one which
would serve the general interest best, or something in-between.

The question, as stated, asks about a social moral code; but a
person might deliberate just about his own moral code; or he
could ask about both, and possibly give somewhat different answers
to the two questions. The question about the social moral code leads
into more important topics, however; and it is a more realistic
question—since we often do have to decide which code to support
in teaching our own children, in public statements, in writing to the
newspapers, at parent-teacher meetings, and so on. Hence I
confine myself to the question about the social moral code.

Since everyone already has the motivations and dispositions
to feel guilt or disapproval which constitute his personal moral
code, why should anyone want to know which code he would
most tend to support if he were fully rational? Part of the answer
is that we are aware of the diversities of moral codes, both
personal and social, and the process by which a given moral
system is perpetuated—what we may roughly call 'socialization' in
the case of the individual, and 'cultural transmission' for the social
code. We would like to know which of these codes is 'correct'—
that is, criticized by facts and logic as far as possible. We do not
like to think that our moral thinking is confined to making our
intuitions coherent; we should like to step outside our tradition,
look at it from the outside, and see where some more basic kind of
criticism would lead. Now identifying the moral code a fully
rational person would support does just this. We shall see how
this process brings to light irrational prohibitions, just as the

identification of a person's rational desires shows which of his desires/aversions fail to reflect sensitive interaction with the actual world. Thus it seems that identifying the social moral code you would tend to support if you were fully rational will recommend it to you (knowing you would support something if rational, we have seen, will have this effect); and will enable you to escape from your own moral tradition to a more objective stance (in the sense of being more in touch with the realities of the situation, as rational desires by definition are) which has been criticized by fact and logic as far as that is possible. Identifying this stance does not rely upon value judgements; much less is it a mere matter of finding a moral position maximally coherent with so-called 'moral intuitions'. Thus identifying it seems to have some importance.

In appraising the importance of identifying this stance, there are some further facts to be considered. Let us ask ourselves: Suppose we succeed in demonstrating to a person that a certain moral code is one he would, if rational, support above every other and in preference to none at all. What effect would this have on him?

First, the effect that he will support such a system, in the same way as his support for any long-range policy would be engaged, if we show him it is what he would adopt if he were rational. What kind of support? For educational projects (e.g. planning a programme for moral education in the early grades), for publicly espousing such a system where that would be a helpful thing to do, for voting for it, and so on.

Second, the effect that if he was previously alienated from morality, he will now tend to be 'disalienated'. What this means is as follows. A person who wants to do a certain thing the moral code of his society prohibits naturally chafes at the restriction; he also dislikes being the target of criticism and disapproving attitudes, particularly if he thinks that morality is just irrational taboo and convention. When a person thinks thus, and chafes under restriction and criticism, we can say he is alienated from morality. But now, if we can show him (1) that the restriction flows from the very moral system he would support above others if he were rational, even in preference to none at all, and (2) that disapproval of him is part of the working of that very moral system, then his feeling of rebellion and his annoyance at criticism are bound to diminish if not disappear, just as fear diminishes when we realize there is no danger, and as anger diminishes when we realize that some hurtful act was intended to promote our good. When we affect a person's response to a moral system in this way, we can say we have 'disalienated' him from morality. Of course, disalienation from an ideal moral system need not disalienate him from the actual moral system of his society, which perhaps no rational person would support. Moreover, disalienation from morality does not imply that the person will never choose to infringe the rules of even an ideal moral system, from reasons of self-interest.

Third, we can expect a change in his behaviour in case of conflict of interest with other persons. Suppose we propose to a person that a conflict of interest be adjudicated by appeal to the principles of the code he knows he would support if he were rational. He will find it difficult to decline. He may decline, just as he may deliberately infringe the injunctions of the system, but it will be hard for him, since if he does he is in the position of publicly refusing to do what he is prepared publicly to advocate that others be encouraged and taught to do. He will be cast in the light of an inconsistent and selfish person, advocating for others what he refuses to accept himself, out of self-interest. In this case the selfish inconsistency will be manifest, because the refusal is to discuss a topic on the basis of principles to which he is in general prepared to agree and urge on others—as contrasted with ordinary infractions of the code which he need not explain and the incompatibility of which with this preferred code will be less blatant.

A fourth impact is obvious. We can expect him to be somewhat motivated to go along with the injunctions of his rationally chosen moral system, more than he would have been if he did not believe that the moral code in question was one he would support if he were fully rational.

Let us bear in mind all these impacts on a person of showing him that a certain moral code is the one he would support if he were fully rational. We remind ourselves that knowing which code he would support is also to know which code would be *best* for him (in a broad sense that goes beyond personal welfare), one which has been arrived at by a process enabling him to step outside and criticize his cultural tradition—bringing logic and facts to bear, apparently, as far as possible. With all this in mind, should we then go on to say that in identifying this moral code for a person, we have justified it to him? 'Justify', as dictionaries testify, is a vague term; but philosophers often talk of 'justification' of belief, desire, fear and so on. I think we should answer the question in the affirmative; indeed, identifying the rationally favoured moral code appears to be the only kind of justification available for educated persons at the present time. One could even sensibly propose to define 'justification of a moral code to a person' as a showing of this sort. Or, doubtless better, one might define 'justification to a person' as some showing, free from factual error and conceptual confusion and fallacious argument, which serves to recommend something to a person, remove his ambivalence about it and arouse his enthusiasm for it, and in general to make him content with it. In that sense of 'justification', the identification of a moral system as the rationally favoured one (for a certain person) is obviously a justification of that social moral code (to that person).

The possibility has been left open that the social moral code which would be supported by one person if he were fully rational is not exactly the same as the one which would be supported by another person if he were fully rational. If so, then the moral code that is justified for one person is not necessarily the same as the one that is justified for another. I have suggested that all fully rational persons would tend to support the same moral code only as a simplifying first approximation. We must examine, and possibly revise, that approximation later.

2. THE CONCEPT OF CHOICE OF (TENDENCY TO SUPPORT) A MORAL CODE

In Chapter 11 I shall explain how we can show someone that, if he were rational, his tendency to support one specific moral system would be greater than his tendency to support any other or none at all, for a society in which he expected to live. I shall view this tendency to support a moral system as like a person's tendency to support any policy or plan of action, and analyse the situation in a way familiar from Chapter 4. The problem of analysis will be complex, but, as we shall see, not unmanageably so. For the present, however, I wish to make one part of this conception clearer: the notion of a *tendency to support* a moral code.

Philosophers in recent years have often spoken of the 'choice' of a moral system. What has been the conception of these philosophers? Sometimes they think of all persons gathering at a supposititious constitutional convention, at which they might bargain with each other and make trade-offs, and end by casting a ballot for one system or another, with the understanding that when there is unanimity all will be bound by its terms. Or, sometimes it is thought that people might be presented with a set of moral principles and asked whether they would agree to live by them, accept them, acknowledge them as binding—on the assumption that all others will do the same. Or we can think of individuals as prospective colonists, given the option of joining only one of a set of societies, of which they know nothing except the moral code— and with each possible moral code being represented by one society.

These conceptions appear at first to be simpler and more natural than they are. If we attempt to specify their detailed character, we are left puzzled. For instance, would a person be free to choose a moral system in which everyone would be so strongly motivated to conform that it would not be necessary to have guilt-feelings, disapproval, or rules of excuse? Are we free to choose a system without choosing the socialization procedures which would be necessary to keep it in being from one generation to another? May we ignore the costs of such procedures? May we assume that whichever system we choose will be complied with by all persons, irrespective of their level of intelligence, however complex the system may be?

A conception is desirable which essentially contains instructions about how to go about answering all such questions. My proposal contains just that, because it includes the notion of 'supporting' a moral system, and we already know that any realistic activity of supporting will be undertaken by a rational person only in view of the probable costs, difficulties and benefits. So the social moral code a person will aim to support is the one he will expend means to bring about; presumably one whose socialization procedures are both feasible and not too expensive; one simple enough to be understood by most people; and probably one with motivation not so strong as to guarantee conformity in the face of unlimited temptation, and so on. With this in mind, we may hope to identify the strength and direction of motivation, guilt-feelings, etc., in the moral system the rational person will support by voting, criticizing conduct so as to discourage it, participating in the education of his children, and so on.

It is essential, however, to refine this concept of 'supporting a moral system' a bit further, and I have therefore, in more careful formulations, spoken of 'tending to support', meaning by 'tending' an action-tendency in the sense explained in Chapters 2 and 3. Thus the precise question I want to raise is which moral code a fully rational person would *tend* in this sense to support *more strongly* than he would tend to support any other moral system, or none at all.

This conception, even when so refined, is more troublesome than might at first appear, and to avoid some problems we must introduce a restriction, which is to be understood throughout. The restriction is that the outcomes, the valence and expectation of which ($V \times E$ in terms of Chapter 3) underlie the tendency to support, are to be only those that are involved in the conception of the moral system itself and its conditions and effects, and not extraneous considerations, such as what disadvantages one might suffer if one incurred the disapproval of others by advocating deviation from the status quo. Thus we are to think of a tendency for or against performing an act of support as arising from expectations about the consequent currency of the code, of behaviour arising from the code, of states of affairs arising from that behaviour, and so on, each with the proper subjective probability attached, and each state of affairs ideally valenced because it is vividly and precisely represented with its equal share of attention.

The proposal is not subject to some objections that might be raised. For instance, one might say that a person could rightly think that his support would have no effect whatever, and hence that he would have no tendency to support any code. But, while the tendencies might be quite small, so small that no action would ever occur because of the effort involved, there will be some, in view of the fact that an individual's support does (slightly) affect the prospects for a moral code. (Of course, a person of bad repute might best 'support' a moral code by announcing that he was opposed to it!) Again, a critic might argue that rational persons would always tend to support the status quo most strongly, since the probability of success would always exceed that of a reforming effort, since an action-tendency is a simple function of the product of the valence of an outcome and the probability of the act producing the valenced outcome. Now I have just admitted that an individual's action-tendencies may be quite small, in view of the fact that his efforts may only affect minimally the prospects of a moral system. But here what we are wanting is to compare the tendencies (admittedly quite small) to act in support of Code A as contrasted with Code B or none at all. Suppose the code which is the status quo prohibits adult homosexual activity, but the chooser has no aversion to this activity or any of its likely consequences. The valence of the consequences of the code will thus be zero, and his tendency to support the existing code in this respect also zero, whatever he thinks about the efficacy of his support. Suppose further that, in contrast, he is averse to needless frustration of homosexuals and also to criticism of any purely self-regarding activity of anyone. So the consequences of a code permissive on this score are positively valenced. However, suppose he also thinks that public opinion is adamant, so that a change will require many years, and the increased probability of its occurrence given his support extremely small. Will there then be an action-tendency to support permissiveness? It will be quite small, but positive. The person will see that his little effort will not have noticeable effects, but that the summation of the support of many like-minded persons over a period of time presumably can have some success. His effort will be his small contribution to the total outcome; it will increase, very slightly, the probability of the novel code. So, while his tendency may be so small that it will not affect conduct on account of contrary motivations (desires to save time and effort), the stronger tendency will be in opposition to the status quo.[2]

It is true, however—and it is an important fact about the present conception—that a rational person would have no tendency to support some feature of a moral code so contrary to human psychology and the interests of all other individuals that its realization in society is a causal impossibility. Thus a moral code which favoured the chooser and his friends is one a person might

[2] I am indebted to George Mavrodes for raising various questions about this concept.

well like to have in his society, but it is not one he would have a tendency to support, since there is no chance that effort on his part would contribute at all to a probability of having it. I shall have a good deal to say later (Chapter 11) about which kinds of moral code a fully rational person would support.

The concept of 'supporting' a moral code is still somewhat vague. In view of the definition of a social moral code in Chapter 9, it will be evident that what is to be supported is the *currency* of a moral code in society in the sense of the currency among individuals of the motivations, tendencies to have guilt-feelings and so on, which are constitutive of an individual moral code. But what degree of currency is a rational person supposed to be aiming for? Is he supposed to be aiming at 100 per cent adoption by individuals of a given code, and its adoption, say, not merely in Ann Arbor but in Los Angeles, Moscow and London? Since it has already been explained that one universal code might not do in all these places, the conception is restricted to the goal for a society in which the individual rational person expects to live and which he understands well enough to have some idea which particular kind of code he is willing to support for it. That seems clear enough. It could be, of course, that he will support one code for absolutely everyone. The more difficult question is which percentage of the society he aims to be persuaded of his preferred code. There is no reason to be unrealistic about this. When we write a letter to the local newspaper advocating a certain moral stance, or urge that certain principles be taught in the early grades, we are presumably wishing (and setting as the optimal goal) a 100 per cent acceptance; but we only display our innocence about social facts if we are unhappy with anything less. A thoughtful person will want the attitude to be widespread, among well over 50 per cent, somewhere near 90 per cent, where moral attitudes towards acts like murder and child-abuse tend to be. But the presence of different segments of the community—physicians, lawyers, small children—complicates the picture. As we shall see later, a rational person may support slightly different moral codes for some of these. Moreover, a person who writes to the local newspaper may well have no idea at all how widespread an acceptance of his moral stance he is aiming at; most likely what motivates him to write is simply the thought that an editorial might create more agreement with his view. If pressed, perhaps he could mention a threshold of acceptance below which he would lose interest and motivation; and if he thought that anything he and others of like mind might do would stand no chance of affecting acceptance at that level, he would lose all motivation to join in. But, on some matters, he might be well-motivated to support a stance even if he believed it would never be shared by more than a few like-minded persons, for instance, some attitude about kindness to birds.

It would be a mistake to press too hard for an exact answer to the question just what a rational person is aiming at when he supports the 'currency' of a certain moral code. What is important to keep in mind is the fact that a rational person may be expected to do certain things—write letters, vote, etc.—with the thought that he is contributing to one ultimate state of affairs in contrast with some other.

3. THE DEFINITION OF 'MORALLY RIGHT'

There is, beyond the question what would justify a moral code to a person, a further question: How should we define the concept of 'morally right' itself?

There are two reasons for considering this issue. First, the terms 'morally right', 'morally obligatory', and so on, and rough synonyms of them in other languages, are in common use, and it would be clarifying to know what might helpfully be meant by them. (I argued in Chapter 1 that they do not have any definite meaning in ordinary use, so that the only serious question is what they might helpfully be employed to mean.) But second, these terms are not only in the language: they serve two highly important ends, that of communicating moral motivations to other persons, and that of mediating reflection which clarifies the individual's own attitudes towards concrete issues. These ends place a restriction on any artificial modification of the meaning or use of the expressions.

What meaning, in a broad sense, then, might 'is morally wrong' most helpfully bear? We want it to continue to have the expressive function it now clearly has; that is, we want it to be true that when it is used normal auditors will take it that the speaker's motivations (etc.) are opposed to a certain action. But there are advantages in the term also having some descriptive meaning, which is quite compatible with its expressive meaning remaining intact. What might this be? One possibility is something like: 'and the attitude hereby expressed is justified'. I suggest, however, that we assign 'is morally wrong' the descriptive meaning 'would be prohibited by any moral code which all fully rational persons would tend to support, in preference to all others or to none at all, for the society of the agent, if they expected to spend a life-time in that society'. If the phrase were used in this sense, it would express the unfavourable moral motivation (etc.) of the speaker, since in the normal case the statement would hardly be made unless the speaker had an anti-attitude towards the behaviour in question and auditors would take it that he did. So the expressive function would not be lost by assigning the term this descriptive meaning. We could add, 'and therefore the attitude hereby expressed is justified'. It would be simpler, however, to omit this, since in the context it would clearly be implied.

This suggested descriptive meaning is only one possibility. There are others, and perhaps better ones. For instance, if it turned out that not all fully rational persons would tend to support the same moral code in preference to all others, it would be better if 'morally wrong' were given a slightly different descriptive meaning, perhaps 'would be permitted by any moral code which I [or you], if I [you] were fully rational, would tend to support, in preference to all others or to none at all, for the society of the agent, if I [you] expected to spend a lifetime in that society'. There are other possibilities too.

Why should we pack my conception of rationally favoured moral codes into the descriptive meaning of 'morally wrong'? After all, the view that such moral codes are justified can be defended independently of the descriptive meaning normative terms have. The reason, however, why it would be better if 'morally wrong' came to bear a descriptive meaning along the lines suggested (and similarly for other terms) is its *educational* value. For at least two beneficial educational effects would accrue. First, whenever a person used a moral term he would be reminded that morality is not a matter of conventions, taboos, or uncriticized traditions of the Establishment, as many people today tend to think; or that it is a system of laws handed down from Heaven or self-evident to the

Wise, as some others think; but that it has, or can have, the status of being rationally preferred, one which deserves respect but is not something above human reflection, sensitivity, and debate. Second, this meaning would remind a speaker of the whole conceptual framework, of how moral issues should be thought through, and hopefully guide his moral reflection, certainly more than the vague, ill-defined descriptive meaning of moral terms as now used.

To say that it would be educationally beneficial if 'is morally wrong' were assigned a certain descriptive meaning needs further explanation. Obviously philosophers should not go about saying that the actual descriptive meaning of this term is the one suggested; that would be false. What I mean is that philosophers should try to make it the descriptive meaning of the phrase. Philosophers may object that this proposal unduly inflates the business of the profession. And in any case philosophers are not in a position to do much about the meaning phrases carry; at least, not unless we enlist the co-operation of teachers in the lower age-groups. But we should not underestimate the possible influence of philosophers. Persons in Washington have introduced horrendous and quite superfluous terms into the language. Moreover, ordinary people, humanists and scientists at least, use terms indigenous to philosophy, like 'persuasive definition' and 'operational definition'. In any case, to restrict a philosopher to the armchair or to passive observation of linguistic behaviour is to define his job narrowly and arbitrarily. Why should philosophers not actively introduce definitions which enable people to think more clearly, and disabuse them of misconceptions?

I have said nothing about other moral terms like 'morally reprehensible' (or 'blameworthy') and 'morally praiseworthy'. My proposal would be the obviously consistent one: an action is 'morally reprehensible' if it 'would be disapproved of by any moral code [viz. any person with that moral code would disapprove of it, all things considered] which all fully rational persons . . .', and so on as before. Since 'has a moral right to' can be defined in terms of 'morally right' or 'morally obligatory', the reader can work out the proposal for that term.

4. A POSSIBLE KANTIAN MODIFICATION OF THE DEFINITION

Some philosophers think that it would be better, if we wish to define 'morally right' by some kind of reference to what rational or fully informed people would want or choose or tend to support, to choose a definition in which reference to a *moral code* drops out in deference to reference to what people are actually to *do*, and in which there are other less important modifications. Thus they in effect suggest that a morally right act is one which rational people would not object to anyone doing, and that a morally wrong act is one which rational people would not want (or choose) everyone, or even anyone, to do. We could say this is a Kantian proposal, if we take Kant to say that an act is morally right only if its 'maxim' is one that the agent—we can here read 'rational persons'—can consistently want everyone to follow. The proposal is also one we might associate with the most recent views of Professor R. M. Hare, taking him to say that a morally wrong act is one of a kind which informed prudential persons would proscribe for absolutely everyone. (In earlier Hare-type terminology, 'Your doing *A* is morally wrong' would become 'Your doing *A* in the circumstances is an instance of a principle which prohibits the doing at any time of anything like *A* in relevantly similar circumstances, to which I hereby subscribe.')

These philosophers seem to suppose that they are actually reporting the meaning of moral terms in ordinary speech, rather than proposing useful meanings for these terms, as I have done (although Kant hints at my suggestion). Since, clearly, these definitions do not report current usage, I shall inquire only whether their proposed type of definition would be a more, or less, useful definition than mine.

I shall concede at once that (as will be fully explained later) the main benefit of having a moral code at all is its influence on actions. If nobody ever paid any attention to his moral code, instilling a moral code in children would be a waste of time. The moral code is an instrument. Of course, in large part human behaviour is an instrument, also. For we care about how people act mainly because of how their behaviour affects other persons for good or ill, by disappointing their expectations, injuring them, and so on. For the most part, actions are important to us because of their consequences. Finally, then, a moral code is important largely because it influences human behaviour in bringing about desirable states of affairs. All these facts can tempt us simultaneously to define 'morally wrong' in terms of the moral code, or of human behaviour, or of the desirable states resulting from human behaviour. I have suggested that the first is the best way, whereas Kant and Hare opt for the second way, and still other philosophers may opt for the third. I omit the third view, and merely explain some objections to the second.

First we should notice that the kind of moral code rational persons might tend to support in preference to any other could comprise just one rule, a rule incorporating the Kant–Hare conception. The entire moral code could just be the rule: 'Don't ever do what rational persons would not want everyone, or anyone, to do'. Perhaps no rational person would want a moral code like that for his society; but this is one of his options. So a person attracted by the Kantian 'categorical imperative' need not on that account reject my proposed definition; indeed, my definition is logically compatible with any set of principles taken as the substantive content of morality.

Now for the objections. First, the Kant–Hare conception appears to ignore the difference between the merely desirable for conduct, and the morally obligatory. It is one thing to know what rational persons would want everyone to do, or no one to do. It is another thing to know what rational persons would want everyone to be *required to do*, by conscience. We must agree with a well-known statement of J. S. Mill: 'We do not call anything wrong, unless we mean to imply that a person ought to be punished in some way or other for not doing it; if not by law, by the opinion of his fellow-creatures; if not by opinion, by the reproaches of his own conscience.'[3] My proposal permits a clear distinction between what rational or informed persons might want everyone to do, and what they might want required to be done by conscientious scruple, or, in my terms, by the agent's moral code. I repeat that this distinction does not imply that rational people want things required just for their own sakes; it may be that rational people want persons required by conscientious scruple to do certain things

[3] J. S. Mill, *Utilitarianism*, Chap. 5. A very similar view is supported by Kurt Baier, 1966.

because that promises to make life better for us all. But the point is that they do want some things required by conscience, and this is tantamount to wanting a moral system; and this conception makes it possible to distinguish between the desirable and the morally obligatory.

This objection suggests that the reason for opting for my definition in preference to the suggested Kant–Hare definition is simply that it enables us to recognize a distinction we are accustomed to make, between acts that are 'desirable' and those that are 'morally obligatory'. But I have not been paying much attention to ordinary language, and do not think any important distinction ought to turn on mere ability to render distinctions made by ordinary speech. There is, however, a corresponding substantive issue which constitutes a second, more potent, objection. For society needs the kind of internal social control of action constituted by a moral code, because it is a condition of a good life, and I suggest all rational persons would want some kind of moral code in society for that reason. And, if we are going to have it, there is a question of what kind of conduct is to fall within the scope of its prohibitions and injunctions. My definition proposes in effect to name the acts that do so fall within its scope by the terms 'morally wrong' or 'morally obligatory'. The conceptual scheme I propose, therefore, has a function within a desirable cultural system, whereas the Kant–Hare alternative is out of touch with this social reality.

A third important reason for keeping the concept of a moral code firmly in the middle of our conceptual framework refers to the cost of moral motivation. We may prefer that people should not do certain things but it is another question whether we want them brought up so as to be forbidden by conscience to do these things. Building in conscientious scruples involves the use of explanations and punishment of some sort in childhood. These methods are rough and the fact of stimulus generalization has the effect that the motivation and tendency to guilt-feelings that we build in are liable to spill over into areas where we do not want them. It is very easy for consciences to prevent people from doing what is in their own best interest, and what rational people think they should be doing. That is just one cost of instituting conscientious scruples. Such costs obviously may not be over-looked. In deciding what is to be morally forbidden—what we shall call 'morally wrong'—we should not only count the advantages of people behaving in a certain way, but the costs of having motivated them to behave in this way on account of conscience. The moral system, like the legal system, should be devised to count the costs as well as the benefits. My proposed conceptual scheme encourages us to keep this consideration in the forefront, whereas the Kant–Hare definition forces us to overlook it altogether—unless it is amended out of all recognition.

CHAPTER XI

RATIONALLY PREFERRED MORAL CODES AND THE GENERAL WELFARE

IF A person knows which moral code he would most tend to support, then (as we saw in the preceding chapter) he knows which moral code is justified for him, and also which kinds of actions he can call 'morally right' in the preferred sense of that phrase. But which moral system would fully rational persons most tend to support? That is the topic of the present chapter.

It would be nice if we could demonstrate that all fully rational persons would support one and the same moral system. We shall in fact have to settle for something short of that. What we can hope for is to identify an area in which all fully rational persons will agree, and an area in which there will probably be disagreement. Perhaps all rational persons will agree that a moral code must prohibit unprovoked assault, but will disagree about whether foetuses have a right to be born, or whether we have an obligation to curtail consumption for the sake of future generations.

The question is not one of purely theoretical interest. We have to raise it frequently in practice: we have to decide what to do about the moral education of our own children at home, of children in the schools, and what letters, if any, to write to the newspaper or to a legislator; and presumably in making such decisions we would like to know what we would do if we were fully rational.

I. AN OVERVIEW OF THE CHOICE PROBLEM

The first step towards finding which moral code a given person, if fully rational, would tend most strongly to support for his society, is to assemble before us the variety of codes from which a selection must be made.

Moral codes differ most obviously in their content: what they prohibit or enjoin, or, in other words, what people are to feel motivated to do on its own account, feel guilty about, and so on.

There are also the rules of excuses—which conduct infringing the primary rules is not disapproved of; and there are the 'supererogatory' actions—those that will be admired and praised but are not required. Codes also differ in the strength of their injunctions: the intensity of the motivations, the guilt-feelings, in general. (Differences in strength of various prohibitions may fix how weighty a given consideration will be in moral deliberation.)

Among how many different systems must a choice be made? Professor Rawls distinguished fourteen possible systems especially important for the theory of justice, but if we do not confine ourselves to recognized types of systems (e.g. forms of utilitarianism, or intuitionistic-pluralism like that of W. D. Ross), but also consider the particular general moral principles which may be different—or the different relative weights that might be assigned to each—the number becomes bewilderingly large. Our task in this chapter is to winnow out the main contenders from this large group, and attempt to identify a narrow range of systems with strong claims to be the winner.

We can happily eliminate those moral systems which are virtually impossible given the facts of human nature and society. For instance, a moral system of complete malevolence is probably impossible; and the same applies for a moral system of perfect compliance—one in which the motivation to do things like keep promises is so strong that no one, for reason of selfish motivation or impulse, ever fails to do what he is required morally to do—the cost of such a system eliminates it from serious consideration. There is also an important limit on complexity. When an item is prohibited there is, we saw, motivation to avoid it on its own account and guilt-feelings when the action is performed without excuse. Now the complex process of teaching these dispositions involves classical conditioning and, unlike the teaching of language, offers relatively few opportunities for correction. Some apparent complexities do not offer difficulty: if benevolence is learned as Chapter 7 affirms, then the aversion to injury to others increases with the magnitude of the anticipated harm, so that virtually a continuous set of reactions presents itself for different situations. Something similar may be true for promises: we may teach what makes a promise more stringent, so that at least a stepped set of responses to different situations is available. It is obvious that teaching injunctions so that each has exactly the desired weight in relation to each of the others, for the possible situations in which they can conflict, would be quite difficult. For the most part morality must consist of general and reasonably simple prohibitions and injunctions, with some built-in degree of motivation. Partly for this reason of complexity a moral system cannot well comprise rules containing proper names. There can be some: 'Act as Jesus (or Buddha) would'; but there cannot be many.

Once we have eliminated the obvious non-contenders from amongst possible moral systems, we must review how rational persons will choose from among the remainder. Fortunately, we can rely on the conceptual frame laid down in earlier chapters, since we have already discussed the theory of fully rational desires, aversions, and decisions. So we think of individuals first undergoing cognitive psychotherapy with respect to the desires and aversions possibly relevant to the present question, to make these rational; and then, with the rectified desires and aversions, we think of them acting to select or support a moral system on the basis of an ideally vivid representation of all relevant available information. The person making the decision will avoid the various errors listed in earlier chapters: he will be disabused of 'unauthentic' desires, and desires based on false beliefs or on childhood deprivations or improper generalization of experiences; he will not overlook outcomes or wrongly estimate their probability, and he will weigh them in an undistorted holistic way, and so on.

The psychological theory of action and the conception of a fully rational action simplify the task at least of determining how nearly individuals will agree in the choice of a moral code. For if all the choosers are fully informed, their deliberations will have some things in common. They will be appraising the same set of possible moral systems; they will identify the same set of outcomes as likely, given any particular moral system; and they will make the same probability judgements about the likelihood of these outcomes. Further, as rational they will have the outcomes equally vividly in mind. How, then, can choices differ?

Obviously because different persons, even when fully rational, attach different valences to the various outcomes. Valences differ because different persons have differing physiological constitutions (I abhor bananas) or because of different life-experiences (traumas, parental preachments, and so on). More important, even when people like the same things they may prefer to have the good experiences themselves and other persons to have the bad ones. Who gets the money or the plaudits is an important matter. So the consequences of a moral system may be differently valenced because of their differential impact on individuals or groups: a moral system which demands equal distribution of income will be unpalatable to a wealthy and successful businessman (it means a decrement of welfare for him), but highly acceptable to an unskilled worker or the unemployed.

I shall now review the various outcomes which probably influence preferences among moral systems. I shall then show that a fully rational person would not be susceptible to certain valences, and further, would reject some options as causally unfeasible. We shall then be in a position to assess residual disagreements among rational persons, and identify the range of serious contenders for top rank.

2. TYPES OF VALENCED OUTCOME RELEVANT TO SUPPORT OF A MORAL SYSTEM

What types of consequence of a possible social moral code might influence a fully rational person's choice of a code? (I shall assume that the properties of the moral code itself may be viewed as a 'consequence' to be considered.)

We must ignore certain desires for and aversions to consequences of moral codes, in particular any pro or con attitude towards some code or its consequences which exists because the person thinks the code or consequence is *morally objectionable*. We must ignore such aversions because we are trying to find out, by inquiring which moral system a fully rational person would support, what is morally acceptable or objectionable. We cannot, then, assume as already known that certain behaviour is wrong; and therefore, since the aversion in question *ex hypothesi* occurs only because the person thinks the conduct wrong, the aversion is based on what is at this stage a groundless belief.

Let us now list considerations which might influence a person's choice of a moral code.

i. Features of a moral code desired just for themselves. Some features of a moral system may be desired just for themselves. What are some examples? A person might conceivably want people in his society to be sympathetic or compassionate, aversive to deceit and to taking one's pledged word lightly, for no further reason. We may question whether any rational person would want these dispositions in members of his society just for themselves; we shall come back to this

ii. Behavioural consequences desired intrinsically. A moral system may elicit support because the kind of behaviour it favours is valenced, directly or indirectly. Obviously if some form of behaviour comes to be prohibited by a moral system, it tends to become less frequent. Now this behaviour may be desired (aversive) in itself and hence affect directly the tendency to support the moral system which produces it; or, while not desired (aversive) in itself, it may bring about other states of affairs which are so, and this fact may affect the choice of a moral system. What are some examples of behaviour affected by a moral system which is desired or aversive intrinsically, for no further reason?

Some people find it aversive that other persons get drunk, gamble, smoke marijuana, or indulge in homosexual acts; some people want young men not to wear their hair long, or women not to smoke a pipe or cigars. In general, some persons want others to adopt a certain life-style, for no further reason. It is not that these behaviours make them uncomfortable, in the sense that smoking by women is offensive because the choosers are allergic to cigar smoke, or that a drunken person arouses anxieties about what he might do next. Some persons apparently just do not want anyone to do these things.

iii. Behavioural consequences of a moral system desired for further reasons.

iiia. Self-regarding outcomes of behaviour. Behaviour encouraged by a moral system may have further consequences desired for themselves, and rational persons might prefer one moral system to another on account of these. It is useful to divide these further consequences into three types: the first type we can call 'self-regarding' consequences; they might also be referred to as 'selfish considerations'. Obviously enhancement of one's enjoyments or reduction in discomforts belong in this class. For instance, a moral code may prohibit unprovoked assault; as a result unprovoked assaults tend to be infrequent; as a further result a person does not get hurt by assaults and does not have to feel unsafe—states of affairs he wants. A rational person will probably want a moral system prohibiting unprovoked assault partly on account of this indirect self-regarding outcome.

It is worthwhile to digress, in view of the concern of some philosophers with what moral system, if any, a purely selfish person would support, and to point out that a person with desires for only self-regarding outcomes will almost certainly want a moral system of a sort in preference to none at all. This fact is Thomas Hobbes's point on government. A purely selfish person will want the protection a moral system can provide against unprovoked assault on one's person, reputation, or basic position in society.

Would absolutely every rational selfish person tend to support a moral system (or legal system) with such safety features? Of course God does not need this protection. Nor does a person with magical self-protective powers. But it is a most unusually situated person who would shun a protective moral code.

Virtually all persons with only self-regarding valences will also take an interest in the currency of some moral system for reasons other than the sheer protection it affords. For they will like the quality of life of a group with a moral system: one with autonomous self-restraint, mutual trust, mutual respect, openness, the absence of need to be on one's guard against malicious or self-serving attacks of any sort. These features characterize a society with at least most kinds of moral system, and not one without. Life is more comfortable in such a society, and a completely selfish man will want a society with a moral code on that account.

Let us call any moral code a perfectly selfish rational person might prefer to no code, a *Hobbesian morality*. I am saying, then, that virtually every perfectly selfish but rational person will tend to support some Hobbesian morality in preference to no morality. Hobbesian moralities need not be identical. But presumably all Hobbesian moral systems will have some features in common, for instance, features protecting against unprovoked assault.

iiib. Other-regarding consequences of behaviour. Behaviour encouraged or discouraged by a moral system may have consequences which are liked or disliked by (enjoyable or unpleasant to) persons other than the chooser among moral systems, and if the rational chooser is benevolent, he will tend to support some moral systems on that account. The conclusion of Chapter 7 was that a benevolent person is concerned only about the happiness of others (not the satisfaction of their desires in so far as it does not affect this), but if one likes one can think of the benevolent interest as extending to all consequences of 'self-regarding' interest to another.

Benevolent persons need not choose exactly the same kind of moral system. For one thing, they also have desires for situations not other-regarding, and these may lead them in different directions. For another thing, they need not be benevolent to the same degree. Children show different degrees of benevolence or sympathy on the playground at quite early ages (Murphy, 1937); it may be that a person's genes and the classical conditioning of the early years bring about a distinctive degree of sympathy or benevolence which is a relatively fixed lifetime trait of personality. Conceivably some fully rational people will have no benevolent desires at all; at the opposite extreme may be persons with perfect benevolence, in the sense that they desire the happiness or welfare of others as much as they desire their own. There may be all degrees in between. Persons with one degree of benevolence might prefer to have art galleries, fine operas, and tree-lined streets rather than food stamps for the poor; those with a different degree of benevolence might reverse this order of priority. Furthermore, as people in fact are, their benevolence differs depending on the individuals involved. Some persons are much concerned about the happiness of their relatives but not much about that of others; some are concerned to alleviate the misery of citizens of the U.S.A., but not of residents of Africa. Some are moved by the misery of animals where others are not. How far would these particular differences survive if a person were rational? An answer to this question must be somewhat speculative. Undoubtedly some of these differences are a function merely of inadequate representation of the situation of the other—for instance, most people do not realize that it causes animals pain of the most severe sort to die in a trap. At least they do not represent the fact vividly, even if verbally they concede the point. But there is another possibility. It follows from the conditioning theory of benevolence (p. 140 f.) that a person will normally be more concerned to relieve his own pain than that of others; for his own pain is an unconditioned stimulus to aversive response, whereas his aversion to others' pain is a two-stage conditioned response, involving stimulus generalization, to the supposed pain of others. For much the same reason a person will normally take more interest in the welfare of persons like himself—same sex, age, and so on. If such differential benevolence is established at a very early age, by the very process of classical conditioning to which we owe the trait of benevolence altogether, it may well be that fully rational persons—those who have undergone relevant cognitive psychotherapy—will still manifest different degrees of benevolence towards different kinds of individual.

Is there anything general we can say, despite these variations, about the difference between a benevolent person's and a selfish person's choice of a moral system? Of course, much depends on how benevolent a benevolent person is. But there are some things we can say. Suppose, of two largely similar moral systems, one would leave at least one person better off than the other, and none worse off (Pareto-optimal as compared with the other). The benevolent person would of course select that one; the selfish person could be indifferent between the two. But to take more interesting differences: we can expect a benevolent person to choose a moral system forbidding cruelty to animals, or enjoining care for future generations or aid to the distressed in distant countries, whereas a perfectly selfish person need not do so—since these features of a moral system do not increase either his safety or his comfort.

iiic. Valenced impersonal consequences of behaviour produced by a moral code. Behaviour encouraged or required by a moral system has certain consequences which may motivate a person to support that code, for neither selfish nor benevolent reasons. Some of these which have figured in the literature of philosophy are: a situation of economic and social equality; a distribution of economic goods (or, sometimes, happiness) in accordance with merit of some sort or effort or productivity; punishment of a wrong-doer in accordance with the heinousness of his offence. Persons who have wanted these things have doubtless sometimes wanted them only because they thought them morally required, in which case, if my earlier argument is correct, that preference must be ignored; but it may be that a person reared in a democratic society might just find social and economic inequalities aversive on their own account.

3. THE IRRATIONALITY OF SOME DESIRES

The states of affairs relevant to choice of a moral system are so numerous, and the likelihood that they will be differently valenced even for rational persons seems so great, that the prospects may seem poor for demonstrating that given rational persons would select the same one. It should be no surprise that writers like Professor Rawls have attempted to reformulate the problem so that such demonstrations become very much simpler—we shall see how in Chapter 12.

Nevertheless I shall now show why, as a result of certain simplifying facts, rational persons would probably opt for one within a narrow range of what we might loosely call 'utilitarian' moral systems; that is, ones the currency of which would maximize the expectable happiness or welfare of some large group, the size of the group depending on the benevolence of the chooser. We must be satisfied with plausibility rather than certainty. I shall make no attempt to work out the details of the moral system that would be chosen, but I shall lay out some guidelines so that an interested individual can determine his own rationally favoured code.

What are the simplifying facts which narrow the range of acceptable alternatives? The first is the irrationality of many desires, so that we may ignore these in deciding which moral code a rational person would support. The second is a requirement, which I shall call 'viability', on the type of moral code a rational person would support—roughly *causal feasibility*.

Many desires which people have in mind when they compare moral systems are desires which would not occur in a fully rational person who had been through cognitive psychotherapy. In fact, many of the desires classifiable in the preceding section under (*i*) and (*ii*), and possibly some under (*iiic*), may be ignored on this account. But what line of reasoning will support such a claim?

In Chapter 6 four ways in which intrinsic desires or aversions can go wrong were identified—desires or aversions which would not occur in a rational person. These were desires/aversions based on false beliefs, those produced artificially in the process of culture transmission (and which could not have developed by experience with their objects), those based on generalization from untypical examples, and those deriving from early deprivations. Now, some valences relevant to the choice of moral systems fall into one or other of these categories. This proposal cannot well be proved; the identification of desires with the above defects is not easy even for one person; nor do we have a complete list of the desires in these several categories. But we can make the conclusion plausible by discussion of some examples.

The aversions to certain sorts of behaviour ((*ii*) above) just for themselves appear all to be produced either by what I called 'desire-arousal in culture transmission' or by false beliefs, and could not be aroused just as a result of familiarity with the type of conduct in question. To see this for himself, the reader must simply review any aversions of this category he finds in himself. I draw some examples, however, from the literature of philosophy. Hastings Rashdall, writing at the beginning of the century (1924, Vol. I, Chap. 7), affirmed that even an occasional drunk is 'intrinsically degrading', and that incest is both 'shocking' and 'revolting', although he himself believed, in my opinion probably wrongly, that such behaviours may not be injurious to anyone's long-range happiness. The reader of Kant's *Lectures on Ethics* (1963, pp. 169 ff.), again, will discover that Kant finds various sexual practices aversive, partly because he thinks them 'contrary to nature' but also because the actions 'degrade' the person to the level of animals and make him 'unworthy of his humanity. He no longer deserves to be a person.' Rashdall, incidentally, concedes that his attitude is one of aversion which might well be only pathological, and says that the test whether it is an acceptable or only pathological attitude is whether it 'disappears after full reflection upon the act itself as well as upon all circumstances and consequences' (1924, Vol. I, p. 212)—an approximation to what I have called 'cognitive psychotherapy'. Let us ask how these philosophers came by these feelings. The suggestion is ludicrous, but one would like to know whether these gentlemen, had they taken the trouble to indulge in these forms of behaviour themselves or at least observed such behaviours or their consequences in the case of others, would have acquired these strong attitudes. One cannot escape the conviction that the aversions were acquired, and could have been acquired, only in the course of socialization in the puritanical atmosphere of the day and would extinguish in cognitive psychotherapy (except to the extent they are supported by objectionable consequences).

Consider suicide. It is not easy to know what people now think about suicide. It seems likely that many people have an intrinsic aversion to the act of committing suicide, on account of which they might wish to include a prohibition in the moral code. The aversion may, of course, result from a belief that the act is wrong, in which case, as noted above, we must dismiss the attitude for present purposes. But many other experiences might produce the attitude by direct conditioning or closely related processes: awareness of the refusal to permit burial or even a funeral service by a prestigious religious group, the expression of horror by one's parents at the suicide of an acquaintance, the grim-faced exercise of authority by one's physician when he refuses information that would be useful for a graceful departure from this life. Desires produced in this way, and which could not be produced by direct acquaintance with the facts, are irrational desires. Another possible source of an intrinsic aversion to suicide is the influence of theological beliefs. As Rashdall remarked: 'A strong feeling against suicide seems to be the spontaneous deliverance of the moral consciousness, wherever the Christian view of life, with its ideas of discipline, education, or moral probation, and its sense of responsibility to a divine Father, is accepted.' (1924, Vol. I, p. 210.) Some of these beliefs were expressed by Kant: 'We have been placed in this world under certain conditions and for specific purposes. But a suicide opposes the purpose of his Creator; he arrives in the other world as one who has deserted his post; he must be looked upon as a rebel against God. So long as we remember the truth that it is God's intention to preserve life, we are bound to regulate our activities in conformity with it. . . . This duty is upon us until the time comes when God expressly commands us to leave this life. Human beings are sentinels on earth and may not leave their posts until relieved by another beneficent hand.' (1963, p. 154.) If such groundless or even unintelligible thoughts create the intrinsic aversion to suicide, we must again criticize it as irrational.

The thought that something is 'contrary to nature' has also created intrinsic aversions and contributed to various moral views. This conception has never been made clear; in one sense, whatever happens, happens according to causal laws, and is therefore 'natural'. To the extent to which this concept nurtures aversions, they are rooted in confusion and must be viewed as irrational attitudes.

These remarks on possible sources of intrinsic aversions hardly show that these examples, much less all the outcomes above classified as (*ii*), are irrational; but I believe that the suggestions do have a strong claim to truth.

There is a complication about some valenced outcomes listed under (*ii*) and also under (*i*). This arises from the fact that when something is a means to, or is thought of as being a means to, something desired for itself, it tends to become wanted for itself (see above, pp. 101, 122). Take speaking the truth. It is normally beneficial to oneself or others when a person speaks the truth. We may expect, then, that by conditioning speaking the truth may come to be valenced for itself. Or, a person may be made to feel uncomfortable by the attentions of drunk people; he may then have an aversion towards drunkenness in itself. In so far as an intrinsic desire or aversion has a source of this kind and would not extinguish in cognitive psychotherapy, it is not irrational. We can understand, then, how some consequences listed under both (*i*) and (*ii*) are desired for themselves: it is a result of being, or being thought to be, means to other outcomes wanted for themselves.

When some consequence is desired, or aversive, for itself in this situation, it is redundant in the choice of a moral system, for there are other consequences listed under (*iiia*) or (*iiib*) which can serve in its stead.

This consideration leads to a result of some significance: a consequence desired or aversive in itself, of the kinds (*i*) or (*ii*), is either redundant in the sense just mentioned, or in all probability is irrational. Why is it probably irrational if not redundant? Obviously the desire or aversion is not native; and if not native it is acquired by conditioning. If it is acquired by conditioning it will extinguish in cognitive psychotherapy by inhibition or counterconditioning (see Chapter 5) unless certain thoughts (true ones) relate it to the satisfaction of other desires, or to enjoyable experiences. There can be such true thoughts if the same outcomes can be supported by valenced outcomes of types (*iiia*) and (*iiib*); otherwise the conditioned desire or aversion will extinguish and must be viewed as irrational. At the least, we can say that if a person tends to support a certain moral code because of valenced outcomes of types (*i*) or (*ii*), then either that support is redundant, or else there is prima facie reason to think that the relevant desire or aversion is irrational.

A desire or aversion of types (*i*) and (*ii*) may in fact be created by parental preachments, identification, and so on. But this fact does not impair their status as rational, provided they could have been acquired by reflection on facts, and from reactions which will not dissipate in cognitive psychotherapy.

Must we really go through such speculative reflection in order to find which moral system, if any, a fully rational person would want for his society? I believe we must. We can ignore desires of types (*i*), (*ii*) and (*iiic*), as we shall see some philosophers do, but only at the cost of arbitrariness or dogmatism. Philosophers sometimes write, for instance, as if aversions of type (*ii*) do not exist, or at any rate merit no attention; but to ignore them is to fail to 'speak to the condition' of many people. If philosophers really wish to show that a fully rational person would not have certain aversions, widespread in the community, it is not obvious how they can avoid considering them, one by one, somewhat in the fashion I have briefly indicated. Probably such discussion takes place best as dialogue in a classroom or tutorial, where real persons with divergent attitudes can engage in candid interchange.

4. THE CONCEPT OF A VIABLE MORAL SYSTEM

The irrationality of some valences, then, reduces the scope of disagreement among rational persons selecting a moral system for their society. Two further facts have the same effect.

The first is simply that the rational person choosing a moral system by definition has available relevant information, but is not omniscient. In particular, he will normally not know certain facts about his own future: when he will die, whether he will lose his money in a stock market crash, whether he will be divorced, and so on. As a result, a person may wisely choose a moral code which will insure his future to some extent, but one that would not be optimal if he were omniscient. Kant made the point, for which he has been unjustly criticized, that a reasonable person will want people generally to give to charity, with the thought that conceivably he might need charitable contributions himself one day. So a rational wealthy man will not object to social security taxes and medicare even if in all probability he will lose by the system in the long-run. The same for various features of a moral code.

The second fact limiting the scope of disagreement is that rational persons will support only a moral system that is viable, or *causally feasible*. This is an important consideration for rational persons, because the tendency to do something is a function of the valence of the prospective outcomes and also the probability that these outcomes will occur, given the occurrence of the act. Hence, in choosing between two moral systems, if the possible outcomes of one are valenced say equally with those of another, but the probability of its valenced outcomes is nearly zero, the tendency to choose the other will be relatively much greater. I have mentioned a system which might be impossible in this sense, a system with motivation sufficient to guarantee strict compliance, that is, so high that no contrary motivation, however strong, could induce deviation. If motivation of that strength is not inherently impossible, still for most cases the various costs would so far outstrip the benefits that thoughtful persons would not advocate the learning of such a system.

This kind of feasibility restriction tends to have the effect that even selfish chooosers of moral systems with special interests to defend might be willing to support a system conducive to the general welfare. Consider an extreme case in which a person wants a moral system requiring everyone's devotion to his personal welfare. It would be pointless to support such a system; our egoist would simply find no one interested, certainly if the others were as rational and selfish as himself. An effective moral system must strike a responsive chord in other people; others must see how they have a stake in it. Once people come to view a provision of a moral code as burdensome, with no benefits to themselves or those they care about, their attachment to it is undermined. It is at least close to the truth that a moral code is not viable unless its provisions can be wanted by most persons in the society. Within limits, people advocating a code protective of their special interests must be ready to make concessions so that its provisions are not in the long-run felt intolerable, or burdensome, or even useless, to most people. In the following section I shall explain why this fact tends to lead even selfish people in the direction of supporting a code for economic allocations which is expectable-welfare-maximizing for the person's society.

The restriction of viability, incidentally, is another reason why rational people will not try to embody irrational aversions to certain sorts of behaviour, for no further reason, in a moral system. For so doing is advocating some restriction on the behaviour of other people, who do not want to be restricted in that way and see no point in it, in terms of interests, their own or other people's. If Mr *A* urges that homosexual behaviour is intrinsically evil, he is advocating a restriction very frustrating to some, and which he cannot recommend to them on the grounds that it injures others or themselves, as he can for assault or libel or smoking cigarettes. He cannot appeal to their self-regarding or other-regarding desires.

A moral code which includes restrictions based on irrational desires need not always be unviable. For instance, it may be sheer irrational preference when people object to marriage between cousins or even siblings, but such a preference can be incorporated into a viable moral system because it causes so little hardship.

5. RATIONAL CHOICE AND UTILITARIANISM

Irrational desires will not influence a fully rational person, then, in his choice of a moral system; not will he support a system which is not viable. Can we, then, draw inferences about the kind of moral system which such a person will support?

We have concluded that desires or aversions of types (*i*) and (*ii*) may be ignored. Either it is irrational for the choice of a moral system to be moved by these desires, or else their influence is redundant in the sense that there are considerations among outcomes of types (*iiia*) and (*iiib*) which will have the same effect. I shall also set aside desires for outcomes of type (*iiic*), although the most important of these—a possible aversion to social and economic inequalities—will in effect be considered in Chapter 16, where I shall argue that this desire is largely if not fully satisfied by principles of economic distribution required by a utilitarian system of morality. We have before us, then, the task of finding which moral system fully rational persons, with possibly varying 'desires for outcomes of types (*iiia*) and (*iiib*), would support for their society.

Let us begin by asking which moral system a rational person would support in either of two conditions of benevolence: perfect benevolence and no benevolence. I shall assume that we can then infer, from answers to this question, which system would be chosen by a person whose benevolence lies somewhere between the two extremes.

Take first the chooser with perfect benevolence. I define a 'perfectly' benevolent person as one who, between two options, always prefers the one associated with the greater long-term sum of expectable net happiness, irrespective of who is to receive it. (A perfectly benevolent person is not an altruist, if an altruist is one who ignores his own welfare altogether.) This conception needs explanation. We think first of any individual liking (or disliking) some experience he is having at the time to a degree k, which can be represented by a cardinal number, representing the distance from the indifference level. The momentary increment of happiness produced by some action is the difference between what his felicity-level k at a particular time would be without the action, and what it would be with the action. Then we draw two curves for a period of his life beginning with the first effects of the action: the time being represented by distance along the x-axis, and the felicity-level represented by distance along the y-axis. We then compute the area between the two curves over the total length of time over which the action makes a difference. (This area may be positive or negative, depending on whether the action produces gain or loss.) Then we sum all these areas over everyone affected. The course of action preferred by the perfectly benevolent man will be the one associated with the larger sum. Obviously this conception supposes that we can assign cardinal numbers to happiness-levels, and that we can make interpersonal comparisons. I defend both these conceptions in Chapter 13. The conception also implies that a perfectly benevolent person will balance losses to some against gains to others, and that he will balance numerous small increments against a few large increments.

This concept of perfect benevolence is somewhat simplified. For one thing, it ignores the fact that a rational benevolent person might weigh irrational pleasures less heavily than rational ones. Again, a rational benevolent person would not count equally gains in happiness achieved by just adding to the population. I have not discussed this point, but it seems clear that benevolent persons are more concerned to enhance the welfare of exisiting persons than to produce more persons who will be happy if they exist. I assume we can incorporate these facts into our total normative conception, although I shall not say how.

There is another simplification which is more puzzling. The above suggestion is that a rational person prefers an option depending on the total increments to happiness produced, whoever gets them. In other words, he wants the happiness of any other person as much as he wants the happiness of himself or his friends. But we have seen that a person wants other things in addition to his own happiness. He may want achievement, to own a grandfather clock, or to have the affection of particular persons. These desires are connected with a person's happiness: if he does not achieve, or obtain the clock he may be dissatisfied, but if he does he will be exhilarated. Now, in Chapter 4, I emphasized that a person's desire for some outcome is different from, or at least additional to, his desire for the happiness of having it. Now, my definition of 'perfect benevolence' ignores this, in assuming that a person's choice will be fixed by prospective happiness-levels of himself and other persons, and not at all by his desire for other things. Of course, the definition might be framed in terms of total desire-satisfaction of all the parties, but we shall see in Chapter 13 why we must avoid this conception.

In view of these simplifications one might hesitate to embrace inferences subsequently drawn about precisely which moral system a fully rational but perfectly benevolent person would support. But in fact there is no reason to think that giving up the simplifications would lead to significantly different results (except the one about population control, which has importance restricted to special issues).

Once these simplifications are allowed, the main inference is quite obvious. For a perfectly benevolent rational person will tend to do whatever will maximize expectable happiness. He will most support that system which as a whole—taking into account probable effects on behaviour and the resulting contribution to happiness, and also the costs of the system such as restriction on individual freedom, the unpleasant pangs of guilt, and the effort of moral education—will maximize the expectable happiness of all sentient creatures. In that sense we can say that he will opt for some kind of 'utilitarian' moral system.

It will be obvious why a perfectly benevolent person will not be influenced by possible special gains to himself because of his special abilities and position in the social–economic system. It is because he wants the largest possible increments of happiness for sentient beings, whoever they are.

Let us now consider which moral code a perfectly selfish but rational person would choose. A completely selfish person presumably takes no interest in the happiness or welfare of others. (I assume he is not sadistic.) Obviously he will choose the one, among the feasible options open, which will maximize his expectable welfare, where we define his 'welfare' in terms of his self-regarding rational desires—his happiness but other satisfactions too.

We would be spared the necessity of this discussion if it could be shown that a fully rational person must be perfectly benevolent —since our aim has been to find which moral system a perfectly rational person would support. Some philosophers have thought this can be shown. Henry Sidgwick might be said to have offered a kind of proof. For he asserted that it is self-evident that 'the good of any one individual is of no more importance, from the point of view ... of the Universe, than the good of any other'; and he also claimed that it 'is evident to me that as a rational being I am bound to aim at good generally' and 'ought not to prefer my own lesser good to the greater good of another'. His first point need not be denied, but admission that from the point of view of Heaven my welfare is not preferable to that of others does not imply that from my point of view my good is not preferable, i.e. not preferred by me when I am fully rational. So there is no proof, and his latter contention need not be accepted as self-evident.[1]

Thomas Nagel has recently argued—inconclusively I think—a point similar to Sidgwick's.[2]

Sidgwick also urged that at least it is as rational to take an interest in the happiness of another person as in one's own future happiness; and John Perry (1976) has suggested that one takes an interest in another person's welfare to the extent that he is like one now—so that Methuselah at twenty-five would take less interest in his own happiness at age one thousand than he would in that of a contemporary exact replica of himself. These suggestions are intriguing, but a careful analysis of the psychological genesis of benevolence, at least as depicted above in Chapter 7, suggests that even a fully rational person will take more interest in his own welfare in normal situations than in that of another person. (This conclusion depends on the fact that there is more opportunity for firm conditioning of valence to the idea of one's own future welfare than to that of the future welfare of another.) So we must reluctantly set aside the idea that a fully rational person would want the happiness of other sentient creatures generally equally with his own.

The serious options open to a perfectly selfish man, however, are restricted by the requirement of viability. Let us suppose, for the moment, that the persons in the group with whom he will interact and with whom he must form a moral community are equally as selfish as himself. Obviously a moral system which serves his interests at their expense would not enlist their loyalty, and there is no point in his supporting it. A moral system which makes moral demands on others in order to produce consequences he will like must, if it is to be viable, at least make the same moral demands on him, thus possibly producing conse-

---

[1] Sidgwick, 1922, p. 382. It is interesting to note that C. D. Broad's intuitions came out differently: 'It does seem to me conceivable, although not self-evident, that I ought to desire *more strongly* the occurrence of a good state of mind in myself than the occurrence of an equally good state of mind in anyone else; whilst it seems self-evident that I ought to desire *to some degree* its occurrence anywhere.' (1934, p. 245.)

[2] Nagel, 1970. See the critical review by Sturgeon, 1973; also Mackie, 1976, p. 32. See also some parallel discussions in Gauthier, 1963, Chaps. 6–9; Parfit, 1971, p. 26; Baier, 1958, pp. 104 f., 118 ff., 156 ff., 298 ff.

quences which they will like. If the selfish chooser wants, as he will, protection against crimes against the person, such as assault, negligent injury, and libel, he must choose a moral system which provides the same protection for others, thereby restricting his activities and giving them what they surely want. A selfish person who supports a rule which provides a desired circumstance for all because it, among feasible options, maximizes expectable welfare for him is inadvertently also supporting a rule which will maximize expectable welfare for the group (put each one on a higher 'indifference curve'). Thus all selfish rational persons, except for magicians and dictators, will support a minimal moral code for selfish reasons, and the code they choose will maximize the expectable welfare of the group.

But, when selfish persons have different or conflicting desires, what will be the status of a moral system which will advantage some at the cost of others? What happens if a feature of a moral system would advantage women, or well-trained persons with skills in short supply as contrasted with less well-trained workers without demanded special skills? What is the impact of the requirement of feasibility for cases of this sort? Can any code get generally accepted, or will each group simply support the morality congenial to its own advantage?

We can view the potential conflict here as a conflict between the better-off and the worse-off, with the worse-off standing to gain by a morality of equality, and the better-off standing to gain by a morality of inequality which let us suppose underwrites the status quo. Is there any reason why selfish persons in either position might find it necessary, in view of the requirement of viability, to make concessions to the other group? We can say, Yes, but only with a number of important reservations which we shall come to shortly; and in principle and in the long-run it is the morality of equality which is more viable. The viability of a moral system will depend, of course, on the distribution of inequalities: if the difference between top and bottom is small, and nearly equal numbers are above and below the average, an unequal system may be stable possibly indefinitely. But if the inequalities are large, and a few individuals are much better off, with the large majority below the average, the morality of inequality will have trouble commanding general loyalty and support. Or, to take specifically economic status, a system of inequality may be viable indefinitely if everyone is reasonably well off. But in a world of scarcity, a person well below the average will not have enough to eat or a decent place to live, and correspondingly if he is rational he will be apt to have fierce objection to the system, not matched by the dedication to it by the better-off, since the advantages of being above the average are not comparably motivating—an effect of the operation of the principle of the declining marginal utility of money. I am assuming, of course, that selfish rational people will question principles that are manifestly in conflict with their own self-interest. The moral principles which will be most viable will be those which arouse least total resentment, counting both numbers and intensity; and hence equalitarian principles will tend to be more viable.

Suppose we agree tentatively that selfish persons would tend to opt for equalitarian moral principles. Would they be moral principles which would be happiness-maximizing, for the group as a whole? In large part they would be. We shall see in Chapter 16 that the more equal distributions of income, assuming that normally the utility-curves of individuals are not known, tend to maximize expectable happiness. On the other hand, a happiness-maximizing system will require some departures from strict equality.

If we take into account the earlier conclusion that rational selfish persons will support a moral system which provides protections all rational persons want, we have the conclusion that roughly, and in the long-run, rational selfish persons will support a happiness-maximizing moral system, not intentionally but inadvertently, since of course each rational selfish person will support his best— his expectable-welfare-maximizing—option among the viable ones open to him.

The reader will have noticed that the assumptions which lead to this conclusion are not quite realistic. A selfish chooser among moral systems need not suppose that others are as rational and selfish as himself; in fact, many in his society may be rather benevolent, or may dislike conflict of any sort and prefer to accept less than an equal share than take a firm public stand in opposition to the status quo, especially if it is a system which does not disadvantage them too markedly. Again, the selfish person may not feel any necessity to support a system convincing to others in the long-run; he may be well-satisfied with the short-run, which may last as long as he will live. If he has an advantage in an existing economic system, why should he support moral principles critical of it, just because those principles will hardly command the allegiance of rational people in the long-term future?

The reasoning I have suggested is the best we can do to justify one moral system to everyone. A happiness-maximizing system may not be fully justifiable to a selfish person, who enjoys an advantageous position, perhaps because of intelligence or inherited wealth. What we can do successfully is justify some part of a Hobbesian morality to all selfish men, rather than no moral system at all. But Hobbesian moralities are of different sorts. A central core—the protective system roughly supportive of the criminal law —can be justified to all selfish persons alike, and indeed to persons of any degree of benevolence; but various possible additions to this may not, any of them, be justifiable to all selfish persons, in view of the fact that support of different ones may promise short-term advantage to some group at a given time. This result, while not ideally gratifying to a philosopher, need not leave him with the feeling that the enterprise of moral philosophy must fail. It is no failure to be unable to demonstrate what in principle cannot be demonstrated. If we succeed in seeing clearly which moral principles can be justified to whom, and why, we have done as much as is humanly possible. In any case we shall discover, in the following chapter, that it is short of catastrophic if one and the same morality is not justifiable to everybody.

In one major respect rational benevolent persons will support a moral system different from that which rational selfish persons support. For the rational selfish person is interested in parts of a moral code which benefit others, only to the extent to which benefit in return is provided for himself. So he supports a system calling on him to submit to moral obligation to others only in so far as those others can help or hinder him. He wants only reciprocal ties. The benevolent man, in contrast, wants the benefits of the moral system extended to those who can do him neither harm nor good: to future generations, to animals, to the mentally defective, small children, and possibly foetuses.

What inference can we draw from the above discussion for the more realistic case of persons whose degree of benevolence falls between these two extremes? It looks as if we might expect these persons to be less willing than perfectly benevolent persons to make sacrifices for future generations and animals—for all those groups in no position to harm or benefit the choosers. They would, like all the others, opt for the protective part of a moral code which would maximize expectable welfare. But, when we come to the part of the moral code which concerns allocation of goods, matters would be more complex. Since they are assumed to have some benevolence, they will be sensitive to those considerations which will lead rational perfectly benevolent persons to opt for an expectable-happiness-maximizing system. Again, if a person has enough benevolence not to wish to take advantage of those who are themselves benevolent, or undisposed to be active in defence of self-interest, he will again tend to give his support to the expectable-happiness-maximizing system. But if he has less than this benevolence, or if he is disinclined to take a long-range point of view, his tendency to support a moral system will be rather like that of some of the purely selfish rational persons.

It would be nice if we could identify a specific level of benevolence for all fully rational persons and provide a behavioural definition of this level. That is too much to hope for; and indeed there are reasons of theory for supposing that different persons would, if fully rational, have somewhat different levels of benevolence. It is obviously quite a difficult question what level of benevolence even some specified individual, like the reader, would attain if he were fully rational. So we must be content with rather abstract reasoning.

The argument is strong enough, however, to warrant raising a question which I shall discuss in three later chapters: 'Which moral system is the one which, taken as a whole, would maximize expectable happiness or welfare?'

The above argument, however, is complex and less than ideally coercive; moreover, the conclusion involves reservations, exceptions, and complexities. Is there not some other line of argument which would do better? Some simpler lines of reasoning have been popular in recent years; and some philosophers have employed forms of them which are claimed to have much more spectacular success—to reach conclusions which are simple, unqualified, and demonstrated. I shall pause in the following chapter and consider whether these types of reasoning really do compare favourably with the complex and untidy argument I have offered.

CHAPTER XII

THREE DIFFERENT DERIVATIONS OF THE RIGHT

I HAVE suggested that the question 'Which actions are morally right?' can best be construed as the question 'Which actions would be permitted by the moral code which a fully rational person would most strongly tend to support, for a society in which he expected to live a lifetime?'. In the preceding chapter I took a first step towards identifying the moral code a fully rational person would most support; but the argument was not ideally coercive. It may have been optimistic in its reliance on the 'requirement of viability', and its claim that many types of desire are irrational was based on plausible analyses of examples, not on a formal demonstration. Its conclusion was that the moral system which would be supported is that one which will maximize welfare or happiness of some group including the chooser, how small or how inclusive the group still to be debated.

Perhaps, however, a change in the question would make things turn out more happily; on the one hand maybe a different question would seem more the one which on full reflection we want to raise when we ask 'Which actions are morally right?', and on the other hand it might permit simpler reasoning to conclusions about specifically what is right or wrong—the deduction would be more straightforward, would require only generally accepted premises, and would be rigorous.

In fact, such a change of question will work no miracles; the major alternative theories are worse. In order to show this I shall briefly examine three theories highly influential at the moment, and see whether the questions raised are more, or at least, equally pertinent, and whether they permit an easier movement to substantive normative conclusions: the ideal observer theory; the present theory of R. M. Hare; and the veil of ignorance theory of John Rawls.

1. THE IDEAL OBSERVER THEORY

I shall propose two versions of the first theory. According to the first version, if we want to know whether something is morally right, the question is: 'Would it be permitted by the moral code which an omniscient, omnipercipient, disinterested, dispassionate, but otherwise normal person would most strongly tend to support as the moral code for a society in which he expected to live?'— a conception close to that of Roderick Firth (1952). The second version differs either in the addition of 'benevolent' to the above qualifications, or in the substitution of it for 'disinterested and dispassionate'. Of course, a precise meaning for that term would have to be supplied.[1]

If we compare the question the ideal observer theory equates with the question 'Which actions are morally right?' with the question I have suggested as a substitute or replacement for this ordinary language question, it is clear that the difference between the two proposals is the difference between the conception of a 'fully rational person' and an 'omniscient, omnipercipient, disinterested, dispassionate, but otherwise normal person'. The essential differences between these two concepts are as follows: (1) A 'fully rational person' is defined as one who makes full use of all available information, but not as a person who is omniscient or omnipercipient. (2) A fully rational person is one whose desires have been fumigated (or enlarged) by cognitive psychotherapy; the alternative conception lays down no such requirement. (3) It is not a conceptual necessity that a fully rational person be either disinterested or benevolent; it is an empirical question whether or to what extent he is. (4) One might question how nearly 'normal' a person who is omniscient and disinterested and dispassionate might be in other respects; but equally one might ask how nearly normal is a person who has undergone cognitive psychotherapy. I shall pay no attention to possible differences at this point.

[1] I have phrased the theory so as to be more similar to my own account than is common. It is usually phrased so as to be about particular cases. My formulation does not make the theory less plausible, and renders the differences more perspicuous.

Writers who have occasionally supported something like this theory, in addition to historical figures like David Hume and Adam Smith, include C. D. Broad, Roderick Firth, Jonathan Harrison, and William Kneale. At one time I defended it myself.

The first version of the theory employs the notion of 'impartiality' or 'disinterest', terms which call for explanation they seldom receive. Firth was precise, and I shall follow his exposition. He defined 'disinterested' as meaning devoid of particular interests, where 'particular interest' is a desire or aversion to something which, at least to the degree to which it occurs, depends on the person's belief that the thing has a property which is not an abstract universal but can be explained only by the use of proper names or indexicals. For instance, if a person favours some action of the United Nations because he thinks it good for the U.S.A., he has manifested a particular interest; if he favours it because it fosters peace for everybody, he has not. Obviously a person with no particular interests will not be inclined to favour himself or his friends in his decisions. Indeed, he might not, as far as the definition goes, have benevolent attitudes either; if he is benevolent, it is because he is a normal person, and not because of anything in the definition. He might be malevolent. It is not surprising that some writers would wish to add 'benevolent' to the conception of an 'ideal observer'.

Let us leave aside benevolence for the moment, and consider how we might infer what kind of moral system an omniscient, disinterested, but otherwise normal person might support. (1) There is a serious obstacle to inferring, from this conception, what kind of moral system would be supported, because of the plethora of desires an omniscient and disinterested being might have, for a reduction in which the theory provides no reason—none, in particular, which is parallel to the reduction required by the conception that the desires involved be 'rational'. There is nothing in the theory which rules out, as irrelevant, such aversions as those to gambling, homosexual behaviour, hair-style, indeed anything at all not conforming to the chooser's own life-style. An omniscient and disinterested person might just be averse to these forms of behaviour for no further reason, and support a moral code which prohibits them. It might be said that such intrinsic aversions could not occur in an omniscient person; but why not? Thus, while it is often counted a virtue of the ideal observer theory that it is not necessarily utilitarian, and that an omniscient and disinterested person might want a moral code which required keeping promises, telling the truth, etc., for no further reason, this very virtue of catholicity in fact apparently prevents any inference at all to which moral code would be supported, because no intrinsic desires are ruled out as irrelevant, on some such ground as irrationality. (2) It is true that an omniscient and disinterested person, if he wanted a moral system at all, would presumably support only one which is viable, which could command the allegiance of people generally, and this fact would set some restriction on the content of a code he might support. (3) It might be supposed that the quality of disinterest would set a restriction on the content of the code. And it is true that a disinterested person would not support a moral system which favoured specific individuals; but he could perfectly well have desires which are partial towards classes of individuals. Thus he might condone inhumane treatment of animals, and he might want special privileges for women or professors. Such preferences are not ruled out by the definition of 'disinterest'. Indeed it is not clear that a purely disinterested being would support a moral system at all. Clearly he would lack one quite good reason normal people have for supporting a moral code: that they themselves would like to be able to rely on promises, to be safe from assault, and to be able to command the assistance of others in times of distress. For a disinterested person would not support a moral system for reasons of personal interest. And it is possible he would not support a moral system for its contribution to human welfare generally; for he might be indifferent to human welfare. It seems, then, that writers including Rawls who have thought there is no way to infer the content of a favoured moral code from this conception of an 'ideal observer', have been correct.

Matters are somewhat altered if we add 'benevolence' to the conception of an ideal observer. Then, at least, we could know that an ideal observer would support some kind of moral system for the sake of the welfare of sentient beings. But for more precise inferences to the content of the code that would be supported, we need to know more precisely how benevolent he is to be. One possibility is to stipulate benevolence in the sense of 'perfect benevolence' explained in the preceding chapter (p. 215). Then we should know that, as benevolent, he would prefer the code which would produce the greater long-term welfare. (We can drop reference to probability, since the choooser is to be omniscient.) This stipulation, however, is still too weak for the conception to yield definite implications about which moral system would be chosen. For benevolence is presumably only one of the motives of an ideal observer; as noted above, he might well have strong aversions for no further reasons to various forms of behaviour such as: homosexuality, long hair for men, and so on. It might be assumed, of course, that the degree of benevolence is so strong that any other desires relevant to the choice of a moral system would always turn out to be weaker than it; then, we could infer that the theory would imply that some kind of welfare-maximizing moral code would be supported. Such an assumption, however, would be out of the spirit of the theory, whose supporters have generally wanted to frame it so that it is neutral among different normative systems; they have wanted to propose it only as a good analysis of 'is morally right'.

Let us leave aside the question of the utility of the conception for deriving any normative results. Let us rather ask whether 'Which kind of moral system would an ideal observer choose?' is somehow a better question for replacement of 'Which kinds of act are morally right?' than the question 'Which kind of moral system would a perfectly rational person choose?'. It is far from evident that it is. It might be said that the former question is a good account, after all, of what we mean when we ask what is morally right; but if the contentions of Chapter 1 are sound, this claim is not one of serious weight. In contrast, if a certain moral system would be chosen by a fully rational person, facts and logic have been taken into account in a maximal way in the choice of the moral system; whereas that is not the case in the choices of an 'ideal observer' because of absence of the requirement of rational desires. Further: Would a given moral code be justified to you if you knew that you would support it if you were fully informed and either completely disinterested or benevolent or both? Suppose a selfish person is told that, if he were an ideal observer, he would choose a moral code of such-and-such a kind. Would that fact necessarily work as a recommendation to him to support such a moral system of that type? Not necessarily.

2. THE THEORY OF R. M. HARE[2]

Professor Hare has sometimes suggested that his theory is extensionally equivalent to some 'benevolence' version of the 'ideal observer' theory, in its implications for action. However, he also thinks that his theory makes possible, given one plausible empirical assumption about human motivation, a defence of utilitarianism, in two senses. On the one hand he thinks he can show that an act is *morally right* if it maximizes utility in the sense of desire-satisfaction of everyone affected; on the other hand he thinks he can show that the moral code it is morally right for educators to teach is a form of rule-utilitarianism: principles the acceptance of which would maximize utility.

It is interesting to compare Hare's derivation with the ideal observer theory. He uses two premisses, the first of which is a claim about the meaning of 'is morally right' in ordinary language. (I shall not attempt to appraise this claim; I have criticized it elsewhere (1964), and Chapter 1 has pointed out why such appeals to ordinary language in any case are not coercive.) This claim, of course, is different from the corresponding analysis of the ideal observer theory. Hare's view is that 'it is morally obligatory for me to do *A* rather than *B* in these circumstances' comes to the same thing as, 'I *prefer* [or, what comes to the same: 'I hereby prescribe'] *A* rather than *B* done in *any* situation just like this, given I am prudent and fully informed and believe that I will occupy seriatim the position (including the likes and dislikes of the person involved) of everyone affected by whether *A* or *B* is done, in a sequence of lives.'

Hare then introduces an empirical premiss (which of course an ideal observer theorist can also employ, if it is true): that, if any person is prudent and fully informed, he will perform that act at any time which will maximize his benefit over his lifetime, where 'maximize benefit' is taken to mean 'satisfy all desires maximally' or in other words 'bring about those events which

---

[2] The following discussion is based on Hare, 1963, Chaps. 6–9; 1972, Chap. 7; 1976; and the sixth lecture of a series given at Notre Dame University in 1973, of which Professor Hare kindly gave me a copy. I rely most on the 1976 paper.

he will most want'.[3] (This is rather similar to my explanation, in Chapter 4, of what I called an act 'rational to a first approximation'.)

Hare infers from his second premiss that, in a choice between A and B, given I am prudent and believe I shall occupy sometime the position of each person affected by my act, I shall prefer A if and only if I believe the aggregate desire-satisfaction, for everyone affected, is greater than the aggregate desire-satisfaction if B is done. But then, by the first premiss, I shall properly say that it is morally obligatory for me to do A. Thus one can say generally: 'It is morally obligatory for me to do A rather than B if and only if the aggregate benefit (= desire-satisfaction) for everyone affected is greater if A is done than if B is done.' But this, Hare says, is the principle of utility.[4]

For the sake of the argument, let us suppose that Hare's conclusion about which acts are morally obligatory is accepted. One might think that the principle of utility in the ordinary sense (say that of Mill or Bentham or Sidgwick) has been established. But in fact matters are more complicated than appears, and the problems which beset inferences to normative conclusions from the ideal observer theory begin to appear, of course in a somewhat different way. The simplicity of Hare's normative theory begins to become rather clouded. For, in order to find which act is morally right, on this view, we must take into account all the

---

[3] Is it the desires I now have for future states of myself which I shall satisfy if I am prudent and well informed, or the desires I shall have later? We saw in Chapter 4 that these are different questions, and that what an informed person will do is not precisely to act as if he now had the desires he will have later, even if he knows he will have them later. Hare's argument seems to require the second interpretation: for it supposes that if I am prudent I shall seek to satisfy the desire I shall have when I am in the shoes of another person, at one of those stages of life when I am to occupy his position.

[4] The reader may wish, in view of the above, to scrutinize the following statements by Hare (1976, pp. 116–18): 'I am prescribing universally [when I say something is morally obligatory] for all situations just like the one I am considering; and thus for all such situations, *whatever* role, among those in the situations, I might myself occupy. I shall therefore give equal weight to the equal interests of the occupants of all the roles in the situation; and, since any of these occupants might be myself, this weight will be positive.... If I am trying to give equal weight to the equal interest of all parties in a situation, I must, it seems, regard a benefit or harm done to one party as of equal value or disvalue to an equal benefit or harm done to any other party. This seems to mean that I shall promote the interests of the parties most, while giving equal weight to them all, if I maximize the total benefit over the entire population; and this is the classical principle of utility.'

basic desires of everybody affected by an act. So doing avoids speculating about which desires would remain after 'cognitive psychotherapy', but it brings in complications arising from the variety of desires needing to be considered, e.g. for other people to wear their hair in a certain way or generally conform to a certain life-style; for achievement for oneself and one's children; for other people's happiness; for social or economic equality, or economic distribution in accordance with some formula or other; or even for the suffering of others. A consequence is that a given action can 'affect' a very large number of people: my divorcing my spouse 'affects' all those persons who prefer that no one gets divorced. Apparently, in order to find the right thing to do, one must proceed as follows: First, for every person the satisfaction of whose desires (in this broad sense) is affected by whether I do A or B, we must get his vote as between A and B, presumably his prudent or rational vote in view of all his desires (perhaps in the sense of Chapter 4). A mere majority vote will not suffice, since on the above supposition the degree to which anyone is affected must be taken into account. So we shall have to weight the intensity of his rational preference for one action rather than the other, for each voter. It is intriguing to consider how this might be done. Are we to count the votes only of people living at the time of the choice? Hare himself is prepared to count the preferences of the dead along with the living, and among the living of those who know nothing about a choice (and its outcomes) along with those who do; indeed, he is willing to count the preferences of purely possible beings. In particular, in order to know if it is right for me to get a divorce, there must be millions both living and dead who have a preference, and whose views require weighing, not to mention possible beings.

If we ask whether it is simpler to identify the morally right act on the basis of Hare's theory, or on mine as indicated in the preceding chapter, it is far from clear that Hare's view gets the palm for simplicity.

It is questionable whether Hare's theory should be classified as a form of utilitarianism. At least it is if we define an 'act-utilitarian' as one who holds that an act is morally obligatory if and only if its performance will maximize future happiness, as compared with the performance of any other act open to the agent.

Hare recognizes one may raise another, easier question: 'On the evidence at the agent's disposal, which act of his is *most probably* right in the foregoing (objective) sense?' Or, alternatively, one might ask: 'On the evidence which is available and which one could obtain with a reasonable amount of effort considering the importance of the issue, which act is more probably right in the objective sense?' Possibly these questions can be answered.

I have already noted that Hare's theory is a two-tier theory: on the one hand there is the question which is the morally right act; on the other there is the question of *morally good* acts—acts it is best, or morally right, to recommend to our children or ourselves. In contrast, my proposal was that the morally right act is the one permitted by the moral code fully rational persons would support; it is a one-level theory. Hare's two-tier theory leads to the conclusion that on occasion the morally good act is one that is not morally right.

His reason for the second tier is that the working morality we teach our children cannot involve the elaborate reasoning sketched above. It must take into account the limited intelligence and other weaknesses of ordinary people; it should be fairly simple and give specific directions for frequent problems; since persons must often act quickly it must be one which a person can apply rapidly; since people tend to rationalize in their own favour it must minimize scope for judgement. It must not set standards too high, since doing so may cause morality simply to fall into disrepute; its formulation must take into account the disadvantages of labouring to instil a moral code. Within these restrictions we are to teach the moral code, the teaching of which will maximize desire-satisfaction as far as we can determine. The aim of teaching will be to attach guilt-feelings to one's own failures to conform to the selected code, and feelings of disapproval to failings of other people. As he puts it, the teachers will 'implant' in their children 'not rules of thumb, but principles which they will not be able to break without the greatest repugnance, and whose breach by others will arouse in them the highest indignation' (1976, p. 124). An act which conforms to the moral code we ought to teach he calls the 'morally good' act. The objectively right will not be forgotten, however; children must be taught something about this since they will some day have to decide which moral code to teach their own children, and they may from time to time need to re-educate themselves morally, when the code they have been taught is no longer the best code to teach. Furthermore, children will be taught to revert to the determination of what will maximize desire-satisfaction when the principles of the code they have been taught conflict, or 'when [p. 124] there is something highly unusual about the case which prompts the question whether the general principles are really fitted to deal with it'.

I have commented on the disadvantages of his conception of the morally *right* in the closing pages of Chapter 10; the two-tier theory tears 'morally wrong' and 'morally bad' apart.

Does Hare's theory as a whole permit simpler, more rigorous derivation of conclusions about what is morally right and morally good, requiring only premisses which are highly plausible? The reader can make up his own mind on this point. But, in addition to the matter of simplicity, there is the problem of whether his main question—stated in his first premiss—formulates the question which on reflection we want to raise. One thing an answer to his question does not do: it does not justify a moral code to a person in the sense of showing him that it is the code he himself would support if facts and logic had been fully brought to bear on his motivational machinery. It is by no means clear why an answer to it should disalienate a person who has become alienated from morality. All that Hare even aims to show is that, if a person uses 'morally ought' in the standard English sense, to be consistent he must say that someone morally ought to do something only if it would conform with the 'aggregated' preferences of everyone affected (in his sense). He hardly attempts to show why a person might be interested in using 'morally ought' in this allegedly standard English sense.

I shall return to this and related matters in the final paragraphs of the present chapter.

3. CHOICE BEHIND A VEIL OF IGNORANCE: THE THEORY OF JOHN RAWLS[5]

A third theory is rather like Hare's in purporting to reach normative conclusions by a simple, reasonably rigorous, and conclusive argument, and, like both theories discussed above, has a proposal somewhat different from mine about what question a philosopher should be asking about a moral code. This is the theory of Professor Rawls. His theory is somewhat similar to the ideal observer theory, but differs, in its conception of a useful meaning for 'morally right', by imposing requirements on the *beliefs* of choosers among moral systems, whereas the other theory imposes requirements on the *motivation* of the choosers (that it be impartial, benevolent). The benevolence requirement is replaced, in the Rawlsian theory, by a 'veil of ignorance'. Whereas my own proposal has roughly been that 'is morally right' be construed as 'would be permitted by any moral system which *fully rational* persons would support . . .', the Rawlsian proposal is roughly that 'is morally right' be construed as 'would be permitted by any moral code which *all rational* self-interested persons behind a "veil of ignorance" would choose. . .*'.[6]

Rawls asserts that his conception of choice behind a veil of ignorance has much the same effects as the concept of benevolence in the ideal observer theory; but he thinks it enjoys very marked advantages. He writes: 'The combination of mutual disinterest and the veil of ignorance achieves the same purpose as benevolence. For this combination of conditions forces each person in the original position to take the good of others into account. . . . This pair of assumptions has enormous advantages over that of benevolence plus knowledge. As I have noted, the latter is so

[5] See Rawls, 1971. Some other writers have employed much the same basic conceptions, but used them to arrive at very different results. See Harsanyi, 1953, 1955; also Vickrey, 1961, 1960. For criticisms of these economists see Rawls, 1971, pp. 162 ff.; also Sen, 1970, pp. 141 ff.

[6] Rawls's conception of 'rational' is different from mine, and I have written 'rational*' to emphasize the fact. It has no element corresponding to my requirement of surviving 'cognitive psychotherapy'. It is close to what I have called 'rational to a first approximation', in the sense of being nearly materially equivalent to that. The central part of the idea is that the rational person seeks to realize his ends at minimum cost, prefers a means which realizes all the objectives of alternative means and more (produces a more inclusive set of desired outcomes), or has the best chance of doing these things. (See Rawls, 1971, pp. 411 ff.)

complex that no definite theory at all can be worked out. Not only are the complications caused by so much information insurmountable, but the motivational assumption requires clarification. For example, what is the relative strength of benevolent desires? In brief, the combination of mutual disinterestedness plus the veil of ignorance has the merits of simplicity and clarity while at the same time insuring the effects of what are at first sight morally more attractive assumptions.' (1971, pp. 148–9.)

For Rawls, then, the important question for appraising moralities is: 'What would be permitted by any moral code which all rational* self-interested persons behind a "veil of ignorance" would choose . . . ?' Why does he think this the important question? His answer seems to be that it is because of the virtues of the corresponding principle: 'An act A is morally right if and only if it would be permitted by any moral code which all rational* mutually disinterested persons behind a veil of ignorance would choose.' This principle is one that has much to be said for it. For one thing, the principle is 'natural', 'plausible', and commands 'a broad measure of agreement'. Further, it serves, he says, to rule out of account (by placing them behind the veil of ignorance) some considerations that are 'irrelevant from the standpoint of justice', such as the natural or social advantages of the chooser. But, more important, when the principle is taken with reasoning about what in fact rational* self-interested persons would choose behind a veil of ignorance, it has implications about which actions or institutions are right or wrong, just or unjust; and these moral principles coincide with our moral intuitions, in so far as they are in a state of 'reflective equilibrium' (see above, p. 17 ff.). He supposes that when moral principles coincide with our intuitions in a state of reflective equilibrium, they are as well justified as moral principles can be. Moreover, the basic principle as formulated permits a relatively simple argument to normative principles, whereas 'without these limitations on knowledge [the veil of ignorance] the bargaining problem of the original position would be hopelessly complicated'. So Rawls thinks we are justified in accepting the basic principle, and the corresponding definition of 'just' or 'right'.[7]

---

[7] For Rawls's discussion touching most nearly on these general issues, see 1971, pp. 17–22, 121–2, 136–42, 577–83.

A typical normative principle Rawls thinks can be derived—and a normative principle he thinks coincides with our intuitions—is the Difference Principle: that 'the social order is not to establish and secure the more attractive prospects of those better off unless doing so is to the advantage of those less fortunate'. (1971, p. 75.)

Two questions arise over this reasoning. First, should we accept a principle because it coincides with our intuitions? Second, does his principle really imply the normative conclusions in a simple way? (A person might just affirm his 'intuitive principles' and refuse to accept the basic principles and the definition of 'just' or 'morally right' which goes with it.)

The answer to the first question has been discussed in Chapter 1, where I argued that consonance with intuitions does not, without a good deal more discussion not so far forthcoming, show a principle to be more credible, and that there are good reasons for not appealing to intuitions as a test of moral truth: the diversity of intuitions around the world, and our knowledge that our intuitions are what they are because of the cultural tradition within which we stand. It is sometimes claimed that the logic or epistemology of moral principles is no worse, in an appeal to intuitions, than is the logic of empirical science; but defenders of this view never remove the difference between observation or experiment—data on which the corpus of scientific theory rests—and moral intuitions. Science is not based on what scientists think but on what they see.

However, it is premature to worry about whether a principle and a definition are supported by the consonance of their implications with our intuitions until it has been shown that they do in fact logically lead to some normative principles, possibly ones to which we are intuitively committed. Does Rawls's conception of self-interested rational* choice of principles behind a 'veil of ignorance' actually do this? Can one derive rigorously some fundamental normative principles from his conception?

A good many writers have thought not. They think, for instance, that Rawls never establishes that rational* persons in this position would adopt a 'maximin' strategy – an essential step in his derivation of the Difference Principle. And, they think, there are comparable gaps in his defence of the lexical priority of liberty (a principle which in any case only very doubtfully corresponds with our intuitions). For a discussion of these issues see Norman Daniels (ed.), 1975.

If we scrutinize the basic conception of choice in the original position, that is choice of principles by rational* self-interested persons behind a 'veil of ignorance', we shall see that this idea is much less simple and 'natural' than might at first appear. I shall not object to the proposal that the choice be by 'mutually disinterested' persons: I have myself raised the question what selfish persons would want in a moral code, and while most persons are not selfish it is interesting to see what can be shown about which normative principles would be chosen by rational* persons who are so. I shall also ignore the fact, noted earlier (p. 189), that there is a puzzling vagueness about his conception of 'choice' of a moral system, which leaves us in the dark over whether to choose a moral system is also to choose all the mechanisms necessary for its continuation and effectiveness as a social reality. I shall concentrate on his conception of a 'veil of ignorance' and his psychology of choice.

Readers of Rawls will recall his concept of choice in the original position: Individuals are conceived to be the same as they in fact now are, except that interest in other persons is not assumed, and it is supposed they are rational* and are deprived of a good deal of information. This is straightforward so far, except we need to know more about choice in a state of 'ignorance'. This state is thought of as a temporary amnesia: the individuals are conceived to have forgotten some things they know or believe, in particular everything which might enable a self-interested person to choose principles favouring himself. How much amnesia is covered? Rawls excludes all knowledge about oneself such as one's abilities, desires, social and economic position (except in so far as these may be inferred from general scientific laws); and he rules out all historical information and information about the economic and social structure of one's own and all other societies (again except in so far as this can be inferred from laws). Some important information is allowed, however—information it would be difficult to 'forget'. For a chooser does know that he does or will exist (he does not know when, that is, where in the stream of generations); and he knows that he is human.

Rawls's point about the relation of the veil of ignorance and the contrasting assumption of benevolence is important, because it follows that exactly how the veil of ignorance is drawn (what it hides) amounts to a stipulation about the directions or extent to which benevolence is extended, fixing the classes of beings towards whom we are to be benevolent. Consider an example. Suppose I am a man, choosing a moral system. If I am self-interested, I shall choose a system which benefits men—say by dropping the idea that men have a duty to equal sharing of household chores with an employed spouse. But if in my choice of a moral system I did not know whether, in the society in which the projected system would operate, I would be male or female, I would refrain from favouring either sex. The choice would be the same as if I knew I were male but had so much benevolence that I did not want to give myself an advantage. Thus the veil of ignorance amounts to perfect benevolence in certain directions: my benevolence towards others is as strong as my love of myself.

We saw earlier that a definition of benevolence is important for the ideal-observer theory in the benevolence form. The same with the veil of ignorance; where it is drawn is very important. And one can ask, in both cases, why at one place rather than another? Here both theories contrast with my proposal, which presumes benevolence only to the extent a given person would have it if he were fully rational. I concede it is difficult to know how much this will be in a given person, and whether different individuals would be benevolent to the same extent if they were fully rational. But my proposal has the virtue of making the issue a matter of fact. How is it decided where the 'veil of ignorance' is to be drawn, in Rawls's case? For instance, why not stipulate that the chooser of a moral system is allowed to know that he is sentient, but not to know whether he is human? Obviously drawing the veil at one place would make a difference to the moral principles that would be chosen to apply to animals. (But see Rawls, 1971, pp. 504 f. and 512.) Again, why might the veil of ignorance not be extended so that the chooser is allowed to know that he has been conceived, but not whether he will be born? Drawing the veil at one place might also make a difference to decisions about the morality of abortion. Some philosophers think that possible beings have a prima facie right to be brought into existence; hence one may ask whether the veil of ignorance should not be extended so that the chooser of a moral system is allowed to know that he is a possible sentient creature, but not that he is or will be actual. I have remarked that Rawls regards his basic principle as 'natural', but it is hardly obvious or a matter of agreement when we come to these details.[8]

More important for the substantive implications of the 'veil of ignorance' is the sweep of the prohibition otherwise: the limitation 'to knowledge of the general laws of science. This far-reaching restriction is clearly a sufficient condition for preventing choosers from advantaging themselves in the selection of a moral system; but is it necessary? It looks as if this restriction functions not only to remove knowledge which would enable a self-serving choice, but also to prevent intelligent choice. Why should the choosers of moral systems be required to make their choice with so little information? In particular, the theory allows no information about the natural resources or economic possibilities of the society in which the chooser is to live; choosers are not permitted even to have before them information about various possible worlds, as to their natural resources, economic systems, and resultant possible distributions of income, so that a separate set of principles might be chosen for each one. The information denied would not enable an individual chooser to advantage himself since he does not know his own talents and status; but it would enable him to choose a system which would make life better for everybody, and it is not clear why that possibility is ruled out. One can understand the motivation of the restriction on the basis of our knowledge of Rawls's own ethical intuitions about the unacceptability of utilitarianism: thus the assumption of extreme ignorance is important in his theory because it is the cornerstone of his argument that the chooser of moral systems will use a maximin strategy for choosing such systems, and will therefore wind up in opposition to utilitarianism.

Before summarizing what these reflections about the 'veil of ignorance' imply about the force of his general argument, I turn to the other part of his conception of choice on which I said I would comment: his psychology of choice. We know from Chapter 3 that decision and action are always a function of at least

[8] Some of these problems have been pursued by G. S. Kavka, 1975.

two things: beliefs and desires. So far we have considered only the beliefs on the basis of which the choice is to be made. We must consider also the desires.

Rawls depicts the choice situation in a very simple manner. We know the information each is to have at his disposal: roughly (we saw the exceptions) the laws of science—a restriction which functions to prevent anyone from advantaging himself. But now he assumes that each person, in making the choice, is self-interested only; each wants to choose a moral system so as to do the best for himself that he can do. Each knows something of his specific desires, but only what he can learn from psychology and economics—which comprise the general laws from which he might draw inferences, and which do not distinguish his desires from those of others. So, Rawls argues: the same information and the same desires; hence the same strategy and the same conclusions in the way of principles of justice and morality. As he says: 'The veil of ignorance makes possible a unanimous choice of a particular conception of justice. Without these limitations on knowledge the bargaining problem of the original position would be hopelessly complicated.' (1971, p. 140.)

This reasoning contains a factual error—that is, if we think of the hypothetical choice of a moral system as conforming to what we know about the psychology of human action. The psychology of action (described in Chapter 3) indicates that the influence of a desire on action-tendency and action does not depend on awareness of it. The effect on behaviour of desires of which we are unconscious is quite familiar. Indeed, it is a well-supported thesis in psychology that some of the most important processes are ones which get no representation in consciousness.[9] If I am thirsty (want a drink), and reflect that going to the kitchen will produce some iced water, the thirst will operate to augment the action-tendency to move towards the kitchen, without my being necessarily aware of what is going on. (The process is built into the wiring of the brain: no more is necessary.) It is not that the causal process is as follows: First, I notice that I want a drink. Second, I reflect that going to the kitchen will produce

[9] See Nisbett and Wilson, 1977. The authors summarize data from experiments on cognitive dissonance, on subliminal perception, on stimuli influencing problem solving, on awareness of group size effects on helping behaviour.

a drink. Third, I infer that, in view of my wanting a drink, getting one via going to the kitchen will satisfy a desire. Therefore I go to the kitchen. Yet, apparently this is the psychology of choice to which the Rawlsian theory is committed. For it is supposed that if I do not know that I desire something, I will not act in such a way as to bring about the desired event. Accordingly, on his view, ignorance of desires prevents their influencing behaviour. And, since it is hypothesized that in the original position a person will know only about his desires for 'primary goods'—things everyone (allegedly) wants either as an end in itself or as a means to other ends, such as income, wealth, authority, liberty, and self-respect—primary goods are the only things a person in the original position will strive to achieve in his choice of a moral system. But, in fact, since this cognitive theory of action is mistaken, the 'veil of ignorance' cannot operate to prevent the influence of desires, other than those for primary goods, on the choice of a moral system.

Rawls's theory here permits him to ignore several whole classes of desire, all ostensibly relevant to choice of a moral system, which are embarrassingly awkward for his deduction—types already mentioned above, (1) desire that conscience be structured in a certain way (e.g. compassionate) for no further reason, (2) desire that people do not behave in certain ways (e.g. have homosexual contacts) for no further reason, (3a) desires for numerous things such as to own a grandfather clock, (3b) benevolent desire for the happiness or satisfaction of self-regarding desires of others, and (3c) desire for such things as economic equality or the compensation of effort by economic reward. These desires do vary from one person to another, and hence we cannot know about them by inference from general scientific laws.

It is clear that Rawls's derivation of normative principles from the concept of choice in the original position would break down in a very serious way, unless this difficulty is remedied. Assuming that he must operate within the framework of an acceptable psychological theory, the only remedy seems to be for him to incorporate into his description of the original position a restriction on desires, say, to desires for the 'primary goods'.

All these specifications about where the veil of ignorance is to be drawn diminish the force of his proposal that 'An act is morally right if and only if it would be permitted by any moral code which all rational* mutually disinterested persons would choose behind a veil of ignorance.' And correspondingly, the proposed definition of 'morally right' or 'just' is less convincing. At least, it does not appear obviously to be 'plausible', 'natural', and to command 'a broad measure of agreement'. Perhaps, when his principle is explained, it is to some extent rendered plausible if it implies normative principles consonant with our intuitions; but it is so contrived a conception that it can hardly add force to any of these intuitions which we might have doubted but for implication of them by his basic principle.

Some philosophers apparently including Rawls himself think it is a virtue of Rawls's conceptual framework that everyone would make the same choice of a moral system—so that what is right or just is so for everyone. The same individuals would presumably view it as a defect of the conceptual framework I have proposed that there is no guarantee that every fully rational person would support one and the same moral system.

How serious a defect is it, if a defect at all, for the conceptual framework I have defended, if it turned out that fully rational persons do not tend to support the same moral system? What is the importance of unanimity? What is the gain in being able to say that one moral system would be supported by all and is justified for everyone? We should make a distinction between the core features of a moral system, and the less central ones. It seems easy to show that all rational persons would agree on some core features—say, prima facie prohibition of unprovoked assault, slander, theft of property, rape, breach of promise—most of the kinds of conduct prohibited by the criminal or tort law. On the other hand, it is more difficult to show that there will be total agreement about other things—say, about the priorities when basic prohibitions conflict, or about the degree of obligation to future generations, and perhaps to animals. However, it is practically less imperative that people agree about the latter items. Social life would be intolerable without general agreement on some basic matters. But we are accustomed to living with people who are insensitive to the suffering of animals and refuse to worry about future generations; and we know how to put up with disagreements about homosexual behaviour, abortion, and marijuana. In fact, fully rational persons with a substantial degree of benevolence will probably agree on almost all of even these latter matters. But, where they do not, persons who have a certain moral commitment and think it justified need not be shaken by the observation, even when they think—although the evidence usually falls short of requiring this thought—that the others would not change with any amount of information and cognitive psychotherapy.

If a person has a certain code of his own and believes it is justified (for him), is anything important added by the thought that all fully rational persons will agree? One might think that then the agreement somehow has the force of contract—it becomes an undertaking each makes in return for a similar undertaking by others—so that the justified code is somehow made more binding or authoritative.[10] It is generally recognized, however, that the fact people would have agreed to certain principles, if they had been in a position they have in fact not been in, does not constitute any kind of contractual obligation; contracts hypothetical in this sense are not binding. In any case, such a contract could not be the source of the bindingness of all moral principles, for the reasoning presupposes that any contract itself is morally binding. In view of these facts, it would seem that talk of the agreement in the original position amounting to a contract were better dropped.

It does not seem, then, that the conceptual framework supported in this book is necessarily defective, in leaving open the possibility that fully rational persons do not acknowledge or agree to the same moral principles.

What is the force of knowing that one would, along with all others, have chosen certain moral principles if one had been making a choice behind a veil of ignorance, in the 'original position'? It is not obvious that information of this sort would justify the supposedly chosen moral code, in the sense of motivating a person to support it, or disalienating him from the actual moral system of his society in so far as it is identical with this code.

All the theories discussed in this chapter have one thesis essentially in common which contrasts with the position taken in this book: they have assumed, in effect, that the important question to ask is what a *benevolent* person (or, what is much

[10] See Rawls, 1974, especially pp. 650–3. Gilbert Harman seems to take this view, 1975.

although not quite the same thing, a person choosing without information which he could use to benefit himself) would choose as the moral system for his society, or all societies. My question has been different: I have asked what a *fully rational* person would choose, and left open the question whether a fully rational person must be benevolent. As a result, I have had to ask what kind of moral system a selfish person who is fully rational would choose. (I have not said a fully rational person could be completely selfish, but I do not believe anyone knows he could not be.) Of course, I could have come closer to these theories by adding the property of benevolence to the framework: I could have asked what fully rational benevolent people (benevolent to what degree?) would choose as a moral system for their society or all societies. I have elected not to do this. Why not? For one thing, it seems an important question how far facts and logic alone can carry us in criticism of a moral system: this is the question my conceptual framework has been designed to answer. For another thing, knowing that something is a fully rational choice justifies it, recommends it, to a person; but knowing what one would choose if one were benevolent to a certain degree need not—unless, of course, one is benevolent to that degree. Both these points appear important.

Why do these other theories give benevolence, in one form or another, the role they do? For some, the answer is that the conception involving benevolence is closer to what we mean by 'is morally right'; it is our linguistic intuitions that lead to the conception. For others, the answer is that the conception involving benevolence leads closer to our 'moral intuitions'. These views, which I criticized in Chapter 1, are important motivations for the conceptual frameworks discussed in this chapter. Another way of putting the argument from linguistic intuitions is to say that if we find which code would be supported by benevolent or disinterested persons, we have found a *moral* code—and a code chosen which did not meet this condition would not be a *morality*. It may be said that the very notion of a morality is of a system which could be chosen from 'the moral point of view', from a position of impartial benevolence. But this point is only a verbal one. We can then put the issue in proper perspective by the following question: 'Is it more important to know which kind of motivation-guilt system is properly called 'moral' in the English language, or is it more important to know which one a person would choose when fact and reason had played a maximal role in the selection—otherwise letting the chips fall where they may—with the result that the so-chosen system is one that is justified for the individual?' There can hardly be doubt how to answer these questions. Which motivation-guilt system deserves the magic name 'morality' appears a trivial question; whereas the question which moral system, if any, a person would support for his society when facts and logic have played a maximal role in the decision seems a highly important question.

It is true that 'moral' and 'morality' and 'moral principle' are words with favourable associations. It may be, then, that certain principles or ideals which could not capture our allegiance on their merits, can capture it if only they become associated for us with the term 'morality'. But what words we use to express our ideas surely cannot make a difference in clear thinking, and if some ideals or principles can be recommended only if we phrase them in certain familiar words, the argument has failed, and the force of the argument is a matter of irrational association, in the sense criticized in Chapter 6.

CHAPTER XIII

WELFARE: THE CONCEPT, MEASUREMENT, AND INTERPERSONAL COMPARISONS

I HAVE argued that fully rational persons will support roughly that moral system which will maximize expectable welfare in some sense of 'welfare', for some group of individuals. Hence if we wish to find which among the types of moral system historically advocated by philosophers rational persons would support, we need to determine which of these would maximize welfare.

This project requires a preliminary decision: what kind of thing is the welfare that is to be maximized. Our conclusions so far have not been univocal on this point. In Chapter 7 I offered reasons for thinking that rational benevolent persons want to increase the happiness or net enjoyment of sentient creatures and not the satisfaction of their desires, as such. On the other hand, we concluded in Chapter 3 that what people generally aim for is roughly to attain that collection of events which they most want; and further we concluded that fully rational persons do not just want happiness for themselves—they may want achievement, the admiration of other persons, and so on. So a decision is called for: whether fully rational persons will support a moral system which promises to *maximize happiness* in a society, or to provide the collection of events which sentient creatures in some sense *most want*. I shall contrast these as the 'happiness theory' and the 'desire theory'.

These two theories are not the only possible ones. Various philosophers have thought that some things, different from happiness and possibly not desired by anyone or everyone, are worthwhile in themselves and worthy of being produced for no further reason, for instance: knowledge and virtue. This view, however, seems to be obsolescent, and I propose to ignore it.

For our purposes a decision between the happiness theory and the desire theory must be made, since otherwise an intelligent discussion of measurement of welfare and interpersonal comparisons would be precluded. For practical purposes, however, it might seem to make little difference which is chosen, at least after some necessary qualifications and restrictions are imposed on the desire theory, in view of the normally close relation between what a person wants and what will make him happy.

At the present time the desire theory enjoys widespread support among both philosophers and economists, in one or other of its possible forms; but I am going to opt for the unpopular happiness theory, on the ground that the other proposal is not a plausible, or even an intelligible one, when we work it out in detail.

1. THE OBJECTION TO DESIRE THEORIES

Let us initially and roughly define the 'desire theory' as the theory which identifies welfare with desire-satisfaction and holds that ideally benevolent people would seek to maximize the desire-satisfaction of everyone. Some philosophers have held this theory in an unqualified form, but it is more usual for some distinctions to be made, for instance to identify welfare with the satisfaction of only some desires: ones that persist in the face of full information, or that occur in a normal (not angry) frame of mind, or, to use a conception discussed in an earlier chapter, ones that survive cognitive psychotherapy. But probably most philosophers would want a further restriction made. They would want to exclude altruistic or, more generally, non-self-interested desires (a conception to be discussed further in Chapter 17), and as a result would want to define 'welfare' in terms of desire-satisfactions that would come about only while the person is still alive, or perhaps only in terms of those about which the person would know when they occurred. There are other possible restrictions.

It may seem inconsistent for desire theories to be rejected here. For the proposal I made about what is the best thing to do, from a person's own point of view, puts his desires squarely in the centre of the account. And I came very close to saying that if something is rationally desired for itself by a person, that thing is intrinsically good for him. Nevertheless, we shall see that the desire theory of welfare becomes elusive when we raise the question which programme of action would maximize the desire-satisfactions of an individual (or collection of individuals) over a lifetime. That question is one we do have to raise when we ask which moral system would produce most welfare for the individuals in a society over their whole lifetime. Whether an individual who visualized this difficulty clearly would experience some change in his own desires, in the direction of aiming at happiness only, is a question I leave to the reader for reflection.

In order to get the difficulty clear, let me first sketch the essence of the happiness theory, for which the problem does not arise. And, in order to simplify the problem to the bare essentials, let us consider just the case of one person X who can do either A or B, and wishes to do what will maximize the welfare of another person, Y, over his lifetime. Let us also ignore the fact that we can know only with probability what will happen, and let us suppose we can talk freely just of what will happen to Y if A is done, as compared with if B is done. We suppose, then, that for every future moment of time we can know what difference it will make to Y's life whether A or B is done, and hence can decide how much happier Y is at that moment given one act occurred than he would have been had the other occurred. Let us represent these results by a curve, plotting the points at which he is happier if A is done above the X axis, the distance above the axis fixed by how much happier he is than he would have been had B been done; and similarly plotting points below the X axis representing how much happier he is if B is done than he would have been had A been done. This operation will give us curve-segments both above and below the line. Let us then compute the area under these curves. When we know whether the area above the curve is larger or smaller than that under the curve, we know which act will contribute more to Y's happiness over his lifetime. Whatever the practical difficulties in measurement, this conception is at least clear.

Two points in support of the happiness theory of welfare were mentioned in Chapter 7. First, that what we seem to care about securing for other persons (e.g. our own children) is their happiness; and we seem to care about getting them what they want (or would want if they knew more, etc.) only to the extent we think that so doing will bring them happiness or avoid distress and depression. Second, the psychological theory of benevolence leads to the conclusion that what we are sympathetically motivated to secure for others is happiness and freedom from distress (although we may want desire-satisfaction because we believe it a means to these).

These two points suggest that a benevolent person will tend to support a moral code which he thinks will maximize expectable welfare in the sense of expectable happiness.

Let us now turn to the central awkwardness of the desire theory. We must first remind ourselves what it is to satisfy someone's desire. Suppose Mr. X at a time t wants an occurrence O at some time t', or at any one of many moments t_i to t_n. Then, if O actually occurs at some one of these times, X's desire has been satisfied. And a greater satisfaction of desire has occurred, if the occurrent O was desired more intensely.

It is clear that the desire theory can take any one of several forms. In its simple unqualified form it affirms that a person's welfare has been increased if an O occurs which was or is or will be desired by him in fact. In a qualified form it affirms that a person's welfare has been increased if an O occurs which was or is or will be desired by him, if he is fully informed, and calm, and if the desire is not altruistic. We need not worry about the various possible forms of qualification. I shall consider the theory only in the simplest form, since the problem I wish to point out arises there (as well as in the other forms).

The desire theory holds, then, that greater welfare corresponds to greater satisfaction of desire, and that a benevolent person, in deciding what to do, does or at least ought to perform that act among the options open to him which will maximize desire-satisfaction. The idea seems to be that we consider all the desires a person has (and everyone has many occurrent desires at every moment), at some time or other, or many times, over a lifetime, and what that person—more particularly, for our problem, a moral code—should aim at is to maximize the satisfaction of these desires. This conception is unintelligible.

That there is a problem begins to appear when we reflect that we think some desires need not count. Suppose my six-year-old son has decided he would like to celebrate his fiftieth birthday by taking a roller-coaster ride. This desire now is hardly one we think we need attend to in planning to maximize his lifetime well-being. Notice that we pay no attention to our own past desires. Are we then to take into account only the desires we think my son will have at the time his desire would be 'satisfied', here at the age of fifty? If we take this line, we come close to the happiness theory—of providing that for each future moment he enjoys himself maximally at that moment.

The problem for the desire-satisfaction theory arises from two facts: first, that occurrent desires at a time t are for something to occur (to have occurred) at some other time; and second, that desires change over time.

The second fact merits dilation. Notice that one acquires some desires and loses others as one matures: loses one's desire to be an airline pilot, perhaps, and acquires one to provide for one's family. There are temporary fancies: a person suddenly wants to learn French, works at it, and then loses interest before achieving mastery. Most notably, some desires are cyclical, in the sense that after satisfaction there is a period of no desire for a whole family of events, followed by a recovery of interest. Some desires, as in morphine addiction, are the result of an earlier sequence of activities. As a person approaches the end of his life, he may lose his hedonic interests and want to make some contribution to the world, and wish perhaps to have done things differently in the past.

In view of these facts, what is a would-be maximizer of satisfaction of desires to do? If the other person's desires were fixed, you could identify his fixed long-term preference ordering of biographies for himself or the world, and then move him up to the highest indifference curve your resources permit. Since the desires are not fixed, you cannot pursue this programme.

Does the length of time a person entertains a desire make a difference, so that a sadistic wish for an angry hour counts less than a wish entertained for a whole month (say, only $1/720$ as much)? You might say that such comparisons are irrelevant; it is desires at the time of satisfaction that count. But consider an objection to this[1]: a convinced sceptic who has rebelled against a religious background wants, most of his life, no priest to be called when he is about to die. But he weakens on his deathbed, and asks for a priest. Do we maximize his welfare by summoning a priest? Some would say not, in view of his past desires. The programme also ignores future regrets.

What, then, is the programme of desire-satisfaction maximization to be, if different from happiness-maximization? As far as I know, no proposal has been put forward by advocates of the desire theory which tells us in principle, and generally, how to decide

[1] For the example, I am indebted to Derek Parfit and James Griffin.

which of two possible courses of action would produce more desire-satisfaction, even if we can predict the impact of the events on the individual, and how long and how intensely each of the several outcomes has been or will be desired.[2] I have the temerity to suggest that the whole concept is unintelligible.

I make this suggestion with hesitation, since someone may produce an intelligible and attractive programme which I have overlooked. And there are intelligible programmes; the only question is, how convincing are they? Let me suggest one. Suppose we give up the idea of an overall general programme which I might adopt now for maximizing the desire-satisfaction of my young son, given information about his future desires. Let us suppose rather that I adopt a flexible plan, and whenever the time comes to make a choice, say, between actions A and B which expectably affect his welfare, I adopt his set of priorities at that time (or, perhaps, his system of ideal priorities). The procedure then, for any choice, is to go along with the other person's vote, or his rational vote, at the time. Thus the procedure is flexible over time: if and when my son's desires shift in intensity, my programme of assistance will shift accordingly. A result of this programme will be that, if and to the extent that he ignores his past desires, I am to ignore them. I also ignore his future desires to the extent that he does (or would, if he were rational). Another implication is that if he is dead on a certain date and has no desires, the programme calls for no satisfaction of earlier desires. In the case of the dying sceptic, the programme calls for a priest to be summoned, since that is what he now wants.

This programme seems arbitrary and unsatisfactory compared with the original tidy goal of satisfying a person's desires, past and future, maximally, based on a picture of all desires he will have at every moment of his life. Nor can it be recommended on the ground that it is the most efficient way to maximize lifetime desire-satisfaction when all desires are taken into account, because we have no general conception of such a programme.[3]

There is another problem about implementing the foregoing desire theory, for the theory must find a plan for aggregating the

[2] Thomas Nagel, 1970, is possibly an exception; R. B. Perry had a solution for certain obvious cases.

[3] For some economic literature on the topic, see Hammond, 1976, Koopmans, 1964, and Gintis, 1972. Also Blackorby, Nissen, Primont, and Russell, 1973; and Peleg and Yaari, 1973.

desire-satisfactions of everybody whose welfare is concerned. How will this be done? Suppose a choice has to be made between plan A and plan B. A prospective beneficiary, Mr. X, votes for A, whereas the other prospective beneficiary, Mr. Y, votes for B. How will a decision be made? Evidently the above plan will need extension. Suppose we are able to compare the intensity of X's preference for A over B, and equally that of Y for B over A. Is the programme to call for acting in line with the stronger preference? This might be unconvincing, say, if Mr. X happens to want a great many things more than Mr. Y, and perhaps more intensely. That would seem strange—although it does not seem strange to adopt a programme which produces the most happiness, however divided between the two. One different programme that might be adopted is simply to allocate to each individual an equal share of the resources of the community over a lifetime. But this is not attractive either, in view of the special claims of the ill or handicapped. I must leave open the question what a desire-satisfaction theorist would say rational bene-volent persons would prefer to do.

The above problems with the desire-satisfaction theory may lead us to opt for the happiness theory, for reasons suggested by Sidg-wick in a slightly different context. He wrote: 'If we are not to systematise human activities by taking Universal Happiness as their common end, on what other principles are we to systematise them? I have failed to find—and am unable to construct—any systematic answer to this question that appears to me deserving of serious consideration.' (1922, p. 406.)

The alternative theory is that fully rational and benevolent persons want a moral code to maximize the happiness, or net enjoy-ment, of sentient creatures. None of the foregoing problems arises for the happiness theory.

A happiness conception of utility or welfare is not popular in some quarters at present. Economists may reject it because it is no longer used in price theory; they can construct the indifference curves needed for prediction with choices or preferences alone. Another thought more widely persuasive is that the happiness theory suggests dictation to others about what they should do—not giving them what they want, but rather what is thought best for their happiness. This thought is seriously mistaken; for, as Mill made clear, it is important for happiness in the long-run that people should be secured in the direction of their own lives, both because this freedom is significant for growth in personal decision-making, and because people like to feel they can make their own decisions.[4]

Defenders of a desire theory need not part company with us at this point. The argument to follow, with a few amendments, could be adapted for their purposes. Moreover, desire and enjoyment are so closely related that both theories reach the same conclusions on many of the basic questions about right action. Further, many of the desires important for the choice of a moral system are fixed over a lifetime, so that the problems emphasized above do not arise.

2. THE MEASUREMENT OF HAPPINESS

Can a benevolent person ever know which moral system—or, indeed, which one of any pair of acts—will produce more happiness than some other? If he can it must be because he can know about the happiness of other people. I shall postpone this problem of interpersonal comparisons until Section 3, and begin with the prior problem of whether he can know that one past event produced more happiness for him, and, by inductive projection, whether a similar future event will produce more happiness for him, as compared with some other event.

We recall the definition (p. 40 f.) of an experience E being pleasant for a person at a time t: 'an experience of the kind E is going on in the person at t, and the experience E is the differential cause at t of an occurrent positive valence of the continuation of E beyond t'. We now extend this definition to the comparative case, and say that 'E is more pleasant than E'' means (roughly) that an experience E produces a *stronger* positive valence for the continuation of E than does the experience E' for the continuance of E'.

We have little difficulty in knowing which of two experiences we enjoy the more. We smell two perfumes and know at once which one has the more pleasant odour—it is the one with which we want to linger more. We find eating a mouthful of pie more pleasant than

---

[4] Some philosophers are moved by some differences between the desire theory and the happiness theory (which desire theory I leave to them). Suppose a man wants his wife to be faithful to him. She commits adultery but sees to it that he never knows about her unfaithfulness. Has his welfare been diminished? The desire theory would say that it has, because something has occurred which he wants not to occur. The happiness theory would say not, by this event in itself, although the question whether the long-range happiness of both has not been subtly damaged is another matter.

eating a mouthful of peas; we want another bite of pie but eat another mouthful of peas out of a sense of duty. There is a bit of an epistemological puzzle here (p. 41 f.), but it need not disturb us.

On the basis of recollections of such facts we can inductively infer that, other things being equal, we shall enjoy eating one kind of pie more than consuming peas. Such inferences to the future must, of course, take contextual facts into account: for instance, satiation effects if one has already had several pieces of a favourite pie.

The situation is complicated by the fact that normally we do not make predictions about one kind of experience at one instant compared with another at another instant. We want to predict about stretches of experience, say about playing two sets of tennis as compared with eating a French meal. Such predictions must be based on the memory of past cases. But how do we make such comparative judgements about the past? How can I compare a French meal at my favourite restaurant in Sausalito with the two sets of tennis last week? The answer is, in part, that sometimes the comparison is in principle the same as the simpler one just discussed. Suppose the game and the meal each occupied two hours. Suppose further that I can take each moment of the tennis game and match it with a moment of the meal, so that the moment of the meal is either equal in enjoyment level or more enjoyed—there being no highlights of the game, such as some very satisfying shot or victory at the end which surpass in ecstasy any moment of the meal. The meal clearly comes out ahead. Of course, we hardly remember past events that well, but the principle is sound and applicable in many cases.

Many comparisons, however, present greater problems. Suppose I have to compare eating a leisurely three-hour French meal with playing a one-hour game of tennis. Suppose in this case the tennis was exhilarating, and the best hour consisting of selected moments of the meal is out-matched by correlated moments of the tennis. So far the tennis comes out ahead. But there are two hours of the meal left over. How do they compare?[5]

---

[5] The total experience of eating a meal or playing tennis is composed of several elements. Each of these has its own pleasantness, but we can also speak of the total net enjoyment at each moment—how much I was 'enjoying myself'. We must be careful to be clear which we are talking of, to avoid confusion. Mostly I shall be talking of the pleasantness of just one element—say the pleasantness of just the eating at a moment—or, in other words, of its addition or increment to the pleasantness of the whole.

Perhaps we can answer this question by assigning numbers to the degrees of enjoyment of the elements of the experiences, if the numbers have sufficiently interesting properties. In order to see how let us think of an example. Suppose I am eating in a restaurant. A good string quartet playing would add more to the enjoyment of my experience than a juke-box would. (I should be reluctant to substitute the latter for the former; I would resist more the cessation of the former than the latter; and I should be more reluctant in general to get up and leave the restaurant with the quartet playing than with the juke-box going.) In other words, the increment to my total enjoyment from the quartet is greater than the increment from the juke-box. Now we can also find experiences which would add approximately *equal* increments, or which are equally enjoyable taken by themselves. For instance, I would say that adding chocolate sauce to vanilla ice-cream might add an increment to the momentary enjoyment-level of the eating experience indistinguishable from that of adding suitable seasoning to unseasoned peas.

Now, if we are justified in saying that one change contributes an increment of enjoyment equal to that of some other change, we can assign some numbers. We can give unit value arbitrarily to one increment (which in some cases will just be the pleasantness of the whole experience). Then we give the same number to all cases of equal increments; and we give the number 2 to any increment just equal to that of the joint increment of two elements already assigned the number 1. (Say, a certain increment from eating parfait is just equal in pleasantness to a combination of hearing the quartet and gazing at an attractive lady, the latter two having already been judged equal and given the number 1.) Minus numbers can be assigned to elements of experience which are unpleasant to a degree equal to elements with positive numbers already assigned (the action-tendency to terminate the former would be equal to the tendency to continue the latter). Some elements of experience are neither pleasant nor unpleasant, e.g. the odour of water. They are assigned the number 0. We can then represent the intensity of pleasantness (or an increment to it) at a moment on a graph, as the *distance* above the x-axis or, in the case of an increment, as distance above a lower point on the graph.[6]

---

[6] For a useful discussion, see Ellsberg, 1954, especially pp. 533 ff. For a proof using a different conceptual scheme, see Suppes and Winet, 1955. See also McNaughton, 1953.

We can compare the three-hour French meal and the one-hour tennis game as follows. In each case we draw a curve, representing the enjoyment (or increment of enjoyment) as distance from the origin parallel to the y-axis (or as distance from the curve below, in the case of an increment), and the successive moments of time parallel to the x-axis. Plotting the intensity-level for each moment gives us a curve. Then we simply compute the area under each curve. If the area under the curve of the meal (or the area between it and the curve below, if we are talking of an increment) is greater, we then say eating the meal 'produced more happiness' —indeed, we can say just how much more in terms of the adopted units.

It may be objected that since 'E is more pleasant than E''' means essentially 'E makes its own continuation more valenced than E' does', we have no right to say that one experience is more pleasant than another when each produces the same valence for its own continuation but the former simply lasts longer. It may be said then, that saying one experience is more pleasant when the positive area under its pleasantness curve is greater than that under the curve of another experience is just a confusion of two quite different senses of 'more pleasant'.

If we view the matter from a larger perspective, however, we see that the idea outlined is essentially correct, although it needs more explanation (and if one wants, a slight change in terminology). To get the larger perspective, let us go back to the conception of what a benevolent person wants for others. Obviously two things: he wants as high a level of enjoyment as possible at any moment, but he also wants the highest level to go on for as many moments as possible (he wishes a long life as well as a happy one). At any rate, it is clear that the benevolent person will act so as to produce an increment of enjoyment-level of two units for ten minutes rather than just for one. But will he be indifferent as between adding one moment of a 2-unit increment and two moments of a 1-level increment? The proper answer to this question seems affirmative. For if we know that the second increment of the 2-unit increment is really identical in magnitude to the first one, what difference would it make whether we add it at the first moment of time, or the second? So long as what a benevolent person wants to produce is enjoyment-increments for moments of time, however short you wish to make them, and it is granted that equal increments can be identified, then it seems to follow that a benevolent person would always prefer to produce the increment of enjoyment over time represented by the larger area under a curve of increments. Hence, while it may be slightly misleading to say that the larger area represents *more happiness* (a term which suggests increases in intensity of valence), it is correct to say that the larger area is what the benevolent person prefers. And, for simplicity, and at the risk of a slight misunderstanding, I am going to use the term 'more happiness' for this very concept. So, if what one wants is to maximize happiness over time, what one has to do is produce increments such that the area under the curve is at a maximum. In that sense welfare, as enjoyment, can be measured quantitatively.

Vagueness in our conception of pleasure complicates the picture. I have said that for an experience to be pleasant at t is for the experience to be causing a positive valence for its continuation beyond t. But how far beyond t? This notion was left vague. If I am enjoying a piece of pie, is what is valenced just one more bite (nothing less than this could well count as a continuation), or to eat the whole piece, or what? If I am enjoying a symphony, is what is valenced ten more seconds of hearing it, hearing to the end, or what? For most purposes we need not specify, and I shall not. An additional problem is the fact that eating a certain piece of pie was positively valenced before I began to eat. We must separate that valence from the momentary valence produced by the eating of it. (My awareness of these problems is due to conversations with Professor Diana Ackerman.)

If we can now make comparisons of experiences in the past, we are justified in making, with suitable adjustments for difference of context and taste (etc.), comparable judgements about future experiences. We can say, then, that probably this kind of experience will be more enjoyable to us than that kind, in the future.

3. INTERPERSONAL COMPARISONS OF ENJOYMENT

We come now to what is generally viewed as the tougher problem: that of interpersonal comparisons. We need to face this, because we want to know which moral system will produce more happiness in general than some, or any, other. We cannot know this unless we can know, in general, whether one kind of event *has* produced more happiness in general than another, and therefore can somehow inductively infer that one kind of event *will* produce more happiness than another. The problem is especially troublesome if an event caused, or is expected to cause, happiness for some persons and unhappiness for others; in that case, how do we estimate the total impact?

There has been understandable scepticism about such estimates. We can observe our own conscious states, and perhaps also the properties and behaviour of physical objects, but we cannot observe the conscious states of others. So how can we hope to compare whether some event has given more happiness to one than to another? This difficulty is less conclusive than it appears at first. For one thing, we can know a great many things about material bodies (including organisms) which cannot be observed, by inference—most of theoretical physics consists of such knowledge. The limits of observation do not set the limits of knowledge. For another, whereas the traditional view of pleasure, as a quality of experience which could be directly inspected by one and only one person, encouraged scepticism about interpersonal comparisons, the present motivational view of pleasure, as the causation of something being valenced in a person, brings it into a network of laws which at least opens the door to interpersonal comparisons.

In what follows I shall claim that, and explain how, we sometimes know that (1) one event caused more enjoyment in another person than a second event; (2) one event caused more enjoyment in one person than another event caused in a second person; and (3) one event did (will) produce more net enjoyment for everyone affected than did (will) another event.

(1) The first claim, although hardly controversial among social scientists, is a useful starting point since its defence requires an account of the kinds of inference employed in showing that the impact of one event produces more enjoyment than another, and this account will be useful in an attack on the more difficult and controversial problems.

We may simplify our problem by asking simply whether some momentary event like sipping a Coca Cola on a hot day is more pleasant for another person than, say, sipping lukewarm water.

If we simplify our problem thus, then according to our definition of 'more pleasant', what we are asking is whether we can know of another person that an experience E (sipping Coca Cola) at a time t makes the continuation of E beyond t more strongly valenced at t than an experience E' (sipping warm water) at a time t' makes the continuation of E' beyond t'. In other words, we are asking whether we can know about the relative *causal power* of a certain kind, of two different experiences in another person. Our question can be raised of animals as well as of human beings.

What sort of reasoning might we deploy in support of a conclusion about this matter? Let us suppose that on two occasions a friend came to our home after three sets of tennis: on the first occasion we gave him a cold soft drink; on the second we gave him warm water. Suppose further that after these visits we have the following facts in hand. First, he drank three times as much of the cold soft drink. Second, he smiled while drinking the soft drink, and made a wry face while consuming the warm water. Third, we know that when he is at the tennis club he always spends money on a soft drink, after playing, rather than drink tap water. These data support the view that he enjoyed the soft drink more.

How? All the observed facts need explaining. If we assume he enjoyed the soft drink more, that would explain why he drank more of it; for something being pleasant *is* making the continuation of the experience positively valenced. Again, we tend to smile when we are enjoying what we are doing and we tend to make a wry face when there is something unpleasant in the mouth; and we assume others do the same. So his liking the soft drink would explain why he smiled; and his disappointment with the warm water would explain the wry face. Finally, we saw in Chapter 5 that incentive value—the preference ranking of objects which will satisfy thirst— is strongly dependent on the pleasantness of previous experiences with the same object. So, if a person has enjoyed soft drinks more than warm water on hot days in the past, our general theory tells us that he will prefer a soft drink to warm water whenever he is thirsty. We assume that likes and dislikes are fairly constant. If his usual preference for soft drinks must be explained by a normally greater enjoyment of soft drinks than of warm water when thirsty on a hot day, we think we can safely infer that probably this time he enjoyed the soft drink more than the warm water.

The essential point is that observable facts require explanations. The hypothesis that he generally enjoys soft drinks more, and that he did so on this occasion, provides an explanation of the data, when taken with reasonably well-established laws. It is doubtful whether anyone but a professional sceptic will question which drink was more enjoyed by our tennis player.

(2) The difficult question is whether we can sometimes know that one event E did (will) produce more enjoyment for one person A than another event E' did (will) for a person B.

In some cases the question can be answered by reasoning essentially like the preceding type: something occurs which is known to increase the enjoyment of A, and something else occurs which is known to decrease the enjoyment of B. For instance, if I give my son a chocolate and accidentally step on my dog, it is clear I have done better by my son's enjoyment than by my dog's.

The difficulty arises when both changes are in the same direction, or when we need to compare changes in opposite directions. Suppose two persons, Friend and Enemy, have just finished three sets of tennis on a hot day. I give Friend a cold soft drink, and I give Enemy warm water. We would normally think the following evidence establishes that Friend's enjoyment was increased more than Enemy's. Suppose Friend smiles, consumes three glasses, and is known always to consume cold soft drinks after tennis, in preference to lukewarm water. Suppose Enemy frowns, takes just enough of the warm water to quench his thirst, politely places his unfinished glass out of sight, and is also known always to consume cold soft drinks after tennis, in preference to lukewarm water. It is clear from Enemy's behaviour that he would have enjoyed a cold soft drink more. But could one not consistently argue that Enemy really got more enjoyment than Friend? It is consistent, at least, to say that Enemy's thirst was highly unpleasant and therefore just assuaging it was producing an increment of enjoyment much more than enough to equal all the increment produced for Friend by his satisfying cold drink. Intuitively, we should not take this proposal seriously unless there was special evidence: say, to the effect that Enemy had consumed no liquid for twelve hours on account of a medical examination, whereas Friend had drunk his fill just before the game.

Nevertheless, despite our intuitions on the matter, there is a serious problem of principle to be faced. For the pleasantness of an experience is definitionally equal to the increment in valence of continuation which the experience causes. This increment in valence effects an increment in the tendency to continue any act which is supporting continuation of the experience; and the strength of the tendency to perform that act is measured by whether it succeeds in controlling behaviour in the face of competing action-tendencies, e.g. one might cease drinking warm water in order to join one's wife digging in the garden, but not cease drinking cold Coca Cola. However, all this tells us nothing about how pleasantness, valence, or action-tendency in one person compares with that in another person, unless we can compare at least one of these, directly, in some instances, with the corresponding feature in another person, and determine whether in one person it is greater than, less than, or equal to the same feature of the other person. We could proceed, for instance, if we knew that the unpleasantness of a small shock for Friend was equal to that of a similar shock for Enemy. We could then determine whether the pleasantness-increment for Friend or Enemy is equal to or greater than the hedonic value of the shock, since we can observe whether each will continue, or discontinue, if he knows that a shock is the price he must pay for continued drinking. If Friend's tendency to continue with his soft drink is so strong that he continues despite the shock, whereas Enemy desists, we can infer that Friend's enjoyment from the soft drink is greater than Enemy's increment from the warm water. But is there any experience, like a shock, the pleasantness of which can be known to be roughly equal for one person to that of the same experience for another? Doubt about this is the serious basis for scepticism about interpersonal comparisons.

Some might like to state this point in a different conceptual framework. Suppose we want to know whether the strength of X's preference for A over B is greater than the strength of Y's preference for B over A. We are in well-known difficulties; but suppose we knew that X and Y want equally to avoid, say, a 120 volt five-second shock. Then, if X would prefer to endure the shock in order to get A rather than B, whereas Y would prefer to forego getting B rather than A in order to avoid the shock, we should have good reason to think X's preference greater.

The most likely candidates for interpersonally equally pleasant/ unpleasant experiences appear to be those produced by some physiological condition, which can be known to be the same in two individuals. Of course individuals need to be matched for features known to influence the pleasantness of an experience: say, for recent experience and 'habituation', or for associations such as ones that may have produced a conditioned anxiety response attached to the experience. Let us suppose this matching is done as carefully as possible. Then consider the discomfort of thirst. Thirst is a response to the triggering of a sensing mechanism by the chemical content of the blood; if the body is dehydrated beyond a certain point, the mechanism is set off and the resulting thirst roughly increases with the dehydration. Knowing this, we can test roughly for sameness of thirst by establishing sameness of dehydration, either by chemical test or by allowing two matched individuals to go without liquids, say for four hours. Can we be sure that the two individuals experience equally unpleasant thirst? There is more checking to be done. Some persons are born with different pain thresholds, and similarly some individuals may have defective triggering systems, so that they do not feel thirsty when they need liquid. A deviant thirst-dehydration system can, however, be identified fairly easily: if one individual fails to report thirst at a stage of dehydration at which normal people do, he is disqualified as a member of our comparison pair. Other features of the individuals may make us suspicious, e.g. bodily weight; so, to be doubly sure, we might pick our individuals roughly identical in weight. May we then infer that when two individuals are so matched, the unpleasantness of their thirst is equal? Similarly, suppose we find that the same individuals, as far as we can tell, are not different in the features relevant to their response to electric shock. May we then infer that the unpleasantness of their shock experiences is equal?

If the answer to these questions is affirmative, and the two individuals set up a personal pleasure ordering, with numbers unique except for the size of the unit (using the method outlined in the preceding section), then they can calibrate their pleasure assignments with each other, just as we calibrate two thermometers by comparing their readings for the temperatures at which pure water begins to freeze and begins to boil.

But what is the serious logical justification for answering the questions in the affirmative? It is as follows: First, we suppose that the unpleasantness of X's thirst is caused somehow, presumably by some events in the brain. This assumption will hardly be questioned. Second, we may assume (which again will not be contested) that same causes produce same effects, so that if the complex cause which produces the unpleasantness of X's experience of thirst is duplicated in Y, then the unpleasantness of Y's experience will be the same. Doubt about the identity of the hedonic tones of the two experiences, then, must arise from doubt whether the causal complex is identical, in Y, with that in X. Now X and Y are both human beings (it might help if they were identical twins) with brain structures roughly the same. We do not know that the particular complex responsible for the unpleasantness of thirst is the same in both; but we have matched them for properties which we think might be relevant, and we know there are many properties which are irrelevant (we can vary them, and neither reports any variation in his unpleasant thirst). Evidently the hedonic tones of the experiences of the two can reasonably be inferred to be identical if we are justified in thinking that two effects are the same if the causes are the same *as far as we know*, at least when enough is known of causal laws relevant to the material so that we would probably know about relevant differences in the causes if there were any. Philosophers will recognize this line of thinking as a form of analogical argument. The doubt about it arises from doubt whether we are in a position to assert that we know enough to justify saying that we have probably not failed to match our individuals in respect of features causally important for the degree of unpleasantness of their thirst. Some ground for doubt of this sort, however, is present in all inductive inference in science.

It appears, then, that in principle we are not debarred logically from believing that we can calibrate the personal hedonic scales of two individuals. And if we can do that, we can develop reasoning along obvious lines (which will show how expressive behaviour can be assessed as an indicator) to support the common-sense belief that Jimmy enjoyed a big-league baseball game more than his sister did, and that she enjoyed watching a ballet more than he did. More important, we seem to know enough to affirm with conviction that a transfer of $200 a year from rich Mr. X to poor Mr. Y would produce a larger increment of enjoyment for Mr. Y than it costs Mr. X. Why? If we happen to know that the transfer will enable Y to raise the temperature of his home from 45° to 65° during the year, whereas X will spend the money on five bottles of fine French wine, it requires very little imagination to see that the area of increment to Y's pleasure curve will be very much larger than the area of decrement to X's curve. Professor Ward Edwards, a distinguished experimenter on decision theory, once wrote (1954) that 'it seems utopian to hope that an experimental procedure will ever give information about individual utilities that could be of any practical use in guiding large-scale economic policy'. He does not specify what kind of information might in principle satisfy him, but it does seem over pessimistic to think there is no foundation for the rough judgements we need to make in decisions on policies or social welfare programmes.

(3) The implications of the foregoing will be clear for our third claim: that sometimes we can know that one event did (will) produce more net enjoyment for everyone affected than did (will) another event.

There are several conditions which are sufficient for knowing that one act increased the net total happiness more than some other act.

(a) The first is obvious: the case in which one act enhanced the enjoyment of everyone affected, and the second act affected the enjoyment of persons adversely if at all. Knowledge that this situation obtains requires at most the simple form of reasoning outlined in (1) above, pp. 258 ff.

(b) The second is equally obvious: the case in which one act increased the happiness of at least one person, while leaving the situation of others equally happy from the point of view of each, and the other act affected the happiness of no one either favourably, or for the worse. Knowledge that this situation obtains requires no more elaborate reasoning than did the first case.

(c) The third condition is best explained by means of an example: it is just a generalization of the example. Suppose there are ten persons in a group, and as a result of an action the happiness-level of three is decreased, that of five increased, and that of two unchanged. When may we say that the total happiness is increased? A sufficient condition is this: that among the five persons whose happiness has increased, we can pick out three, and match them with those whose happiness has declined, and know that, for each point of time when the hedonic level has been changed, the happiness of the one of a pair has gone up more than, or at least as much as, the happiness-level has declined for the person matched with him. In this situation, adjudication does require interpersonal comparisons, but not assignment of cardinal numbers to anyone's happiness-level or increment.

(d) The final condition requires both interpersonal comparison and the assignment of cardinal numbers. What might be a practical judgement that requires this? Apparently asking whether punishment of a criminal does more harm than good: counting the distress caused him, the costs of the system, the probable reduction in crime-caused distress as a result of his punishment, and the improved hedonic level arising from the reduction of the threat of crime. In this situation we have to determine the (probable) net increase or decrease of happiness for each individual involved, add them up, and sum. In principle, if my argument is sound, this could be done. Further, a person with broad experience and sensitivity can probably predict with good accuracy how such a determination would come out. That is all we need for purposes of policy.

If all this argument is sound then we can know, with reasonable accuracy, after careful reflection and observation, which moral system for a given society will maximize expectable welfare or happiness.

CHAPTER XIV

THREE MONISTIC MORAL CODES

MY EARLIER conclusion, that fully rational benevolent persons would support a moral code the currency (pp. 215 ff.) of which they believed would maximize welfare and that fully rational selfish persons would support a code the currency of which in fact would turn out to be beneficial for members of the moral community, leaves open the question which specific kind of moral code different kinds of rational person would support. The question was also left open whether they would all support the same moral system.

In this chapter reason will be given for thinking rational persons would not support three kinds of moral code—certain one-principle or monistic moralities. These three possible codes are important because of their historical connections. Each is associated with a tradition in normative ethics: one with egoism, one with act utilitarianism, and one with utilitarian generalization.

In asking whether fully rational persons would support a certain moral code we must bear in mind what it is for an individual to have a moral code, or a moral principle (Chapter 9). It is primarily for something to be true about his motivation and emotions: that he is intrinsically averse to his (or, usually, anyone else) acting in certain ways; that he feels uncomfortable (guilty or remorseful) if he acts in one of these ways except in special excusing circumstances, and has an anti-attitude towards anyone else who does so except in excusing circumstances. He also believes this motivation and attitude justified in some sense, and thinks the corresponding restriction on behaviour an important one.

All three theories to be evaluated are consequential, or 'result' theories. That is, according to them an act is wrong only on account of its *consequences for welfare*, or on account of the consequences for welfare of a related class of actions. In this respect they differ from most historical moral codes, which have regarded a variety of kinds of action as prima facie objectionable in themselves: incest, telling lies, breaking promises, injuring people. Our three theories, in contrast, hold that the only prima facie objectionable feature of an action is its producing, or probably producing, or tending to produce, harm or at least less good than some alternative possible action; or else its belonging to a class of actions of which the same is true—a class of actions such that if they were performed in place of some other class of actions, harm or less good would be produced, or probably produced, and so on. Accordingly, all these theories consist in effect of advocating, or claiming to be justified, a one-principle moral code—a code in which there is one basic aversion, an aversion to doing something that in some way fails to maximize something.

In what follows I shall describe, as sympathetically as possible, the kind of moral code an advocate of one of these traditional theories might espouse, and shall ask about it whether a fully rational person, whether benevolent or selfish, would support it for a society in which he expected to live.

1. EGOISM

The general idea of egoism historically has been that what any person ought to do is maximize his own welfare. But this vague thesis may be interpreted in a number of different ways. (a) An egoist might not be saying that anything at all is morally right or wrong, and hence making no claim about which moral code a rational person would support; what he might be saying by 'any person *ought*' is simply that the *best thing* for anyone to do, from his own point of view, is to maximize his own welfare— or better, to remove vagueness along lines discussed earlier, that what a fully rational person would do is maximize his own welfare. (2) Alternatively, an egoist may combine the last part of the above thesis with a minimal claim of a moral sort, namely, that a person has a moral right to do whatever will probably maximize his own welfare or self-interest. In the context of the egoist theory, however, 'moral right' cannot mean what it normally does—that other persons are at least enjoined not to interfere with the person who has the right, in his exercise of it. For if it is to the self-interest of one person to interfere with another person's doing what is best for him, the person who interferes has a perfect moral right of his own so to do. Thus the most that would be morally prohibited, on this interpretation, is one person's interference with another's pursuit of his own good, when the interference is not in the self-interest of the one who interferes. (3) Or, the egoist might be making a strong moral claim, that an act is morally right for an agent if and only if it will probably maximize his own welfare. He will say that a rational person would support a moral code which positively enjoins maximizing one's own welfare: that is, intrinsic motivation to seek one's own welfare, a tendency to be uncomfortable (feel guilty) when one fails to do this without excuse, a tendency to have an anti-attitude towards others when they fail without excuse, and so on. For instance, one recent self-styled egoist says that 'an individual always has a duty, from his own point of view, to attain as nearly as possible his highest good ...'. And another says: 'A man is subject to moral censure for performing an act if and only if he has good reason to regard that act as detrimental to his own best long-range interests, and a man is entitled to moral commendation for performing an act if and only if he has good reason to regard that act as favouring his own best long-range interests.'[1]

How is the term 'self-interest' or 'own welfare' to be construed, on any of these egoistic theories? This conception has not been as fully discussed as one might expect. I shall come back to it in the final chapter. For now, let us say that a state of affairs is 'in a person's self-interest' if (1) that person would want it if he were fully rational and if (2) it entails the existence of himself, as enjoying himself or having wealth or power does, but as the happiness of others does not. We shall see later that this definition is not entirely satisfactory, but it will do for our present purposes.

Which of the three egoistic theses should we examine? The first and second theses I shall pass by, since it may be objected to both that a selfish person would want a moral code of some sort, for his own protection, unless he were most unusually situated. The very thin moral claim of the second thesis is too eccentric, when we try to spell out what it comes to, to merit careful attention.

[1] G. Williams, 1948, Olson, 1961. See also a series of helpful papers by Kalin, 1969 and 1975; also Brandt, 1972.

The third theory, however, is clear and interesting; and an examination of this one will be instructive.

This third theory affirms that a rational person would support a moral code which could be expressed by saying 'An action is morally right if and only if it maximizes the expectable welfare of the agent'. What kind of moral code might this be? The morally well-developed person in a society with such a code will be intrinsically averse to neglecting his long-range interest in favour of impulse or sentimental benevolence, and in that sense will be a prudent man. He will feel guilty about such lapses when there is no excuse; he will disapprove of others who manifest the weaknesses of impulsiveness or altruism when the targets of it are not persons whose happiness is important to him, except when there is excuse; and he will think all these attitudes justified in some appropriate sense.

Philosophers have usually supposed that a utilitarian moral code could consistently include some 'secondary' moral rules, or rules of thumb; and an egoistic code could do the same. That is, it might be that, in view of temptations to undervalue benefits or costs in the remoter future, and in view of the time involved in estimating whether a certain kind of act would produce long-range benefits, children might be taught that certain rules are good ones to live by. For instance, 'Never smoke cigarettes' or 'Don't drive after drinking more than two martinis' or 'Don't eat cholesterol-rich foods like eggs'. Indeed, it might be that good rules, from the point of view of long-range-benefit, are 'Keep your promises' or 'Don't make promises you don't intend to keep' or 'Don't injure other people'. The latter, social secondary rules might be included in view of the fact that other persons do not like to be injured or to have promises to them broken, and are apt to retaliate.

Would a fully rational person support a moral code of this sort for his society, in preference to none at all and to any other? He might support it rather than none at all, since a person's life is better if guided not by whims and passions but by a view of his own long-range good. But a rational person would hardly support it as compared with some other codes.

Why not? One reason is that an egoist moral code would have difficulty in sustaining itself, once established. For persons whose basic moral motivation is directed at their own long-range interests would hardly be concerned with the perpetuation of their code with the next generation, especially in view of the fact that their own self-interest would be best served by others around them not subscribing to an egoist moral code but to some more altruistic type— the fewer selfish people around, the better for other selfish people.

There are more potent reasons. Let us consider what the attitudes of both benevolent and selfish persons will be to an egoist moral code, beginning with a benevolent person. He will not want an egoist code because there are other codes, of a more utilitarian sort, which will do better for those whose welfare he wishes to protect. An egoist moral code gives no protection to individuals who are in no position to retaliate against maltreatment: animals, future generations who may be left unprovided for by the egoist who would waste natural resources, under-developed nations, or even powerless needy persons in one's own community. The egoist code advises the agent to ignore the welfare of such groups except when there are special circumstances connecting their welfare to his own. But apart from these classes of individuals, the egoist code generally advises one to seek one's own welfare even at catastrophic cost to others. It apparently advises people not to pay legally uncollectable debts, to plagiarize where there can be no proof, to ignore commitments by pleading forgetfulness when the other person cannot prove that one did remember, to pass on work to others under the pretence of being very busy, and so on. An egoist moral code would maximize expectable utility for all only by the most miraculous contingencies. A rational benevolent person would hardly favour this.

However, neither will a selfish person want an egoist moral system, unless he is in a special position of power, in which case he may not care about a moral system at all. For one thing, he will not want to be liable to assault whenever it may maximize the utility of another to assault him; he would like assault forbidden. Further, he will want to be able to rely on the promises of others when he is in no position to require performance. More generally, he will want to live in a society in which there is mutual trust, no need to be on one's guard, and friendly warmth among persons. An egoist moral code is inimical to this.

2. ACT UTILITARIANISM

A second monistic moral code is act utilitarianism (hereafter AU), according to which an act is morally right if and only if the total welfare-expectation for everyone affected by it is at least as great as from any alternative action open to the agent.

We should remind ourselves of the question we are asking about this principle. We are concerned with it as a moral code for a society: that is, with many people in the society being intrinsically motivated to perform any act believed to have optimal welfare-expectation, feeling guilty if they have failed to perform such an act (except with an excuse), having anti-attitudes towards other persons if they fail (again, except with an excuse), and so on. Our question about this moral code is whether fully rational persons would support it for their society—or more precisely would tend most strongly to support it, in preference to other codes or none.

There are some explanations needed to make the above principle clear. (1) An 'act' is construed so as to include doing nothing (inaction) as well as doing some specific thing; and so as to include compound acts of any length, i.e. sequences of simple acts. (Thus it is convenient to count as an act not just backing my car out of the garage, but the compound act of doing this and then driving someone to a hospital.) (2) Where do we draw the line between an act and its consequences? Does an 'act' include only the movement of one's body (or intentional mental occurrences, such as thinking of a certain thing)? It normally makes no difference where we draw the line (as long as any utility of the act itself is counted along with the utility of the consequences), but it is convenient to include not only bodily movements but the changes they effect in the surrounding world, when these are essentially under the agent's control. (3) An 'alternative' to an act is one which is incompatible with it; two acts are incompatible with each other if it is impossible to perform both. (4) What is the total welfare-expectation? To get this concept clear, let us contrast performing an act A with an alternative B. Consider then the possible events subsequent to the onset of A or B. We separate and ignore those events the probability of which is unaffected by the performance of either A or B. Then we take the set of remaining possible events, and, on the assumption that A is performed, we determine how probable (p) each of these is. We then decide the increment to welfare if that event occurs, and assign it a corresponding number, positive or negative. For each event we then multiply the probability of its occurrence if A is done, by the increment of welfare, positive or negative, and we sum these products. (If we are identifying 'welfare' with happiness or enjoyment, we have seen that the utility numbers can be assigned, in principle.) We repeat the process for B. Obviously the above principle says that A is right if and only if this sum of products is at least as great as the corresponding sum for any alternative act B open to the agent at the time.[2]

The above concepts are also important for egoism—indeed, for any moral code which will be taken seriously by rational persons —but I have chosen to introduce them here.

One of the alternatives a person always has is to stop and get more information relevant to his estimate of the probable benefits of his options. He may get more information, or take more time to reflect. How much more? Searching for information and reflecting are themselves actions with costs, and are themselves subject to the basic principles. Some writers have purported to find a vicious regress here (Duncan-Jones, 1957), but it is sometimes or usually obvious when further reflection would cost more than expectable benefits from it (or the reverse).

The above statement of the AU moral code gives no clue to how intense the motivation and guilt-feelings are to be. Historically defenders of the theory have had little to say about this. Some discussions appear to assume that the motivation might be so strong as always to override that of personal interest; but this supposition is unrealistic, especially in view of the psychological costs of teaching such motivation. One possible proposal is that the level of intensity is to be set by inquiring which acts of teaching the code would satisfy the principle itself; the optimal level of motivation is the one it would maximize expectable welfare to teach.

The internalization of the main feature of an AU code in a child —the internalization of aversion to producing anything less than

---

[2] Readers interested in problems leading to and connected with these ideas can profitably consult Bergstrom, 1966, 1968, and 1976; von Wright, 1963a, Chaps. 4–8; Castaneda, 1968, 1969, and 1972; Horwich, 1974; Cornman and Dirnbach, 1973.

the most good or expectable benefit possible—is consistent with learning that certain specific types of act are likely to do good or harm, e.g. telling certain kinds of lies, and breach of promises. This teaching may prevent mistakes about what will do most good, when the person has little time to think or is tempted to follow inclination. If such learning occurs, some intrinsic motivation will tend to develop in connection with these behaviours; but we can say a person's code is AU if the overriding motivation remains, to maximize welfare or happiness, on the basis of available information.

Would fully rational persons want a moral system of this sort for their society? There is initial plausibility in an affirmative answer. At least, if those fully rational persons who are benevolent do, as argued earlier, want a welfare-maximizing moral system, would they not want a moral code which consisted primarily of everyone being motivated to act so as to contribute maximally to welfare?

An important distinction, however, must be emphasized. What a moral system provides is motivation in a certain direction, and guilt-feelings and anti-attitudes towards others in certain cir-cumstances. But to be motivated to perform acts with maximal welfare-expectation by no means guarantees that the agent will perform acts with maximal welfare-expectation. A given individual may be hopelessly incompetent to identify which acts have this feature; he may be quite confident, but confidently mistaken, in almost every case. The rules of thumb he is taught about which types of act are likely to have maximal welfare-expectation may be good ones, but a person may often think he has good evidence for thinking these rules misguided in a given case. An AU moral system in a society like ours, with persons of average intelligence (by definition), may fare as badly as a legal system with just one law: 'Always act so as to maximize welfare-expectation!' Suppose the instructions from the Internal Revenue Service contained only one rule: 'Pay the amount of tax which on your evidence will maximize expectable welfare!'

If the motivation provided by an AU moral code promised to affect actual behaviour in a relatively unfortunate way, fully rational persons might prefer some other kind of moral system, e.g. a morality of specific rules, just as they might prefer the specific rules provided by the Internal Revenue Service to the suggested directive just to pay what would maximize expectable welfare.

Philosophers at least as early as Bishop Berkeley (1712) have thought that more good would be produced by a morality prohibiting or enjoining specific types of act as compared with one simply enjoining the performance of whatever act each person, at each moment, judged likely to maximize the good. Recently D. H. Hodgson (1967) has argued, more strongly, that everyone actually following the directive of AU in an ideal society of logically competent and well-informed persons all of whom know that everyone is an AU in moral code, would have catastrophic consequences for the quality of life, since the practices of promise-keeping and reliably telling the truth would not exist. The literature elicited by Hodgson's book has made it clear that his particular reasoning is inconclusive (Lewis, 1972; Peter Singer, 1973; Mackie, 1973), but has left open the possibility that Hodgson was right in thinking an AU moral code would be unfortunate, as compared with some kind of morality of rules.

I have pointed out that an AU morality may include believing that certain specific types of act (e.g. breach of promise) normally lead to loss of welfare. These beliefs (and associated probable intrinsic motivations) may have the effect that the moral code approximates the morality of 'rules' to be discussed in the following chapter. In so far as that happens, both the special attractions and special disadvantages of an act utilitarian morality tend to disappear. But let us consider the disadvantages of an AU morality, assuming that it involves a case-by-case cost-benefit analysis of prospective acts.

(1) The reasoning required will often be complex, and hence will be open to self-interested rationalization. Suppose a prospective tax-payer considers whether he should conceal income so as to save $1,000. He asks himself which course of action will maximize benefit. Non-payment will obviously produce much enjoyment for him, say a vacation in Greece. What will be the benefit of payment? Perhaps a slight increase in the prospect of a tax-reduction with an attendant small increase in happiness for many. Considering the reasons for which tax-cuts are made, and their improbability, this gain is highly speculative. (Remember, we are not

asking what the effect would be if everybody followed his example.) The required reasoning must be subtle, quite unlike what occurs if all one has to notice is whether one's prospective action would be a case of untruthfulness, theft, or perjury; and the individual will find it easy to conclude that he should not pay the extra tax.

(2) It is important to be able to know in advance what other people will do, partly just for peace of mind, but also for efficient planning. The case-by-case cost-benefit analysis by individuals, required by the AU code, makes such assurance impossible for many types of case. (a) Sometimes this will be because the reasoning must be subtle, as explained in the preceding paragraph. (b) But consider forms of 'institutional' behaviour, like keeping promises, parents caring for their children, and police enforcing the law and insuring any accused person treatment in accordance with his legal rights. In an AU society, if something has been promised me (say in return for a service), even if I know the other person believes I am expecting him to perform, there must be some doubt since his personal situation may be such that he will not quite maximize the general welfare by doing so. It is manifestly useful for people to feel bound to do certain things unless there is very pressing reason of public benefit (etc.) to the contrary. (c) Uncertainty can arise from differences of valuation, what we may call 'conservative' and 'revolutionary' values. Consider the execution of a will. There is a long-term advantage in individuals being able to control the disposition of their property after death, both from the lifetime satisfaction of knowing that certain things will happen, and from the motivation to be in a position to provide for these things from one's estate. Conservatives will value this advantage heavily, even while admitting the system can be abused (providing for the life-long luxury of one's cats). Revolutionaries will not; they will think people should write wills with the public good in mind and should not be permitted to expect that their testaments will be respected when they do not. With both conservatives and revolutionaries in the field, what is one to expect? A similar conflict of values about euthanasia will make an elderly and infirm person in an AU society wonder whether his consent will be necessary if a morally enterprising relative is in a position to see to his demise. (I am assuming that no AU morality will prevent persons from wanting to see to the future

welfare of their children, or from wanting to continue living when it is for the public benefit that they pass on.) In general, then, it appears that there will be a considerable advantage in knowing that moral people will not do certain things, and will discharge certain recognized obligations, except in exceptional circumstances; these will be impossible with an AU morality.

It is interesting to note that an avowed act utilitarian, evidently of a somewhat 'conservative' sort, writes as follows, although it is surprising that he thinks it consistent for him to do so:

A direct and immediate attempt to teach only the act-utilitarian principle itself to the child would obviously be disastrous. . . . It is reasonable for adult act-utilitarians to continue to enforce those norms which they have been taught as children, not only against others, but against themselves. . . . A system of shared social morality is thus seen to be quite analogous to a legal system constructed on an act-utilitarian basis. Considerations of utility lead to the participation of each in the creation and support of a system of norms which bar direct appeals to utility and which are backed by sanctions.[3]

We need not question that careful deliberation and discussion can show which is the correct solution in the case of conflicts between conservative and revolutionary. We need not question the possibility of identifying and teaching an expectable-benefit-maximizing moral code; in fact, I shall be arguing precisely that in the following chapter. What is costly is leaving all decisions, to be made on a case-by-case basis, to persons often incompetent to make a careful analysis.

(3) Act utilitarianism makes extreme and oppressive demands on the individual, so much so that it can hardly be taken seriously; like the Sermon on the Mount, it is a morality only for saints. For instance, according to it I should give my salary to charity until the benefit to me of the last dollar I keep for myself is no larger than someone else might get from it if it were given to him. (How much motivation would there be to work, if morality demanded this degree of charity?) AU permits no clear distinction between duty (what morality requires) and 'works of supererogation'—acts not morally required but desirable in view of the benefits they confer. According to it, if I leap on a live hand-

[3] Sartorius, 1972, especially pp. 208, 212. For a similar view see Peter Singer, 1972, especially pp. 101–2.

grenade which someone has dropped and lose my life on behalf of others, I have only done my duty. It appears a disadvantageous defect in a morality not to retain that distinction. Moreover, there is much to be said for the charge made by M. G. Singer (1961, p. 184), that AU leads to 'moral fanaticism, to the idea that no action is indifferent or trivial, that every occasion is momentous'. The statement is perhaps extreme: an AU need not be vastly excited by the prospect of doing either a minor harm or a minor good, and the 'rules of thumb' will tell one that in certain situations it is not worth one's time to explore what good for others one might be producing. But, with our present kind of moral code, I know that at the present moment none of my obligations is undischarged—except for more generous charity— and that I am morally free to be reading a novel. Whereas if I really thought I ought to be doing the most good I can, I would be inquiring into the circumstances of the men engaged at this moment in cleaning a piece of furniture in my living room. Doubtless the world would be better off it there were more of this; but a moral code is oppressive if it leaves no area of freedom, to do what one wants to do to achieve one's own goals, and simply enjoy oneself. With the AU code there is no finite set of obligations, which one can know have all been discharged.

What would it be like for there to be a thoroughly AU moral code in our society? Not what some act utilitarians may think —that the only difference would be modifying the present system slightly in the direction of less attention to rules and prohibitions, and more in the direction of human welfare.

Fully rational persons who are benevolent would, I suggest, not be convinced by an AU moral code, and would look for some alternative which might combine the benefits without the disadvantages—as does the system I shall be describing in Chapter 15; and fully rational selfish people would be equally unconvinced.[4]

---

[4] Some philosophers have thought to avoid some of these problems by a variant often called 'negative utilitarianism'. The essential difference of this view is a limitation on the kind of welfare relevant to right and wrong action. Specifically, the welfare to be counted as relevant to right and wrong action is restricted to (1) reductions in welfare as a result of the action, and (2) improvements in welfare, but only up to the point where 'relief from misery' has been accomplished. There also tends to be an understanding that the impact on persons below the above-misery level counts more heavily than that on persons above this level. (It is usually not discussed when a person is above

3. UTILITARIAN GENERALIZATION

It seems worthwhile, in view of the bulk of recent literature on the topic, to discuss a third theory alongside egoism and act utilitarianism, a theory closely related to AU, invented with the aim of being an alternative proposal without the objectionable features of AU. Roughly, it prescribes your doing A if and only if everyone in a relevantly similar situation doing A, instead of something else you might do, would maximize expectable long-run welfare. Let us call this proposal the 'utilitarian generalization' theory—UG for short. The UG proposal is reminiscent of Kant, if we construe him as saying that an act is right if and only if its 'maxim' is one the agent can reflectively accept as a law for the action of everyone; for by substituting the notion of maximizing welfare for the agent's reflective acceptance, we get: an act is right if and only if everyone acting on its 'maxim' would be beneficial to society.

Rather different theories qualify as variants of the UG type. For instance, M. G. Singer (1961, p. 73) wrote: 'If the consequences of everyone's doing x would be undesirable, while the consequences of no one's doing x would not be undesirable, then no one has the right to do x' (without a special reason). Again, B. Gruzalski proposed: 'An act is wrong if and only if the proportional value of the consequences of everyone (who can) doing that kind of act would be less than the proportional value of the consequences of everyone (who can) doing some alternative open to the agent.'[5]

---

the misery level: whether it is enough to be at an average state of happiness so that the specified level varies from time to time and place to place, or whether it should be at what the Department of Labor has called 'a modest but adequate standard of living', or simply above a level neither aversive nor attractive to the person concerned.) Roughly, then, the idea is that a person is morally bound to maximize welfare in general except that increases in welfare above the misery level do not count.

This proposal does imply a reduction in the scope of a person's obligations. Indeed, so much so that many will not like the proposal: it implies that there is no obligation to provide education which will add to the happiness of people when it is not necessary to bring them above the misery level; and that there is no obligation to redistribute income from the very well-off to the rest, if the others are already above the misery level, irrespective of how great the gain otherwise.

Apart from this, the proposal does nothing to mitigate the disadvantages pointed out above.

5 In a paper read at a meeting of the American Philosophical Association in 1975.

There have been other variants in the last fifty years (Harrod, 1937; Harrison, 1952–3). Writers who have supported such theories have generally regarded them as having whatever epistemological status, or truth-status, is available to normative statements, and they have defended them by arguments, by appeal to 'our intuitions', and so on. The theories are here, however, being construed in an entirely different way—as proposals for a *one-principle moral code*, one a subscriber to which might express by one of these statements. And the question, if my whole argument is correct, that we want to have answered about these proposals is whether fully rational persons would support one of them for their society. Obviously a closely related question is whether the currency of one of these codes would maximize expectable welfare in the world as compared with alternative moral codes.

It is important to distinguish two questions about the 'currency' of such codes. One is the question what would be the actual utility of everyone following the prescription of the code accurately (as an omniscient person might do). The other is the question what would be the expectable utility of everyone being motivated to follow the code up to some specified ideal level, but his actual conformity to the code being restricted by his level of logical acumen, the available information, and his human weaknesses. It is possible that the answer to the first question would be: exactly the same utility as that of following the AU code since everyone who followed the UG code would do exactly the same thing as he would if he followed the AU code. Whereas the answer to the second question might be: either more or less than that of everyone being motivated, up to some specified ideal level, to follow the AU code. The second question is the one we need to answer, to determine whether fully rational persons might support some form of the UG code. A great many recent discussions have addressed the first of these questions, and the consequent debates are of limited importance for an answer to the second question.[6]

---

[6] See Lyons, 1965; Sobel, 1970; H. S. Silverstein, 1974; Feldman, 1974; Goldman, 1974. Earlier useful discussions include: Broad, 1915–16; Harrod, 1937; Harrison, 1952–3; Ewing, 1953; A. K. Stout, 1954.

So far I have stated the UG principle only 'roughly'. Let us now see if we can state a plausible one more precisely. Obviously the principle talks about everybody in *relevantly similar* circumstances performing the *same action*. The italicized expressions must be explained. Let us begin with 'same action'. Suppose I am considering performing an action of the kind A (bringing about some change—but see above, p. 271) at time t; then anyone who performs an action of the same description A at any time t' performs the same act. But what is to go into the act-description 'A'? Obviously the properties I suppose necessary to reach the objectives on account of which I perform it; but also any properties which, as far as I can see, make a difference to the expectable utility of its being performed. Let us suppose these properties are FG ... M. Then my act will be described as doing something of the form FG ... M. Anyone at any time who performs an act of the kind FG ... M has done the same act. One could, of course, offer some different proposal for 'same act', but the suggested one seems reasonable for a person primarily concerned about the utility of acting.

The notion of 'relevantly similar circumstances' can be spelled out in much the same way. A person will properly identify two situations as relevantly similar if, as far as he can see, the second has in it all the properties of the first which affect the expectable utility of the action being performed, and no others which will affect the expectable utility of the same act being performed.

It is sometimes easy to confuse what is part of the description of an act with what is part of the description of the circumstances of an act. The decisive difference is that the description of the act can include only an account of the change the agent can bring about, whereas the circumstances are what remains fixed, irrespective of which of the alternative actions under consideration the agent performs.

Given these conceptions, we may propose a variant of the UG theory (or imperative) as follows: 'Do A if and only if, as far as you can see, there is no alternative B open to you, such that as much expectable net benefit would be produced if everyone in relevantly similar circumstances, who could perform either A or B (or some other action with expectable utility equivalent to that of

B in your case), performed *B* (or the equivalent).[7] Essentially this is what some UG theorists have apparently wanted to prescribe. Obviously the implications for action of the UG prescription will differ from those of the AU prescription only in special cases. Suppose I am considering drinking a quart of skimmed milk daily instead of a quart of beer, for the sake of my health. Obviously if this is better for me in my state of health, and we (for the sake of the argument but perhaps for no better reason) exempt effects on the dairy and beer industries, it will be better if everyone in my state of health were to do the same; the recommendations of the two codes will be identical. Indeed, the serious question is whether the recommendations can ever be identified by an agent as being different, for if the actions of several persons are the same in respect of their apparently utility-relevant features, and performed in contexts identical in their apparently utility-relevant features, then if act *A* will have better expectable consequences than *B*, in the case of one agent, must not everyone performing *A* have total expectable consequences greater than the total expectable consequences of everyone doing *B*?

So far I have ignored one important and controversial problem about the interpretation of 'same circumstances'. The question is whether the behaviour of other persons, and especially other persons doing *A* (or *B*) is to be included among the circumstances of an individual's act. Obviously what others are doing affects the consequences of the individual act. For instance, suppose a nation is considering (*A*) disarming versus (*B*) keeping up its armed forces. The expectable consequences will be different if the disarmament is unilateral from what they will be if all others go along. Hence, some supporters of the UG principle wish to construe it so as to imply, not 'Disarm if and only if it would have best consequences for all nations to disarm' but 'Disarm if and only if it would have best consequences for all those nations to disarm, who are in the situation of being surrounded by

[7] Compare Lyons, 1965, pp. 25, 54. With some trepidation I am stating the UG conception in such a way as not to narrow the class of relevant persons (1) to those who have precisely the option *B* also open, much less (2) to those who have precisely the *whole set* of options the agent has before him.

This formulation avoids puzzles which may arise because different numbers of persons have *A*, or *B*, as options.

hostile and well-armed neighbours who will not disarm.' Or, to take a different case, suppose I am considering whether to do A (push a stalled car) or B (not push), when I believe that no one else is going to push and I cannot move the car by myself. We do not want to accept a general principle which implies that I must do A (push) just because it would have best consequences if all others pushed. It appears that the only realistic thing to do is to read the UG code so as to include in the agent's 'circumstances' all the facts about the *known or* (*to him*) *reasonably expected* behaviour of others relevant in the sense that they bear on the expectable benefits of the agent's action; so that what is to be estimated, in order to know what the agent should do, is the expectable benefits of everyone in that situation doing A versus doing B.

Let us now return to the question whether an intelligent subscriber to the UG code would be morally inclined to behave in a way different from the way an intelligent subscriber to the AU code would behave. It seems there would sometimes be a difference. Consider voting. Suppose I am pondering whether to go out and vote for a bond issue to support construction of playgrounds which I think important for the community. On the AU principle, I must compare the prospective benefits of voting and staying at home. If I vote, I shall have to stay up late reading a dissertation, and will be both tired and unable to criticize it effectively. If I vote, there will be one more vote for the bond issue but it is extremely unlikely that my vote will affect the outcome. I conclude that the expectable benefit from voting is less than that from working at home, and decide not to vote. (Things are more evenly balanced if the election promises to be close and my vote could be crucial.) An example below will suggest what a more sophisticated analysis might be like. What should I do if I apply the UG principle? I consider the class of persons who, like me, will support the bond issue if they vote, and each of whose individual votes is, on the evidence available, no more likely to be crucial than mine is. We restrict the class further to those who probably, on my evidence, have an alternative action promising as much benefit as my staying at home. Suppose I estimate that most prospective pro-voters are in that position. It may then be clear that if none of these votes, the bond issue will probably lose, and this expectable loss will be substantially greater than the total expectable benefit of all the non-voters performing their alternative actions. Hence I conclude that the UG code requires me to vote. A UG subscriber may properly come to one answer, the AU subscriber to another.

Matters would be different, however, if I happen to have good reason to think a large proportion of supporters of the bond issue in fact will vote. In that case I should ask myself what would happen if none of the prospective supporters, who may not vote in view of some disadvantage, were to vote. If this group is small, no harm would be done if they failed to vote and it is right for me to stay home. In this situation AU and UG would agree. (In reality, the envisaged information is unlikely to be available.)

Is there a fairly large range of cases for which the two codes would lead to different actions? Supporters of the UG principle have thought so. They have thought there are various kinds of act, e.g. a physician lying to his patient about his physical condition, which would individually cause only small expectable losses, on the evidence, although general performance of them would be most unfortunate.

It will clarify the contrast to present a more detailed analysis of one simple situation. Suppose an innocent man is accused of a crime, and four persons can testify to his innocence. The testimony of any two will certainly free him. (If the effect is only probable, the following must be complicated correspondingly.) But suppose each has to come some distance in order to testify. Let us suppose the disutility of any one coming is L (loss), and that the utility to the accused of being freed is G (gain), which is equal to $8L$. Let us suppose no communication is possible and that randomizing procedures are not allowed. On the UG theory, we need only estimate the expectable utility if all go, and if no one goes. In this case the theory prescribes that all go, since G is greater than $4L$. (Things are different if it is known someone *will* go.) On the AU theory matters are less simple, since whether an agent should go depends on the expectable net utility of his going rather than not, and this depends on his probability estimate whether others will go. So he must sum the products of the utilities, if he goes, given that one other goes, or two others, or three, and the corresponding probabilities which are, if the probability of each other going is judged the same and to be p, respectively $(1-p)^3$, $3p(1-p)^2$, $3p^2(1-p)$, and p^3. The respective utilities are $-L$, $6L$, $5L$, and $4L$. He will similarly sum the products if he does not go; in this case the utilities will be 0, $-L$, $6L$, and $5L$. More simply, since there is a net payoff in his going only if exactly one other person goes, there is expectable benefit in his going only if $[3p \times (1-p)^2] \times (B-2L)$ is greater than 0. When the relative values of B and L are set as suggested, this will occur when p is greater than 0.05 and less than 0.76. Evidently whether the AU and the UG principles prescribe the same action depends on the estimated benefits/losses and the estimated probabilities.

Evidently the UG subscriber, in the voting case, must decide the number of supporters who may not vote and will suffer approximately his loss if they vote; he will have to decide how probably their all voting for the bill will decide the issue, and compare the expectable benefit of passage against the expectable loss in their voting. Contrariwise, the AU subscriber will have to decide, along the above lines, and in view of the probabilities of voting he assigns to all others, whether the expectable payoff from his voting is greater than 0.[8]

So much for the statement of the UG principle, and for whether its implications for action are the same as those of the AU principle. The question now confronts us of whether the currency of the UG code would be optimal, or at least better than the currency of the AU principle.

(1) The UG code is less simple to apply. The agent subscribing to it must get clear what his circumstances are (including what conduct by other persons is to be taken as a given), and how large is the class of persons in his situation able to perform his act and some comparably beneficial alternative; and must make an estimate of expectable costs and benefits of everyone doing his action A as compared with other possible courses of action having a utility-expectation equivalent to that of one's own alternative B.

(2) Nevertheless, a subscriber to the UG code will tend to avoid a likely effect of the AU code—to confine reflection to short-range consequences. For the 'what if everybody did' criterion as

---

[8] The reasoning would be different if the UG principle is construed to allow random strategies, or if the principle were complicated so as to allow probability estimates of the size of the 'same circumstances' group.

it were puts the long-range social effects of an action under a magnifying glass. Hence there will be less of a tendency to rationalize in one's own favour.

(3) Subscribers to the UG code will still employ a case-by-case cost-benefit analysis, just like subscribers to the AU code. This fact will be a source of uncertainty for others needing to anticipate his behaviour. This will be partly because of the complexity of the reasoning involved, partly because another person will not know the 'circumstances' of the other person or at least what the other person thinks they are and hence will not know how he will go about his calculation, and partly because (as with the AU code) it makes a difference whether the agent is a revolutionary or a conservative in his evaluation.

(4) Does the UG code make as extreme and oppressive demands on a person as does the AU code? Subscribers to the UG code, no more than those to the AU code, can enjoy no sphere of freedom, no time when they can know they have discharged all their obligations and do as they wish. For one can always ask of any action being contemplated, whether there is not some other action one could be performing, such that more benefit would be produced if everyone did that rather than the contemplated alternative. And it is not clear that the UG code leaves room, more than does the AU code, for the distinction between the obligatory and the supererogatory.

I shall not attempt to weigh the relative long-range expectable utilities of subscription to these two theories. Both of them suffer from such serious problems that it is worth considering whether some different type of moral system might not produce more considerable benefits and thereby engage the support of fully rational persons more than do these.

CHAPTER XV

THE CONCEPT OF A PLURALISTIC WELFARE-MAXIMIZING MORAL SYSTEM

IT IS possible that a system of several moral rules, properly selected, might maximize welfare, and hence be the kind of moral system fully rational persons would support. This chapter will explore that possibility.

Such a conception is not novel. It was put forward by Bishop Berkeley and theological utilitarians: the idea was that God wishes to maximize the happiness of sentient creation and to that end has promulgated certain laws fitted to that purpose, and has revealed them to man either in the Bible or through conscience or reason in some sense.[1] An analogue of this theological moral utilitarianism has been devised by utilitarian reformers of the criminal law including Bentham. They have thought of the ideal criminal code as a complex system of prohibitions, penalties, and procedures such that the operation of the whole system will maximize welfare.

We have, then, a general idea of such a plural moral system. This chapter will work out some details. (1) First it will review the ways in which moral codes can differ: the various parts of a moral code which can be varied so as to get a welfare-maximizing system as a whole. (2) It will discuss in more detail how an ideal system of injunctions should be identified: what they will regulate, the level of abstraction at which they should be framed, whether and how the several rules may be assigned weights and how probability estimates might be used in applying them. It will show how historical moral codes can serve as a guide in fixing the basic rules of an 'ideal' code. All of this discussion will provide reason for thinking that the currency of a code so devised would

---

[1] Berkeley gave the theory an interesting statement, supported by arguments, in 1712, in *Passive Obedience, or the Christian Doctrine of Not Resisting the Supreme Power, Proved and Vindicated upon the Principles of the Law of Nature.*

in fact maximize social welfare. (3) It will conclude by replying to some apparently serious objections.

1. THE VARIABLE FEATURES OF PLURAL MORAL SYSTEMS

i. Intrinsic motivation. The most important part of a moral code is the basic desires for (aversions to) certain kinds of behaviour .for themselves, like the prohibitions and injunctions of the criminal and civil law. A basic aversion to some form of behaviour will, in English, normally be expressed by 'It is (prima facie) wrong to ...' (The words 'prima facie' indicate that the prohibition can be overridden by stronger prima facie injunctions.) These motivations can vary in three respects: the kind of behaviour involved; whether the behaviour is desired or is aversive; and the strength of the motivation. The kinds of behaviour in question need not be simple. Take promises. A code may require that promises be kept, prima facie, but only certain kinds of promise, perhaps ones not made under duress, or ones not made on the basis of a misrepresentation of facts given deliberately in order to extract the promise. Such exceptions might be made because it would be socially harmful for people to feel obligated to keep such promises.

Not all logically possible 'rules of obligation' of this sort are causally possible. Obviously the basic motivations cannot be very numerous, since they have to be instituted by a process of conditioning, or some such device (e.g. the use of prestigious persons as models). Again, the complexity of the conduct enjoined or banned is limited by the intellectual capacities of the average person. What these rules may require is limited by the strain of self-interest in everyone, and the specific desires and aversions bound to develop in nearly everyone, including some degree of benevolence; and they are also limited by the fact that these other desires are prior in the sense that the basic moral motivations can be acquired by conditioning only by building essentially on them.

ii. Justifications. What if these basic motivations conflict in a given situation? What if the basic code prohibits both breaking promises and injuring others, but in a given case injuring another can be avoided only by breaking a promise? A complete moral system will ideally answer these questions. How can this be done? One possibility is that the particular built-in strength of each motivation decides the issue in each case in favour of the stronger: so a person 'ought' to do what he is most motivated (morally) to do. These strengths could be built in so that conflicts of obligations decided in this way would come out as the code-builder wanted; a utilitarian, for instance, might reflect on how great an injury to others might just balance the loss from a breach of promise in cases of a certain type, and set the motivation to avoid that much injury so as just to match an already set aversion to that kind of breach of promise. (Of course we can hardly in practice tune the consciences of people finely enough so that they come out exactly as we might want.) But there is a second possibility: introducing a special moral rule (motivation) restricted to conflicts of the primary rules, or at least to severe conflicts.

iii. Guilt-feelings, disapproval of others, and excuses. Responses by guilt feeling or disapproval, to breaches of the rules of obligation, are another variable of a moral code. To some extent the responses are fixed by the basic motivations: for instance, if aversion to injuring others is built in on the basis of underlying benevolence, a person will have a tendency to feel remorse if he injures another, and to have anti-attitudes towards someone else who does. In some cases, however, the disposition to have guilt-feelings must be learned separately, and then it is variable independently of the basic motivations. Variations are also possible through cognitive changes: the intensity of a young child's guilt-feelings seem often a function of how much damage his wrong-doing caused; later by acquiring discriminations based on concepts like intention, inadvertence, and mistake, his guilt-feelings (and anti-attitudes towards others) are reduced. Persons can be trained to perceive the acts of another not in terms of the objective change he caused, but in terms of intention and motives. Evidently the relation between intrinsic motivation and the feelings of guilt or disapproval—what we may call the 'system of excuses'—is variable, just as in the criminal law the relation between commission of a forbidden act and the punishment varies.

iv. Admiration, praise, and pride. There is another variable. At least in the Anglo-Saxon world some types of action are not required morally, but their performance is praised and arouses respect or admiration: acts of heroism (like falling on a live hand-grenade in order to save one's comrades), or of saintliness (like caring for a cantankerous relative through a long illness, with patience and without complaint). Although admiration and respect are native responses to certain sorts of situation and are not learned by conditioning, the frequency and expression of these attitudes can be varied: people can be taught to recognize the rare, difficult, and socially beneficial traits of character which some actions normally express; and they can be taught to express favourable attitudes in praise. If people are taught to respond with praise to such actions, the actions are encouraged; and people may come to value the traits of character they express, to develop a corresponding self-ideal, and to take pride in behaving in such a manner.

This variable feature of moral codes may be of interest to a utilitarian, because he may think it beneficial to encourage such supererogatory actions, but not to require them.

2. THE CONTENT OF A WELFARE-MAXIMIZING MORAL SYSTEM

Let us confine attention to the intrinsic motivation of a moral system, the system of injunctions and prohibitions. I shall suggest some directives about how to identify welfare-maximizing injunctions and prohibitions. This will give us clues to what the rules will be; but we cannot state them precisely without a specific society and set of institutions before us.

If we assume that the rules of the code are not to be just directives to produce welfare, directly or indirectly, they must be rules enjoining or prohibiting act-types. But which ones? The most expeditious first move is to find areas of behaviour needing regulation, by consulting our actual moral code, the codes of criminal law and tort law, and so on. We can then decide which items on this list of actually regulated behaviours it would maximize utility for a moral code to prohibit, and ideas for additions may occur to us. For instance, such a survey will indicate some need for morality to regulate fulfilling contracts and promises, and risking injury to others. The older manuals of casuistry, or a treatise like Sidgwick's *Methods of Ethics*, comprise a mine of information about the structure of conscience of at least some people. These sources will not only provide suggestions about which act-types probably need regulation; they will also provide information about what exceptive clauses may be useful.

The ideal rules are presumably some not very distant variant of some present rules. Like 'incrementalists' among political scientists we should frame our ideal code by improving the present rules. How? For one thing, some, having lost their function, should be scrapped. The present moral or legal rules may not reflect recent technological or institutional changes, and where we know such changes have occurred, reflection about the creation of quite new rules, doubtless analogous to some old ones, will be in order.

At what level of abstraction should the rules regulating act-types be framed? Should there, for instance, be a basic rule forbidding carrying a revolver? Or is it enough if there is a rule prohibiting risking injury to others? One advantage to abstract rules is increased applicability—perhaps world-wide. Abstract rules can also be few in number, and that is an advantage since the basic motivations have to be established by conditioning. On the other hand, the conditions and exceptions of the abstract rule, as well as the inference from it to the concrete application may be too complex for the average person. A reasonable compromise is to propose that the code contain fairly concrete rules for frequent situations, especially ones for which predictability of behaviour is important to many persons. For less frequent or less important matters, more abstract regulations requiring some inference may be sufficient.

These facts suggest that the moral code taught or emphasized may vary somewhat from sub-group to sub-group in a society. Children may need to be taught not to cheat in examinations and to be honest about money and perhaps to respect the morality of queues; but they need not hear about pacifism or tax-evasion. Physicians and lawyers frequently face moral problems of special and complex kinds, and possibly it is useful for them to be taught special rules about obligations to patients/clients, or at least careful accounts of the connection between general moral rules and the special situations they meet frequently: hence the need for codes of medical and legal ethics. The same for various other professions, and for business men. We can leave open the question whether these various 'ethics' for special groups can all in principle be deduced as special cases of the rules to be taught to society as a whole, or whether they must be justified by direct appeal to welfare-maximization.

If a moral code is to maximize welfare, it must be suited not only to the intellectual capacities of the average person, but also to his degree of selfishness, impulsiveness, and so on. Possibly some rules will be welfare-maximizing, not because strict adherence to them would be, but because the actual imperfect response to them will be, just as a speed limit of 55 m.p.h. is consistent with information that more benefit is gained if traffic moves at 60 m.p.h., because the thinking and habits of motorists are such that with an advertised speed limit (enforced as nearly as personnel and finances permit) of 55 m.p.h., the traffic will actually move at approximately the ideal speed.[2]

Should, or can, a plural system of moral principles incorporate a feature, analogous to the act utilitarian injunction to maximize expectable (as contrasted with actual) utility, which allows the specific implications of the code for action to be sensitive to the fact that different actions are more or less likely to realize a desired outcome? It should, and it can. It should, because if a utility-maximizing code is devised to prevent injury to others, an expectable utility-maximizing code will also prohibit in appropriate ways the taking of risk of injury. It should, because if such a code is devised to accomplish execution of promises (to return a book, perhaps), it should direct whether the borrower must return it personally or whether he may trust it to the postal services. The moral system can incorporate such a feature, and in a fairly simple way. For subscription to a moral principle, I have argued, is essentially a matter of intrinsic motivation; and it follows from the psychological theory explained in Chapter 3 that, given an aversion of a certain strength, the tendency to perform an action will be a multiplicative function of the strength of that aversion and the degree of expectation that the act will enable avoidance of the aversive outcome. Thus, if there is an intrinsic aversion to the failure to return a book, and posting it makes the pro-

---

[2] I am indebted, for this example, to an unpublished version of Irving Seldin, 1977. He also points out that juries are required to swear that they will accept the judge's interpretation of the law and confine their decisions to the factual question whether, on courtroom evidence, the case is covered by the law—even though everyone expects and hopes that in extreme cases juries will simply follow their own sense of justice.

bability of loss as high as 40 per cent, the consequent tendency to post it will be weaker than the tendency to return it personally. Similarly, if there is an aversion to injuring another person, the resulting tendency to avoid that act will be stronger than the tendency to perform an act believed to pose only a small risk of injury. (Matters will be complicated if the code contains a 'right' permitting a small risk when the cost to the agent of avoiding it is considerable. In any case, the adequate teaching of a moral code must include some teaching of probability reasoning.) To accomplish the objective of a system of principles sensitive to the above considerations, all that needs to be done is to set the degree of intrinsic motivation at an appropriate level— ideally a motivation such that the consequent tendencies to avoid acts with various degrees of risk will be at approximately welfare-maximizing strength.[3]

The problem of what ought to be done when two of the basic rules of obligation conflict has already been mentioned. One solution is simply to rely on the built-in weights of the rules, just mentioned. (This seems to be the one actually used in our society.) Another possibility already mentioned is to invoke the UG or AU principle for such cases. I shall not try to suggest which procedure would be welfare-maximizing.[4]

A similar problem arises for situations for which the basic rules of obligation do not provide at all. Possibly there are no such cases, for a novel situation might not require evaluation unless good or harm is involved, and there will be rules about this. But there may be novel questions, as, for instance, control over how a baby's genes develop. Might every baby have a right to be as bright as Einstein? This type of problem is not well covered either by the Ten Commandments or by W. D. Ross. How would the welfare-maximizing code provide for it? One option is to follow legal practice and decide by the rule covering most nearly analogous

---

[3] The possibility that numbers must be assigned in some sense to the strength of prima facie obligations is mentioned by Frank Snare, 'The definition of *prima facie* duties', *The Philosophical Quarterly* 24 (1974), p. 243. The idea has been discussed at some length by Holly Goldman in her Ph.D. dissertation, 'The Generalization Principle in Ethics', 1972, deposited in the University of Michigan Graduate Library.

[4] P. H. Nowell-Smith has argued that we must despair of finding any reasonable device for adjudicating between different rules. If I am right, there are several sensible options. See his interesting 'Some reflections on utilitarianism', 1973.

cases. Or the UG rule might be specified. Another possibility is that we should get away from thinking of the 'ideal' moral code as something static, as it certainly is not. The code ideal today will probably not be welfare-maximizing a hundred years from now. Perhaps we should think simply of background teaching so that future rational persons will recognize and support a moral code ideal for their day.

The above remarks on how to identify a welfare-maximizing code will give a reasonably good idea what such a system would be like. Indeed, there seems no doubt that we know what some of the relatively specific rules in such a moral system would be: rules safeguarding personal security, requiring fulfilment of contracts and promises, and so on. Our discussion does suggest that many options are open and debatable; most of these options, however, are not very different from one another, and they usually correspond to murky areas in ordinary moral thinking, where people are confused about what is right and would like the guidance of a definite principle. Nothing prevents us, however, from learning more about the optimal specific rules; philosophers, psychologists, and other social scientists could co-operate in determining what a welfare-maximizing moral code would be. Indeed, it is not clear why much greater effort is not being made in this direction.

The fact that we start with our present rules does not imply that a complete code would simply reflect our long-established 'intuitions'. On the contrary, the conception of a happiness-maximizing moral code can have rather revolutionary implications. This would be clear in any country where the moral code forbids racial intermarriage. Moreover, it is clear that there is a prima facie case against the moral code prohibiting anything—which may be quite surprising. For what someone wants to do there is (at least normally) some benefit in permitting: he will enjoy doing it, and feel frustrated in being prevented on grounds of conscience. If something is to be prohibited or enjoined, a case must be made out for the long-range benefit of restricting the freedom of individuals, making them feel guilty, and utilizing the teaching resources of the community. Without proof of long-range benefit, any restriction lacks justification.

Is there a fatal logical flaw in the present conception, set by the fact that two different moral systems might be equally bene-ficial? This possibility is no mere speculation, for it looks very much as if two quite similar codes, say with different emphases on the obligation to keep promises, might not offer noticeably different effects on welfare. Or, different systems might adopt dif-ferent ones of the options mentioned for adjudicating between conflicting rules, or for dealing with situations not specifically mentioned in the rules; again, there might be no demonstrably different promise for welfare. Of course, it would seem that the greater the disparity, the larger the chance of demonstrating different effects on welfare. But suppose that two some-what different codes would promise approximately equal benefits. Then we could say of some rules that they comprise part of a welfare-maximizing system, but of the others only that they comprise parts of alternative systems, each of which would do equally well in producing welfare, and better than the rest. Which one would then be taught? It would make no difference, as long as there could be agreement—just as with rules of the road. If two moral rules promised equal benefits on other grounds, the fact that one was already 'conventional' should turn the scales in its favour. Until such agreement is reached, however, there would be no definite correct answer to the question of which rule would be supported by rational persons. Individual moral deliberators would presumably emerge with different answers. But we have already learned to tolerate different people acting conscientiously on different systems of moral principles; in this situation, no one could be criticized for sticking to his favoured moral system, among the optional alternatives.

A natural mistake about the content of the 'ideal' code is to assume that the welfare-maximizing code which rational people would support would be a one-principle code after all, like act utilitarianism, just one principle: 'Do whatever would be required by the moral code the currency of which would maximize wel-fare.' Is this the whole moral code which rational people would support? The answer to the question is: 'No, rational persons would not support that one-principle moral code.' We can see why not if we try to spell it out. Suppose it were true that the moral code the currency of which would maximize welfare is just this one-principle code. Then what we should have to teach is: 'Do whatever would be required by the moral code, "Do what would be required by the moral code ..."' and so on infinitely. In other words: 'Follow the principle which is to follow the principle....' Either there is some other specifiable set of rules the currency of which would maximize welfare, or there is not. If there is not, then the one-principle becomes, in the phrase of C. I. Lewis, a 'perpetual stutter'. If there is, then *it* is the set of principles rational persons would want taught, and is the moral code the currency of which would maximize welfare.

Currency of the type of plural moral code here envisaged can be shown by a cost-benefit analysis to produce more benefit, as shown by a total cost-benefit analysis, than any of the one-principle codes discussed in Chapter 14. For a system of plural rules, specifically built in for situations of importance and frequency in the society, avoids the major difficulties of the other theories. When individuals are deciding what is the right thing to do, in the normal case they need not engage in elusive calculations which tempt them to decide in favour of what they want to do. A principle about promise-keeping, with rules about possible exceptions, is built in. The individual need not deliberate about whether in this case it would do a little more good to break the promise—and because he need not, other individuals can predict reliably what a moral man will do. Others will be able to plan on specific behaviour by moral persons. Moreover, they need not worry about the outcomes of others' moral deliberations: they will feel personally secure, and secure about promised activity taking place. Furthermore, the agent benefits from his ability to know at any time whether his role, or prior behaviour, or his general obligation to help others in severe need, places him under an obligation at any given moment. Knowing that no such obligation is undischarged, he is free to do as he pleases as long as he does not risk injury or cause inconvenience to others. For the most part he can quietly go about his business. There are nice things he can do for us, even heroic and saintly things, and if he does these things he is properly admired or even loved by others; but he is not obligated to do them.

Evidently, then, there is strong reason to think that the currency of a carefully selected plural code in a society will produce considerably more welfare or happiness, on balance, than any of the one-principle codes that historically have been advocated.

We have the conception, then, of a welfare-maximizing moral code for a given society. We do not know exactly what its injunctions and prohibitions would be, but we have some guidelines for identifying it, and presumably co-operation among various disciplines would come very close to determining the ideal code which fully rational persons would support and teach, in preference to one of the one-principle codes.

3. PARADOXES FOR THE PLURAL IDEAL-CODE UTILITARIAN?

Philosophers critical of utilitarianism have usually been less unhappy with a 'rule-utilitarian' conception like the foregoing, than with the conception of an act utilitarian code for society (see Donagan, 1968). Nevertheless, many have been critical of the present conception; and some of the objections have sufficiently wide currency that it seems necessary to consider them. The objections are roughly the following: (a) that a code like the foregoing can hardly maximize welfare, and hence a person of utilitarian persuasion is defeating his own purposes if he espouses it; (b) that there are circumstances in which the following of such a code even by a good many persons in our actual society could only be harmful; and (c) that conformity to such a code would necessarily result in significant unfairness. Let us look at the reasoning.

(a) The first argument is an abstract a priori argument. It urges that if this code makes recommendations for behaviour different from AU—and they must be different, or the theory loses all its claim to fame—it must be telling people to do something different from producing the very best consequences, which is what the AU code recommends. So following it must be producing less than the very best.[5] Much the same point is made by others who say that rule-utilitarians must be rule-worshippers, since they advocate following a rule even when so doing would fail to maximize utility. (Smart, 1961 and 1956.) These points, however, rest on a confusion. For to have an AU code is to be motivated (basic motivations) to do what one thinks will have best conse-

---

[5] Lyons, 1965, p. 144. David Lyons does not endorse this point; he states it in order to introduce a complex and thoughtful discussion.

quences, so that doing what one is thus motivated to do is not at all necessarily to do what will have best consequences, assuming that agents are not omniscient. Whereas persons committed to the ideal code are motivated (basic motivations) to do what they think will be the keeping of a promise, the avoidance of causing injury, etc., and doing what they are thus motivated to do will be to do what in the long-run will have the best consequences, even if some such acts do not. Non-omniscient persons acting to keep their promises (of certain kinds) will actually succeed in producing more welfare than those who are aiming at maximizing welfare directly.[6] So this first line of reasoning may be dismissed.

(b) A second argument commences by conceding that at least normally welfare is maximized by everyone following the recommendations of an ideal code. Roughly, the 'ideal' code is picked with that end in mind, so that it can be no surprise that it succeeds. But suppose the currency of a code in a certain society would maximize welfare; it does not follow that some people acting in accordance with it will maximize welfare, irrespective of what other people are doing. Consider an example:[7] There is a society in which violence on the streets is common, everyone carries a weapon, and the ability to use it is the only guarantee of safety. In this society, universal following of the rule: 'Do not carry a weapon' would maximize benefits, but for only one person to follow such a rule would merely endanger his life.

This argument depends on an unduly simple conception of what an optimal set of rules would be like. Two points need to be made. (1) The first is that the unfortunate behaviour suggested above might be required by one rule with prima facie force, but there will usually or always be other rules. One of these might well be: 'Defend yourself and your wife and children against unjustifiable violent attack with effective means.' Both of these rules have only prima facie force, but the second might have more stringency than the first in the ideal code. If so, then, if one

---

[6] David Braybrooke has a nice way of putting this (1967).

[7] The example is drawn from Hodgson, 1967, p. 169; see also pp. 32 ff., Chap. 3 and Appendix. Also Lyons, 1965, pp. 143–60 and Chap. 5; and Feinberg, review of Lyons, 1967, especially pp. 373–8.

could not discharge the second obligation compatibly with following the first rule, one would be morally bound to infringe the rule against carrying a weapon. (2) But in any case an unrestricted prohibition against carrying weapons could hardly be even a prima facie rule of a welfare-maximizing code for that society. We must remember that an ideal moral code will be devised somehow to deal optimally with problems that actually will arise, and hence with the fact that many persons will be carrying lethal weapons in the streets. (Even if the 'rule' were for no one ever to carry a weapon, we should have to expect some weapons in the streets, for even if the rule is 'current' to the extent that the most widely accepted ones are, there will be some who do not accept it, and others who will not follow it, out of self-interest. We must recall that for a person to subscribe to a code is only for him to be motivated in the appropriate direction, not necessarily always to follow it.) One of the reasons, we recall, why the construction of an ideal code should begin with actual codes is that the latter draw attention to situations which need regulation. Now, obviously, one thing an optimal moral code would aim to avoid is moral people being the prey of unscrupulous or morally weak persons; and it would be a deterrent to potential criminals not to be sure, when attacking a moral man, that he would be defenceless. So everything considered, what kind of moral rule would be welfare-maximizing? Apparently an alternative rule, something like: 'Do not carry a weapon when there is no significant personal risk in not doing so; if there is significant personal risk, you may carry a weapon but use it only for self-protection, and meanwhile you should work to enlist co-operation in reducing violence in the streets.'[8] The currency of this rule would have virtually all the advantage of the unrestricted prohibition, and bring the further benefit that it provides for expectable contingencies.

What this example shows is that an ideal moral rule will not permit catastrophes arising (1) from the behaviour of those who do not accept the rule, or (2) from the behaviour of those who do accept it but fail to follow it because of stronger contrary motivation, or (3) from other predictable or probable situations. An ideal code might, of course, make some risky demands; if it

[8] I am indebted to David Benfield for improvement of an earlier formulation.

would be welfare-maximizing for behaviour to meet a certain standard, it might be best to teach a code requiring some risk of harm, in order for the society to get started on the ascent to ideal behaviour.

(c) A third line of reasoning aims to show that sometimes following the ideal rules would be unfair, in what Professor Lyons has called 'maximizing' situations. We can develop the basic ideas most simply in an example. Suppose I am on board ship, travelling tourist-class. The promenade deck of tourist-class is unsuitable for exercise, whereas the first-class deck is excellent. A sign at the staircase which leads to the first-class promenade deck reads: 'First-class passengers only'. Now, even if long-range welfare is maximized by most tourist-class passengers respecting the sign, would it not be better if a few venturesome souls, so few that their presence on the first-class deck would not be a nuisance or even noticed, were to ignore the sign and enjoy the amenities of the first-class deck? Let us assume that there are benefits in the general system of segregation and of voluntary conformity and that in the circumstances violation of the rules by a few would do no harm and would benefit the violators. Might the ideal rule then be: 'Respect the ship's rules about the segregation of the classes of passengers, except when the preceding clause is so generally obeyed that a few visitors in the first-class deck would not be harmful, and when such persons would enjoy the exercise'?

The answer is that the currency of such a rule could not be welfare-maximizing, as contrasted with the rule without the excepting clause. It is true that more good might be produced by a few people secretly behaving immorally, for there is benefit in a few enjoying the first-class deck with no harm done; but it would not be maximally helpful for the above rule to be a publicized and respected moral rule. (1) Such a rule would only promote confusion and discontent. Every tourist-class passenger would be encouraged by it to look around and notice who is doing what, perhaps breakfasting early in order to be one of the 'early-birds' who could claim to be in the unobjectionable quota; and, human nature being what it is, there would be a gradual and eventually intolerable increase in the number of visitors in the first-class facilities. (2) If there is a benefit here which can be distributed, it should be divided in accordance with welfare-maximizing rules which remove confusion—perhaps by taking turns, or issuing special passes to persons under medical orders to walk six miles a day. One of the advantages of a plural utilitarian ideal code is that it can provide rules, for a case of more people doing a certain thing than are necessary for maximizing the good which arises from conformity, and for dividing the 'surplus' in an optimal manner, with a licence to be excused to those who can benefit most. Of course, such an arrangement may not be possible in every case. In that case the 'surplus' benefit is lost.

In general, an ideal moral code will not contain clauses inviting just anyone to make himself a benefit-producing exception to a rule, the general observance of which is important for the public good, when sufficiently numerous others are conforming to the rule. (See Lyons, 1965, especially pp. 172 ff.)

4. A FINAL PUZZLE

We have the conception, then, of a plural moral system—of basic motivations, justification, rules of excuses, and so on—subscription to which by a large majority of the adult population of a given society would result in more welfare than subscription to any other moral system. Not only do we have the idea of such a system; we know what some of its main features would be, and we know in principle how to go on to find as precise details as need be. In the preceding section I argued that, if we understand what the details of such a system really would be, we can see that only a few persons conforming to it in the society where its currency would be welfare-maximizing would almost always be doing what would produce as much good as anything they might do instead.

I have argued that fully rational persons would support such a moral system for a society in which they expected to live. But we must be careful to notice that in fact probably no one is living in a society with a moral code exactly ideal in that sense. If such a code were current in a given society, the ideal motivations etc. would be built in. As a result, if a practical problem arose for a person in that society, he would need roughly only to follow conscience (his built-in moral motivations, responding to his intellectual analysis of his situation), perhaps assisted by a background explanation of the welfare-maximizing purpose of moral codes, in order to do the right thing. But probably a code exactly like the ideal one is not current anywhere; and it is highly doubtful whether many parents or teachers in the early grades of school have any such thing in mind as something they should be teaching.

One might therefore feel inclined to ask: 'Granted that if I were fully rational I would support a moral code for my society requiring action A in circumstances C, in the absence of such a code (or at least of a code requiring A in C), would I, if I were fully rational, advise a person in C to do A?'

One is at first, at least, inclined to be doubtful whether the answer to this question would be affirmative. For the answer, it appears, must depend on one's own motivations, and furthermore on the state of mind of the other person: what kind of conscience he in fact has, and what he thinks he is morally bound to do. Suppose, for instance, that you are a selfish person and want a moral code of a certain kind only because it will afford you certain protections and other benefits. In that case you might care little whether a given individual conforms to the ideal code now, since his conforming will not give you any of this protection or other benefit. Presumably you will want an agent to do what will promote your own selfish set of objectives best, and if whichever action he takes will not affect your realization of your objectives either way, you will not care what he does. On the other hand, if you are a perfectly benevolent person, you may be inclined to want the agent to do just whatever will do most good now, and hence possibly not perform the action A which a welfare-maximizing moral code would call for in his circumstances. There is of course the possibility that a rational person, whether selfish or unselfish, would in certain circumstances believe that a given agent's doing A would be a step in the formation of an ideal moral code in his society, in which case he would advise doing A as part of his support of his preferred moral code for that society. Another possibility is that, if you are deeply concerned about the institution of morality, you might encourage the agent just to follow his own moral code, whatever that might happen to be, with the thought that his act will at least support his own commitment to morality.

Nevertheless, I believe that a perfectly rational person would answer our original question in the affirmative, and would advise the suppositious agent to do A in C, just as the ideal moral code requires. Why? As a rational person, you can identify which moral code a rational person would support by noticing which moral code you do support. Furthermore, if you agree with an earlier argument that a moral code is justified to a person if he, were he fully rational, would support it more strongly than any other code, and that an optimal definition of 'morally ought to' is 'is required to, by a justified moral code', you will then at least emerge with the view that the agent is morally obligated to do A, as the ideal code prescribes. (There are complications for provisions in the code on which fully rational persons do not agree.) Hence, assuming that you take an interest in whether people discharge their moral obligations, you will encourage and advise our agent to do A. It does not follow from this that you will necessarily hold the agent morally blameworthy, subject to moral reproach, if he fails to do A when his own conscience prescribes doing something else; for obviously the ideal code, like the Western moral tradition, will hold that an agent is morally blameless for following his own conscience unless there is something culpable, something indicative of a defect of character, in his subscribing to the code he does subscribe to.

Some philosophers, however, think that a person cannot be *morally obligated* to do what conforms to a moral code which would be welfare-maximizing if it were current (and the currency of which is supported by fully rational persons), but is not in fact current, in force, in the community of the agent. Some philosophers think that an agent in this situation is morally obligated just to do what good he can. Others think a person should always conform to his own personal moral commitments, whatever they are. Still others think that if a moral system is actually in force in a society —and is one from which everyone benefits—everyone is bound to conform to it, and not to the ideal code, since everyone is receiving benefits.[9]

What kind of reasoning might lead a person to say that an agent

---

[9] This last doubt seems to be expressed by B. J. Diggs, 1970. Diggs concedes there may be reason to follow an ideal code if there is some likelihood that it can be adopted, and especially if the action in question would contribute to its adoption, pp. 313, 315.

can be obligated to conform to a welfare-maximizing or rationally-supported code, only if that code is actually in force? One possibility is that the person is confusing two different concepts; he takes 'is morally obligated to do A' to mean the same as 'is morally blameworthy (culpable) if he fails to do A'. Then, if he thinks (correctly) that an agent is normally not culpable if he .follows the dictates of his own conscience, or conforms with the standards accepted in his community, he wrongly infers that an agent cannot have failed to do what he is morally obligated to do in these circumstances. In fact, however, 'morally obligated' and 'morally blameworthy if he fails' are far from synonyms. In any system that would be welfare-maximizing, moral appraisals will recognize certain kinds of *excuses*; for instance, mistake of fact, not being oneself owing to, say, fright, being temporarily of unsound mind; and when one of these situations is present it is said that the agent's behaviour, in view of the excuse, is not morally blameworthy, but nevertheless it may be consistently affirmed that the behaviour is objectively wrong. If we make this distinction, then we may concede that a person is not morally blameworthy for not conforming with a welfare-maximizing code he has not even thought about much less subscribed to, but we can still inquire whether a person might not be failing in his objective moral obligation if his conduct deviates from that of the rationally-supported code.

What would philosophers accept as a proof of my view that a person is objectively morally obligated to act according to the requirements of a rationally-supported code? Usually when philosophers raise questions about a normative thesis, they are assuming that there is some alternative view about what is morally obligatory, which is self-evident, analytically true, or favoured in some way. One way of defending the present view against attack is to show that the critics' alternative proposals do not stand up. For instance, we could repeat the good reasons for rejecting act utilitarianism as analytically true, or self-evident, or a coherent normative theory. Or, if someone says a person should conform to the 'moral principle by which' he chooses 'to live his life' (Feinberg, 1967, p. 377), we could point out (1) that presumably he means the principles he is prepared to recommend for everyone and (2) that good reasons were given, in Chapter 10, for thinking that one must then go on and say that what a person should do is conform to the principles he is prepared to support as the ones all persons should follow in conduct for reasons of conscience; and, if the reasoning of Chapter 11 is accepted, the result is substantially what has here throughout been defended. Or, if someone proposes that it is morally obligatory to do what is required by an operating moral system from which one benefits, as a matter of doing one's fair share, we can answer by pointing out (1) that this claim seems to be underwriting conventional morality, whatever it is, and (2) that the principle seems itself to be a normative principle and one wonders if it is supposed to be self-evident. Obviously a person is not morally obligated to do something only if he lives in a moral community in which there will be actual criticism of him if he fails; if this were true, a reformer would never be discharging his real moral obligation when he deplored, and flaunted, the moral standards of his community.

There is no way to prove a blanket rejection of all the theories, about when some action is morally obligatory, which conflict with my proposal; but it is obvious that mere *obiter dicta* on the part of some philosopher are nothing we need take seriously. Contrary views require support by a systematic theory.

My view, that in a situation like the present in which the 'ideal' moral code is not generally accepted (at least in its details and the details not even known by anyone) a person is nevertheless morally obligated to do what would be required by the rules of a rationally-supported code for his society, rests upon the main argument of this book. My defence, in brief, is this: a set of moral motivations is justified if it is what it would be if facts and logic were brought to bear on its 'choice' to a maximal extent— that is, if fully rational persons would tend to support it in preference to any other system and to none. I have argued that when we have identified such a system of motivations, we have found one which is 'justified' for us in the only sense in which a moral system can be justified at the present time. Further, I have proposed (Chapter 10) that we define 'is morally obligatory' as 'would be called for by the moral system which is justified, and which fully rational persons would most tend to support'. If this is accepted, then what is called for by justified moral motivations, or by the justified moral code, is morally obligatory. I have argued, with some reservations, that at least for benevolent people this system will be a welfare-maximizing one. We have hardly discussed which principles a welfare-maximizing moral code would contain, but we know some of them roughly, and know how to go on to identify such principles for specific types of situation.

Let us look finally at how an actual agent may reasonably make a decision, if he is convinced about the above-supported general description of what he is obligated to do (say, what a welfare-maximizing system would require) but is not sure of the precise requirement of such a system for a situation he is in. He thinks, however, after careful reflection that such a system would require that he do so-and-so. For instance, suppose an agent thinks that a welfare-maximizing system would call on people to keep their promises in the kind of situations he takes himself to be in, so that, as far as he can see, justified moral principles require him to keep his promise. In that situation, given the proposed meaning for 'moral obligation' it would not be misleading for him unqualifiedly to assert: 'I am morally obligated to keep my promise.' But, if he wishes to be very circumspect, he might say 'It is possible that I am not really obligated to keep my promise, but as far as I can see, on the facts I know and in the light of the reasoning I have gone through, I am obligated.' He can say this correctly, even if in fact he is mistaken about what the principles of a welfare-maximizing moral code would require. And, if he then follows his own moral conclusion, he is morally blameless for doing the objectively wrong thing (barring some morally culpable error in his total reasoning); and if he does not follow it he morally deserves reproach, even if what he then does is objectively right. The moral status of his action would not be altered by the fact that most of the persons in his society would disagree with his conclusion and would not disapprove if he failed to keep his promise.

CHAPTER XVI

JUSTICE, EQUALITY, AND THE MAXIMIZATION OF WELFARE

WHAT IS morally right or obligatory for an agent to do, then, is fixed by which moral system a fully rational person would support for his society in preference to any other or to none, if he expected to live in it. There are good reasons to think that the moral system a fully rational person would support is roughly a welfare or happiness-maximizing system, although it may be suggested that a fully rational person would want, say, a more egalitarian or meritarian system for the distribution of welfare than is compatible with a welfare-maximizing system. In a recent volume it is claimed that utilitarianism emerges as 'absurdly primitive' in view of its (alleged) implication that 'questions of equitable or inequitable distribution do not matter'. (B. Williams, 1973, p. 142; also Sen, 1973.) Other philosophers have phrased much the same point by saying that utilitarianism has no adequate theory of justice.

The conclusions of earlier chapters in this book, however, are compatible with thinking that the moral system a fully rational person would support is a system of rules which is not precisely welfare-maximizing. For the reasoning of Chapter 11, aimed to determine what kind of moral system fully rational persons would support, did not exclude the possibility that they would be moved by some considerations in addition to welfare-production, such as equality of welfare. In that chapter we simply set aside the possibility for the moment, with the thought of returning to it, as we now shall.

I. THE PROBLEM ABOUT JUSTICE

When critics object that the ideal of a welfare-maximizing moral code overlooks or makes mistakes about justice, what do they have in mind? Usually they believe there is a group of principles about the *distribution* of good and evil which are sound principles, and that the utilitarian theory either has no implications for such principles, or has mistaken implications. Which principles of distribution? Ones like the principle that an equal distribution (or one in accordance with need, or in accordance with one's contribution to society, and so on) is prima facie right.

The charge sometimes runs deeper than this: it is claimed that even if one has a sound theory about what is morally right to do, it is not yet a theory of *just* action, which is what we want for a normative theory of justice. But this charge is a puzzling one. If we already know what it is morally right to do, how can there be some further, quite different task, to find out what is *just*? It is true, however, that 'is unjust' is not equivalent to 'is morally wrong', and that an action can be morally wrong but not unjust, and can be unjust but not morally wrong. How is this? The most plausible suggestion[1] is that 'is unjust' means approximately 'is prima facie morally wrong, *and because* [although perhaps this should be construed as what is implied rather than what is said] it would produce an unequal allocation of good and evil' (or defective in some of the other ways mentioned above). 'Unjust' is a strong word, and it may be that normally when we say something is unjust we mean not merely that it is prima facie morally wrong for certain reasons, but that it is actually morally wrong. It seems, however, that we do not always use the term in this way: sometimes we say that something is unjust but concede that nothing else is feasible and therefore on the whole it is morally justified.

If this proposal is accepted, then 'is unjust' would make a somewhat different point from 'is morally wrong' or even 'is prima facie morally wrong'. But it is clear that if this account is correct, then 'just' is not so utterly different a term from 'right' and 'obligatory' that we have to begin our account of morality all over again, with a quite new and different conception added to all the rest. Indeed, we could drop the terms 'just' and 'unjust' from our moral vocabulary altogether, using the definiens instead. And furthermore, it follows that if utilitarianism has a correct account of whether certain allocations of good and evil are prima facie

[1] By W. K. Frankena, 1962, p. 25. This is substantially the same as, but simpler than, my proposal, 1959, p. 410.

obligatory or wrong on account of certain considerations (such as whether the allocation would be an equal one) then it is already a correct theory of justice.

The 'deeper' charge, then, is misguided; and the serious objection is that a welfare-maximizing moral code is incompatible with certain allocations of good and evil being prima facie obligatory, whereas in fact they are. If we are to appraise this charge, there are two things we must do. First, we must examine what principles about welfare-distribution would be contained in a welfare-maximizing moral system and what kind of institutional structure would be pressed by a person who demanded that institutions be welfare-maximizing;[2] and second, we must recall the force of the charges. Suppose it should turn out that a welfare-maximizing moral system would not require, prima facie, that income or welfare be distributed equally; and suppose we reached similar results about a welfare-maximizing educational system, and so on for other institutional systems. What follows? If the critics were in a position to assert that we know that a satisfactory moral system or institutional system would have these features, then it would follow that the conception of a welfare-maximizing moral or institutional system is not ideal in some way or other. But how are the critics supposed to show that we know this? This question takes us back to issues discussed much earlier in this book. One thing is clear: it is not enough for the critics to tell us about their moral intuitions. What they must show is that (say) an egalitarian ideal going beyond the provisions of a welfare-maximizing moral system will make a strong appeal to fully rational persons.

---

[2] The last clause may seem mysterious; for until now we have been considering only moral systems, so why this sudden expansion to talk of institutional systems? The answer is that if there is reason to think that a moral code would be supported by fully rational persons only if it is welfare-maximizing, there is equal reason to think that the same applies to an institutional structure. So, much of my argument about morality can be transposed to institutional systems. This fact means that there may be dual demands on institutions: first, that they measure up to the demands of the moral code fully rational persons would accept, and second, that they be of a sort fully rational persons can accept directly, irrespective of morality. It could be that the latter critique is more exacting—that there are features of an institutional system acceptable to morality but not ideal, in the sense that full rational persons would not support them.

2. A WELFARE-MAXIMIZING PRINCIPLE ABOUT ALLOCATIONS OF INCOME AND GOODS

What principles about welfare-distribution, then, would be contained in a welfare-maximizing moral system? One might say: none at all, on the grounds that it is undesirable to burden a moral code with a principle people seldom have occasion to apply—since they can perfectly well, on the few occasions on which such issues come up, infer what they ought to do from other moral principles. But problems of allocation and income do arise frequently, for instance, in the family. If the male member of a married pair does not work, does he have a right to some or an equal share of his wife's income? Or, whether he does or does not work outside the home, what is a fair distribution of the chores? Should children have equal allowances? Should equal provision be made for higher education, or if not equal provision, then provision on what principle? If a girl is given the money to attend a big-league baseball game, should her brother be given the money to attend a ballet? Outside the home, if one runs a business or is the director of a company, one must face decisions about wage levels for one's employees; and if one is a worker, there is the problem of what would be a fair contract between union and employer. Then, in one's role as citizen and voter, one must decide whether to favour extra taxation to provide more parks, improve the streets, or improve the level of education in the schools; or the reduction of real estate taxes and the imposition of a local income tax, and so on.

It looks, then, as if one faces problems involving income-and-goods allocations about as frequently as one faces any other type of moral decision, perhaps more often. Furthermore, the relevant lines of reasoning from other moral principles are not obvious, so there is reason to think a welfare-maximizing moral code must include some principle or principles directly about this matter.

It should be emphasized that welfare-maximizing principles about distributions have only prima facie force, of whatever degree of strength would be welfare-maximizing. Other moral principles may conflict in various situations. What I shall propose is a principle, then, with a prima facie force only, and which may not tell us what must be effectuated, everything considered.

The principle about income-allocation which I propose seems to ignore intra-family distributions but in fact has implications for them. It is as follows: *The real income* (monetary income adjusted for differing price-levels) *after any taxes should be equal, except (a) for supplements to meet special needs, (b) supplements recompensing services to the extent needed to provide desirable incentive and allocate resources efficiently, and (c) variations to achieve other socially desirable ends such as population control.* The principle requires elaboration, to make clear how to determine the size of the supplements and variations; but the basic idea is clear enough, as can be seen when we think how it might be applied in an institutional structure like that of the U.S.A. There the equality of basic income would take the form of an identical tax-credit (with some complications so as to permit population control). The first supplement would provide for health care, among other things, and could be implemented either by a health service or by a universal 'insurance' plan. The second supplement would take the form of job-incomes (not to be wholly absorbed by taxes). In different institutional structures the principle could be implemented in quite different ways. It may be that a further principle about the allocation of educational opportunities is needed, but the stated principle has implications for this, if we attach monetary value to education, as to some extent can be done.[3]

The above principle will tend very strongly towards the equalization of welfare: by its requirement for a basic equal (adjusted) monetary income, by the supplements to meet special needs so that the inequalities brought about by health disasters are removed or mitigated, and by the job-income supplement which compensates those who are willing to work rather than enjoy leisure time. However, the principle does not specify equality of welfare, but only what monetary income is to be. Moreover, it is justified not by derivation from a higher-level ideal of equality of welfare, but from the higher-level ideal of maximizing welfare. In this respect it is within the tradition of utilitarian political economics and tax theory, going back to the economics at least of J. S. Mill. So, on the one hand, the equal-welfare tendency of the principle gives much of what some critics of utilitarianism who have demanded equality of welfare have wanted, such as Nicholas

[3] See Coleman, 1968; Arrow, 1971; Green and Sheshinski, 1975; Morgan and David, 1963.

Rescher (1966); and on the other hand, the principle is strictly in the utilitarian tradition because it can be derived by showing that the currency of the principle would maximize welfare. So maximizing and equalizing are not necessarily antithetical principles: a principle the currency of which would maximize happiness or welfare will at the same time at least strongly tend to produce equality of happiness or welfare. (The principle does not attempt to attain this completely; for instance, it does not attempt to recompense for their loss people who are ill, crippled, chronically depressed, or otherwise handicapped, by providing extra income to make their happiness-level equal to that of others; it mitigates it only to an extent that will be explained below.) Perhaps, then, a happiness-maximizing principle will provide all the equality that a fully rational person would want in a moral principle for income-allocation.

3. WHY EQUAL MONETARY INCOME?

In order to show that this moral rule would be part of a welfare-maximizing moral code, we must show that its currency would maximize expectable utility. Approximately, this means we must show that its implementation in the institutional system would maximize happiness, with such adjustments as may be called for by other principles also having prima facie weight.

Why should the principle be about the allocation of money? One practical reason is the matter of simplicity: money is something we can easily hand out in equal amounts. More important, however, is the fact that we are apt to maximize happiness if what we allocate is money. We know an individual must buy certain things in order to maximize his net enjoyment, but on the whole it is more efficient to leave to him the decision about how to use it in making purchases, since he is normally better placed to know what will give him enjoyment than other persons are, not to mention rationing boards. Of course, it is cheaper and less chaotic for society to purchase some things which we assume almost everyone wants, such as roads, an educational system, a police force, a postal system, and so on. But for our present purposes, we can ignore this kind of allocation.

If we are to maximize happiness, why not give most money to

those who will enjoy it most? The answer is that this should be done in special cases; as we shall see later in the case of the ill or handicapped. But there are two reasons why it should not be done generally. One is that individuals cannot show, in any reasonably simple way, that they are the ones who would benefit relatively more from extra income. People's tastes and needs differ, and the correlation between income and happiness-level also varies from one person to another, depending on personality. It simply would not be feasible to allocate income in this way: there are not publicly identifiable classes into which these types of individuals fall. The second reason is that an equal distribution is the best strategy for maximizing happiness, in view of the declining marginal utility of money, and in the absence of reliable information about individuals' income-utility curves. We must explain why.

It has been questioned whether the marginal utility of money does decline, that is, whether expenditure of successive increments to one's income produces less happiness or welfare than that of preceding increments, on the average and in the long-run. But that it does decline follows from the fact that outcomes are preferentially ordered, some being more strongly wanted than others. (As we have seen, the intensity of desire may not always be a reliable clue to how enjoyable the outcome will be, but since desires are generally fixed by enjoyable experiences with the relevant kind of outcome in the past, there will be a rough correlation.) So a person, when deciding how to spend his resources, picks a basket of groceries which is at least as appealing as any other he can purchase with the money he has. The things he does not buy are omitted because other things are wanted more. If we double a person's income, he will spend the extra money on items he wants less (some special cases aside), and which will give less enjoyment than will the original income. The more one's income, the fewer preferred items one buys and the more preferred items one already has. On the whole, then, when the necessities of life have been purchased and the individual is spending on luxury items, he is buying items which will give less enjoyment, so that if we represent income and enjoyment on a graph, with income measured along the x-axis and enjoyment on the y-axis, the curve will slope upwards steeply beginning at the subsistence level, and then gradually flatten out. (The derivative of this curve, which is the marginal utility of income, will be concave, sloping down only slightly at first.) This conclusion corresponds well with common-sense reflection and practice.

Obviously the ideal happiness-maximizing strategy for dividing the national income (aside from incentive effects, etc.) would be to do so in such a way that the extra enjoyment produced by the last dollar each person receives is exactly the same. But, in the absence of information about the utility-curves of individuals, we are in no position to adopt this strategy. The best strategy, given our happiness-maximizing objective and the fact of the declining marginal utility of income, is to divide income equally (except for the supplementary payments to be discussed below). The reasoning for this conclusion may not be obvious, and is as follows. (It was, as far as I know, first developed by A. P. Lerner.)[4]

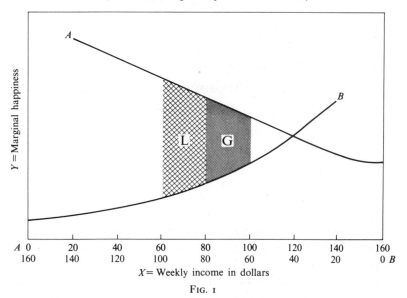

FIG. 1

Consider Figure 1. The curves marked 'A' and 'B' represent supposititious income-marginal utility-curves for Mr. A and Mr. B respectively, where for convenience the curve of A has the lower

[4] Lerner, 1944, Chap. 3; see also Sen, 1973, pp. 83 ff.; Friedman, 1947; Sidgwick, 1929, Chap. 10; Pigou, 1932, Pt. I, Chap. 8; Blum and Kalven, 1953.

left-hand corner as the point of origin, and the corresponding curve of *B* the reverse, with the lower right-hand corner as the point of origin. So *A*'s curve shows how much utility is being added per dollar corresponding to the $20, or $40 (etc.) level of income; the same for *B*'s, except that his *x*-axis carries values in the reverse order. (The curves suppose that *B* gets less happiness from his income than does *A*, so his curve is lower.) Both curves begin at about the $30 level, on the assumption that there is no life or happiness at all until a person has a subsistence level, say of $30; thereafter, in accordance with the theory (above) of the declining marginal utility of money, each curve slopes downwards.

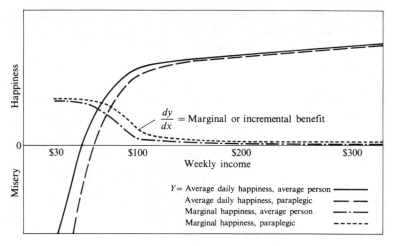

FIG. 2

It may be helpful in understanding the meaning of this curve to look at the happiness-misery-income curve of Figure 2, which depicts the average daily happiness (measured along the *y*-axis) corresponding to different weekly income levels. This curve rises throughout, but at first slopes up sharply, gradually flattening out at around $100 per week. The curves of Figure 1, which represent the contribution to happiness of an additional dollar at each income level, represent the first derivative of the happiness-income curve of Figure 2; thus, corresponding to the initial steep slope in Figure 2, the curve is high; and when the curve in Figure 2 rises less rapidly, the curve in Figure 1 falls. Presumably there is some equation for the curve in Figure 2, in which y is some function of x; and, given this, there is a derived equation for Figure 1 which, for instance, might be '$y = \log x$'. The area under a curve of Figure 1, between two points (say bounded by A's curve, the x-axis, and vertical lines say above \$60 and \$80), represents the addition of happiness by income increasing from the first point to the second. (This area is the integral of, say, $y = \log x$, between \$60 and \$80.) This, of course, corresponds to the $y_b - y_a$ difference corresponding to an increase from salary x_a to x_b, in Figure 2.

The argument, then, goes as follows. We ask ourselves how to divide an income of \$160 per week between two individuals, Mr. A and Mr. B, so as to maximize enjoyment. Evidently we do this if we divide income at the point on the x axis below the point of intersection of the curves (where the marginal utility of a dollar is equal); the area under the segments of the two curves, from the beginning to the point of intersection (= the happiness purchased by the two incomes), is maximal. But we are assuming that for the normal case we do not know what the curves are (we know only the general shape: that they decline from their starting points); hence we do not know where this point of intersection is, and are in no position to divide income at the optimal point. Note, however, that if we did know the point of intersection, we would lose by dividing income equally, since we would lose all the area (= happiness) between the two curves between the points above \$80 and the point of intersection. Nevertheless, we will probably gain, given our ignorance, if we divide income equally. For suppose we divide it unequally. If we give an extra \$20 (viz. \$100) to A, we gain the shaded area G, as contrasted with an equal division; if we give an extra \$20 to B, we lose the hatched area L as contrasted with an equal division. Since we, in our ignorance, do not know which way to move away from equality for the sake of maximizing happiness, presumably we shall, in our blindness, go the right way half the time and the wrong way half the time. But, unfortunately for an inegalitarian system of division, as Lerner puts it (1944, p. 32), 'every time a movement is made away from an equalitarian division the probable *size* of the loss is greater than the probable size of the gain. This is shown by the figure where, because of the slopes of the curves, given by the principle of diminishing utility of income, the double-hatched area L (which represents the *loss*) is greater than the shaded area G (which represents the *gain*).' The same reasoning can be applied to the division of income among any number of persons; thus an equal distribution of income will produce a maximal expectation of happiness or welfare. Notice that the argument so far makes no use of any interpersonal comparisons.

4. WHY SUPPLEMENTS FOR THE ILL AND HANDICAPPED?

The moral principle for allocation of income formulated above provides for 'supplements to meet special needs', with the term 'special need' referring to illness, physical handicap, and so on. But it has been argued by A. K. Sen (1973, pp. 16 ff.) that a welfare-maximizing system would assign less income to the crippled, on the ground that such persons would get less utility from it than would the normal person. It is important to see that his reasoning is mistaken, and that a welfare-maximizing system would include the indicated clause because supplements for such cases are a best buy. However, the reasoning and interpretation of the principle are not simple, and merit discussion.

It will hardly be denied that medical and hospital care are best buys; most people will agree that the relief from pain, the saving of life, the return to health so that one can enjoy life and perform the duties of one's job are considerable benefits. Hence $100 spent for these will purchase more than $100 spent to improve the quality of life of an already well and happy person. Everyone who purchases medical and hospital insurance in order to guarantee such care agrees with this since evidently he thinks these benefits are worth more than the enjoyment which could be bought with the money saved by buying no insurance (and fore-going such care when one is ill).

It is the status of a supplement for the handicapped in a welfare-maximizing scheme which Professor Sen has questioned. His argument is, roughly, that it is not implausible to suppose that a cripple will get (say) only half as much utility out of any income we give him as will a normal person, and therefore that a utilitarian must provide a smaller income for the cripple than for others. (His curve might be like that of *B* in Figure 1.)

Sen's argument relies on assumptions about utilities and marginal utilities which are untrue to the facts. In order to see this, we must take a more careful look than seems ordinarily to be done, at curves which represent the relation of income and happiness, and income and marginal contribution to happiness. Let us look, then, at Figure 2, which shows curves representing both these relations, for both a normal person and a paraplegic. The rationale for the curve representing the relation of income and happiness for the normal person is as follows: if I had less than $30 a week I would simply die of starvation or exposure; so I have no position on the map at all, at an income below that point. I enter the map at a point where I am badly nourished, live in an unheated room with no hot water, with no books or TV, and so on. At this point my life is well below the indifference level; if I had no better future in prospect, I would be better off dead. So the happiness-level which correlates with $30 per week income is far down below the *x*-axis. From there on up the improvements are rapid. I suppose that at $50 a week I am at the indifference-level. Thereafter the increases are still steep until, say, $100 a week, after which they become much smaller until, beyond $300, they are hardly discernible.

On the same map is a curve representing the marginal contribution of each additional dollar of income. It is not easy to see how to represent the contribution of the first $30, which serves merely to put one on the happiness map. It seems best not to represent its contribution at all. (This, of course, is the reason the first parts of the curves are missing in Figure 1.) After the first $30 the contributions are positive, and considerable. They remain great (and the curve nearly a straight line) until shortly before the point of $100 a week is reached, after which the curve slopes downwards, becoming nearly flat and virtually parallel to the *x*-axis beyond the $300 a week point.

Suppose, now, we compare all this with the happiness-income curve of a paraplegic, in order to find the optimal 'supplement', if any. More money for special transportation devices, and so on, is required to put him on the happiness map at all. Let us say he must have $40 a week just to survive. There is no particular reason to think that his happiness curve from there to the indifference point will differ from mine: he will benefit from more heat, and better food, as much as I do. So his curve parallels mine up to the indifference point, only moved to the right. Beyond that point, how do the curves compare? The paraplegic will not spend money on a tennis racquet and membership in a tennis club; but he may buy records or improve his hi-fi system. Since there are restrictions on what he can do, must his happiness level off at a point below where mine does? Not obviously: it may be that available time rather than scope of activities is what limits happiness, but even if his curve does not ever quite touch mine, its height is equal to mine, only ten dollars later, until after a great deal of income has been expended. Up until that point, he simply spends his money on enjoyments different from mine. It is only when income is well past, say, $300 a week, that his curve is lower because of the restricted range of his activities. How will his incremental or marginal happiness curve compare with mine? It will begin to the right of the point at which mine begins, and thus at the $40 point. Otherwise it is the same until very far out to the right: until then we get his curve simply by transposing my curve to begin ten units to the right.

In what way, then, should available total income be optimally divided between us? For happiness-maximization, it will be divided at the point at which the incremental or marginal benefits are equal. Now whatever function the marginal happiness is of the income, we know that—since one curve is identical with the other except that the paraplegic's is displaced ten units to the right— my marginal utility will be the same as his when his income is just $10 greater than mine. So, whatever income we have to divide, he will receive just $10 more of it than I will. Evidently a welfare-maximizing principle will not imply that the handicapped person gets less than the normal person; on the contrary, he gets more.

Some assumptions about the happiness curves of handicapped persons would lead to Sen's conclusions. If, for instance, the handicapped person's happiness curve flattened out and remained flat shortly after the indifference point, his marginal or incremental happiness curve would fall steeply—more than mine—shortly after the $50 point, and would cross mine say at the $100 point. Then he would get less income. But what kind of handicap might this be? Not chronic depression, for if a person is merely depressed, lithium treatments or visits to the psychiatrist will hopefully cause his happiness-level to skyrocket, and the above assumptions about the curves will be mistaken. In the case of an imbecile Sen's argument might work, but the result is not outrageous. It would be stupid to spend much money when more than a little will add no further enjoyment.

My principle for income-allocation may, then, require interpretation for various kinds of handicap, each associated with a different happiness curve, with consequent different conclusions about the size of any supplement. There are other problems too: for example, whether to expend large sums of money merely to prolong a person's life at an uncomfortable level.

5. RECOMPENSE FOR SERVICES

Philosophers who allege more than one principle for proper income-allocation face the problem of fixing the relative force of the various principles. It is easy to say that equality should be a factor; it is not easy to say exactly how big a factor. The problem is raised by all the supplements mentioned above. Of course, the utilitarian theory has a vast advantage over many, since on it in principle we know how to go about assigning weights: the divisions must be made so as to maximize welfare in the long run.

What follows concentrates on just one of these supplements, that of providing incentive and optimal allocation of manpower resources; but the type of argument is proper for adjudicating other types of case as well.

There are two reasons for providing a supplement in connection with a person's occupation. First, people will work well, at least at many boring and monotonous jobs, only if they expect to gain more income; and they will sacrifice enjoyments and prepare to perform difficult tasks (e.g. neurosurgery) more readily if there is the expectation of financial reward. This economic motivation might not be necessary in a social-economic system, or value-system, different from that familiar in the West (given that it is possible, as it is thought to be, to endow even monotonous jobs with meaning), but one of the lessons of the failure of 'The Great Leap Forward' experiment in China was that some economic incentives are needed until further 'moral education' of the workers has been provided. It was Marx's view that such incentives can be dropped only in the final stages of development of a Communist society.[5]

Second, differential incentives motivate people to enter occupations which are thought to be less pleasant than others but where additional personnel are required. Presumably in the long run workers may be expected to compare the money incentives of various jobs with their inherent utilities and disutilities, and take a job, among those for which they qualify, which offers the best total opportunities. Hence, in order to obtain a maximally efficient economic system (one in which, among other things, what consumers want gets done) extra compensation will be given, normally, for unpleasant or dangerous work. This feature of a welfare-maximizing economic system will also tend to equalize welfare, since the extra compensation for unpleasant or dangerous work tends to make the total prospects for different persons equal. (Incidentally, the differential retirement programmes in China recognize the above principle.)

Inequalities of income, then, are necessary for utilitarian reasons: to motivate persons to work well and enter occupations where they are needed. But how much inequality? And how does one decide how much? This depends partly on the economic-political system of the society. There could, for instance, be centrally decided incomes for all jobs, perhaps with specified minima for each type and a set of steps above the entering level, each associated with a fixed salary, so that an individual moves upwards, by anticipatable steps, hopefully on the basis of merit. In order to know what we are doing, however, I shall assume a free-market economy for jobs and job-incomes as is standard in the West, and that a rational individual will decide which occupation (or firm) to enter on the basis of the prospective inherent utility of the job for him, the expected economic reward, the cost and unrecompensed time in education he must have before entry, and the size and progressivity of income tax. I shall assume that the only centrally regulated device for achieving equality of in-

[5] Marx, *Critique of the Gotha Programme*, Selected Works II, Foreign Language Publishing House, Moscow. (Quoted in Sen, 1973.)

come and other social objectives is the tax system. (For simplicity, I shall assume that corporate taxes are abolished. I shall also be silent on the sources and cost of risk capital.) The tax system is obviously very important for the whole economy: if a tax system took 100 per cent of all income above a certain level and nothing at all below that level, the economic incentive to perform well, or to go into one occupation rather than another, might be virtually abolished.

For the purpose of attacking the problem at hand it is convenient to make a further simplifying assumption: that decisions about the revenues needed for public services (the police force, road construction, etc.) and for health and old-age care, have already been made, although rational decisions about these matters would presumably take the form of the analysis to follow. I assume that the budget must be in balance, so that these fixed sums must be raised. The remaining problem to be solved is what proportion of the residual taxable income should be taken in taxation in order to provide some level of equal negative income tax-credit for all, and how progressive the tax on job-income is to be.

What we need to know, then, is which mix of the variable tax policy (the total amount of the net national income to be taken for the negative tax-credit—and this will fix the size of the credit—and the progressivity of the tax schedule) would maximize the total social welfare.

We can find this as follows. (1) We must find what the net national income will be for each mix considered. The mix will make a difference if increases in taxation affect negatively (as it is supposed they will, although perhaps not as much as commonly thought) the productivity or efficiency of workers, and the success with which workers are lured into occupations where they are most needed. How shall we find this? Of course, it is known what the net national income was the preceding year, with a given mix. We shall have to rely on the speculations of economists, based on this and other similar data, for projections of the net national income for various mixes, for, say, the five years ahead. (2) How this total national income will be divided among workers is determined by the market. Presumably figures are available, for preceding years, about the percentages of workers at various income levels; and again we must rely on economists for pro-jections for the years ahead. (3) Given the information just described, we can determine for each mix of tax policy the per-centages of workers with various after-tax disposable incomes. So we have a number of workers specified, for each net income level (bottom 5 per cent, next 5 per cent, and so on), for each tax policy mix. (4) Now if we had an income-welfare curve for individuals, we could then infer how many workers would be at various welfare levels, which would be represented ideally (if the conclusions of Chapter 13 are sound) by a cardinal number. We could then infer the total welfare at each income level by multiplying this number by the number of workers at that level. We do not actually have such curves; hence I shall come back to the matter. (5) If we sum these products over all income levels we get the total social welfare—a somewhat different one for each tax policy mix under consideration. The tax policy mix which gives the largest social welfare is the one to be selected.[6]

The source of the complexity of the above is the requirement of a welfare (happiness)-maximizing mix which takes fully into account both the benefits of equal incomes and possible losses from production-reducing lack of incentive. Other schemes for income distribution, which do not aim at a careful balancing of the costs and benefits, can be simpler. Rawls, for example, proposes that we simply identify the economically worst-off segment of the working public, and then adopt a tax system most to their advantage: make their income, either by a negative tax or fixing of job-income, maximal, up to the point where the effect on pro-duction of the size of their income is so great that any further increase in their percentage of the national income would be costly to them because the increase would reduce significantly the total income pie to be divided. This proposal requires no knowledge of income-welfare (happiness) curves—indeed no interpersonal comparisons of utilities at all beyond identification of the worst-off group—in order to determine the size of the income of (or tax-credit to) the lowest group. However, Rawls's proposal is not of a welfare-maximizing system, and there is no reason to think fully rational persons would support it (unless they were selfish and at the bottom of the income ladder).

[6] For a recent less complex solution, see Fair, 1971.

Are the various projections on which is based the supposititious calculation of optimal tax policy, sketched above, actually possible or available, or is such information beyond the powers of economics? We should admit that the projections are not going to be very reliable; but we do have figures showing what has happened in countries which have modified their tax policies drastically (e.g. Sweden). In any case, in the absence of such data, we are hardly in a position to regard the present tax structure as optimal. It may have the support of special interest groups who think they would lose by a large increase in either total tax take or progressivity, but that is no substitute for a serious argument that the present structure is welfare-maximizing.

One of the parts of the above calculation, however, has a quite different status and we must consider it: the assumption that we know income-welfare curves, and that they are substantially the same for everyone. Actually, we do not have such knowledge about these curves in general, much less about their being the same for all. In fact, I argued earlier that an equal distribution of income is justified precisely because we do not know the income-welfare curves of individuals, so that any claim now that we do have such knowledge constitutes a partial restriction of the basis of that argument for equality.

What I want to point out now is that Congress (or whatever authority sets the tax policy of the nation) is actually in a position to make some comparative judgements of the welfare-producing properties of different tax schemes, without knowledge of income-welfare curves generally. How? First, two obvious ways. (1) Of two tax schemes, it is irrational to prefer one which would so affect production that the after-tax income would be smaller for many and larger for none. (2) It would be rational to prefer one if the after-tax income is not lower for anyone, but is larger for some, even if the latter are in the higher income brackets. But, second, what of the unobvious cases, e.g. a choice between allocating 40 per cent of the net national income for the basic negative tax-credit, as against allocating 60 per cent (holding the progressivity curve constant)? In this case the 40 per cent allocation will presumably yield a smaller real income for persons in the lower half of the population, a larger one for the upper half of the population, as compared with the 60 per cent allocation. Now, a comparative judgement of the welfare-maximizing properties of these two schemes does not require a knowledge of the shape of income-happiness curves generally. Let us see how Congress might adjudicate this matter in the absence of a full picture of income-welfare curves.

Suppose Congress learns, as it well could, that the effect of the 60 per cent allocation will be that everyone among the poorest 10 per cent after taxes will gain the equivalent of a 1978 sum of $500, and that the wealthiest 10 per cent after taxes will lose rather more than that, say the 1978 equivalent of $1,000. In order to make a choice, Congress might inquire what an extra $500 means to people in the lowest group, and what the loss of $1,000 means to people in the top group. Suppose the gain of $500 to the lowest 10 per cent means only that the typical person can buy a new car every fourth year instead of every sixth year: that is not a big gain in welfare. On the other hand, matters would be very different if an extra $500 meant that the typical man could now heat his home to 70° rather than 50°, have some entertainment beyond his TV set, and enjoy a diet richer than rice and oatmeal. Now, the larger allocation for the negative income tax would not be justified if persons in the top 10 per cent would lose more from sacrificing $1,000 than the increments just described for those in the lowest 10 per cent. Of course, we would not have a nearly equal loss among the higher group from a mere loss of $500, on account of the declining marginal utility of money; but might they not suffer a loss equal to the gain for the lower group, if they had to give up $1,000? In essence, the question is whether the additional commodities purchased by the $500 at the lower level are less happiness-productive than the additional commodities purchased by an extra $1,000 at the higher level. In order to answer this question, we do have to make a comparison of happiness increments from certain purchases; and, as we saw in Chapter 13, this is in principle possible. Obviously the comparisons will be rough, but it is not self-evidently beyond the powers of Congress to come to the right answer.

It is apparent that interpretation of part (b) of our basic principle, calling for supplements to provide incentive and allocate manpower efficiently, is not simple. Presumably the details of how the principle is to be interpreted or implemented could not themselves be taught as parts of the moral code. But they need not be, as long as the welfare-maximizing idea behind the code is understood. Those persons charged with implementing the code will know what to do.

Let us now ask ourselves how nearly equal the welfare of different persons will be, if public policy follows the lines of the foregoing proposal. The ill and the handicapped will not be compensated for their bad luck, except in the sense that extra income will be diverted in their direction as long as alleviation of their situation makes the diversion worthwhile. People with high native ability and the good fortune to be reared in an intelligent and loving family will do well in the job market; but they will receive more income than others only to the extent it is shown that the gain in incentive and efficient allocation of manpower resources justify it—and the evidence seems to show that the amount of income advantage needed for these purposes is quite small, far smaller than exists at present. People are not to be compensated for being less intelligent, for having had less good fortune in their family environment, etc. than others. There are other qualities, apparently a result of birth or early environment, which confer unfair advantages: physical attractiveness, native energy, quick wit and a sense of humour, and so on. No attempt is made to gain equality by taxing income in the light of these advantages. So the welfare-maximizing system of income-allocation works in the direction of equality of welfare, but it does not pretend to provide equal happiness for all.

Is this enough? It seems true that we (and the same might be true of fully rational persons) tend to sympathize with the position of the worst-off, want them brought up to the level of others, and especially do not want them made even worse off than they already are. It may be that this attitude on our part is psychologically necessary, in view of how benevolence gets instituted by classical conditioning (we are more averse to worse states of ourselves). Such aversion to the position of the worst-off is presumably what is behind the view of philosophers who say that equality of welfare is to be valued on its own account. Should we seek to gain more equality at the cost of sacrificing happiness in general? One might do this; one might set aside a fund for compensation of individuals for natural ill-luck in life, and treat it as a public benefit like national defence or the construction of roads. (See Thurow, 1971.) There are problems over how to implement such an idea in detail; and how do we want to strike a balance? The suggestion of my foregoing discussion is that the above-stated principle of allocation, when interpreted and implemented, does not involve arrangements manifestly less egalitarian than fully rational persons would want, or at least would want as compared with the other options, with their sacrifices.

If the foregoing reasoning is sound, we must conclude that the large literature on 'social choice theory' is less important for a normative theory of allocation of income than has often been thought to be the case.

The above reasoning is valid not only for the distribution of income within a nation, but for all living persons in the world. Implementation of the scheme on a world-wide basis raises special problems, especially for the period of transition. But transposition of the scheme to the larger problem can be made by steps which will be fairly obvious to the reader.[7]

---

[7] An interesting study which comes to slightly different conclusions, the critical parts of which I mostly accept, is by L. O. Ericsson, 1975.

CHAPTER XVII

IS IT ALWAYS RATIONAL TO ACT MORALLY?

PHILOSOPHERS SINCE Socrates have been interested in two questions: (1) whether it always pays to act morally, and (2) whether, if not, it is rational to do the moral thing. Sometimes it has just been assumed that moral action is irrational except as it promises to serve the agent's long-range interest. Bishop Butler remarked that 'though virtue or moral rectitude does indeed consist in affection to and pursuit of what is right and good as such; yet, when we sit down in a cool hour, we can neither justify to ourselves this or any other pursuit till we are convinced that it will be for our happiness, or at least not contrary to it' (Sermon 11).

Both of the above questions need to be formulated more clearly, in a way which gives sympathetic expression to the underlying puzzlement. Obviously the first question, about whether it always pays to act morally, is inquiring whether moral action is always at least not contrary to long-range self-interest. Clarification demands an explanation of 'self-interest' and this will be undertaken in the following section. The second question can be given clear formulation more easily. For instance, 'Is it rational to do the moral thing?' has been construed as 'Ought one, morally, do to ... ?' and also as 'Ought one, from the point of self-interest always do ... ?'. Formulated in these ways, the question is also easy to answer: affirmatively if we choose the first construction, negatively if we choose the second. But both reformulations are unsympathetic. What questioners want to know is whether, in case of an ultimate clash between morality and self-interest, a rational person would give higher priority to one or the other. But 'rational' in what sense?

The conceptual framework developed in this book may permit us to reformulate the second question in a clear way and sympathetically, so that knowing the answer to it would remove the dissatisfaction which has been felt by those who have been puzzled by the issue. The question is this: 'Would you, the reader, if you were *fully rational*, always do what you know to be morally right even when you know that so doing conflicts with your long-range self-interest?' The right answer to this question is not obvious.

It may help to deal with two side issues at the outset, before attacking the main problems. These matters should not be controversial.

First, even if it is not rational for a person to discharge what he knows is his moral obligation when so doing conflicts with his self-interest, it may be rational for others to disapprove, criticize, and punish him if he does not. We have seen that part of what it is for there to be a moral system is for people to be disposed to disapprove of others for showing motivation insufficient to do what the system requires. The purpose of this criticism and punishment, to enhance motivation to act morally, may be served in the case of an agent, even if it was irrational of him to act morally in the particular case. What it is rational for an agent to do in a given situation is one thing: what it is rational for moral persons in society to do in response to his action is quite another.

A second point to be noted is that it does not follow from the fact that a fully rational person supports a certain kind of moral code—promulgates it, praises it, votes for its being taught in the schools, and so on—that he would on all occasions restrict his own conduct to that code. A person can sometimes rationally preach what he has no intention of practising, and even do so effectively.

I. THE CONCEPT OF SELF-INTEREST

The question whether it is rational to follow duty when it conflicts with long-range self-interest cannot be answered until we have made up our minds what we mean by 'self-interest'. If we define self-interest as that which a fully rational person would seek, then it would be contradictory to suppose that a rational person would forsake self-interest for the call of duty; correspondingly, it would be contradictory to propose that a fully rational person would sacrifice himself for any reason. Hence this proposal will not do as a definition of self-interest. So let us try another approach in the hope that we can come closer to rendering the essential content of the concept of self-interest—although the term 'self-interest' (and also 'self-sacrifice') is hardly used precisely in ordinary speech.

Let us consider the class of desires (aversions) a given person would have if he were fully rational. We may be able to define a sub-class of these rational desires, and call them self-interested desires. Then we could define a person's self-interest as the target of his rational self-interested desires.[1] The problem of defining self-interest then resolves into the problem of defining 'self-interested desire'.

Clearly the desires to get pleasure for oneself and to avoid painful or unpleasant experiences are central to the concept of self-interested desire. Further, desires for states of affairs which are normally means to enjoyment or the avoidance of distress (for example, income, wealth, power, and social status, for oneself) should also be counted as self-interested. Should we add more, thereby broadening the concept of self-interest? The suggestion has been made (Overvold, 1976) that any desire is self-interested if its target is a state of affairs at some time which logically cannot be realized in case the subject of the desire does not exist at that time. On this view, a desire for my mother's happiness is not self-interested, whereas desires for various states of myself are. This suggestion has much to be said for it. Consider the desire to be respected or admired by others, or for the affection or friendship of others, or for personal achievement or a demonstration of superiority. These desires are not just desires for one's own enjoyment or happiness, but they are desires for states of affairs which cannot occur unless the subject is living at the time. And we do count all these as self-interested. But there are some implications of the definition which are not so plausible. For instance, a desire to be a generous or conscientious person counts as self-interested by the definition; but it is doubtful if we want to classify it thus. Again, the definition classifies desires

---

[1] I am drawing heavily, in these remarks on self-interest, on the dissertation of Mark C. Overvold, 'Self-Interest, Self-Sacrifice and the Satisfaction of Desires', 1976, deposited in the Graduate Library of the University of Michigan. A paper still very much worthy of study is C. D. Broad's 'Egoism as a theory of human motives', 1952.

to be remembered or respected after death as not self-interested because they are desires for states of affairs which can be the case even if the subject of the desire is no longer alive; but we would definitely tend to call them self-interested.

These reflections do not point to what seems a definitive definition of 'self-interested desire', but I shall be content with the result for now. I propose then, that self-interested desires include desires for one's own happiness, wealth, power and status, and indeed, desires for any states of affairs which imply the existence of the person, except the desire to have benevolent desires, and the desire to act morally or to have moral qualities of character for their own sake (and not just as a mark of superiority or achievement). We can still discuss our problem even if we do not clarify the concept more sharply.

Obviously not all desires are self-interested in this sense: the desire for one's daughter to be happy, or for a student to get his personal problems solved, or for the tennis underdog to win, for example. Some non-self-interested desires are impersonal, such as wanting the state of the arts to flourish in one's city, or for there to be an egalitarian society.

It is not only self-interested desires that can conflict with the requirements of morality. Indeed, a person's kindly desires, for instance too much love for somebody else, may render him unwilling to perform some harsh act required by duty.

The question whether acting morally pays can now be broken into two questions. The first is: 'Would having the intrinsic motivations (traits of character) you would, if you were fully rational, want adults in your society to have, be contrary to your long-range self-interest over your lifetime, on the evidence available to you now?' The second is: 'Would conforming to the moral code you yourself would choose if you were rational, in this instance, be contrary to your long-range self-interest, on the evidence available?'

Argument is hardly necessary to show that acting morally does not pay in all possible situations. Some obvious cases are: paying more income tax than one need, because one thinks it wrong to perjure oneself on the tax declaration, even when one knows a misrepresentation of income cannot possibly be detected; and covering the retreat of one's comrades by manning a machine gun, when flight is the only route to personal safety. Let us tentatively suppose that specific moral actions in some cases do not promise to pay, in terms of long-range self-interest, on the available evidence. With that understanding, let us now return to our original question about the rationality of acting morally. We can now reformulate this as: 'Would you, the reader, if you were *fully rational*, always do what you think to be morally right even when you know that so doing probably conflicts with long-range self-interest, viz. is not what you would do if you were moved solely by self-interested desires, or rational self-interested desires?' I suggest that this question gives explicit expression to the puzzle which often bothers people when they wonder if it is not foolish to sacrifice self for the sake of moral principle.

2. WOULD A RATIONAL PERSON EVER ACT MORALLY CONTRARY TO SELF-INTEREST?

People often knowingly risk their own welfare or long-range interest by doing what they view as their duty: they get killed when organizing demonstrations favouring minority voting registration; they go to jail for a principle when they could have avoided it by telling a lie. What we want to know is whether such things would still happen if the agents were fully rational. Let us list some situations in which it is psychologically possible for people to act contrary to their own self-interest.

Sometimes this will occur because the action is impulsive. A person may act out of benevolence or other moral motivation before his self-interested desires (which would incline successfully in the opposite direction) can become fully engaged. We might say he acts morally before he thinks—at least before he counts the cost in the sense of representing vividly the outcomes sacrificed by the moral action. Such impulsive action probably happens quite often. A soldier is killed when he falls on a live hand-grenade which someone has accidentally dropped; if he had had time to think vividly of what he would be losing, he might have fallen to the ground in the opposite direction and perhaps would have saved his life at the cost of the lives of others. Impulsive actions of this sort may, of course, be irrational; they might not have occurred if the person had had all the relevant facts vividly represented at the time of action. Such actions throw no light on the problem of concern to us.

There is a second type of case. Sometimes the morally right triumphs over long-range self-interest because a person happens to have non-self-interested desires which motivate him to do what is morally right. For instance, if someone involved is a friend or lover or one's pet dog; or if the issue arouses one's interest in some movement in art or literature or music; or if it touches on one's political loyalties. In such cases morality has powerful allies. This situation is doubtless rather special, but it does seem that if these non-self-interested desires are rational, then a fully rational person would do what is contrary to self-interest.

The third and most interesting type of case is that of straight conflict between moral motivations and self-interested desires, when the agent does not fail to represent the relevant outcomes, and has no other types of relevant desire. Let us suppose that the moral motivations are of superior strength, and the person does the moral thing. Now, if this could not happen in a fully rational person, it must be because the moral motivations, or at least these motivations with the strength they have, are themselves irrational. Must this be the case?

We saw earlier (p. 111) that a desire might be 'mistaken' in the sense that its satisfaction is so incompatible with the satisfaction of other major desires—like a desire for alcohol in the case of an ambitious politician—that a rational person would take steps to rid himself of it. Could the moral motivations, at least when they exceed a certain strength, be in this position? It seems unlikely. At least, many books on moral philosophy contain detailed and apparently well-taken reasoning, to the effect that normally a life of concern for others, and of strong moral commitments, is a richer and more enjoyable life than one that is merely self-interested. To decide the matter, one would need to obtain and choose between two world-biographies, one that would probably occur if one divested oneself of one's benevolence and moral attitudes, and the other that would probably occur if these remain as they are, or were at the level one would want such attitudes to attain among adults in one's community, if one were fully rational. It seems unlikely that it will be seriously urged that life would be better in the absence of benevolence and moral motivations in the way it would be better without addiction to alcohol.

The moral motivations might be irrational in the quite different sense that they would disappear in cognitive psychotherapy. Are there facts which, if repeatedly brought to mind, would sever the associative bonds on account of which these desires and aversions exist? This question seems to me the central one, the answer to which will resolve the puzzlement people feel about the clash between self-interest and morality.

Let us begin with benevolence which, if not itself to be counted as a moral motivation (since it may be considered to be directed at states of affairs and not at actions), is psychologically one of the foundations of morality. Is benevolence possibly irrational? At an earlier stage (p. 130 f.) we concluded that if it is *native* it would not extinguish by inhibition or discrimination; and that if, as is probably the case, it is a result of Pavlovian conditioning at a very early age, again it would almost certainly not extinguish as a result of either inhibition or discrimination, especially not in the presence of clear discrimination between one's own welfare and that of others. One possibility, however, we did not consider there: the possibility of functional extinction by counterconditioning. Might not a person bring to mind thoughts such as that the welfare of others often stands in one's own way, and so on? Might not such reflections, repeatedly occurring at optimal moments, undermine benevolent motivation? It seems doubtful. Partly because the age of the development of benevolence is so early; partly because it normally receives continuous support later in life, of the very kind that established it in the first place. Moreover, a rational person would not have these thoughts, since it is just not true that the happiness of others usually stands in one's way. It is true that going to the aid of another may be costly in some cases, but it would not be hard to show, by many examples, that benevolence-expressing behaviour normally pays in terms of self-interest, as does having moral attitudes in general, provided the degree of benevolence does not go beyond a certain point. It would seem, then, that sympathy and benevolence pass the test of rationality.

How about the strictly 'moral' motivations—the desires and aversions directed towards certain kinds of actions on their own account, with the associated guilt-feelings and attitudes of disapproval? Would they survive in a fully rational person? This is more doubtful; it depends on what they are and how they can be acquired. I have claimed, in Chapter 11, that some moral motivations are irrational—such as Kant's or Rashdall's aversion to homosexual behaviour, on grounds that have nothing to do with human happiness. But what about those moral motivations which would comprise the main part of a welfare-maximizing moral code, one which I have argued would be supported by fully rational people? Take for instance one's aversion to committing perjury, or to breaking promises and contracts, or to injuring other people. Are these rational?

Let us first remind ourselves how these motivations may be taught—by the 'inductive' method, that is, by pointing out to already sympathetic children how these behaviours lead, or tend to lead, to injury of other persons. The inductive method is parasitic on benevolence, but since we have just seen that benevolence is a rational motivation, this is no objection. These motivations, then, are conditioned aversions, acquired because of the association between the kind of action and the already aversive concept of distress in others. We need not say that this process is the only one involved in learning these motivations; presumably it is not. In my review of how desires and aversions are acquired (pp. 98 ff.), I discussed various other factors which may play a role, and the account was developed further (p. 174 f.) in the chapter on the nature of a moral code. But the 'inductive' method appears to be central. And in any case it seems to be most important when a person's motivation in a certain direction is weak; if a person asks 'What's wrong with perjury?', the pertinent answer appears to be an account of how harmful perjury tends to be.

In so far as the inductive account of the genesis of important moral motivations is correct, they are rational. For the conditioning can be based on pointing out correct information about the relation of perjury, breach of promise, etc. to the welfare of other people. And the sympathy-benevolence on which the aversion to these things is built by conditioning is itself a perfectly rational motivation. In so far, then, as morality is a welfare-maximizing system of motivations (etc.) it appears to be perfectly rational. Indeed, it would seem that an already sympathetic-benevolent person who underwent an appropriate process of cognitive psycho-therapy would actually develop these motivations to a consider-able extent, if he did not have them before.

It does not follow that moral motivations will always control conduct when they conflict with self-interest in a perfectly rational person. His moral motives may not be as strong as his self-interested desires and aversions, in which case it may not be possible to show that if only he were rational—had undergone cognitive psychotherapy—they would be strong enough to control conduct. Even if his moral motives would have been strong enough, if they were at the level rational persons including himself would want for persons living in their society (e.g. a level which would maximize the general welfare), it does not follow that he is irrational if he lacks that degree of moral motivation. Moreover, a rational person's moral motivations might not always control conduct, even if they had the strength characteristic of a welfare-maximizing moral system. For this optimal welfare-maximizing degree of moral motivation might be weaker than self-interested motives in some situations. Just as it is uneconomic to punish a theft of one dollar by a twenty-year prison sentence, so it may be uneconomic for moral motivations to be developed adequately to ensure that the moral motivation will be superior in absolutely every case.

Nevertheless, when the moral motivations in conflict with self-interested desires do control conduct, in the absence of a specific indication that there was mistake in factual belief or reasoning, or that the motivation would have been weaker in a person who had undergone cognitive psychotherapy, it is not irrational that they do so. If this very modest conclusion is sufficiently supported by the above considerations, the worries of some philosophers can properly be set at rest.

REFERENCES

ALEXANDER, FRANZ (1956). *Psychoanalysis and Psychotherapy*. Norton, New York.

ALLAIS, M. (1953). 'Le comportement de l'homme rationnel devant le risque: critique des postulats et axiomes de l'école americaine', *Econometrica* 21, 503–46.

ALSTON, W. P. (1967). 'Pleasure', in Paul Edwards (ed.), *The Encyclopedia of Philosophy* I, pp. 341–7. Macmillan, New York.

AMSEL, A. (1952). 'Motivational properties of frustration', *Journal of Experimental Psychology* 43, 363–8.

—— (1958). 'The role of frustrative nonreward in continuous reward situations', *Psychological Bulletin* 55, 102–19.

—— (1972). 'Behavioral habituation, counterconditioning, and a general theory of persistence', in W. K. Prokasy, *Classical Conditioning* II. Appleton-Century-Crofts, New York.

ARISTOTLE (1954). *Nicomachaean Ethics*, translated by W. D. Ross. Oxford University Press.

ARONFREED, JUSTIN (1968). *Conduct and Conscience*. Academic Press, New York.

ARROW, K. J. (1951). 'Alternative approaches to the theory of choice in risk-taking situations', *Econometrica* 19, 494–537.

—— (1971). 'A utilitarian approach to the concept of equality in public expenditures', *Quarterly Journal of Economics* 85, 409–15.

ATKINSON, J. W. (ed.) (1958). *Motives in Fantasy, Action, and Society*. D. van Nostrand, New York.

—— (1964). *An Introduction to Motivation*. D. van Nostrand, New York.

—— and BIRCH, D. (1970). *The Dynamics of Action*. John Wiley and Sons, New York.

—— and FEATHER, N. (1966). *A Theory of Achievement Motivation*. John Wiley and Sons, New York.

—— and RAYNOR, J. O. (1974). *Motivation and Achievement*. John Wiley and Sons, New York.

—— and REITMAN, W. (1958). 'Performance as a Function of Motive Strength and Expectancy of Goal-Attainment', in J. W. Atkinson (ed.), *Motives in Fantasy, Action and Society*, pp. 278–87. D. van Nostrand, New York.

BAIER, KURT (1958) *The Moral Point of View*. Cornell University Press, Ithaca, New York.

BAIER, KURT (1966). 'Moral obligation', *American Philosophical Quarterly* 3, 210–26.

BALDWIN, A. L. (1968). *Theories of Child Development*. John Wiley and Sons, New York.

BANDURA, A. (1969). *Principles of Behavior Modification*. Holt, Rinehart and Winston, New York.

—— and HUSTON, A. C. (1961). 'Identification as a process of incidental learning', *Journal of Abnormal and Social Psychology* 63.

BECKER, G. M. and McCLINTOCK, C. G. (1967). 'Value: behavioural decision theory', *Annual Review of Psychology* 18.

BEEBE-CENTER, J. G. (1932). *The Psychology of Pleasantness and Unpleasantness*. D. van Nostrand, New York.

BERGSTROM, LARS (1966). *The Alternatives and Consequences of Actions*, Stockholm Studies in Philosophy 4. Almqvist and Wiksell, Stockholm.

—— (1968). 'Utilitarianism and deontic logic', *Analysis* 29.

—— (1976). 'On the Formulation and Application of Utilitarianism', *Nous* 10, 121–44.

BERKELEY, GEORGE (1712). *Passive Obedience, or the Christian Doctrine of Not Resisting the Supreme Power, Proved and Vindicated upon the Principles of the Law of Nature.*

BERKOWITZ, L. (1964). *The Development of Motives and Values in the Child.* Basic Books, New York.

BERLYNE, D. E. and MADSEN K. E. (eds.) (1973). *Pleasure, Reward, Preference.* Academic Press, New York.

BINDRA, DAVID (1968). 'Neuropsychological interpretation of the effects of drive and incentive-motivation on general activity and instrumental behavior', *Psychological Review* 75, 1–22.

—— (1969). 'The interrelated mechanisms of reinforcement and motivation, and the nature of their influence on response', *Nebraska Symposium on Motivation.*

—— (1972). 'A unified account of classical conditioning and operant training', in W. K. Prokasy (ed.), *Classical Conditioning* II. Appleton-Century-Crofts, New York.

—— (1974). 'A motivational view of learning, performance, and behavior modification', *Psychological Review* 81, 199–213.

BIRK, L. and BIRK, A. W. (1974). 'Psychoanalysis and behavior therapy', *American Journal of Psychiatry* 131.

BITTERMAN, M. E. (1967). 'Learning in animals', in H. Helson and W. Bevan (eds.), *Contemporary Approaches in Psychology.* D. van Nostrand, Princeton, New Jersey.

BLACK, MAX (1964). 'The gap between "is" and "should" ', *Philosophical Review* 73.

BLACK, R. W. (1969). 'Incentive motivation and the parameters of reward in instrumental conditioning', *Nebraska Symposium on Motivation.*
BLACKORBY, C., NISSEN, D., PRIMONT, D., and RUSSELL, R. R. (1973). 'Consistent intertemporal decision making', *Review of Economic Studies* 40, 239–48.
BLUM, W. J. and KALVEN, H. (1953). *The Uneasy Case for Progressive Taxation.* University of Chicago Press.
BOLLES, R. C. (1967). *Theory of Motivation.* Harper and Row, New York.
BRADY, J. P. (1967). 'Psychotherapy, learning theory, and insight', *Archives of General Psychiatry* 16.
BRANDEIS, R. and LUBOW, R. E. (1975). 'Conditioning without awareness—again', *Bulletin of Psychonomic Science* 5.
BRANDT, R. B. (1959). *Ethical Theory.* Prentice-Hall, Englewood Cliffs, New Jersey.
—— (1964). Review of *Freedom and Reason,* by R. M. Hare, *The Journal of Philosophy* 61.
—— (1967). 'Happiness', in Paul Edwards (ed.), *The Encyclopedia of Philosophy.* Macmillan, New York.
—— (1970). 'Traits of Character: A Conceptual Analysis', *American Philosophical Quarterly* 7, 23–37.
—— (1972). 'Rationality, egoism, and morality', *The Journal of Philosophy* 69, 681–98.
—— (1976). 'The psychology of benevolence and its implications for philosophy', *Journal of Philosophy* 73.
BRAYBROOKE, DAVID (1967). 'The choice between utilitarianisms', *American Philosophical Quarterly* 4.
BRESNAHAN, J. L., HILLIARD, J. P., and SHAPIRO, M. M. (1973). 'Reinforcement in children: received and expected', *Bulletin of Psychonomic Science* 2, 195–7.
BROAD, C. D. (1915–16). 'On the function of false hypotheses in ethics', *Ethics* 26, 377–97.
—— (1934). *Five Types of Ethical Theory.* Harcourt, Brace and Co., New York.
—— (1952). 'Egoism as a theory of human motives', The Marrett Memorial Lecture at Exeter College, Oxford. Printed in *Ethics and the History of Philosophy,* Routledge and Kegan Paul, Ltd., London, 1952.
BROWN, J. S. (1961). *The Motivation of Behaviour.* McGraw-Hill, New York.
—— and FARBER, I. E. (1968). 'Secondary motivational systems', *Annual Review of Psychology* 19.
BUCHWALD, A. M. and YOUNG, R. D. (1969). 'Some comments on the

foundations of behavior therapy', in C. R. Franks (ed.), *Behavior Therapy: Appraisal and Status*. McGraw-Hill, New York.

BUTLER, BISHOP JOSEPH (1729) (first published). *Sermons*. Many editions.

CAMPBELL, DONALD (1972). 'On the genetics of altruism and the counter-hedonic components in human culture', *Journal of Social Issues* 28.

CARTWRIGHT, DORWIN (1942). 'The effect of interruption, completion, and failure upon the attractiveness of activities', *Journal of Experimental Psychology* 31, 1–16.

—— and FESTINGER, LEON (1943). 'A quantitative theory of decision', *Psychological Review* 50, 595–621.

CASTANEDA, H. (1968). 'A problem for utilitarianism', *Analysis* 28, 141–2.

—— (1969). 'Ought, value, and utilitarianism', *American Philosophical Quarterly* 6, 257–75.

—— (1972). 'The problem of formulating a coherent act-utilitarianism', *Analysis* 32, 118–24.

COFER, C. N. and APPLEY, M. H. (1967). *Motivation: Theory and Research*. John Wiley and Sons, New York.

COLE, S. N. and SIPPRETH, C. N. (1967). 'Extinction of a classically conditioned GSR as a function of awareness', *Behaviour Research and Therapy* 5.

COLEMAN, J. S. (1968). 'The concept of equality in educational opportunity', *Harvard Educational Review* 38, 14–22.

COOKE, G. (1968). 'Evaluation of the efficacy of the components of reciprocal inhibition psychotherapy', *Journal of Abnormal and Social Psychology* 73.

CORNMAN, J. W. and DIRNBACH, B. J. (1973). 'Utilitarianism and the obligation to do exactly one act', *Analysis* 34, 20–23.

CRESPI, L. P. (1942). 'Quantitative variation of incentive and performance in the white rat', *American Journal of Psychology* 55, 467–517.

DANIELS, NORMAN (ed.) (1975). *Reading Rawls: Critical Studies of 'A Theory of Justice'*. Basic Books, New York.

DAVIDSON, D., SUPPES, P., and SIEGEL, S. (1957). *Decision Making*. Stanford University Press, California.

DAVIES, D. R. and TRINE, G. S. (1969). *Human Vigilance Performance*. American Elsevier Publishing Co., New York.

DAVISON, G. C. (1968a). 'Elimination of a sadistic fantasy by a client-controlled counterconditioning technique', *Journal of Abnormal and Social Psychology* 73.

—— (1968b). 'Systematic desensitization as a counterconditioning technique', *Journal of Abnormal and Social Psychology* 73.

DEUTSCH, J. A. (1960). *The Structural Basis of Behavior*, chap. 3. University of Chicago Press.

DEUTSCH and DEUTSCH, D. (1966). *Physiological Psychology*. Dorsey Press, Homewood, Illinois.

DIGGS, B. J. (1970). 'A comment on "Some merits of one form of rule-utilitarianism"', in K. Pahel and M. Schiller, *Readings in Contemporary Ethical Theory*. Prentice-Hall, Englewood Cliffs, New Jersey.

DONAGAN, ALAN (1968). 'Is there a credible form of utilitarianism?', in Michael Bayles (ed.), *Contemporary Utilitarianism*. Anchor Books, New York.

DUNCAN-JONES, A. (1957). 'Utilitarianism and Rules', *Philosophical Quarterly* VII, 364–67.

DUNCKER, KARL (1941). 'On pleasure, emotion, and striving', *Philosophy and Phenomenological Research* I.

EDWARDS, WARD (1954). 'The theory of decision making,' *Psychological Bulletin* 51, 380–417. Reprinted in Ward Edwards and Amos Tversky, *Decision Making*. Penguin Books, Baltimore, Maryland, 1967.

—— and TVERSKY, AMOS (eds.) (1967). *Decision Making*. Penguin Books, Baltimore, Maryland.

EISENBERGER, R. (1970). 'Is there a deprivation-satiation function for social approval?', *Psychological Bulletin* 74, 255–75.

ELLIS, ALBERT (1962). *Reason and Emotion in Psychotherapy*. Lyle Stuart, New York.

—— and HARPER, R. A. (1961). *A Guide to Rational Living*. Wilshire Book Co., New York.

ELLSBERG, D. (1954). 'Classic and current notions of "measurable utility"', *Economic Journal* 64.

EPSTEIN, S. (1962). 'The measurement of drive and conflict in humans', *Nebraska Symposium on Motivation*, pp. 127–205.

—— and FENZ, W. D. (1962). 'Theory and experiment on the measurement of approach-avoidance conflict', *Journal of Abnormal and Social Psychology* 64, 97–112.

ERICSSON, LARS O. (1975). *Justice in the Distribution of Economic Resources*. Almqvist and Wiksell, Stockholm.

ERNEST, C. H. and PAIVIO, A. (1969). 'Imagery ability in paired-associate and incidental learning', *Psychonomic Science* 15, 181–2.

EVANS, D. R. (1968). 'Masturbatory fantasy and sexual deviation', *Behavior Research and Therapy* 6.

EWING, A. C. (1953). 'Suppose everybody acted like me', *Philosophy* 28, 16–29.

EYSENCK, H. J. (1973). 'Personality and the law of effect', in D. E. Berlyne and K. E. Madsen, *Pleasure, Reward, and Preference*. Academic Press, New York.

EYSENCK, H. J. and BEECH, H. R. (1971). 'Counter conditioning and related methods', in A. E. Bergin and S. L. Garfield (eds.), *Handbook of Psychotherapy and Behavior Change: An Empirical Analysis*. John Wiley and Sons, New York.

FAIR, R. C. (1971). 'The optimal distribution of income', *Quarterly Journal of Economics* **85**.

FEINBERG, JOEL (1967). 'Review of The Forms and Limits of Utilitarianism', in *Philosophical Review* **76**.

FELDMAN, FRED (1974). 'On the extensional equivalence of simple and general utilitarianism', *Nous* **8**, 185–94.

FESTINGER, LEON (1957). *A Theory of Cognitive Dissonance*. Stanford University Press, California.

FIRTH, RODERICK (1952). 'Ethical absolutism and the ideal observer', *Philosophy and Phenomenological Research* **12**.

FOLEY, A. and BANFORD, J. L. (1968). 'Validation of a psychophysical test of aptitude for learning social motives', *Psychophysiology* **5**, 316–32.

FRANKENA, W. K. (1962). 'The concept of social justice', in R. B. Brandt (ed.), *Social Justice*. Prentice-Hall, Englewood Cliffs, New Jersey.

—— (1963). *Ethics*. Prentice-Hall, Englewood Cliffs, New Jersey.

—— (1968). 'Obligation and motivation' in A. I. Melden (ed.), *Essays in Moral Philosophy*. University of Wasington Press, Seattle.

FRIEDMAN, MILTON (1947). 'Lerner on the economics of control', *Journal of Political Economy* **55**, 405–16.

GALE, D. S., STURMFELS, G., and GALE, E. N. (1966). 'A comparison of reciprocal inhibition and experimental extinction in the psychotherapeutic process', *Behavior Research and Therapy* **4**.

GALLISTEL, C. R. (1964). 'Electrical self-stimulation and its theoretical implications', *Psychological Bulletin* **61**, 23–34.

GAUTHIER, DAVID (1963). *Practical Reasoning*. Clarendon Press, Oxford.

GEORGESCU-ROEGEN, NICHOLAS (1968). 'Utility', in *International Encyclopedia of the Social Sciences* **16**, p. 250. Macmillan, New York.

GEWIRTZ, J. L. and BAER, D. M. (1958). 'Deprivation and satiation of social reinforcers as drive conditions', *Journal of Abnormal and Social Psychology* **57**, 165–72.

GIBBARD, ALLAN (1976). 'Natural property rights', *Nous* **10**, 77–88.

GINTIS, H. (1972). 'A radical analysis of welfare economics and individual development', *Quarterly Journal of Economics* **86**, 572–99.

GLICKMAN, S. E. and SCHIFF, B. B. (1967). 'A biological theory of reinforcement', *Psychological Review* **73**, 81–109.

GOLDFRIED, M. R. and MERBAUM, M. (eds.) (1973). *Behavior Change Through Self-Control*. Holt, Rinehart and Winston, New York.

GOLDMAN, ALVIN I. (1970). *A Theory of Human Action*. Prentice-Hall, Englewood Cliffs, New Jersey.

—— (1976). 'The volitional theory revisited', in Myles Brand and Douglas Walton (eds.), *Action Theory: Proceedings of the Winnepeg Conference on Human Action*. Reidel, Amsterdam (Synthese Library).

GOLDMAN, H. S. (1972). 'The Generalization Principle in Ethics', unpublished Ph.D. dissertation, the University of Michigan.

—— (1974). 'David Lyons on utilitarian generalization', *Philosophical Studies* 26, 77–95.

GOODMAN, NELSON (1965). *Fact, Fiction, and Forecast*. Bobbs-Merrill, Indianapolis, Indiana.

GOSLING, J. C. B. (1969). *Pleasure and Desire*. Clarendon Press, Oxford.

GREEN, J. R. and SHESHINSKI, E. (1975). 'A note on the progressivity of optimal public expenditures', *Quarterly Journal of Economics* 89, 138–44.

GRINGS, W. W. (1965). 'Verbal-perceptual factors in the conditioning of autonomic responses', in W. K. Prokasy (ed.), *Classical Conditioning*. Appleton-Century-Crofts, New York.

—— (1973). 'Cognitive factors in electro-dermal conditioning', *Psychological Bulletin* 79.

—— and UNO, TADAO (1968). 'Counterconditioning: fear and relaxation', *Psychophysiology* 4.

GROSSMAN, S. P. (1973). *A Textbook of Physiological Psychology*. John Wiley and Sons, New York.

HALLAM, R. and RACHMAN, S. (1972). 'Theoretical problems of aversion therapy', *Behavior Research and Therapy* 10, 341–53.

HAMMOND, P. J. (1976). 'Changing tastes and coherent dynamic choice', *Review of Economic Studies* 43, 159–73.

HARE, R. M. (1963). *Freedom and Reason*. Oxford University Press.

—— (1972). 'Rules of war and moral reasoning', *Philosophy and Public Affairs* 1.

—— (1976). 'Ethical theory and utilitarianism', in H. D. Lewis (ed.), *Contemporary British Philosophy*. Allen and Unwin, London.

HARGRAVE, G. E. and BOLLES, R. C. (1971). 'Rats' aversion to flavors following induced illness', *Psychonomic Science* 23.

HARMAN, GILBERT (1975). 'Moral relativism defended', *Philosophical Review* 84, 3–22.

HARRISON, J. (1952–3). 'Utilitarianism, universalization, and our duty to be just', *Proceedings, The Aristotelian Society*.

HARROD, R. F. (1937). 'Utilitarianism revised', *Mind* 45, 137–56.

HARSANYI, JOHN (1953). 'Cardinal utility in welfare economics and in the theory of risk-taking', *Journal of Political Economy* 61.

HARSANYI, JOHN (1955). 'Cardinal welfare, individualistic ethics, and interpersonal comparisons of utility', *Journal of Political Economy* **63**.

—— (1973). 'Cardinal welfare, individualistic ethics and interpersonal comparisons', reprinted in E. S. Phelps, *Economic Justice*. Penguin Education, Harmondsworth, Middx. (Penguin Books, Baltimore, Maryland.)

HEBB, D. O. (1968). 'Concerning imagery', *Psychological Review* **75**, 466–77.

HECKHAUSEN, H. (1968). 'Achievement motive research', *Nebraska Symposium on Motivation*, pp. 103–74

HEIDER, FRITZ (1959). *The Psychology of Interpersonal Relations*. John Wiley and Sons, New York.

HELLER, KENNETH and MARLATT, G. A. (1960). 'Verbal conditioning, behavior therapy, and behavior change', in Cyril Franks (ed.), *Behavior Therapy: Appraisal and Status*. McGraw-Hill, New York.

HILGARD, E. R. (1969). 'Pain as a puzzle for psychology and physiology', *American Psychologist* **24**.

—— and BOWER, G. H. (1975). *Theories of Learning*. Prentice-Hall, Englewood Cliffs, New Jersey.

HILL, W. F. (1968). 'Sources of evaluative reinforcement', *Psychological Bulletin* **69**.

HODGSON, D. H. (1967). *Consequences of Utilitarianism*. Clarendon Press, Oxford.

HOFFMAN, MARTIN (1970). 'Moral development', in P. Mussen (ed.), *Carmichael's Manual of Child Psychology* II, pp. 261–359. John Wiley and Sons, New York.

—— (1975). 'Developmental synthesis of affect and cognition and its implications for altruistic motivation', *Developmental Psychology* **11**, 607–22.

HORWICH, P. (1974). 'On calculating the utility of acts', *Philosophical Studies* **25**, 21–31.

HULL, CLARK (1952). *A Behavior System*. Yale University Press, New Haven, Connecticut.

HUME, DAVID (1854). *Treatise of Human Nature*. Little, Brown and Co., Boston.

—— *An Inquiry Concerning the Principles of Morals*, Section 9 (many editions).

HUNT, J. M. (1941). 'The effects of infant feeding-frustration upon adult hoarding behaviour', *Journal of Abnormal and Social Psychology* **36**.

—— (1960). 'Experience and the development of motivation: some reinterpretations', *Child Development* **31**. Reprinted in P. H. Mussen, J.

J. Conger and J. Kagan, *Readings in Child Development and Personality*, 1965. Harper and Row, New York.

HUNT, J. M. SCHLOSBERG, H., SOLOMON, R. L. and STELLAR, E. (1947). 'Studies of the effects of infantile experience on adult behavior in rats. I. Effects of infantile feeding-frustration on adult hoarding', *Journal of Comparative Physiological Psychology* 40.

IRWIN, F. W. (1971). *Intentional Behavior and Motivation: A Cognitive Theory*. J. B. Lippincott, Philadelphia.

JACKSON, J. A. (ed.) (1972). *Role*. Cambridge University Press.

JAMES, WILLIAM (1913). *The Principles of Psychology* II. Henry Holt, New York.

JOHNSON, C. D. (1975a). 'Toward a cautious return to natural law: some comments on moral and legal obligation', *Western Ontario Law Review* **14**, 31–49.

—— (1975b). 'Moral and legal obligation', *Journal of Philosophy* **72**, 315–33.

JONES, E. C. (1970). 'A facilitating effect of latent extinction', *Psychonomic Science* **18**, 143–4.

JONES, M. C. (1924). 'A laboratory study of fear', *Journal of Genetic Psychology* **31**.

JOURNAL OF SOCIAL ISSUES (1972). Vol. 28, No. 3. Issue is devoted to altruism.

KAGAN, JEROME (1958). 'The concept of identification', *Psychological Review* **65**.

KALIN, J. (1969). 'On ethical egoism', *American Philosophical Quarterly Monograph* **1**, 26–41.

—— (1975). 'Two kinds of moral reasoning: ethical egoism as a moral theory', *Canadian Journal of Philosophy* **5**, 323–56.

KANT, IMMANUEL (1963). *Lectures on Ethics*. Translated by Louis Infield. Harper and Row, New York.

KAVKA, G. S. (1975). 'Rawls on average and total utility', *Philosophical Studies* **27**.

KELLEHER, R. T. and GOLLUB, L. R. (1962). 'A review of positive conditioned reinforcement', *Journal of the Experimental Analysis of Behavior* **5**, 543–97.

KIM, JAEGWON (1971). 'Causes and events: Mackie on causation', *Journal of Philosophy* **68**, 426–41.

KIMBLE, G. A. (1961). *Hilgard and Marquis' Conditioning and Learning* (2nd edn.). Appleton-Century-Crofts, New York.

KIMBLE, G. A. (1962). 'Chemical conditioning and the problem of awareness', in C. W. Erickson (ed.), *Behavior and Awareness*. Duke University Press, Durham, N.C.

KOHLBERG, L. (1969). 'Stage and Sequence: The cognitive-developmental approach to socialization', in D. Goslin (ed.), *Handbook of socialization theory and research*. Rand McNally, Chicago.

—— (1971). 'From Is to Ought', in T. Mischel (ed.), *Cognitive Development and Epistemology*. Academic Press, New York.

KOOPMANS, R. C. (1964). 'On flexibility of future preferences', in M. W. Shelly and G. L. Bryan (eds.), *Human Judgments and Optimality*. John Wiley and Sons, New York.

KREBS, D. L. (1970). 'Altruism—an examination of the concept and a review of the literature', *Psychological Bulletin* 73.

LANG, P. J. (1969). 'The mechanics of desensitization and the laboratory study of human fear', in C. R. Franks (ed.), *Behavior Therapy: Appraisal and Status*. McGraw-Hill, New York.

LAVERTY, R. (1975). 'On the roles of dopamine and noradrenaline in animal behavior', *Progress in Neurobiology* III, 31–70.

LAZARUS, A. A. (1964). 'Crucial Procedural Factors in Desensitization Therapy', *Behaviour Research and Therapy* 2, 65–70.

LEE, E. G. (1967). 'Early conditioning of perceptual preference', *Child Development* 38, 815–24.

LERNER, A. P. (1944). *The Economics of Control*. Macmillan, New York.

LEVY, B. and MARTIN, IRENE (1975). 'Chemical conditioning of human "evaluation" responses', *Behavior Research and Therapy* 13, 271–6.

LEWIN, K. (1938). *The Conceptual Representation and the Measurement of Psychological Forces*. Duke University Press, Durham, N.C.

LEWIS, DAVID (1972). 'Utilitarianism and Truthfulness', *Australasian Journal of Philosophy* 50, 17–19.

LINTON, RALPH (1936). *The Study of Man*. Appleton-Century-Crofts, New York.

LITTIG, L. W. and PETTY, R. M. (1971). 'Effects of multiply aroused motives on behavior', *Journal of Experimental Research in Personality* 5, 139–44.

LOGAN, F. A. and WAGNER, A. R. (1965). *Reward and Punishment*. Allyn and Bacon, Rockleigh, New Jersey.

LONDON, PERRY (1964). *The Modes and Morals of Psychotherapy*. Holt, Rinehart and Winston, New York.

LUCE, R. D. and RAIFFA, HOWARD (1957). *Games and Decisions*. John Wiley and Sons, New York.

—— and SUPPES, PATRICK (1965). 'Preference, utility, and subjective probability', in R. D. Luce, R. R. Bush, and E. Galanter (eds.), *Handbook of Mathematical Psychology*. John Wiley and Sons, New York.

LYONS, DAVID (1965). *The Forms and Limits of Utilitarianism*. Clarendon Press, Oxford.

—— (1976). Review of Robert Nozick, *Anarchy, State, and Utopia*, *Philosophical Review* 85, 208–15.

MABBOTT, J. D. (1953). 'Reason and desire', *Philosophy* 28, 112–23.

MACAULEY, J. and BERKOWITZ, L. (eds.) (1970). *Altruism and Helping Behavior*. Academic Press, New York.

MACCORQUODALE K. and MEEHL, P. E. (1953). 'Preliminary suggestions as to a formalization of expectancy theory', *Psychological Review* 60, 55–63.

—— (1954). 'Edward C. Tolman', in W. K. Estes, *et al.*, *Modern Learning Theory*. Appleton-Century-Crofts, New York.

MACINTYRE, A. (1957). 'What morality is not', *Philosophy* 32, 325–35.

MACKIE, J. L. (1965). 'Causes and conditions', *American Philosophical Quarterly* 2, 245–64.

—— (1973). 'The disutility of act-utilitarianism', *Philosophical Quarterly* 23, 289–300.

—— (1976). 'Sidgwick's pessimism', *Philosophical Quarterly* 26, 317–27.

MARMOR, J. (1971). 'Dynamic psychotherapy and behavior therapy', *Archives of General Psychiatry* 24

MARTIN, W. E. (1954). 'The development of values in children', in *Symposium on Learning Theory and Identification, Journal of Genetic Psychology* 84.

MARX, KARL (1973). *Critique of the Gotha Programme*, Selected Works II. Foreign Language Publishing House, Moscow. Quoted in A. K. Sen, *On Economic Inequality*. W. W. Norton, New York, 1973.

MCCLELLAND, D. C. (1951). *Personality*. William Sloane Associates, New York.

—— (1958). 'The importance of early learning in the formation of motives', in J. W. Atkinson (ed.), *Motives in Fantasy, Action, and Society*. D. van Nostrand, New York.

—— (1965). 'Toward a theory of motive acquisition', *American Psychologist* 20.

—— ATKINSON, J. W., CLARK, R. A., and LOWELL, E. L. (1953). *The Achievement Motive*. Appleton-Century-Crofts, New York.

—— and MCGOWN, D. R. (1953). 'The effect of variable food reinforcement on the strength of secondary reward', *Journal of Comparative and Physiological Psychology* 46.

MCNAUGHTON, ROBERT (1953). 'A metrical conception of happiness', *Philosophy and Phenomenological Research* 14.

MELZACK, RONALD (1961). 'The perception of pain', *Scientific American* 204.

MELZACK, RONALD and WALL, P. B. (1965). 'Pain mechanisms: a new theory', *Science* 150.

MILL, J. S. (1861, first published). *Utilitarianism*. Many editions.

MILLER, NEAL (1944). 'Experimental studies of conflict', in J. M. Hunt (ed.), *Personality: The Behavior Disorders*, Vol. 1, pp. 431–65. Ronald Press, New York.

—— (1951). 'Learnable drives and rewards', in S. S. Stevens (ed.), *Handbook of Experimental Psychology*. John Wiley and Sons, New York.

—— and DOLLARD, JOHN (1941). *Social Learning and Imitation*. Yale University Press, New Haven, Connecticut.

MILLER, P. M. *et al.* (1973). 'Electrical aversion therapy with alcoholics: an analogue study', *Behavior Research and Therapy* 11, 491–7.

MISCHEL, WALTER (1974). 'Cognitive appraisals and transformations in self-control', in Bernard Weiner (ed.), *Cognitive Views of Human Motivation*, pp. 33–50. Academic Press, New York.

—— and METZNER, R. (1962). 'Preference for delayed reward as a function of age, intelligence, and length of delay interval', *Journal of Abnormal and Social Psychology* 64, 425–31.

MITCHELL, T. R. (1974). 'Expectancy models of job satisfaction, occupational preference and effort', *Psychological Bulletin* 81, 1153–77.

MOORE, G. E. (1903). *Principia Ethica*. Cambridge University Press.

MORGAN, C. T. (1947). 'The hoarding instinct', *Psychological Review* 54.

—— and STELLAR, ELIOT (1950). *Physiological Psychology*. McGraw-Hill, New York.

MORGAN, JAMES and DAVID, MARTIN (1963). 'Education and income', *Quarterly Journal of Economics* 77, 923–37.

MURPHY, LOIS B. (1937). *Social Behavior and Child Personality*. Columbia University Press, New York.

MURRAY, E. J. and JACOBSEN, L. I. (1971). 'The nature of learning in traditional and behavioral psychotherapy', in A. E. Bergin and S. L. Garfield (eds.), *Handbook of Psychotherapy and Behavior Change*. John Wiley and Sons, New York.

MUSSEN, P. H. and CONGER, J. J. (1956). *Child Development and Personality*. Harper and Row, New York.

NAGEL, THOMAS (1970). *The Possibility of Altruism*. Oxford University Press.

NEISSER, ULRIC (1970). 'Visual imagery as process and as experience', in J. S. Antrobus (ed.), *Cognition and Affect*. Little, Brown and Co., Boston.

NELSON, F. (1966). 'Effects of two counterconditioning procedures on the extinction of fear', *Journal of Comparative and Physiological Psychology* 62.

NEVIN, J. A. (1966). 'Generalized conditioned reinforcement in satiated rats', *Psychonomic Science* 5.

NISBETT, R. E. and WILSON, T. D. (1977). 'Telling more than we can know: verbal reports on mental processes', *Psychological Review* 84, 231–59.

—— BORGIDA, E., CRANDALL, R., and REED, H. (1975). 'Popular induction: information is not necessarily informative', in M. V. Carroll and J. Payne (eds.), *Cognition and Social Behavior*. Lawrence Erlbaum Associates, Hillsdale, New Jersey.

NOWELL-SMITH, P. H. (1973). 'Some reflections on utilitarianism', *Canadian Journal of Philosophy* 2, 417–31.

NOZICK, ROBERT (1974). *Anarchy, State and Utopia*. Basic Books, New York.

OLDS, J. (1956). *The Growth and Structure of Motives*, Free Press, Glencoe, Illinois.

OLSON, R. G. (1961). 'Ethical egoism and social welfare', *Philosophy and Phenomenological Research* 21, 528–36.

OVERVOLD, MARK (1976). 'Self-Interest, Self-Sacrifice and the Satisfaction of Desires.' Unpublished Ph.D. dissertation, the University of Michigan.

PARFIT, DEREK (1971). 'Personal identity', *Philosophical Review* 80, 3–27.

PAYNE, J. W. and BRAUNSTEIN, M. L. (1971). 'Preferences among gambles with equal underlying distributions', *Journal of Experimental Psychology* 87, 13–18.

PELEG, B. and YAARI, M. E. (1973). 'On the existence of a consistent course of action when tastes are changing', *Review of Economic Studies* 40, 391–401.

PENELHUM, T. (1957). 'The logic of pleasure', *Philosophy and Phenomenological Research* 17, 488–503

PERRY, JOHN (1976). 'The importance of being identical', in Amelie O. Rorty (ed.), *The Identities of Persons*. University of California Press, Berkeley.

PIGOU, A. C. (1932). *Economics of Welfare*. Macmillan, London.

PROKASY, W. K. (1965). *Classical Conditioning*. Appleton-Century-Crofts, New York.

QUANDT, R. E. (1956). 'A probabilistic theory of consumer behavior', *Quarterly Journal of Economics* 70, 507–36.

QUINN, WARREN (1974). 'Theories of intrinsic value', *American Philosophical Quarterly* 11, 123–32.

RACHMAN, S. J. and TEASDALE, J. (1969). 'Aversion therapy: an appraisal', in C. M. Franks (ed.), *Behavior Therapy: Appraisal and Status*. McGraw-Hill, New York.

RAMSEY, F. P. (1928). 'A mathematical theory of saving', *Economic Journal* **38**, 543–59.

RAPAPORT, A. and WALLSTEIN, T. W. (1972). 'Individual decision behavior', *Annual Review of Psychology* **23**.

RAPHAEL, D. D. (1974–5). 'The standard of morals', *Proceedings. The Aristotelian Society* **75**, 1–12.

RASHDALL, HASTINGS (1924). *The Theory of Good and Evil*. Oxford University Press.

RAWLS, JOHN (1971). *A Theory of Justice*. Harvard University Press, Cambridge, Mass.

—— (1974). 'A reply to Alexander and Musgrave', *Quarterly Journal of Economics* **88**, 633–55.

RAYNOR, JOEL (1974). 'Future orientation in the study of achievement motivation', in J. W. Atkinson and Joel Raynor (eds.), *Motivation and Achievement*. John Wiley and Sons, New York.

RESCHER, NICHOLAS (1966). *Distributive Justice*. Bobbs-Merrill, Indianapolis, Indiana.

RESHEVSKY, S. H. (1967). 'Hunger level during food consumption: effects on subsequent performance', *Psychonomic Science* **7**.

REVENSKY, S. and GORRY, TOM (1973). 'Flavor aversions produced by contingent drug injection', *Behavior Research and Therapy* **11**.

ROLLS, E. T. (1975). 'The neural basis of brain stimulation reward', *Progress in Neurobiology* **III**, 71–162.

ROSEN, B. C. and D'ANDRADE, ROY (1959). 'The psychosocial origins of achievement motivation', *Sociometry* **22**, 185–218. Reprinted in P. H. Mussen, J. J. Conger, and J. Kagan (eds.), *Readings in Child Development and Personality*. Harper and Row, New York, 1965.

ROTHENBERG, J. (1961). *The Measurement of Social Welfare*. Prentice-Hall, Englewood Cliffs, New Jersey.

ROTTER, J. B. (1954). *Social Learning and Clinical Psychology*. Prentice-Hall, Englewood Cliffs, New Jersey.

RYAN, T. A. (1970). *Intentional Behavior*. Ronald Press, New York.

SARTORIUS, ROLF (1972). 'Individual conduct and social norms: a utilitarian account', *Ethics* **82**, 200–18.

—— (1975). *Individual Conduct and Social Norms*. Dickenson Publishing Co., Encino, California.

SCHACHTER, S. (1959). *The Psychology of Affiliation*. Stanford University Press, California.

SCHEFFLER, I. (1954). 'Justification and Commitment', *Journal of Philosophy* **51**, 180–90.

SEARS, R. R. (1942). 'Success and failure: a study in motility', in *Studies in Personality*. McGraw-Hill, New York.

SELDIN, IRVING (1977). 'Laws that are made to be broken: adjusting for anticipated noncompliance', *Michigan Law Review* 75, 687–716.

SEN, A. K. (1970). *Collective Choice and Social Welfare*. Holden-Day, San Francisco.

—— (1973). *On Economic Inequality*. W. W. Norton, New York.

SHEFFIELD, F. D. (1965). 'Relation between Classical Conditioning and Instrumental Learning', in W. K. Prokasy (ed.), *Classical Conditioning*. Appleton-Century-Crofts, New York.

—— (1966). 'A Drive-Induction Theory of Reinforcement', in R. N. Haber (ed.), *Current Research in Theory of Motivation*. Henry Holt, New York.

SHEPARD, R. N. (1964). 'On subjectively optimum selections among multi-attribute alternatives', in M. W. Shelley and G. L. Bryan (eds.), *Human Judgments and Optimality*, pp. 257–81. John Wiley and Sons, New York.

SIDGWICK, HENRY (1922). *The Methods of Ethics*. Macmillan, London.

—— (1929). *Elements of Politics*. Macmillan, London.

SILVERSTEIN, ALBERT (1973). 'Acquired pleasantness and conditioned incentives in verbal learning', in D. E. Berlyne and K. B. Madsen (eds.), *Pleasure, Reward, Preference*. Academic Press, New York.

SILVERSTEIN, H. S. (1974). 'Simple and general utilitarianism', *Philosophical Review* 83, 339–63.

SIMON, HERBERT A. (1955). 'A behavioral model of rational choice', *Quarterly Journal of Economics* 69.

—— (1957). *Models of Man*. John Wiley and Sons, New York.

SINGER, J. L. (1970). 'Drives, affects and daydreams: the adaptive role of spontaneous imagery or stimulus-independent mentation', in J. S. Antrobus (ed.), *Cognition and Affect*. Little, Brown and Co., Boston.

SINGER, M. G. (1961). *Generalization in Ethics*. Alfred A. Knopf, New York.

SINGER, PETER (1972). 'Is act-utilitarianism self-defeating?', *Philosophical Review* 81, 90–104.

—— (1973). 'The triviality of the debate over "is-ought" and the definition of "moral" ', *American Philosophical Quarterly* 10, 31–6.

—— (1974). 'Sidgwick and reflective equilibrium', *The Monist* 58, 490–517.

SKINNER, B. F. (1971). *Beyond Freedom and Dignity*. Alfred A. Knopf, New York.

SLOVIK, PAUL (1964). 'Assessment of risk-taking behavior', *Psychological Bulletin* 61, 220–33.

SMART, J. J. C. (1956). 'Extreme and restricted utilitarianism', *Philosophical Quarterly* 6.

SMART, J. J. C. (1961). *An Outline of a System of Utilitarian Ethics.* Melbourne University Press, Australia, and Cambridge University Press.

SNARE, FRANK (1974). 'The definition of *prima facie* duties', *The Philosophical Quarterly* 24.

SOBEL, J. H. (1970). 'Utilitarianism: simple and general', *Inquiry* 13, 394–449.

SPENCE, K. W. (1956). *Behavior Theory and Conditioning.* Yale University Press, New Haven, Connecticut.

STAATS, A. W. (1970). 'Social behaviorism, human motivation, and the conditioning therapies', *Experimental Personality Research* 5, 111–68.

STEIN, LARRY (1969), in J. T. Tapp (ed.), *Reinforcement and Behavior.* Academic Press, New York.

STERNBACH, R. A. (1968). *Pain: A Psychophysiological Analysis.* Academic Press, New York.

STOCKER, MICHAEL (1970). 'Moral duties, institutions, and natural facts', *The Monist* 54, 602–24.

STOKE, S. M. (1950). 'An inquiry into the concept of identification', *Journal of Genetic Psychology* 76.

STOUT, A. K. (1954). 'Suppose everybody did the same', *Australasian Journal of Philosophy* 32, 1–29.

STRAWSON, P. F. (1974). *Freedom and Resentment.* Methuen, London.

STURGEON, N. L. (1973). 'Altruism, solipsism, and the objectivity of reasons', *Philosophical Review* 74, 374–402.

SUPPES, PATRICK and WINET, MURIEL (1955). 'An axiomatization of utility based on the notion of utility differences', *Management Science* 1.

TAYLOR, C. C. W. (1963). 'Pleasure', *Analysis*, supplement.

THORPE, J. E., SCHMIDT, E., BROWN, P. T., and CASTELL, D. C. (1964). 'Aversion-relief therapy: a new method for general application', *Behavior Research and Therapy* 2.

THUROW, L. C. (1971). 'The income distribution as a pure public good', *Quarterly Journal of Economics* 85.

TOLMAN, E. C. (1932). *Purposive Behavior in Animals and Men.* Appleton-Century-Crofts, New York.

—— (1954). 'A Psychological Model', in T. Parsons and E. A. Shils (eds.), *Toward a General Theory of Action*, pp. 279–364. Harvard University Press, Cambridge, Mass.

—— (1955). 'Principles of performance', *Psychological Review* 62, 315–26.

—— (1959). 'Principles of purposive behavior', in S. Koch (ed.), *Psychology: A Study of a Science*, pp. 92–157. McGraw-Hill, New York.

TOULMIN, STEPHEN (1950). *An Examination of the Place of Reason in Ethics.* Cambridge University Press.

TREBILCOT, JOYCE (1974). 'Aprudentialism', *American Philosophical Quarterly* 11, 203–10.

TRIGG, ROGER (1970). *Pain and Emotion*. Clarendon Press, Oxford.

TRIVERS, R. L. (1971). 'The evolution of reciprocal altruism', *Quarterly Review of Biology* 46.

TROLAND, L. T. (1967). *The Fundamentals of Human Motivation*. Hafner Publishing Co., New York. (Reprint of 1928 edition.)

URMSON, J. O. (1968). *The Emotive Theory of Ethics*. Hutchinson University Library, London.

—— (1974–5). 'A defence of intuitionism', *Proceedings*, The Aristotelian Society 75, 111–20.

VICKREY, W. S. (1953). 'The goals of economic life', in A. D. Ward (ed.), *Goals of Economic Life*. Harper and Row, New York. Reprinted in E. S. Phelps, *Economic Justice*. Penguin Books, Baltimore, Maryland, 1973.

—— (1960). 'Utility, strategy, and social decision rules', *Quarterly Journal of Economics* 74.

—— (1961). 'Risk, utility, and social policy', *Social Research*, reprinted in E. S. Phelps (ed.), *Economic Justice*. Penguin Modern Economics Readings, New York, 1973.

—— (1973). 'Risk, utility, and social policy', reprinted in E. S. Phelps, *Economic Justice*. Penguin Books, Baltimore, Maryland.

VON NEUMANN, J. and MORGENSTERN, O. (1944). *Theory of Games and Economic Behavior*. Princeton University Press, New Jersey.

VON WRIGHT, G. H. (1963a). *Norm and Action*. Routledge and Kegan Paul, London.

—— (1963b). *The Varieties of Goodness*. Routledge and Kegan Paul, London.

VROOM, V. H. (1964). *Work and Motivation*. John Wiley and Sons, New York.

WAGNER, M. J. and CAREY, R. J. (1973). 'Basic drives', *Annual Review of Psychology*.

WARNOCK, G. J. (1971). *The Object of Morality*. Methuen, London.

WATKINS, J. W. N. (1963). 'Negative utilitarianism', Supplementary Vol. 37, The Aristotelian Society.

WATSON, J. B. and RAYNOR, R. (1920). 'Conditioned emotional reactions', *Journal of Experimental Psychology* 3, 1–14.

WEINER, BERNARD (1973). *Theories of Motivation*. Rand McNally, Chicago.

WEITZMAN, B. (1967). 'Behavior therapy and psychotherapy', *Psychological Review* 74.

WHITE, MORTON (1956). *Toward Reunion in Philosophy*. Harvard University Press, Cambridge, Mass.

354   REFERENCES

WHITE, R. W. (1959). 'Motivation reconsidered: the concept of competence', *Psychological Review* **66**.
WHITELEY, C. H. (1976). 'Morality and egoism', *Mind* **85**, 90–6.
WIKE, E. L. (1966). *Secondary Reinforcement*, chap. 3, also pp. 25–7. Harper and Row, New York.
WILLIAMS, BERNARD (1973). In J. J. C. Smart and Bernard Williams, *Utilitarianism: For and Against*. Cambridge University Press.
WILLIAMS, GARDNER (1948). 'Individual, social, and universal ethics', *The Journal of Philosophy* **45**, 645–55.
WINTERBOTTOM, M. R. (1958). 'The relation of need for achievement to learning experiences in independence and mastery', in J. W. Atkinson (ed.), *Motives in Fantasy, Action and Society*. D. van Nostrand, New York.
WOLPE, J. (1958). *Psychotherapy by Reciprocal Inhibition*. Stanford University Press, California.
YOUNG, P. T. (1961). *Motivation and Emotion*. John Wiley and Sons, New York.
ZAJONC, R. B. (1968). 'Attitudinal effects of mass exposure', *Journal of Personality and Social Psychology* **9**, no. 2, pt. 2, monograph supplement.

INDEX